T0202769

Communications
in Computer and Information Science   1944

Rationale

The CCIS series is devoted to the publication of proceedings of computer science conferences. Its aim is to efficiently disseminate original research results in informatics in printed and electronic form. While the focus is on publication of peer-reviewed full papers presenting mature work, inclusion of reviewed short papers reporting on work in progress is welcome, too. Besides globally relevant meetings with internationally representative program committees guaranteeing a strict peer-reviewing and paper selection process, conferences run by societies or of high regional or national relevance are also considered for publication.

Topics

The topical scope of CCIS spans the entire spectrum of informatics ranging from foundational topics in the theory of computing to information and communications science and technology and a broad variety of interdisciplinary application fields.

Information for Volume Editors and Authors

Publication in CCIS is free of charge. No royalties are paid, however, we offer registered conference participants temporary free access to the online version of the conference proceedings on SpringerLink (http://link.springer.com) by means of an http referrer from the conference website and/or a number of complimentary printed copies, as specified in the official acceptance email of the event.

CCIS proceedings can be published in time for distribution at conferences or as postproceedings, and delivered in the form of printed books and/or electronically as USBs and/or e-content licenses for accessing proceedings at SpringerLink. Furthermore, CCIS proceedings are included in the CCIS electronic book series hosted in the SpringerLink digital library at http://link.springer.com/bookseries/7899. Conferences publishing in CCIS are allowed to use Online Conference Service (OCS) for managing the whole proceedings lifecycle (from submission and reviewing to preparing for publication) free of charge.

Publication process

The language of publication is exclusively English. Authors publishing in CCIS have to sign the Springer CCIS copyright transfer form, however, they are free to use their material published in CCIS for substantially changed, more elaborate subsequent publications elsewhere. For the preparation of the camera-ready papers/files, authors have to strictly adhere to the Springer CCIS Authors' Instructions and are strongly encouraged to use the CCIS LaTeX style files or templates.

Abstracting/Indexing

CCIS is abstracted/indexed in DBLP, Google Scholar, EI-Compendex, Mathematical Reviews, SCImago, Scopus. CCIS volumes are also submitted for the inclusion in ISI Proceedings.

How to start

To start the evaluation of your proposal for inclusion in the CCIS series, please send an e-mail to ccis@springer.com.

Zhiping Cai · Mingyu Xiao · Jialin Zhang
Editors

Theoretical Computer Science

41st National Conference, NCTCS 2023
Guangzhou, China, July 21–23, 2023
Revised Selected Papers

 Springer

Editors
Zhiping Cai (iD)
National University of Defense Technology
Changsha, China

Mingyu Xiao (iD)
University of Electronic Science
and Technology
Chengdu, China

Jialin Zhang (iD)
Chinese Academy of Sciences
Beijing, China

ISSN 1865-0929   ISSN 1865-0937 (electronic)
Communications in Computer and Information Science
ISBN 978-981-99-7742-0   ISBN 978-981-99-7743-7 (eBook)
https://doi.org/10.1007/978-981-99-7743-7

This Springer imprint is published by the registered company Springer Nature Singapore Pte Ltd.
The registered company address is: 152 Beach Road, #21-01/04 Gateway East, Singapore 189721, Singapore

Paper in this product is recyclable.

Preface

The National Conference of Theoretical Computer Science (NCTCS) has become one of the most important academic platforms for Theoretical Computer Science in China. So far, NCTCS has been successfully held in more than 20 regions of China, providing a place for exchange and cooperation for researchers in theoretical computer science and related fields.

NCTCS 2023 was hosted by China Computer Federation (CCF), organized by Theoretical Computer Science Committee of China Computer Society and School of Computer Science of South China Normal University from July 21 to July 23, 2023 in Guangzhou, Guangdong. This conference invited famous scholars in the field of theoretical computer science to give presentations, and carried out a wide range of academic activities and showed the latest research results. 291 people registered for NCTCS 2023, of which 276 authors submitted 127 papers (44 papers were finally accepted). We invited 99 reviewers from colleges and universities for peer review (single blind), where the average number of papers assigned to a reviewer was 3, and the average number of reviews per paper was 3. All papers were processed through the Online Submission System (CCF Consys); more details can be seen: https://conf.ccf.org.cn/TCS2023.

This volume contains 16 NCTCS 2022 accepted papers, under 4 topical headings (Computational Theory and Models, Approximation Algorithms, Artificial Intelligence, Networks and Security).

The proceedings editors wish to thank the dedicated Program Committee members and external reviewers for their hard work in reviewing and selecting papers. We also thank Springer for their trust and for publishing the proceedings of NCTCS 2023.

September 2023

Zhiping Cai
Mingyu Xiao
Jialin Zhang

Organization

General Chairs

Xiaoming Sun   Chinese Academy of Sciences, China
Yuncheng Jiang   South China Normal University, China

Program Committee Chairs

Zhiping Cai   National University of Defense Technology, China
Mingyu Xiao   University of Electronic Science and Technology, China
Jialin Zhang   Chinese Academy of Sciences, China

Steering Committee

Xiaoming Sun   Chinese Academy of Sciences, China
Jianping Yin   Dongguan University of Technology, China
Lian Li   Hefei University of Technology, China

Area Chairs

Kerong Ben   Naval University of Engineering, China
Kun He   Huazhong University of Science and Technology, China
En Zhu   National University of Defense Technology, China
Yitong Yin   Nanjing University, China
Yijia Chen   Shanghai Jiao Tong University, China
Lvzhou Li   Sun Yat-sen University, China
Yuhao Zhang   Shanghai Jiao Tong University, China

Program Committee

Jigang Wu	Guangdong University of Technology, China
Lei Luo	National University of Defense Technology, China
Zhaoming Huang	Guangxi Medical University, China
Zhiyi Huang	University of Hong Kong, China
Xin Han	Dalian University of Technology, China
Zhigang Chen	Central South University, China
Juan Chen	National University of Defense Technology, China
Jun Long	Jide Technology Company, China
Cheng Zhong	Guangxi University, China
Zhanyou Ma	North Minzu University, China
Huanlai Xing	Southwest Jiaotong University, China
Kerong Ben	Naval University of Engineering, China
Yicheng Xu	Shenzhen Institutes of Advanced Technology, CAS, China
Mengting Yuan	Wuhan University, China
Jinyun Xue	Jiangxi Normal University, China
Zhiping Cai	National University of Defense Technology, China
Naijie Gu	University of Science and Technology of China, China
Meihua Xiao	East China Jiaotong University, China
Biaoshuai Tao	Shanghai Jiao Tong University, China
Jiaohua Qin	Central South University of Forestry and Technology, China
En Zhu	National University of Defense Technology, China
Feng Shi	Central South University, China
Guojing Tian	Institute of Computing Technology, CAS, China
Changjing Wang	Jiangxi Normal University, China
Gang Wang	Nankai University, China
Haiyu Pan	Guilin University of Electronic Technology, China
Hong Zheng	East China University of Science and Technology, China
Dantong Ouyang	Jilin University, China
Shenggen Zheng	Pengcheng Laboratory, China
Yu Yang	Pingdingshan University, China
Ming Zhao	Central South University, China
Yan Yang	Southwest Jiaotong University, China

Yuncheng Jiang	South China Normal University, China
Qian Li	Shenzhen Institute of Computing Sciences, China
Dongjing Miao	Harbin Institute of Technology, China
Yongzhi Cao	Peking University, China
Zhengwei Qi	Shanghai Jiao Tong University, China
Qi Fu	Hunan University of Science and Technology, China
Peng Zhang	Shandong University, China
Chihao Zhang	Shanghai Jiao Tong University, China
Yong Zhang	Shenzhen Institutes of Advanced Technology, CAS, China
Yong Gan	Zhengzhou University of Light Industry, China
Zhao Zhang	Zhejiang Normal University, China
Jialin Zhang	Institute of Computing Technology, CAS, China
Hao Liao	Shenzhen University, China
Zhengkang Zuo	Jiangxi Normal University, China
Yitong Yin	Nanjing University, China
Penghui Yao	Nanjing University, China
Feng Qin	Jiangxi Normal University, China
Zhihao Tang	Shanghai University of Finance and Economics, China
Mengji Xia	Institute of Software, Chinese Academy of Sciences, China
Chang Tang	China University of Geosciences, China
Nan Wu	Nanjing University, China
Shuai Lu	Jilin University, China
Liwei Wang	Wuhan University, China
Wenjun Li	Changsha University of Science and Technology, China
Zhanshan Li	Jilin University, China
Zhendong Liu	Shandong Jianzhu University, China
Jin Wang	Changsha University of Science and Technology, China
Xiaofeng Wang	North Minzu University, China
Qiang Liu	National University of Defense Technology, China
Zhen You	Jiangxi Normal University, China
Aiguo Wang	Foshan University, China
Jiaoyun Yang	Hefei University of Technology, China
Qilong Feng	Central South University, China
Kun He	Huazhong University of Science and Technology, China
Kun He	Institute of Computing Technology, CAS, China

Hengfu Yang	Hunan First Normal University, China
Min-ming Li	City University of Hong Kong, China
Yongming Li	Shaanxi Normal University, China
Tongyang Li	Peking University, China
Jian Li	Tsinghua University, China
Kuan Li	Dongguan University Of Technology, China
Bo Li	Hong Kong Polytechnic University, China
Daming Zhu	Shandong University, China
Liming Zhang	Jilin University, China
Yuhao Zhang	Shanghai Jiao Tong University, China
Lei Zhuang	Zhengzhou University, China
Zhengjun Xi	Shaanxi Normal University, China
Shaofeng Jiang	Peking University, China
Xiaoyan Kui	Central South University, China
Xiaoyong Tang	Changsha University of Science and Technology, China
Qingyang Zhou	National University of Defense Technology, China
Yi Zhou	University of Electronic Science and Technology of China
Rigui Zhou	Shanghai Maritime University, China
Jinzhao Wu	Guangxi Minzu University, China
Yuxin Ye	Jilin University, China
Panyu Liu	National University of Defense Technology, China
Yuling Liu	Hunan University, China
Xinwang Liu	National University of Defense Technology, China
Peiqiang Liu	Shandong Technology and Business University, China
Shengxin Liu	Harbin Institute of Technology, Shenzhen, China
Huawen Liu	Zhejiang Normal University, China
Zhenyan Ji	Beijing Jiaotong University, China
Cai Dai	Shaanxi Normal University, China
Hai Wan	Sun Yat-sen University, China
Chau Vincent	Southeast University, China
Haihe Shi	Jiangxi Normal University, China

Contents

Networks and Security

Computational Theory and Models

Nonmonotone Submodular Maximization Under Routing Constraints

Haotian Zhang[1], Rao Li[1], Zewei Wu[2], and Guodong Sun[1(✉)]

[1] CS Department, Beijing Forestry University, Beijing 100083, China
{cs_haotian,liraorr57,sungd}@bjfu.edu.cn
[2] CS Department, Macao Polytechnic University, Macao 999078, China
zewei.wu@mpu.edu.mo

Abstract. In machine learning and big data, the optimization objectives based on set-cover, entropy, diversity, influence, feature selection, etc. are commonly modeled as submodular functions. Submodular (function) maximization is generally NP-hard, even in the absence of constraints. Recently, submodular maximization has been successfully investigated for the settings where the objective function is monotone or the constraint is computation-tractable. However, maximizing nonmonotone submodular function with complex constraints is not yet well-understood. In this paper, we consider the nonmonotone submodular maximization with a cost budget or feasibility constraint (particularly from route planning) that is generally NP-hard to evaluate. This is a very common issue in machine learning, big data, and robotics. This problem is NP-hard, and on top of that, its constraint evaluation is likewise NP-hard, which adds an additional layer of complexity. So far, few studies have been devoted to proposing effective solutions, leaving this problem currently unclear. In this paper, we first present an iterated greedy algorithm, which offers an approximate solution. Then we develop the proof machinery to demonstrate that our algorithm is a bicriterion approximation algorithm: it can accomplish a constant-factor approximation to the optimal algorithm, while keeping the over-budget tightly bounded. We also look at practical concerns for striking a balance between time complexity and over-budget. Finally, we conduct numeric experiments on two concrete examples to show our design's efficacy in real-world scenarios.

Keywords: Submodular maximization · Routing constraint · Nonmonotonicity · Bi-criterion approximation

1 Introduction

Submodularity fundamentally captures a diminishing-return property of set function: the reward of adding an item into a set will decrease as this set grows. Submodular maximization aims at finding a subset of some ground set such that the submodular objective function can be maximized with some (or without any) constraints on cost or feasibility. Submodular maximization appears in a wide

Z. Cai et al. (Eds.): NCTCS 2023, CCIS 1944, pp. 3–17, 2024.
https://doi.org/10.1007/978-981-99-7743-7_1

variety of scenarios, from combinatorics to machine learning, such as the coverage problem, facility location planning, information gathering, feature selection, data summarization, factorization in graphical models, and so forth [1–3].

In general, submodular maximization problems are NP-hard, regardless of whether they are constrained or not. A lot of approximation algorithms with guaranteed performance have been presented to maximize unconstrained or constrained-but-monotone functions. So far, however, the *constrained nonmonotone submodular maximization* has not been fairly well understood. Recently, a number of studies maximize nonmonotone submodular functions with additive or cardinality-based constraints, and presented algorithms with provable guarantees. In practical settings, however, the constraints are often more complex, or even infeasible to evaluate in poly-time [4–7]. For instance, in the big-data system with networked processors, multiple processors are often selected to concurrently execute a computation task on their local datasets. For timely applications, these selected processors are orchestrated as a delay-minimum multicast routing tree and expected to return to the user more representative results within a time threshold. Another example of nonmonotone submodular maximization is to complete an informative data collection with an energy-budgeted robot, which passes through a TSP route on some points of interest to collect data. These two examples will be detailed in Sect. 3.3. Their objective functions are nonmonotone submodular; their constraint evaluation is a cost-minimization problem, more complex than evaluating additive or cardinality-based constraints.

In this paper, our goal is to maximize nonmonotone submodular function with the constraints that need to be evaluated by some route planning. To the best of our knowledge, no literature has investigated such a submodular-maximization setting constrained by a routing budget. Part of our problem's difficulty stems from its submodularity, but a great deal more of the difficulty is attributed to its computationally-intractable routing constraints, which hinder the development of constant-factor approximate solution. In response to this issue, we present an iterated two-stage algorithm framework, which uses any poly-time, $(1+\theta)$-approximation algorithm to evaluate whether the routing cost stays under budget. We elaborately draw a connection between the error parameter θ and our algorithm's overall performance. Additionally, by exploring the routing cost function, we prove that it belongs to a kind of k-independence system, where k is loosely upper-bounded by the ground set's size and usually a positive constant in practical settings. Such exploration offers our algorithm a lower bound for performance guarantee. Based on all the above, we develop the proof machinery that proves our algorithm can achieve a $[1/4k, 1 + \theta]$-bicriterion approximation solution; that is, our objective value is at least as good as $1/4k$ of the optimal one, while the ratio of over-budget is upper bounded by θ (which is usually less than one or can be any small in some cases).

The remainder of this paper is organized as follows. Section 2 discusses the related works. Section 3 gives the necessary preliminaries and formulates our problem. Section 4 details the designs of our algorithm and analyze its performance bound. Finally, Sect. 5 concludes this paper.

2   Related Work

2.1   Monotone Submodular Maximization

In literature, most of efforts are put on maximizing monotone submodular functions with various types of constraints, and constant-factor approximation algorithms are presented.

Cardinality Constraint. Nemhauser and Wolsey [8] first give the near-optimal solution for the cardinality setting, with an approximation ratio of $(1 - 1/e)$. Krause and Guestrin [9] give a randomized algorithm to achieve $(1 - 1/e + \varepsilon)$-approximation with high probability (here $\varepsilon > 0$ can be any small). Balkanski and Singer [22] study the adaptive complexity of maximizing a submodular function with a cardinality constraint, and prove that there exists $\mathcal{O}(\log n)$-adaptive algorithm to achieve a $(1/3 - \varepsilon)$-approximation for any small $\varepsilon > 0$. In [23], the authors introduce a parallel algorithm, and the performance is arbitrarily close to $(1 - 1/e)$.

Matroid or Knapsack Constraint. Calinescu et al. [10] give a $(1 - 1/e)$-approximation algorithm for monotone submodular maximization subject to a general matroid constraint. For the settings with k-matroid constraints, Nemhauser and Wolsey [8] proposes a $1/(k + 1)$-approximation algorithm. Badanidiyuru and Vondrak [11] use the continuous greedy policy to design a $1/(k + 2l + 1 + \varepsilon)$-approximation for the intersection of a k-system and linear l-knapsack constraints.

More Complex Constraint. A more recent work [12] considers the monotone submodular maximization with an α-submodular constraint (such as routing constraint), where evaluating the constraint is assumed to be NP-hard. The authors give a bi-criterion algorithm (i.e., their solution is bounded in performance, though it will to some extent disagree with the original constraint), with an approximation ratio of $(1 - 1/e)/2$; the constraint violence is bounded by a polynomial $p(\alpha, k_c, \psi)$, where k_c is the curvature of the constraint function and ψ, the approximation ratio of the algorithm used to evaluate the constraint. Wu et al. [4] model their wireless charging scheduling problem as a monotone submodular maximization problem restricted by TSP routing; they replace their objective function with a surrogate function and propose a $(1 - 1/e)/4$-approximation bi-criterion algorithm. Nevertheless, these two studies' objective functions are monotone, and their analytical machinery cannot be applied to nonmonotone cases at all.

2.2   Nonmonotone Submodular Maximization

Maximizing nonmonotone submodular functions is generally more difficult and usually investigated in the cases without any constraints, or just with cardinality, convex-set, or packing-type constraints. For the unconstrained nonmonotone cases, Buchbinder et al. [13] propose a local search-based exact algorithm and a randomized algorithm, both of which can achieve approximation ratios of $1/2$

and 2/5, respectively. Next we give main results of maximizing constrained non-monotone submodular functions.

Cardinality Constraint. Buchbinder et al. [15] present an algorithm with constant factor ranging from $(1/e + 0.004)$ to $1/2$, and a 0.356-approximation algorithm under an exact cardinality constraint. Wang et al. [24] investigate the submodular partitioning problem with cardinality constraint, which divides a ground set into m blocks to maximize the evaluation of the minimum block under constraints. They propose a greedy-based algorithmic framework to achieve an $\Omega(1/m)$-approximation.

Matroid or Knapsack Constraint. In the case with a single matroid constraint, Feldman et al. [14] design a $1/e$-approximation greedy algorithm. Lee et al. [16] give the first constant-factor results for nonmonotone settings under k-matroid or k-knapsack constraints; the approximation ratios are $1/(k + 2 + 1/k + \epsilon)$ and $(0.2 - \epsilon)$ for the k-matroid and k-knapsack cases, respectively, where $\epsilon > 0$ is any small.

k-Independence System Constraint. Gupta et al. [17] investigate the algorithmic framework of nonmonotone submodular maximization constrained by a k-independence system (k-system, in short), which is a generalization of intersection of k matroids. Their algorithm achieves an approximation ratio of $\frac{k}{(1+1/\alpha)(k+1)^2} \approx \frac{1}{(1+1/\alpha)k}$, where $0 < \alpha < 1$ is the approximation guarantee for unconstrained nonmonotone submodular maximization. This result has remained competitive until now, and has motivated a number of studies focusing on the nonmonotone settings with k-system constraint. Mirzasoleiman et al. [18] follow the above algorithm and slightly reduce the above approximation ratio down to $\frac{k}{(k+1)(2k+1)}$. Also adopting the iterative algorithmic framework of [17], Feldman et al. [19] propose a deterministic algorithm that achieves an approximation ratio of $\frac{1}{k+\mathcal{O}(\sqrt{k})}$, and furthermore, they propose a randomized $\frac{k}{(k+1)^2}$-approximation algorithm for the nonmonotone settings with k-extensible constraint. Shi et al. [20] extend the approach in [16] to make it suitable to the k-system constraint, and present an algorithm with the factor of $\frac{1}{2k+3+1/k}$; the authors also show that, if $k < 8$, their algorithm will outperform that of [19]. Tang [21] proposes a sampling-based randomized algorithm for maximizing the k-system-constrained nonmonotone adaptive submodular function, and this algorithm achieves an approximation ratio of $1/(2k + 4)$.

To date, the algorithms for nonmonotone submodular maximization under k-system have almost followed the seminal framework proposed in [17]. All these algorithms are $\frac{1}{\Omega(k)}$-approximation, merely with slightly-different time complexities. In particular, their constraint functions are assumed to be computationally tractable. However, it is not always true; for instance, evaluating routing restriction is generally NP-Hard. Until now, there have not been any algorithmic frameworks and analytical machinery that can achieve a constant-factor or bi-criterion approximation for the nonmonotone submodular maximization with an intractable routing constraint.

3   Preliminaries and Problem Statement

In this section, we first introduce some preliminaries as well as notations, and then, formalize our problem along with two motivating examples. Finally we analyze the intractability of our problem.

3.1   Submodular Maximization

Given the ground set Ω of n items, we say that a utility function $f : 2^{\Omega} \to \mathbf{R}$ is a *submodular set function* if and only if we have

$$f(A \cup B) + f(A \cap B) \leq f(A) + f(B) \tag{1}$$

for any $A \subseteq \Omega$ and $B \subseteq \Omega$ [25]. Commonly, f is nonnegative and $f(\emptyset) = 0$. The submodularity of f can be equivalently expressed with

$$f(A \cup \{x\}) - f(A) \geq f(B \cup \{x\}) - f(B) \tag{2}$$

for any $A \subseteq B \subset \Omega$ and $x \in \Omega \backslash B$. Submodular function $f(A)$ has a diminishing marginal gain as A grows. We hereafter use $f_A^+(x) \triangleq f(A \cup \{x\}) - f(A)$ to denote the marginal gain of f on $x \in \Omega$ with respect to $A \subset \Omega$, unless otherwise noted. A submodular function f defined on 2^{Ω} is monotone if for all $A \subseteq B \subseteq \Omega$, we always have $f(A) \leq f(B)$ or a nonnegative marginal gain. In a nonmonotone submodular case, however, $f_A^+(x)$ could be negative.

A constrained submodular maximization problem can be defined by $\max\{f(S) \mid g(S) \leq c, S \subseteq \Omega\}$, where f is the objective function, and g, the cost function. In practice, cost functions are usually positive and monotone increasing.

3.2   Routing-Based Cost Function

Given a ground set Ω of items, a weighted graph abstraction can be drawn over Ω—the graph vertices are the items, and an edge exists between two items if both of them have a connection in some way. In such a graph, vertices (items) and edges are all associated with positive weights to represent the costs of visiting vertices and passing through edges.

With a nonnegative function $\rho : 2^{\Omega} \to \mathbf{R}_{\geq 0}$ and any $S \subseteq \Omega$, if $\rho(S)$ is mapped to the least total cost of the route that visits all the vertices of S in some way, we say ρ is a *routing-based cost function*. More specifically, the routing-based cost function on S can be commonly written as $\rho(S) = \sum_{s \in S} c_s + r^*(S)$, where $c_s \geq 0$ is the cost in visiting s and $r^*(S)$ is the minimum cost of traversing each vertex of S at least once. In general, $r^*(S)$ is infeasible to compute within poly-time; clearly, it is the $r^*(S)$ term that makes it NP-hard to determine $\rho(S)$.

To simplify notation, we also use ρ to represent the optimal algorithm of achieving the least cost. In most real-life applications, we have $\rho(T) \leq \rho(S)$ for $T \subseteq S$, i.e., ρ is nondecreasing. Specifically, it is easy to prove that for any $S, T \subseteq \Omega$ with $S = T \cup \{s\}$, we have $\rho(S) - \rho(T) \geq c^{\min}$ where $c^{\min} = \min\{c_s \mid s \in \Omega\}$, i.e., the gradient of function ρ is at least $c^{\min}$. In this paper we assume $\rho(\emptyset) = 0$ and ρ is nondecreasing.

3.3   Problem Definition and Examples

Given a nonempty ground set Ω and a nonmonotone submodular set function $f : 2^\Omega \rightarrow \mathbf{R}_{\geq 0}$, we aim at finding a subset $S^* \subseteq \Omega$ such that

$$S^* = \arg\max_{S \subseteq \Omega}\{f(S) \mid \rho(S) \leq \mathbf{c}\}, \tag{3}$$

where $\rho(S)$ is a routing-based cost function defined on 2^Ω and $\mathbf{c}$ is the budget (a positive constant). Here, $\rho(\cdot) \leq \mathbf{c}$ is a *routing constraint* to the objective function $f(\cdot)$. We assume that $\rho(\{s\}) \leq \mathbf{c}$ for any singleton $s \in \Omega$. Followed are two motivating examples of our problem.

Example-1: Diversified Task Offloading in Big Data. Big Data system is a networked distributed computing environment, in which each processor can store and process data, and processors are connected with delaying links. To effectively complete a computation task within a given time, users usually offload the task down to a subset of processors whose data is more representative. These selected processors can, in parallel, run the task on their local data sets, and return results to users for further combination. In machine learning [18,26,27], the functions of evaluating data representativeness are commonly nonmonotone and submodular. The user can calculate (foreknow) the time of each processor running a task before offloading it. Given a subset of processors, therefore, the completion time heavily depends on how long the in-network data transfer will take. Equivalently, what the user needs is find a delay-minimum multicast routing tree that is rooted at the user and spans all the selected processors, which is an NP-Complete task in general. Obviously, this example can be modeled as a nonmonotone submodular maximization with a multicast routing restriction.

Example-2: Informative Data Collection with a Robot. In this example, an on-ground or aerial robot departs from a depot and moves through some points of interest (already specified in a certain monitoring area) to capture data. The robot's objective is collect as informative data as possible, while not running out of its energy before returning to the depot. This scenario often falls into the category of informative path planning in robotics. The robot cannot visit all points due to its limited energy capacity. It has to select an informative subset of points, and visit them along a TSP tour that starts and ends at the depot. In real-life applications [28–30], "informative" can be measured with the mutual information between the visited and unvisited points; and mutual information is of nonmonotone submodularity. So, this example can be naturally modeled as a nonmonotone submodular maximization with TSP constraint.

3.4   Hardness of Our Problem

The computational intractability of our problem stems from three aspects. First, even if we ignore the constraint on our problem (for example, $\mathbf{c}$ is very large), maximizing a (nonmonotone) submodular function remains NP-hard. It is quite straightforward to know that our problem is NP-hard, too. Second, for a given subset of Ω, we need to evaluate its feasibility by solving the routing-based cost function that is NP-hard in general settings. Third, our problem's objective function and constraint evaluation cannot be solved separately, because each is coupled with the other.

There have been lots of efforts to optimize monotone and nonmonotone submodular functions without constraints. In the past few years, however, there has been a surge of interest in applying constrained submodular maximization to machine learning. But most of these prior works usually focus on the maximization with computationally tractable constraints, such as cardinality, knapsack, and matroid constraints [15,16,31]. They, however, cannot be directly applied to our problem to achieve bounded performance.

4 Our Algorithm

The seminal work [17] propose an iterative greedy algorithm (called SMS, for convenience) to maximize nonmonotone submodular function with k-system constraints. SMS can provide an approximation ratio of $\frac{k}{(1+1/\alpha)(k+1)^2} \approx \frac{1}{(1+1/\alpha)k}$, which remains competitive for general settings until now. Here, parameter α $(0 < \alpha < 1)$ is the approximation guarantee for unconstrained nonmonotone submodular maximization. Each iteration of SMS covers two stages: (1) selecting as many items from available ones as possible, until the k-system property cannot hold, and (2) applying an unconstrained nonmonotone submodular maximization algorithm to those selected items. SMS repeats the two stages k times. During iterations, it stores all the feasible solutions determined by the second stage, and the best one will be returned at last.

Our algorithm follows the algorithmic framework of SMS, and it can achieve at least the same performance as SMS's, while only needing polynomial time cost. Our basic idea is as follows. First, we prove the routing constraint on our problem is a kind of k-system, which transforms our problem into a k-system-constrained nonmonotone submodular maximization problem. This enables SMS's approximation ratio to work for our algorithm. Second, we recruit an algorithm $\tilde{\rho}$ to approximate ρ in evaluating the routing cost, such that our algorithm can terminate in poly-time with an over-budget. Third, we prove that the amount of over-budget is bounded, by analyzing the performance gap in cost evaluation between $\tilde{\rho}$ and ρ.

4.1 Algorithm Description

Our algorithm is outlined in Algorithm 1, and it is an iterative procedure. Each iteration includes two stages which are described below in detail.

Stage-1: Maximization with Constraint Relaxed. In the i-th iteration, the items, yet unexamined so far, form the set S_i. Stage-1 uses the `whileloop` iteratively to examine all the items of S_i, picking out s^*, the item bringing the highest marginal gain. During the cherry-picking, our algorithm uses a $(1+\theta)$-approximation poly-time algorithm $\tilde{\rho}$ in place of optimal algorithm ρ to verify whether the routing cost is under constraint, where θ is usually within $(0, 1)$.

Algorithm 1: our algorithm

---

    input : Ω, $\mathbf{c}$, k, θ, α
    output: $T^* \subseteq \Omega$ and $f(T^*)$

1 $S_1 \leftarrow \Omega$ and $\mathcal{T} \leftarrow \emptyset$ // two sets
2 **for** $i = 1$ up to k
3      $X_i \leftarrow \emptyset$ and $Y_i \leftarrow \emptyset$ // two sequences
       $\triangleright$ Stage 1: add as many items as possible
4   **while** $S_i \neq \emptyset$
5          $s^* \leftarrow \arg\max\{f_{X_i}^+(s)|s \in S_i\}$
6   **if** s^* exists and $\tilde{\rho}(X_i + s^*) \leq (1 + \theta)\mathbf{c}$ **then**
7             $X_i \leftarrow X_i + s^*$ and $S_i \leftarrow S_i \backslash s^*$
8   **if** $\tilde{\rho}(X_i) > \mathbf{c}$ **then**
9                $Y_i \leftarrow Y_i + s^*$
10   **else**
11   break the while-loop (line 4)

       $\triangleright$ Stage 2: find the best from a set of local optima
12   **if** $X_i \neq \emptyset$ **then**
13         $T_i^* \leftarrow \mathsf{UNS}_\alpha(X_i)$
14   **while** $y \leftarrow$ the last item of Y_i exists
15            $X_i \leftarrow X_i \backslash y$ and $Y_i \leftarrow Y_i \backslash y$
16            $T_y \leftarrow \mathsf{UNS}_\alpha(X_i)$ and $\mathcal{T} \leftarrow \mathcal{T} \cup \{T_y\}$
17         $\mathcal{T} \leftarrow \mathcal{T} \cup \{T_i^*\}$
18   **else**
19   break the for-loop (line 2)
20      $S_{i+1} \leftarrow S_i$ // the i-th iteration stops here
21 **return** $f(T^*) = \max\{f(T)|T \in \mathcal{T}\}$ and T^*

In the `whileloop`, the constraint is relaxed from $\mathbf{c}$ to $(1 + \theta)\mathbf{c}$, and the `whileloop` continues until the routing cost evaluated by $\tilde{\rho}$ is beyond $(1+\theta)\mathbf{c}$. If the cost stays under the relaxed budget, s^* will be moved from S_i into the rear of X_i, which is an ordered set or a sequence; otherwise, the `whileloop` breaks, and then, Stage-1 is over in the current iteration and outputs X_i and Y_i. As shown on lines 8 and 9, Y_i is also a sequence and only stores the items that are examined after the original budget $\mathbf{c}$ is violated. The `whileloop` tries to maximize f with its original constraint slightly relaxed, and therefore, $\tilde{\rho}(X_i)$ output by Stage-1 may be larger than $\mathbf{c}$. But the over-budget can remain under $\theta \cdot \mathbf{c}$.

Stage-2: Maximization Without Constraints. Once Stage-1 stops with $X_i \neq \emptyset$ as output, Stage-2 is prompt to take over the unfinished task. Stage-2 tries to employ the UNS_α procedure to dig out a more profitable subset out of X_i. Here, UNS_α can be any solvers that maximize a general unconstrained nonmonotone submodular function, with a bounded approximation ratio α ($0 < \alpha < 1$). In this paper, UNS_α is fulfilled by the deterministic algorithm proposed in [13], which can use $\mathcal{O}(n)$ value oracles to achieve $1/3$-approximation for unconstrained nonmonotone submodular maximization problem.

Stage-2 first uses UNS_α to pick out T_i^* from X_i. However, T_i^* is not necessarily the best because of f's non-monotonicity. As shown on lines 15 and 16, therefore, Stage-2 continues to curtail X_i until $X_i \backslash Y_i$ is reached, and in the meantime, it repeatedly recruits UNS_α to explore for the solution T_y that is possibly better than T_i^*.

After the `forloop` completes at $i = k$ or $X_i = \emptyset$, our algorithm will immediately scan through all the routes in $\mathcal{T}$ and then return the ultimate winner and its objective value. The `forloop` goes ahead as i increases from 1 to k. Here, k is an integer constant, loosely upper-bounded by $|\Omega| - 1$, and it will be discussed later in Sect. 4.3.

4.2 Theoretical Performance

Given a set function $f : 2^\Omega \to \mathbf{R}_{\geq 0}$, we say $(\Omega, \mathcal{I} \subseteq 2^\Omega)$ is an *independence system* if the following two properties are satisfied: I (non-emptiness) $\emptyset \in \mathcal{I}$, i.e., $\mathcal{I}$ is not empty per se, and II (heredity) if $S_1 \in \mathcal{I}$ and $S_2 \subset S_1$, then $S_2 \in \mathcal{I}$. The heredity of independence system makes $\mathcal{I}$ exponential in size in the worst case, and therefore, the optimization via exhaustive search over $\mathcal{I}$ is infeasible in terms of computation.

Given $S \subseteq \Omega$ and $S_1 \subseteq S$, we say S_1 is a *base* of S, if $S_1 \in \mathcal{I}$ and we cannot find other $S_2 \in \mathcal{I}$ such that $S_1 \subseteq S_2 \subseteq S$. An independence system $(\Omega, \mathcal{I})$ is called a *k-independence system* (*k-system*, in short), if and only if there exists an integer k such that $|B_1|/|B_2| \leq k$ for any two bases, B_1 and B_2, of Ω. As a special case, a matroid is a 1-independence system.

Theorem 1. *Let $\mathcal{I}_\rho = \{S | S \subseteq \Omega$ and $\rho(S) \leq \mathbf{c}\}$ and $\mathcal{I}_{\tilde{\rho}} = \{S | S \subseteq \Omega$ and $\tilde{\rho}(S) \leq (1 + \theta)\mathbf{c}$ with $\theta > 0\}$. Both $(\Omega, \mathcal{I}_\rho)$ and $(\Omega, \mathcal{I}_{\tilde{\rho}})$ are a kind of k-system.*

Proof. We first prove that $\mathcal{I}_\rho$ is an independence system. Since $\emptyset \subset \Omega$ and $\rho(\emptyset) = 0$, we have $\emptyset \in \mathcal{I}_\rho$. Consider $S \in \mathcal{I}_\rho$ and a subset $T \subset S$. We know $\rho(T) < \rho(S) \leq \mathbf{c}$, which means $T \in \mathcal{I}_\rho$. Thus $(\Omega, \mathcal{I}_\rho)$ is an independence system.

For any item $s \in \Omega$, we have assumed $\rho(\{s\}) \leq \mathbf{c}$, indicating that each base of $\mathcal{I}_\rho$ is not less than one in size. On the other hand, it is easy to prove, by contradiction, that if Ω has a base of size n, then all its bases are of size n. That said, there must exist an integer k_ρ $(1 \leq k_\rho < n)$ such that $|B_1|/|B_2| \leq k$ for any two bases, B_1 and B_2, of Ω. Hence $\mathcal{I}_\rho$ is a k_ρ-system. Applying similar analysis to $(\Omega, \mathcal{I}_{\tilde{\rho}})$, we can conclude that there exists an integer $k_{\tilde{\rho}}$ $(1 \leq k_{\tilde{\rho}} < n)$ such that $(\Omega, \mathcal{I}_{\tilde{\rho}})$ is a $k_{\tilde{\rho}}$-system. ∎

Theorem 1 implies that our problem is also a nonmonotone submodular maximization problem with k-system constraint. That said, SMS's approximation ratio is hopefully true for our algorithm. However, SMS requires that its k-system cost function be exactly evaluated. Such a requirement cannot be satisfied in our setting, because our cost function is more complex and generally intractable. In exchange for polynomial computation complexity, our algorithm replaces ρ with $\tilde{\rho}$. Recall that $\tilde{\rho}$ is a $(1+\theta)$-approximation to ρ. Now, the crux of analyzing our algorithm's competitiveness is to profile how differently Stage-1 will perform when it uses $\tilde{\rho}$ under a relaxed budget and ρ under the original budget.

Without loss of generality, we focus on Stage-1 of the i-th iteration of our algorithm. Suppose that we can, in parallel, run ρ and $\tilde{\rho}$ in the cost evaluation (line 6 of Algorithm 1), with $\mathbf{c}$ and $(1+\theta)\mathbf{c}$ as their budgets, respectively. For convenience, Stage-1's `whileloop` is called ρ-`whileloop` if ρ is used in cost evaluation, and it is called $\tilde{\rho}$-`whileloop` if $\tilde{\rho}$ is used.

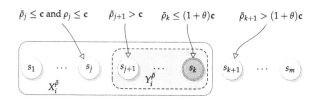

Fig. 1. Demo of our algorithm's Stage-1 selecting $X_i^{\tilde{\rho}}$ out of $S_i = \{s_1, s_2 \ldots s_m\}$, where $j < k \le m$.

Theorem 2. Given S_i at the beginning of Stage-1, assume the $\tilde{\rho}$-`whileloop` stops with $X_i^{\tilde{\rho}} \subseteq S_i$. If ρ-`whileloop` can stop with $X_i^{\rho} \subseteq S_i$, then we always have $X_i^{\rho} \subseteq X_i^{\tilde{\rho}}$ for any $\theta > 0$.

Proof. In line 5 of our algorithm, picking s^* (i.e., the item with the highest marginal gain) out of S_i has nothing to do with the solver used by the cost evaluation (line 6). Without considering the routing constraint, the sequence of best vertices chosen in the `whileloop` would be always the same. We denote this sequence by $\langle s_1, s_2, \cdots s_m \rangle$, where $m = |S_i|$ and s_j is picked ahead of s_k if $j < k$.

Consider a general case: $\tilde{\rho}$-`whileloop` stops at s_k ($k < m$), while returning a route of cost $\tilde{\rho}_k$. As shown in Fig. 1, in such a case, we have $\tilde{\rho}_k \le (1+\theta)\mathbf{c}$ but $\tilde{\rho}_{k+1} > (1+\theta)\mathbf{c}$. Now suppose that optimal solver ρ can stop at s_{k+1} with the best route of cost ρ_{k+1}, meaning $\rho_{k+1} \le \mathbf{c}$.

Since $\tilde{\rho}$ approximates ρ with a factor of $(1+\theta)$, we readily have

$$(1+\theta)\rho_{k+1} \ge \tilde{\rho}_{k+1} > (1+\theta)\mathbf{c}, \tag{4}$$

which means $\rho_{k+1} > \mathbf{c}$. That contradicts. Hence, ρ cannot stop at s_{k+1} under budget $\mathbf{c}$, if $\tilde{\rho}$ stops at s_k under budget $(1+\theta)\mathbf{c}$. Clearly, ρ cannot stop at any s_j for $k+2 \le j \le m$, too. We thus have $X_i^{\rho} \subseteq X_i^{\tilde{\rho}} \subseteq S_i$ for any $\theta > 0$. ∎

Theorem 2 shows that, in Stage-1, ρ cannot pick more items out of S_i under the budget of $\mathbf{c}$ than $\tilde{\rho}$ does under the budget of $(1+\theta)\mathbf{c}$.

Theorem 3. Given S_i at the beginning of Stage-1, if ρ-`whileloop` stops with X_i^{ρ}, then our algorithm must be able to meet X_i^{ρ} in the subsequent Stage-2, and determine a subset of X_i^{ρ} as a candidate solution.

Proof. We resort to Fig. 1 to finish this proof. Assume that the $\tilde{\rho}$-whileloop stops in Stage-1 with $X_i^{\tilde{\rho}}$ and $Y_i^{\tilde{\rho}}$, and that $\tilde{\rho}_j \leq \mathbf{c}$ but $\tilde{\rho}_{j+1} > \mathbf{c}$. This means $Y_i^{\tilde{\rho}} = \langle s_{j+1}, s_{j+2} \dots s_k \rangle$, according to our algorithm's lines 8 and 9.

Since $\tilde{\rho}$ approximates ρ and $\tilde{\rho}_j \leq \mathbf{c}$, we have $\rho_j \leq \mathbf{c}$, i.e., that ρ will not stop earlier than meeting item j. Additionally, we know $X_i^{\rho} \subseteq X_i^{\tilde{\rho}}$ by Theorem 2. Thus ρ must stop at some item of $\{s_j\} \cup Y_i^{\tilde{\rho}}$. If $X_i^{\rho} = X_i^{\tilde{\rho}}$, obviously, our algorithm can meet X_i^{ρ} on Stage-2's line 13. Moreover, in Stage-2's line 14, we continue to shrink $X_i^{\tilde{\rho}}$ (i.e., X_i), by deleting its last item, until $X_i^{\tilde{\rho}} \backslash Y_i^{\tilde{\rho}}$ is hit. During such a shrinking process, we apply UNS_α to each of the intermediate subsets. Clearly, X_i^{ρ} is either among these subsets, or equivalent to $X_i^{\tilde{\rho}}$, i.e., our algorithm cannot miss X_i^{ρ}. ∎

Theorem 2 and Theorem 3 have paved the way to prove our algorithm's bicriterion competitiveness. Next we introduce the formal definition of *bicriterion approximation* as follows. For a problem of $\max\{f(X)|g(X) \leq c\}$, a (p, q)-bicriterion approximation algorithm can output a solution X that guarantees $f(X) \geq p \cdot f(X^{\text{opt}})$ and $g(X) \leq q \cdot \mathbf{c}$, where X^{opt} is an optimal solution, $0 < p < 1$ and $q > 1$. These two parameters p and q approximately measure the optimality and the feasibility of approximation algorithm, respectively.

Theorem 4. Using a $(1 + \theta)$-approximation algorithm $\tilde{\rho}$ to evaluate the cost constraint under budget $(1 + \theta)\mathbf{c}$, our algorithm can at least achieve a $\left[\frac{k}{4(k+1)^2}, 1 + \theta\right]$-bicriterion approximation.

Proof. In each iteration's Stage-1, our algorithm always stops adding items when its budget is violated. So, any routes in $\mathcal{T}$ are not beyond $(1 + \theta)\mathbf{c}$ in total cost; in other words, the over-budget amount of our solution is at most $\theta \cdot \mathbf{c}$.

Theorem 3 ensures that our algorithm with $\tilde{\rho}$ in cost evaluation can still achieve an approximation ratio that is at least as good as SMS's $\frac{k}{(1+1/\alpha)(k+1)^2}$. Our algorithm's Stage-2 invokes the UNS_α procedure, whose approximation ratio is $0 < \alpha < 1$. It is proven in [13] that there exist a deterministic and a randomized algorithms for general unconstrained submodular maximization, which both need linear time and can achieve $1/3$-approximation and $1/2$-approximation (in expectation), respectively. If taking $\alpha = 1/3$, our algorithm can achieve an exact approximation ratio of at least $\frac{k}{4(k+1)^2} \approx \frac{1}{4k}$. In [13,32], two elegant deterministic $1/3$-approximation UNS_α algorithms are presented. ∎

4.3 Asymptotic Time Complexity

Without loss of generality, we first analyze the asymptotic time complexity in the i-th iteration with S_i at the beginning.

Time Cost in Stage-1. The whileloop of Stage-1 will stop, if S_i turns empty or if the relaxed constraint is violated; consequently, Stage-1 examines at most $|S_i|$ items. In Stage-1, determining all possible s^* on line 5 needs $\Theta(|S_i|^2)$ calls of f-oracles in total. In addition, it is easy to know that Stage-1 needs $\Theta(|S_i|)$ calls of $\tilde{\rho}$-oracles in constraint evaluation.

Time Cost in Stage-2. In Stage-2, UNS_α is called $|Y_i|$ times, and every call for UNS_α needs $\mathcal{O}(|X_i|)$ f-oracles. With $Y_i \subseteq X_i \subseteq S_i$, therefore, Stage-2's time cost can be loosely upper bounded by $\mathcal{O}(|S_i|^2)$ calls of f-oracle.

Besides involving the two-stage `forloop` as the protagonist, our algorithm in its last step sorts through the collection $\mathcal{T}$ to return the best solution, and clearly, this process needs $\Theta(|\mathcal{T}|)$ time. Stage-2 of iteration i adds into $\mathcal{T}$ at most $|Y_i|$ local optima; thus, the size of $\mathcal{T}$ is far less than $k|\Omega|$.

To sum up, the time complexity of our algorithm is upper bounded by $\mathcal{O}(kn^2)$ f-oracles plus $\mathcal{O}(kn)$ $\tilde{\rho}$-oracles, where $n = |\Omega|$. We will in future give each stage a tighter analysis that can further reduce this time complexity.

For the settings with k-system constraint, we cannot easily know k in advance because determining k often requires exponentially exhaustive computation. In literature, k is usually replaced by the size of Ω. Although doing so will not worsen the theoretical time complexity too much, less k is preferable in practice. In [17], the authors recommend that k can be set to two—running their SMS's iteration only twice instead of $|\Omega|$ times—in order to considerably reduce the run-time. In [19], the authors find that, in the SMS-like algorithms, reducing k down to $\sqrt{k}$ will not impact the algorithm approximation performance; that is, in our algorithm's implementation, k can be safely replaced by $\sqrt{|\Omega|}$, thereby leading to a significant reduction in computational time.

4.4   Remark About the Over-Budget

Our algorithm's solution may be beyond the original budget $\mathbf{c}$, and the amount of over-budget is at most $\theta\mathbf{c}$. Recall that the error parameter θ is the approximation factor of algorithm $\tilde{\rho}$ evaluating the routing cost. Obviously, the smaller θ is, the less the over-budget will be.

In many practical routing constraint settings, there exist $(1 + \theta)$-approximation algorithms, where θ values are very small numbers, often less than one. For instance, there exists 1.55-approximation algorithm (i.e., $\theta = 0.55$) for minimum-weight multicast routing problem [33]. If the routing cost is determined by Euclidean TSP, for instance, we can recruit a PTAS (Polynomial Time Approximation Scheme) for TSP problem and set its θ to be any small to control the over-budget below a very small scale. In detail, PTAS is a type of approximation algorithm for computation-intractable problems. A PTAS algorithm can achieve $(1 + \theta)$-approximation for minimization, or $(1 - \theta)$-approximation for maximization, where $\theta > 0$; and for any fixed $\theta > 0$, it runs in time polynomial in the input instance's size. For instance, there exists PTAS for Euclidean TSP problems, which finds a $(1 + \theta)$-approximation solution in time of at most $\mathcal{O}(n(\log n)^{o(1/\theta)})$; there exists PTAS for Subset-Sum problems, in time of $\mathcal{O}(n^3(\log n)^2/\theta)$.

In our algorithm, though a smaller θ of PTAS might lead to more computation time in Stage-1's cost evaluation, it can in some degree reduce the time cost in Stage-2 by reducing the size of Y_i. The following theorem gives an explanation about such a run-time reduction.

Theorem 5. Given S_i, if the ρ-`whileloop` stops with $X_i^\rho \subseteq S_i$ and the $\tilde{\rho}$-`whileloop`, with $X_i^{\tilde{\rho}} \subseteq S_i$, then we always have $|X_i^{\tilde{\rho}} \backslash X_i^\rho| \leq 1$ for any feasible $0 < \theta \leq c^{\min}/\mathbf{c}$, where θ is the error parameter of $\tilde{\rho}$.

Proof. Since Theorem 2 has proven $X_i^\rho \subseteq X_i^{\tilde{\rho}}$ for any θ, we here suppose that, given S_i, the ρ-`whileloop` can stop at s_k if the $\tilde{\rho}$-`whileloop` stops at s_{k+2}. We next complete this proof by contradiction.

From the conditions in which ρ and $\tilde{\rho}$ stop, we have (1) $\tilde{\rho}_{k+2} \leq (1+\theta)\mathbf{c}$, and (2) $\rho_k \leq \mathbf{c}$ but $\rho_{k+1} > \mathbf{c}$. According to the property of routing cost function, it is easy to know $\rho_{k+2} \geq \rho_{k+1} + c_{k+2} > \mathbf{c} + c^{\min}$, where c_{k+2} is the visiting cost at item s_{k+2}. Because $\tilde{\rho}$ approximates ρ and $\theta \leq c^{\min}/\mathbf{c}$, we have $\tilde{\rho}_{k+2} \geq \rho_{k+2}$, which further leads to

$$\tilde{\rho}_{k+2} \geq \rho_{k+2} > \mathbf{c} + c^{\min} \geq \mathbf{c} + \theta\mathbf{c}. \tag{5}$$

This inequality contradicts $\tilde{\rho}_{k+2} \leq (1+\theta)\mathbf{c}$. If $\tilde{\rho}$-`whileloop` stops at s_{k+2}, therefore, ρ-`whileloop` cannot stop at s_k. Moreover, the ρ-`whileloop` cannot stop at s_j for any $j < k$, too. Thus, ρ-`whileloop` can only stop either at s_{k+1} or at s_{k+2}. This theorem holds true. ∎

If $\tilde{\rho}$ is a PTAS with $\theta \leq c^{\min}/\mathbf{c}$, then we will have $|Y_i| = |X_i^{\tilde{\rho}} \backslash X_i^\rho| \leq 1$ at the end of Stage-1. It means that Stage-2 can finish with at most two calls of UNS_α. So a PTAS of ρ with small θ can lower Stage-2's time cost. With Theorem 5, we can readily have Corollary 1: the run-time and the budget control can be traded off according to practical settings and resource supply.

Corollary 1. Given S_i, if the ρ-`whileloop` stops with $X_i^\rho \subseteq S_i$ and the $\tilde{\rho}$-`whileloop`, with $X_i^{\tilde{\rho}} \subseteq S_i$, then we always have $|X_i^{\tilde{\rho}} \backslash X_i^\rho| \leq r$ for any $0 < \theta \leq r \cdot c^{\min}/\mathbf{c}$, where r is a positive integer ranging in $[1, \mathbf{c}/c^{\min})$.

5   Conclusion

In this paper, we have investigated the nonmonotone submodular maximization with routing constraint, proved it to be a k-system-constrained nonmonotone submodular maximization problem, and proposed a $[1/4k, 1+\theta]$-bicriterion approximation algorithm. Considering the intractability of constraint evaluation, we draw an elegant connection between the constraint evaluation's error parameter (i.e., θ) and the overall performance. Further, we have developed the machinery for proving the performance guarantee; we believe it can shed light on maximizing nonmonotone submodular function whose constraint evaluation is generally NP-hard. We have numerically evaluated our algorithm under the motivating examples mentioned in Sect. 3.3. Due to page limit, we omit the results and analyses, which can be seen in our previous report[1].

---

[1] https://arxiv.org/abs/2211.17131.

References

1. Krause, A., Golovin, D.: Submodular function maximization, chapter tractability: practical approaches to hard problems, pp. 3–19. Cambridge University Press (2012)
2. Wu, K., Cai, D., He, X.: Multi-label active learning based on submodular functions. Neurocomputing **313**, 436–442 (2018)
3. Bilmes, J.: submodularity in machine learning and artificial intelligence (2022). https://arxiv.org/pdf/2202.00132v1.pdf
4. Wu, T., Yang, P., Dai, H., Xu, W., Xu, M.: Collaborated tasks-driven mobile charging and scheduling: a near optimal result. In: IEEE Conference on Computer Communications (INFOCOM), pp. 1810–1818 (2019)
5. Amantidis, G., Kleer, P., Schafer, G.: Budget-feasible mechanism design for non-monotone submodular objectives: offline and online. In: the 2019 ACM Conference on Economics and Computation, pp. 901–919 (2019)
6. Jakkala, K., Akella, S.: Probabilistic gas leak rate estimation using submodular function maximizationwith routing constraints. IEEE Robot. Autom. Lett. **7**(2), 5230–5237 (2022)
7. Durr, C., Thang, N., Srivastav, A., Tible, L.: Non-monotone DR-submodular maximization over general convex sets. In: The Twenty-Ninth International Joint Conference on Artificial Intelligence (IJCAI), pp. 2148–2157 (2020)
8. Nemhauser, G., Wolsey, L.: Best algorithms for approximating the maximum of a submodular set function. Math. Oper. Res. **3**(3), 177–188 (1978)
9. Krause, A., Guestrin, C.: Near-optimal nonmyopic value of information in graphical models. In: The Nineteenth International Joint Conference on Artificial Intelligence (IJCAI), pp. 324–331 (2005)
10. Calinescu, G., Chekuri, C., Pal, M., Vondrak, J.: Maximizing a monotone submodular function subject to a matroid constraint. SIAM J. Comput. **40**(6), 1740–1766 (2011)
11. Badanidiyuru, A., Vondrak, J.: Fast algorithms for maximizing submodular functions. In: The 25th Annual ACM-SIAM Symposium on Discrete Algorithms (SODA), pp. 1497–1514 (2014)
12. Zhang, H., Vorobeychik, Y.: Submodular optimization with routing constraints. In: AAAI (2016)
13. Buchbinder, N., Feldman, M., Naor, J., Schwartz, R.: A tight linear time (1/2)-approximation for unconstrained submodular maximization. In: The 53rd Annual Symposium on Foundations of Computer Science (FOCS), pp. 649–658 (2012)
14. Feldman, M., Naor, J., Schwartz, R.: A unified continuous greedy algorithm for submodular maximization. In: IEEE 52nd Annual Symposium on Foundations of Computer Science (FOCS), Palm Springs, CA, USA, pp. 570–579 (2011)
15. Buchbinder, N., Feldman, M., Naor, J., Schwarts, R.: Submodular maximization with cardinality constraints. In: Proceedings of the Twenty-Fifth Annual ACM-SIAM Symposium on Discrete Algorithms (SODA), pp. 1433–1452 (2014)
16. Lee, J., Mirrokni, V., Nagarajan, V., Sviridenko, M.: Non-monotone submodular maximization under matroid and knapsack constraints. In: STOC, Bethesda, Maryland, USA (2009)
17. Gupta, A., Roth, A., Schoenebeck, G., Talwar, K.: Constrained non-monotone submodular maximization: offline and secretary algorithms. In: Saberi, A. (ed.) WINE 2010. LNCS, vol. 6484, pp. 246–257. Springer, Heidelberg (2010). https://doi.org/10.1007/978-3-642-17572-5_20

18. Mirzasoleiman, B., Badanidiyuru, A., Karbasi, A.: Fast constrained submodular maximization: personalized data summarization. In: The 33rd International Conference on Machine Learning (ICML), New York, USA (2016)
19. Feldman, M., Harshaw, C., Karbasi, A.: Greed is good: near-optimal submodular maximization via greedy optimization. Proc. Mach. Learn. Res. **65**, 1–27 (2017)
20. Shi, M., Yang, Z., Kim, D., Wang, W.: Non-monotone submodular function maximization under k-system constraint. J. Comb. Optim. **41**(1), 128–142 (2020)
21. Tang, S.: Beyond pointwise submodularity: non-monotone adaptive submodular maximization subject to knapsack and k-system constraints. Theoret. Comput. Sci. **936**, 139–147 (2022)
22. Balkanski, E., Singer, Y.: The adaptive complexity of maximizing a submodular function. In: The 50th Annual ACM SIGACT Symposium on Theory of Computing (STOC), pp. 1138–1151 (2018)
23. Breuer, A., Balkanski, E., Singer, Y.: The fast algorithm for submodular maximization. In: The 37th International Conference on Machine Learning (ICML), Venna, Austria (2020)
24. Wang, S., Zhou, T., Lavania, C., Bilmes, J.: Constrained robust submodular partitioning. In: 35th Conference on Neural Information Processing Systems (NeurIPS), vol. 34, pp. 2721–2732. Curran Associates Inc. (2021)
25. Fujishige, S.: Submodular Functions and Optimization. Elsevier Science, Amsterdam (2005)
26. Lin, H., Bilmes, J.: A class of submodular functions for document summarization. In: The 49th Annual Meeting of the Association for Computational Linguistics: Human Language Technologies, vol. 1, pp. 510–520 (2011)
27. Mirzasoleiman, B., Jegelka, S., Krause, A.: Streaming non-monotone submodular maximization: personalized video summarization on the fly. In: The Thirty-Second AAAI Conference on Artificial Intelligence (AAAI), pp. 1379–1386 (2018)
28. Sharma, D., Deshpande, A., Kapoor, A.: On greedy maximization of entropy. In: The 32nd International Conference on Machine Learning (ICML), Lille, France (2015)
29. Bachman, P., Hjelm, D., Buchwalter, W.: Learning representations by maximizing mutual information across views. In: 33rd Conference on Neural Information Processing Systems (NeurIPS) (2019)
30. Tschannen, M., Djolonga, J., Rubenstein, P., Gelly, S., Lucic, M.: On mutual information maximization for representation learning. In the 8th International Conference on Learning Representations (ICLR) (2020)
31. Iyer, R., Bilmes, J.: Submodular optimization with submodular cover and submodular knapsack constraints. In: NIPS, Lake Tahoe, Nevada, USA (2013)
32. Feige, U., Mirrokni, V., Vondrak, J.: Maximizing non-monotone submodular functions. SIAM J. Comput. **40**(4), 1133–1153 (2011)
33. Du, D., Ko, K., Hu, X.: Design and Analysis of Approximation Algorithms. Springer, New York (2012). https://doi.org/10.1007/978-1-4614-1701-9

A Formal Approach for Traceability Preservation in Software Development Process

Hao Wen[1,2], Jinzhao Wu[1,2], Jianmin Jiang[3(✉)], Jianqing Li[3], and Zhong Hong[4]

[1] Chengdu Institute of Computer Applications, Chinese Academy of Sciences, Chengdu, China
`wenhao21@mails.ucas.ac.cn`, `himrwujzh@aliyun.com`
[2] University of Chinese Academy of Sciences, Beijing, China
[3] College of Software Engineering, Chengdu University of Information Technology, Chengdu, China
`jjm@cuit.edu.cn`, `1102418305@qq.com`
[4] College of Mathematics and Informatics, Fujian Normal University, Fuzhou, China
`fjfzhz@fjnu.edu.cn`

Abstract. Traceability is the ability to trace the usage of artifacts during the software lifecycle process. Though the benefits of establishing a traceability software system have been widely recognized, it is difficult to be applied well in actual development. In this paper, we propose a new method for traceability preservation which may be used in the practical software development process. A formal model for the traceability of software artifacts is first presented, which consists of variable traceability relations, classification and version number controls. We then present the composition, restriction and refinement operations in the software development process. Next, the preservation of traceability under these three operations is discussed respectively. To demonstrate the effectiveness of our approach, we finally develop a prototype tool named Formalized Software Management System (FSMS).

Keywords: Traceability · Preservation · Formal method · UML

1 Introduction

Traceability software refers to a system where artifacts at each phase of the software lifecycle process can be traced by other artifacts, and is now considered as a representation of high-quality software [21,42,50]. For example, source code in the implementation phase needs to be traced to artifacts in the maintenance and testing phases, while it can also trace artifacts from previous phases, such as requirement and design phases.

This work is supported by National Key R&D Program of China (No. 2022YFB3305104), National Natural Science Foundation of China (Nos. 61772006, 61772004 and 12261027) and Scientific Research Foundation for Advanced Talents of Chengdu University of Information Technology (No. KYTZ202009).

Z. Cai et al. (Eds.): NCTCS 2023, CCIS 1944, pp. 18–35, 2024.
https://doi.org/10.1007/978-981-99-7743-7_2

During the development of complex software, traceability plays an important role in reducing maintenance cost and analyzing change impact, but it is difficult to achieve in practice. There are several major challenges as follows: (1) In the software lifecycle process, it is hard to represent traceability between large number of artifacts [50] in a non-formal language (see Fig. 1); (2) Since various types of artifacts and relations are involved in different software systems [12,42], the abstraction level of a formal model is not easy to determine; (3) The scalability of traceability models may be impacted as the software becomes progressively larger [12,36].

When dealing with the above challenges, the main approaches of most studies are as followed: (1) Abstraction of artifacts and relations at different phases [19,20,26,30]; (2) Establishment of relations between artifacts in non-adjacent phases, such as the link between source code and requirements [43]; (3) Recording of traceability using different storage structures, such as matrix [25] and hierarchical tree [37]. However, these existing approaches face some problems, such as the potential loss of information about the relations between artifacts in non-adjacent phases, and the large computational burden imposed by the operations of the matrix. To solve the above problems, we propose a formal model called a *structure model* [48] to describe traceability, which follows the actual software development process to directly establish different types of relations between artifacts.

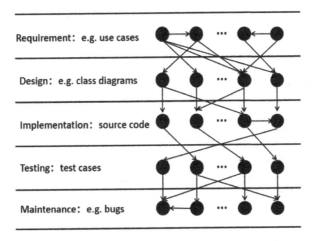

Fig. 1. Traceability links among artifacts in the software lifecycle process

In some early studies on traceability modeling (e.g. [32,42]), the types of traceability links are fixed, and then as the research progresses, most of the studies (e.g. [19,20,26]) consider abstracting similar types of links into more general relations between artifacts. However, these approaches are somewhat constrained when the types of traceability links in actual development are extended or modified. Furthermore, although some studies [4,18] achieve the extensibility and customization of traceability links, they do not support well the many-to-many relationship between two artifacts. Another interesting direction is to retrieve traceability links between source and target artifacts based on the probability [6,24]. In spite of the results showing that the majority of relevant artifacts can be retrieved, some incorrect links are also generated. Moreover, the visualization of traceability is one of the most significant aspects of modeling. Matrices, as two-dimensional structures, are commonly used in commercial tools because they can intuitively portray traceability and can be easily understood by non experts [12,33]. In addition, linear [44], hierarchical [37], graph-based [3,41] and cross-referenced [13,28] representations are also general methods. Nevertheless, the issues related to scalability have not been well addressed in previous work.

Instead of using dynamic behavior to study traceability systems, the structure model is based on the static system structure (a view similar to the structural models in UML [22] and SysML [39]), thus it avoids complex reachability algorithms when analyzing a software system. For convenience, we adopt a similar concept as in SysML [39], considering all the artifacts of different phases as *model elements* named with various labels in a structure model. Since the structure model does not limit the number of types of relations between model elements and supports the many-to-many relation, developers can automatically or semi-automatically assign relations between model elements according to the real development process using a prototyping tool called Formalized Software Management System (FSMS) where traceability can be simply visualized. Compared to the previous definition of the structure model [48], we introduce version number controls and delete the set λ used for modeling constraints.

For a given structural model, composition and restriction are a kind of operations in horizontal direction, and refinement is a kind of operations in vertical direction [31]. However, to the best of our knowledge, only few studies [11,34,38] focus on whether traceability is preserved in different scenarios. This paper discusses in detail whether traceability is preserved under these three operations.

Contribution. This paper makes the following contributions.

- We propose a novel formal model named structure model to describe different types of artifacts and relations in the software development process. In contrast to classical formal models (such as Petri nets and transition systems) that describe systems from a behavioral perspective, our structure model can better represent traceability from the static structure of the system and do not need to use a complex reachability algorithm.
- We study three basic operations composition, restriction, and refinement between structure models, respectively. The results show that combination and refinement do not affect traceability, however restriction only preserves traceability in the vertical direction.
- To support our work, we develop a prototype tool which can visualize traceability.

The remainder of this paper is structured as follows. Section 2 introduces the structure model and presents the definition of traceability. Section 3 discusses the preservation of traceability based on three basic operations. Section 4 introduces our prototype tool. Section 5 is the related work. Section 6 concludes the paper and discusses the future work.

2 Traceability

In this section, we will introduce a formal model called a structure model [48] which is used to model and analyze traceability in the software development process. The structure model consists of model elements, variable traceability relationships between model elements, classifications and version numbers of model elements. Model elements are similar to those in SysML [39]. Based on the above concepts, developers can model and analyze traceability without diving deep into the specific implementation details of a software artifact.

In order to cope with the variable number of relation types between model elements, we choose to represent the structure model with a tuple of variable length. And the concept of version number is introduced in this model for the sake of subsequent analysis of traceability. Some assistant definitions are given below. Let **VN** be the set of version numbers such that $\forall R \subseteq$ **VN** $\times$ **VN**, R is a strict total order. Note that ∞ is a special version number which means a *undetermined* version number, and $\infty \notin$ **VN**.

Definition 1. *A* ***structure model*** *($\mathcal{SM}$) is a tuple* $\langle \text{ME}, \prec, \overset{1}{\hookrightarrow}, \cdots, \overset{n}{\hookrightarrow}, \overset{1}{\tau}, \cdots, \overset{m}{\tau}$ *, $vs, ve\rangle$ with*

- ME, *a finite set of the model elements,*
- $\prec \subseteq$ ME $\times$ ME, *the* containment relation *such that it is a (irreflexive) partial order,*
- $\forall i \in \{1, \cdots, n\}, \overset{i}{\hookrightarrow} \subseteq$ ME $\times$ ME, *the* dependency relation,
- $\forall j \in \{1, \cdots, m\}, \overset{j}{\tau} \subseteq$ ME, *the* type set *of model elements such that* $\forall e \in$ ME, $\exists \tau \in \{\overset{1}{\tau}, \cdots, \cdots, \overset{m}{\tau}\} : e \in \tau$.
- $vs :$ ME $\longrightarrow$ **VN** $\cup \{\infty\}$, *the* initial version function, *and*
- $ve :$ ME $\longrightarrow$ **VN** $\cup \{\infty\}$, *the* final version function.

A model element is assigned the initial version number when it is created, whereas it is assigned the final version number when it is inactivated. If the version number of a model element is not determined, it is assigned ∞.

In order to better understand the definition, we use the structure model to represent a simple student information management system in the following example.

Example 1. We here present the example shown in Fig. 2. In this example, the initial requirements of a student information management system are as follows.

- R: The system shall be able to manage students' information.
- $R1$: The system shall allow students to choose course.
- $R2$: The system shall allow students to check their course scores.

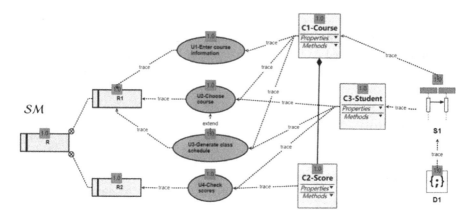

Fig. 2. The partial relations among software artifacts in a system

Obviously, the requirements $R1$ and $R2$ are both contained in R. In addition to requirements, the other model elements in Fig. 2 correspond to artifacts at different phases of software development. $U1$, $U2$, $U3$, $U4$ represent use cases, $C1$, $C2$, $C3$ denote classes, $S1$ denotes the sequence diagram, and $D1$ is the corresponding implementation code of $S1$. For convenience, the specific detail for each artifact is not given in Fig. 2.

There exist four types of relations between model elements: *containment, trace, extend, composition.* Note that the relations between these model elements are assigned by the software engineer. Thus the student information management system can be represented by a structure model $\mathcal{SM} = \langle \text{ME}, \prec$, $\overset{trace}{\hookrightarrow}, \overset{extend}{\hookrightarrow}, \overset{composition}{\hookrightarrow}, \overset{requirements}{\tau}, \overset{design}{\tau}, \overset{implementation}{\tau}, vs, ve \rangle$ with $\text{ME} = \{R, R1, R2, U1, U2, U3, U4, C1, C2, C3, S1, D1\}$, $\prec= \{(R1, R), (R2, R)\}$, $\overset{trace}{\hookrightarrow} = \{(U1, R1), (U2, R1), (U3, R1), (U4, R2), (C1, U1), (C1, U2), (C1, U3), (C2, U4), (C3, U2), (C3, U3), (C3, U4), (S1, C1), (S1, C3), (D1, S1)\}$, $\overset{extend}{\hookrightarrow} = \{(U3, U2)\}$, $\overset{composition}{\hookrightarrow} = \{(C2, C1)\}$, $\overset{requirements}{\tau} = \{R, R1, R2, U1, U2, U3, U4\}$, $\overset{design}{\tau} = \{C1, C2, C3, S1\}$, $\overset{implementation}{\tau} = \{D1\}$. Here, we may suppose that the current version number is 1.0, thus $\forall e \in \text{ME}, vs(e) = 1.0$ and $ve(e) = \infty$.

This example shows that developers can visually represent the model elements and their relations using a structure model. Note that the version numbers are attributes of model elements.

Moreover, in order to make the paper more readable, we summarize some notations which will be used later (see Table 1).

Definition 2. *Let* $\mathcal{SM} = \langle \text{ME}, \prec, \overset{1}{\hookrightarrow}, \cdots, \overset{n}{\hookrightarrow}, \overset{1}{\tau}, \cdots, \overset{m}{\tau}, vs, ve \rangle$ *be a structure model.*

(1) A sequence $rc = x_1 \cdots x_p(p > 1)$ *is called a* relation chain *in* $\mathcal{SM}$ *iff* $\forall i \in \{1, \cdots, p-1\}, x_i, x_{i+1} \in \text{ME}, (x_i, x_{i+1}) \in (\prec \cup \overset{1}{\hookrightarrow} \cup \cdots \cup \overset{n}{\hookrightarrow}) \vee (x_{i+1}, x_i) \in (\prec \cup \overset{1}{\hookrightarrow} \cup \cdots \cup \overset{n}{\hookrightarrow})$. $RC(\mathcal{SM})$ *denotes all possible relation chains in* $\mathcal{SM}$.

Table 1. Notations.

Symbol	Description
$\mathcal{SM}$	A structure model
rc	A relation chain in $\mathcal{SM}$
$RC(\mathcal{SM})$	A set contains all possible relation chains in $\mathcal{SM}$
dc	A dependency chain in $\mathcal{SM}$
$DC(\mathcal{SM})$	A set contains all possible dependency chains in $\mathcal{SM}$
$\mathcal{SM}_1 \sqsubseteq \mathcal{SM}_2$	$\mathcal{SM}_1$ is a substructure of $\mathcal{SM}_2$
$\mathcal{SM}_1 \uplus \mathcal{SM}_2$	The composition of $\mathcal{SM}_1$ and $\mathcal{SM}_2$
$\mathcal{SM}\vert_X$	The restriction of $\mathcal{SM}$ to a given set X
$ref(e)$	A function that refines a model element e
$\mathcal{SM}[e.ref(e)]$	The refinement of $\mathcal{SM}$ under $ref(e)$

(2) A sequence $dc = x_1 \cdots x_p (p > 1)$ is called a dependency chain in $\mathcal{SM}$ iff $\forall i \in \{1, \cdots, p-1\}, x_i, x_{i+1} \in \text{ME}, (x_i, x_{i+1}) \in (\prec \cup \overset{1}{\hookrightarrow} \cup \cdots \cup \overset{n}{\hookrightarrow})$. $\hat{dc}$ denotes the model elements in the dependency chain $dc = x_1 \cdots x_p$, that is, $\hat{dc} = \{x_1, \cdots, x_p\}$. $DC(\mathcal{SM})$ denotes all possible dependency chains in $\mathcal{SM}$. $[dc]$ denotes the number of model elements in the dependency chain dc, that is, $[dc] = p$.

Clearly, a relation chain does not distinguish the direction of relations, while a dependency chain is a directed sequence. For instance, there exists a dependency chain $D1S1C3U3U2R1R$ in Example 1, and this dependency chain is also a relation chain.

Proposition 1. *If $\mathcal{SM}$ is a structure model, then $DC(\mathcal{SM}) \subseteq RC(\mathcal{SM})$.*

Proof. This proof is straightforward.

Proposition 1 states that the dependency chain is a special type of the relation chain.

Traceability is one of the significant criteria for assessing software quality [42]. Since there exist several different model elements (artifacts) for each phase of the software lifecycle process, and these model elements are largely isolated, it is necessary to correlate between various model elements through traceability [2]. Next, we will present some related concepts and give a formal definition of traceability.

The traceability of software systems can be classified as horizontal or vertical traceability [35, 36, 49]. The definition of traceability is as follows.

Definition 3. *Let* $\mathcal{SM} = \langle \text{ME}, \prec, \overset{1}{\hookrightarrow}, \cdots, \overset{n}{\hookrightarrow}, \overset{1}{\tau}, \cdots, \overset{m}{\tau}, vs, ve \rangle$ *be a structure model and specify a system. Let* $\overset{requirements}{\tau} \in \{\overset{1}{\tau}, \cdots, \overset{m}{\tau}\}$ *and* $\overset{requirements}{\tau}$ *be the set of the model elements for representing requirements.*

(1) $\mathcal{SM}$ *is said to be* horizontally traceable *iff* $\forall e \in \text{ME}, \exists dc = x_1 \cdots x_p \in DC(\mathcal{SM}) : e \in \hat{dc}$ *and* $x_p \in \overset{requirements}{\tau}$.

(2) $\mathcal{SM}$ *is said to be* vertically traceable *iff* $\forall e \in \text{ME}, \exists dc = x_1 \cdots x_p \in DC(\mathcal{SM})$: $e \in \hat{dc}$ *and* $\forall i \in \{1, \cdots, p-1\}, vs(x_{i+1}) \leq vs(x_i)$.

(3) $\mathcal{SM}$ *is said to be* traceable *iff* $\forall e \in \text{ME}, \exists dc = x_1 \cdots x_p \in DC(\mathcal{SM}) : e \in \hat{dc}, x_p \in \overset{requirements}{\tau}$ *and* $\forall i \in \{1, \cdots, p-1\}, vs(x_{i+1}) \leq vs(x_i)$.

Here, horizontal traceability considers that all software artifacts directly or indirectly depend on requirements artifacts, whereas vertical traceability focuses on the version changes of model elements [43], that is, the version number of a model element is greater than or equal to that of its dependent model elements. Obviously, though dependency chains are directed, they can be reversely traversed based on directed graphs. Thus, forward traceability and backward traceability [5,51] are both contained in this definition. The definition considers not only the inner traceability of a model, but also the traceability among multiple models. Note that as long as there is an isolated artifact in a software system, the software system is not traceable.

Example 2. For each model element of the structure model $\mathcal{SM}$ in Fig. 2, there is a dependency chain containing this model element such that the elements of this chain are directly or indirectly related to requirements. Therefore according to Definition 3(1), $\mathcal{SM}$ is horizontally traceable. In addition, since all model elements in the structure model $\mathcal{SM}$ have the same version number, by Definition 3(2), $\mathcal{SM}$ is vertically traceable. Thus, by Definition 3(3), $\mathcal{SM}$ is traceable.

3   The Preservation of Traceability

In this section, we will introduce three common operations, and explore the preservation of traceability in the software development process.

A large-scale software project is often divided into several smaller projects which are developed concurrently in practice. A structure model is used to model and analyze the traceability of each project whichever is large or small. Thus, from the perspective of traceability, every project corresponds to a structure model. The decomposition of a complex software system into multiple subsystems can correspond to that of a structure model into multiple substructure models.

Definition 4. *Let* $\mathcal{SM}' = \langle \text{ME}', \prec', \overset{1}{\hookrightarrow}', \cdots, \overset{n}{\hookrightarrow}', \overset{1}{\tau}', \cdots, \overset{m}{\tau}', vs', ve' \rangle$ *and* $\mathcal{SM}'' = \langle \text{ME}'', \prec'', \overset{1}{\hookrightarrow}'', \cdots, \overset{n}{\hookrightarrow}'', \overset{1}{\tau}'', \cdots, \overset{m}{\tau}'', vs'', ve'' \rangle$ *be two structure models.*

A structure model $\mathcal{SM}'$ *is called a* substructure *of* $\mathcal{SM}''$, *denoted as* $\mathcal{SM}' \sqsubseteq \mathcal{SM}''$, *iff* $\text{ME}' \subseteq \text{ME}''$, $\prec' \subseteq \prec''$, $\forall i \in \{1, \cdots, n\}, \overset{i}{\hookrightarrow}' \subseteq \overset{i}{\hookrightarrow}''$, $\forall j \in \{1, \cdots, m\} : \overset{j}{\tau}' \subseteq \overset{j}{\tau}''$ *and*

$\forall e \in \text{ME}' : vs'(e) = vs''(e) \wedge ve'(e) = ve''(e)$. *A structure model* $\mathcal{SM}'$ *is called a* proper substructure *of* $\mathcal{SM}''$, *denoted as* $\mathcal{SM}' \sqsubset \mathcal{SM}''$, *iff* $\mathcal{SM}' \sqsubseteq \mathcal{SM}''$ *and* $\mathcal{SM}' \neq \mathcal{SM}''$.

Proposition 2. *Let* $\mathcal{SM}'$ *and* $\mathcal{SM}''$ *be two structure models. If* $\mathcal{SM}' \sqsubseteq \mathcal{SM}''$, *then* $DC(\mathcal{SM}') \subseteq DC(\mathcal{SM}'')$.

Proof. According to Definition 4, all model elements and relations of $\mathcal{SM}'$ are in $\mathcal{SM}''$. Therefore, all dependency chains of $\mathcal{SM}'$ are in $\mathcal{SM}''$. By Definition 2(2), $DC(\mathcal{SM}') \subseteq DC(\mathcal{SM}'')$.

3.1 Composition

Once all subsystems of a system are completed, all software artifacts in the subsystems should be composed. The model elements and relations in every subsystem should be preserved.

Definition 5. *Let* $\mathcal{SM}' = \langle \text{ME}', \prec', \overset{1}{\hookrightarrow}', \cdots, \overset{n}{\hookrightarrow}', \overset{1}{\tau}', \cdots, \overset{m}{\tau}', vs', ve' \rangle$ *and* $\mathcal{SM}'' = \langle \text{ME}'', \prec'', \overset{1}{\hookrightarrow}'', \cdots, \overset{n}{\hookrightarrow}'', \overset{1}{\tau}'', \cdots, \overset{m}{\tau}'', vs'', ve'' \rangle$ *be two structure models.*

If $\forall e \in \text{ME}' \cap \text{ME}'', vs'(e) = vs''(e) \wedge ve'(e) = ve''(e)$, *and* $\prec' \cup \prec''$ *is a (irreflexive) partial order, the composition of* $\mathcal{SM}'$ *and* $\mathcal{SM}''$ *is defined as* $\mathcal{SM}' \uplus \mathcal{SM}'' = \langle \text{ME}, \prec, \overset{1}{\hookrightarrow}, \cdots, \overset{n}{\hookrightarrow}, \overset{1}{\tau}, \cdots, \overset{m}{\tau}, vs, ve \rangle$ *where* $\text{ME} = \text{ME}' \cup \text{ME}''$, $\prec = \prec' \cup \prec''$, $\forall i \in \{1, \cdots, n\}: \overset{i}{\hookrightarrow} = \overset{i}{\hookrightarrow}' \cup \overset{i}{\hookrightarrow}''$, $\forall j \in \{1, \cdots, m\}: \overset{j}{\tau} = \overset{j}{\tau}' \cup \overset{j}{\tau}''$, $\forall e \in \text{ME}' : vs(e) = vs'(e) \wedge ve(e) = ve'(e)$, *and* $\forall e \in \text{ME}'' : vs(e) = vs''(e) \wedge ve(e) = ve''(e)$. $\mathcal{SM}', \mathcal{SM}''$ *are said to be* composable.

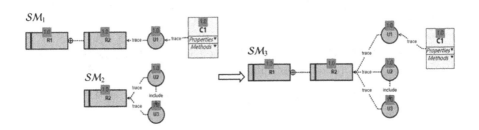

Fig. 3. The composition of two structure models

Here, when there are different types of relations between model elements in two composable structure models, we need to equivalently translate them into the two structure models which have the same relations before composition. For instance, in Fig. 3, there exist two types of relations in $\mathcal{SM}_1$: *containment* and *trace*, while there exist two types of relations in $\mathcal{SM}_2$: *trace* and *include*. $\mathcal{SM}_1$ and $\mathcal{SM}_2$ can be translated into the following two structure models $\mathcal{SM}'$ and $\mathcal{SM}''$, respectively.

$$\mathcal{SM}' = \langle \text{ME}', \prec', \overset{trace}{\hookrightarrow}', \overset{include}{\hookrightarrow}', \overset{requirements}{\tau'}, \overset{design}{\tau'}, vs', ve' \rangle \text{ with } \overset{include}{\hookrightarrow}' = \emptyset,$$

$$\mathcal{SM}'' = \langle \text{ME}'', \prec'', \overset{trace}{\hookrightarrow}'', \overset{include}{\hookrightarrow}'', \overset{requirements}{\tau''}, \overset{design}{\tau''}, vs'', ve'' \rangle \text{ with } \prec'' = \emptyset.$$

Obviously, $\mathcal{SM}_1 = \mathcal{SM}'$ and $\mathcal{SM}_2 = \mathcal{SM}''$. Thus $\mathcal{SM}_1$ and $\mathcal{SM}_2$ have the same type of relations after translation. Note that we need to perform a similar translation when composing two structure models with different types of classifications. By Definition 5, $\mathcal{SM}_1$ and $\mathcal{SM}_2$ are composable. The structure model $\mathcal{SM}_3$ is the composition of $\mathcal{SM}_1$ and $\mathcal{SM}_2$ in Fig. 3.

Proposition 3. *Let $\mathcal{SM}, \mathcal{SM}'$ and $\mathcal{SM}''$ be three structure models. And let every two of the three structure models be composable. Then*

(1) $\mathcal{SM}' \uplus \mathcal{SM}''$ is a structure model.
(2) $\mathcal{SM}' \uplus \mathcal{SM}'' = \mathcal{SM}'' \uplus \mathcal{SM}'$.
(3) $(\mathcal{SM} \uplus \mathcal{SM}') \uplus \mathcal{SM}'' = \mathcal{SM} \uplus (\mathcal{SM}' \uplus \mathcal{SM}'')$.

Proof. This proof is straightforward.

Proposition 3 states that the composition of structure models has closure, commutativity and associativity.

Theorem 1. *Let $\mathcal{SM}, \mathcal{SM}'$ be two composable structure models. If $\mathcal{SM}$ and $\mathcal{SM}'$ are traceable, then $\mathcal{SM} \uplus \mathcal{SM}'$ is traceable.*

Proof. Assume that $\exists \mathcal{SM}'' = \mathcal{SM} \uplus \mathcal{SM}' = \langle \text{ME}'', \prec'', \overset{1}{\hookrightarrow}'', \cdots, \overset{n}{\hookrightarrow}'', \overset{1}{\tau''}, \cdots, \overset{m}{\tau''}$, $vs'', ve'' \rangle$ and $\overset{requirements}{\tau''} \in \{\overset{1}{\tau''}, \cdots, \overset{m}{\tau''}\}$. By Definition 5, $\forall e \in \text{ME}'' : e \in$ $\text{ME} \vee e \in \text{ME}'$. When $e \in \text{ME}$, since $\mathcal{SM}$ is traceable, according to Definition 3 (3), $\exists dc_1 = x_1 \cdots x_p \in DC(\mathcal{SM}) : e \in \hat{dc_1}, x_p \in \overset{requirements}{\tau}$ and $\forall i \in$ $\{1, \cdots, p-1\}, vs(x_{i+1}) \leq vs(x_i)$. When $e \in \text{ME}'$, since $\mathcal{SM}'$ is traceable, according to Definition 3 (3), $\exists dc_2 = y_1 \cdots y_q \in DC(\mathcal{SM}') : e \in \hat{dc_2}, y_q \in \overset{requirements}{\tau}$ and $\forall i \in \{1, \cdots, q-1\}, vs'(y_{i+1}) \leq vs'(y_i)$. By Proposition 2, $\mathcal{SM} \sqsubseteq \mathcal{SM}'' \wedge$ $\mathcal{SM}' \sqsubseteq \mathcal{SM}'' : DC(\mathcal{SM}) \subseteq DC(\mathcal{SM}'') \wedge DC(\mathcal{SM}') \subseteq DC(\mathcal{SM}'')$. Moreover, $vs''(e) = vs(e) \vee vs''(e) = vs'(e)$, thus $\exists dc_3 = z_1 \cdots z_k \in DC(\mathcal{SM}'') : e \in$ $\hat{dc_3}, z_k \in \overset{requirements}{\tau}$ and $\forall i \in \{1, \cdots, k-1\}, vs''(z_{i+1}) \leq vs''(z_i)$. By Definition 3 (3), $\mathcal{SM} \uplus \mathcal{SM}'$ is traceable.

This theorem shows that the composition of two traceable structure models is traceable.

3.2 Restriction

In Sect. 3.1, we have introduced the composition operation which describes a structure model becoming increasingly large and complex. By contrary, there exists some research on model decomposition [1,9,45], which can automatically or semi-automatically obtain sub-models. Thus, we next discuss how to decompose a structure model by restriction.

Definition 6. *Let* $\mathcal{SM} = \langle \text{ME}, \prec, \overset{1}{\hookrightarrow}, \cdots, \overset{n}{\hookrightarrow}, \overset{1}{\tau}, \cdots, \overset{m}{\tau}, vs, ve \rangle$ *be a structure model.* *For* $X \subseteq \text{ME}$, *the restriction of* $\mathcal{SM}$ *to* X *is defined as a structure model* $\mathcal{SM}|_X = \langle \text{ME}', \prec', \overset{1}{\hookrightarrow}', \cdots, \overset{n}{\hookrightarrow}', \overset{1}{\tau}', \cdots, \overset{m}{\tau}', vs', ve' \rangle$ *with*

- $\text{ME}' = X$,
- $\prec' = \{(x, y) | \forall x, y \in X, (x, y) \in \prec\}$,
- $\forall i \in \{1, \cdots, n\} : \overset{i}{\hookrightarrow}' = \{(x, y) | \forall x, y \in X, (x, y) \in \overset{i}{\hookrightarrow}\}$,
- $\forall j \in \{1, \cdots, m\} : \overset{j}{\tau}' = X \cap \overset{j}{\tau}$,
- $\forall x \in X, vs'(x) = vs(x)$, *and*
- $\forall x \in X, ve'(x) = ve(x)$.

Here, we can obtain various substructures of a structure model by restriction.

Proposition 4. *Let* $\mathcal{SM} = \langle \text{ME}, \prec, \overset{1}{\hookrightarrow}, \cdots, \overset{n}{\hookrightarrow}, \overset{1}{\tau}, \cdots, \overset{m}{\tau}, vs, ve \rangle$ *be a structure model. Then* $\forall X \subseteq \text{ME}, \mathcal{SM}|_X \sqsubseteq \mathcal{SM}$.

Proof. According to Definition 4 and Definition 6, the result obviously holds.

The restriction of a structure model must be the substructure of the original structure model, but the substructure of a structure model may not be the restriction of the original model. For example, both $\mathcal{SM}_2$ and $\mathcal{SM}_3$ are obviously proper substructures of $\mathcal{SM}_1$ (see Fig. 4) and thus $\mathcal{SM}_2 \sqsubset \mathcal{SM}_1, \mathcal{SM}_3 \sqsubset \mathcal{SM}_1$. Then $\mathcal{SM}_2$ is obviously a restriction of $\mathcal{SM}_1$ to $X = \{R, U1, U2\}$, but $\mathcal{SM}_3$ is not $\mathcal{SM}_1|_X$.

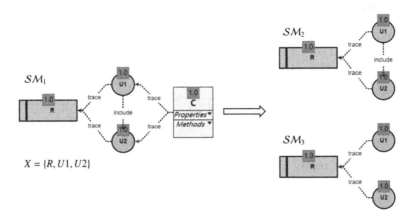

Fig. 4. An example for explaining the restriction of a structure model

Proposition 5. *Let* $\mathcal{SM} = \langle \text{ME}, \prec, \overset{1}{\hookrightarrow}, \cdots, \overset{n}{\hookrightarrow}, vs, ve \rangle$ *be a structure model. If* $\forall X, Y \subseteq \text{ME} : \mathcal{SM}|_X \uplus \mathcal{SM}|_Y = \mathcal{SM}$, *then* $X \cup Y = \text{ME}$.

Proof. According to Definition 5 and Definition 6, the result clearly holds.

This proposition shows that when two substructures are composed to obtain the original structure model, the two substructures necessarily contain all the model elements of the original structure model.

Theorem 2. *Let* $\mathcal{SM} = \langle \mathrm{ME}, \prec, \overset{1}{\hookrightarrow}, \cdots, \overset{n}{\hookrightarrow}, \overset{1}{\tau}, \cdots, \overset{m}{\tau}, vs, ve \rangle$ *be a structure model and* $\mathcal{SM}$ *be traceable. Then* $\forall X \subseteq \mathrm{ME}$, $\mathcal{SM}|_X$ *is vertically traceable.*

Proof. This proof is straightforward.

Theorem 2 states that vertical traceability can be preserved after the restriction. However, when the restricted structure model contains isolated elements or does not contain requirements, horizontal traceability is obviously influenced.

3.3   Refinement

Refinement is another important operation during the software development process. It means that a model at higher abstraction level is transformed into the corresponding concrete one at lower abstraction level. Many researchers have studied the refinement operation based on different models [1, 14, 46]. We here investigate the refinement operation between structure models in this subsection.

We assume a fixed set **ME** of model elements. Let **SM** denotes the set of all structure models. The empty structure model $\langle \emptyset, \emptyset, \emptyset, \cdots, \emptyset, \emptyset, \emptyset \rangle$ is denoted by $\varnothing$.

Definition 7. *(1) A refinement function for structure models is a total function* $ref :$ $\boldsymbol{ME} \rightarrow \boldsymbol{SM} \backslash \{\varnothing\}$ *such that* $\forall e \in \boldsymbol{ME}, ref(e) = \langle \mathrm{ME}, \prec, \overset{1}{\hookrightarrow}, \cdots, \overset{n}{\hookrightarrow}, \overset{1}{\tau}, \cdots, \overset{m}{\tau}, vs, ve \rangle$ *where*

- $\exists e' \in \mathrm{ME}, e'$ *is a copy of* $e, \prec = \{(x, e') \mid x \in \mathrm{ME} \backslash \{e'\}\}$, *and*
- $\forall x, y \in \mathrm{ME}, vs(x) = vs(y) \wedge ve(x) = ve(y)$.

(2) Let $\mathcal{SM} = \langle \mathrm{ME}, \prec, \overset{1}{\hookrightarrow}, \cdots, \overset{n}{\hookrightarrow}, \overset{1}{\tau}, \cdots, \overset{m}{\tau}, vs, ve \rangle$ *be a structure model. Let* $e \in \mathrm{ME}, ref(e) = \langle \mathrm{ME}', \prec', \overset{1}{\hookrightarrow}', \cdots, \overset{n}{\hookrightarrow}', \overset{1}{\tau}', \cdots, \overset{m}{\tau}', vs', ve' \rangle$ *such that* $\forall x \in \mathrm{ME}', vs'(x) \geq vs(e) \wedge ve'(x) \geq ve(e)$. *Moreover, let* $\mathrm{ME} \cap \mathrm{ME}' = \emptyset$. *The refinement of* $\mathcal{SM}$ *under* $ref(e)$ *is the structure model* $\mathcal{SM}[e.ref(e)] = \langle \mathrm{ME}'', \prec'', \overset{1}{\hookrightarrow}''$ $, \cdots, \overset{n}{\hookrightarrow}'', \overset{1}{\tau}'', \cdots, \overset{m}{\tau}'', vs'', ve'' \rangle$ *with*

- $\mathrm{ME}'' = \mathrm{ME} \cup \mathrm{ME}'$,
- $\prec'' = \prec \cup \prec'$,
- $\exists i \in \{1, \cdots, n\} : \overset{i}{\hookrightarrow}'' = \overset{refine}{\hookrightarrow}'' = \overset{refine}{\hookrightarrow} \cup \overset{refine}{\hookrightarrow}' \cup \{(e', e)\}$,
- $\forall j \in \{1, \cdots, n\} \backslash \{i\} : \overset{j}{\hookrightarrow}'' = \overset{j}{\hookrightarrow} \cup \overset{j}{\hookrightarrow}'$,
- $\forall k \in \{1, \cdots, m\} : \overset{k}{\tau}'' = \overset{k}{\tau} \cup \overset{k}{\tau}'$,
- $\forall p \in \mathrm{ME}' : vs''(p) = vs'(p) \wedge ve''(p) = ve'(p)$, *and*

- $\forall q \in \text{ME} : vs''(q) = vs(q) \wedge ve''(q) = ve(q)$.

Definition 7 shows that if the model element of a structure model is refined, then the newly obtained structure model is the refinement of the original one. In order not to pollute the relations between model elements in the original structure model [7,40], we choose to first copy the model element to be refined and then create new relations based on the replica. Thus the refinement operation includes the following steps:

(1) copy e as the new model element e'.
(2) assign e' a new version number, then create the *containment* relation between e' and all model elements of $ref(e)$ respectively (although the model elements of $ref(e)$ are a more concrete representation of e, they may be regarded as descendants of e).
(3) establish the *refine* relation between e and e'.

The refinement operation between structure models can be clearly represented graphically. For distinguishing between different version numbers, once a model element is assigned to a new version number, the old version number will become grey in our tool.

For example, we assume that the model element $U1$ of $\mathcal{SM}_1$ needs to be refined in Fig. 5 and there exists a structure model $\mathcal{SM}_2 = ref(U1)$, then the refinement of $\mathcal{SM}_1$ under $ref(U1)$ can be represented by a new structure model $\mathcal{SM}_3 = \mathcal{SM}_1[U1.ref(U1)]$.

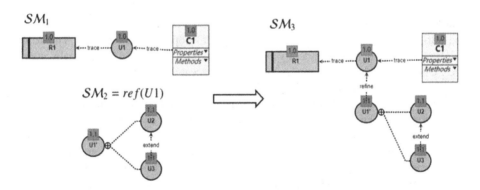

Fig. 5. An example for interpreting the refinement of a structure model

Proposition 6. *Let* $\mathcal{SM}_1 = \langle \text{ME}_1, \prec_1, \overset{1}{\hookrightarrow}_1, \cdots, \overset{n}{\hookrightarrow}_1, \tau_1, \cdots, \overset{m}{\tau}_1, vs_1, ve_1 \rangle$ *be a structure model. Moreover, let ref be a refinement function for structure models. If* $\forall e \in \text{ME}_1 : \mathcal{SM}_2 = \mathcal{SM}_1[e.ref(e)]$, *then* $\mathcal{SM}_1 = \mathcal{SM}_2|_{\text{ME}_1}$.

Proof. Since $\mathcal{SM}_2$ is a refinement of $\mathcal{SM}_1$ under $ref(e)$, by Definition 7 (2), all model elements and relations in $\mathcal{SM}_1$ are not change. Assume $X = \text{ME}_1$, since $X \subseteq \text{ME}_2$, by Definition 6, $\mathcal{SM}_1$ is a restriction of $\mathcal{SM}_2$ to X. Thus $\mathcal{SM}_1 = \mathcal{SM}_2|_{\text{ME}_1}$.

This proposition states that if a structure model is refined, then the newly obtained structure model preserves all the model elements of the original structure model.

Theorem 3. *Let* $\mathcal{SM}_1 = \langle \mathrm{ME}_1, \prec_1, \overset{1}{\hookrightarrow}_1, \cdots, \overset{n}{\hookrightarrow}_1, \overset{1}{\tau}_1, \cdots, \overset{m}{\tau}_1, vs_1, ve_1 \rangle$ *be a structure model and* $\mathcal{SM}_1$ *be traceable. Moreover, let* ref *be a refinement function for structure models. If* $\forall e \in \mathrm{ME}_1 : \mathcal{SM}_2 = \mathcal{SM}_1[e.ref(e)]$, *then* $\mathcal{SM}_2$ *is traceable.*

Proof. Assume that $\mathcal{SM}_2 = \langle \mathrm{ME}_2, \prec_2, \overset{1}{\hookrightarrow}_2, \cdots, \overset{n}{\hookrightarrow}_2, \overset{1}{\tau}_2, \cdots, \overset{m}{\tau}_2, vs_2, ve_2 \rangle$. Since $\mathcal{SM}_2$ is a refinement of $\mathcal{SM}_1$ under $ref(e)$, by Definition 7, $\forall x \in \mathrm{ME}_2 : x \in \mathrm{ME}_1 \vee x \in \mathrm{ME}_2 \setminus \mathrm{ME}_1$. When $x \in \mathrm{ME}_1$, since $\mathcal{SM}_1$ is traceable, by Definition 3 (3), $\exists dc_1 = x_1 \cdots x_p \in DC(\mathcal{SM}_1) : x \in \hat{dc}_1, x_p \in \overset{requirements}{\tau}$ and $\forall i \in \{1, \cdots, p-1\}, vs_1(x_{i+1}) \le vs_1(x_i)$. Moreover, by Proposition 4 and Proposition 6, $\mathcal{SM}_1 \sqsubseteq \mathcal{SM}_2$. According to Proposition 2, $DC(\mathcal{SM}_1) \subseteq DC(\mathcal{SM}_2)$, thus $dc_1 \in DC(\mathcal{SM}_2)$. When $x \in \mathrm{ME}_2 \setminus \mathrm{ME}_1$, by Definition 7, $\exists dc_2 = y_1 \cdots y_q \in DC(\mathcal{SM}_2) : y_q = e \wedge y_1 = x$ and $vs_2(e) \le vs_2(x)$. Thus $\exists dc_3 = z_1 \cdots z_k \in DC(\mathcal{SM}_2) : x \in \hat{dc}_3, z_k \in \overset{requirements}{\tau}$ and $\forall i \in \{1, \cdots, k-1\}, vs_2(z_{i+1}) \le vs_2(z_i)$. By Definition 3 (3), $\mathcal{SM}_2$ is traceable.

This theorem states that the refinement operation does not change traceability in the software development process.

4   Tool: Formalized Software Management System

In order to facilitate the investigation of traceability, a prototype tool named Formalized Software Management System (FSMS) was developed with JavaScript. This tool mainly consists of two independently developed modules (See Fig. 6 for the main interface). One is a draggable drawing modules with traceability management, the other is the consistency management module. This paper is dedicated to the former.

Developers can use different components in the toolbox to visualize the artifacts and the relations between them in the software system, and then the graphic representation of this system can be automatically converted to JSON format for storage. Moreover, this tool implements several analysis functions based on the structure model, such as change impact analysis. The tool has been deployed on the website http://124.220.63.75/ now. More functions will be added to this tool step by step.

5   Related Work

Software traceability has been studied for many years (see References [2,36,51] for surveys). Most of the studies (see References [4,8,15] for surveys) involving traceability do not apply formal methods, but our work is based on formal methods to rigorously model traceability and to analysis traceability. Therefore, we only provide some comparisons between our work and the most related work on traceability modeling and change impact analysis.

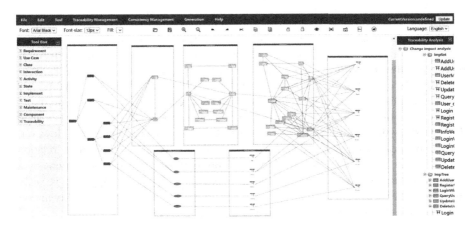

Fig. 6. The main interface of the prototype tool

Goknil et al. [19, 20] mainly focus on the well-defined traceability between the requirement (R) and architecture (A), and they have investigated the reasoning, consistency checking and automatic generation of trace relations based on the system's specifications. Rempel and Mader [43] focus only on the relations between the requirement and implementation (code) phases. However, we hold that the artifacts in the following phases depend on those in the preceding phases, so traceability between non-adjacent or abstract phases may be less practical to lose some implicit details in software lifecycle process.

In [26], six types of traceability relations, which are used to analyze the evolution of the requirement and architecture, are introduced: goal dependency, temporal dependency, service dependency, conditional dependency, task dependency and infrastructure dependency. Lago et al. [30] give a scoped approach to identify core traceability paths and distinguish four relations in R&A: drive, depend-on, modify and influence. Based on the above two studies, Goknil et al. [20] generalize these trace types into within-model traces (refines, requires) and between-model traces (satisfies, allocatedTo). Spanoudakis et al. [47] propose a rule-based method for establishing traceability. This method contains two rules: requirements-to-object-model (RTOM) and inter-requirement traceability (IREQ). Then based on RTOM and IREQ, four different types of traceability relations can be generated between requirement statements and use cases. Cleland-Huang et al. [10] present a novel concept. They consider that the relations between various software artifacts as a direct or indirect link which can be dynamically modified by event notifications. Obviously, neither the different number of relations nor event-based links can be applied to a large-scale development with a very large variety of traceability relations between artifacts. However, our structure model does not limit the number of relation types.

Antoniol et al. [6] propose a seminal approach to retrieve traceability relations between documentation and code based on probability. Their work uses the information retrieval algorithm to calculate the similarity between two artifacts to establish links between them. However, the precision is not high enough, resulting in the possibility of generating incorrect links. In order to establish high quality links, De Lucia et al. [16] introduce a method to understand the semantic context between artifacts using Latent Semantic Indexing, and in [23,47], how to connect heuristic rules with link retrieval is discussed. Obviously, these methods can reduce the number of incorrect links, but cannot avoid the error. In [17], a platform called Tarskil is used to build the semantics of interactive traceability, which is based on first-order relational logic, thus simplifying the reasoning of relations and consistency checking. Santos et al. [44] use a tool named TIRT to show data with list, which is a kind of one-dimensional approach. However, these two researches mentioned above do not well support the many-to-many relation between artifacts. In Holten's work [25], he propose to store adjacency relations by a two-dimensional approach, such as traceability matrix. Although this approach is easily understood by the stakeholder and saves storage space, the change of traceability matrix becomes complicated when the structure of the system is changed.

Laghouaouta et al. [29] use the softgoal tree to manage the traceability of the composition of multi-view models in the Model Driven Engineering (MDE). In [7,27], some approaches to merging trackable links on-demanded are discussed. Obviously, these studies are completely different from our work.

6   Conclusion and Future Work

In this paper, we have investigated how to ensure traceability under the operations such as composition, restriction and refinement in software development process. To demonstrate the availability of these results, we have developed a prototype tool called FSMS that enables traceability visualization.

In future work, we will explore how to make the visualization of our tool better. We also wish to integrate our tool with other software development platforms. On the other hand, automated code generation is another important field of our research based on formal methods. Since automated code generation techniques heavily rely on the traceability, we will focus on how to automatically generate high quality code in the software development process.

Acknowledgements. We would like to thank the anonymous reviewers for their very valuable comments and very helpful suggestions.

References

1. Abrial, J.R., Hallerstede, S.: Refinement, decomposition, and instantiation of discrete models: application to event-B. Fund. Inform. **77**(1–2), 1–28 (2007)
2. Aizenbud-Reshef, N., Nolan, B.T., Rubin, J., Shaham-Gafni, Y.: Model traceability. IBM Syst. J. **45**(3), 515–526 (2006)
3. van Amstel, M.F., van den Brand, M.G.J., Serebrenik, A.: Traceability visualization in model transformations with TraceVis. In: Hu, Z., de Lara, J. (eds.) ICMT 2012. LNCS, vol. 7307, pp. 152–159. Springer, Heidelberg (2012). https://doi.org/10.1007/978-3-642-30476-7_10
4. Anquetil, N., et al.: A model-driven traceability framework for software product lines. Softw. Syst. Model. **9**(4), 427–451 (2010)

5. ANSI/IEEE: IEEE guide to software requirements specification, ANSI/IEEE std 830-1984 (1984)
6. Antoniol, G., Canfora, G., Casazza, G., De Lucia, A., Merlo, E.: Recovering traceability links between code and documentation. IEEE Trans. Softw. Eng. **28**(10), 970–983 (2002)
7. Barbero, M., Fabro, M., Bézivin, J.: Traceability and provenance issues in global model management. In: 3rd ECMDA-Traceability Workshop (2007)
8. Carlshamre, P., Sandahl, K., Lindvall, M., Regnell, B., och Dag, J.N.: An industrial survey of requirements interdependencies in software product release planning. In: Proceedings Fifth IEEE International Symposium on Requirements Engineering. IEEE (2001). https://doi.org/10.1109/isre.2001.948547
9. Chen, H., Jiang, J., Hong, Z., Lin, L.: Decomposition of UML activity diagrams. Softw. Pract. Exp. **48**(1), 105–122 (2018)
10. Cleland-Huang, J., Chang, C., Christensen, M.: Event-based traceability for managing evolutionary change. IEEE Trans. Softw. Eng. **29**(9), 796–810 (2003). https://doi.org/10.1109/tse.2003.1232285
11. Cleland-Huang, J., Chang, C.K., Ge, Y.: Supporting event based traceability through high-level recognition of change events. In: Proceedings 26th Annual International Computer Software and Applications, pp. 595–600. IEEE (2002)
12. Cleland-Huang, J., Gotel, O.C., Huffman Hayes, J., Mäder, P., Zisman, A.: Software traceability: trends and future directions. In: Future of Software Engineering Proceedings, pp. 55–69 (2014)
13. Cuadrado, J.S., Molina, J.G., Tortosa, M.M.: RubyTL: a practical, extensible transformation language. In: Rensink, A., Warmer, J. (eds.) ECMDA-FA 2006. LNCS, vol. 4066, pp. 158–172. Springer, Heidelberg (2006). https://doi.org/10.1007/11787044_13
14. Cusack, E.: Refinement, conformance and inheritance. Form. Asp. Comput. **3**(2), 129–141 (1991). https://doi.org/10.1007/bf01898400
15. Dahlstedt, Å.G., Persson, A.: Requirements interdependencies: state of the art and future challenges. In: Aurum, A., Wohlin, C. (eds.) Engineering and Managing Software Requirements, pp. 95–116. Springer-Verlag, Heidelberg (2005). https://doi.org/10.1007/3-540-28244-0_5
16. De Lucia, A., Fasano, F., Oliveto, R., Tortora, G.: Enhancing an artefact management system with traceability recovery features. In: 2004 Proceedings of 20th IEEE International Conference on Software Maintenance, pp. 306–315. IEEE (2004)
17. Erata, F., Challenger, M., Tekinerdogan, B., Monceaux, A., Tüzün, E., Kardas, G.: Tarski: a platform for automated analysis of dynamically configurable traceability semantics. In: Proceedings of the Symposium on Applied Computing, pp. 1607–1614 (2017)
18. Espinoza, A., Garbajosa, J.: A study to support agile methods more effectively through traceability. Innov. Syst. Softw. Eng. **7**(1), 53–69 (2011)
19. Goknil, A., Kurtev, I., van den Berg, K., Veldhuis, J.W.: Semantics of trace relations in requirements models for consistency checking and inferencing. Softw. Syst. Model. **10**(1), 31–54 (2009). https://doi.org/10.1007/s10270-009-0142-3
20. Goknil, A., Kurtev, I., Berg, K.V.D.: Generation and validation of traces between requirements and architecture based on formal trace semantics. J. Syst. Softw. **88**, 112–137 (2014). https://doi.org/10.1016/j.jss.2013.10.006
21. Gotel, O., Finkelstein, C.: An analysis of the requirements traceability problem. In: Proceedings of IEEE International Conference on Requirements Engineering. IEEE Computer Society Press (1994). https://doi.org/10.1109/icre.1994.292398
22. Group, O.M.: Omg unified modeling language tm (OMG UML): Version 2.5. Needham: OMG (2015)

23. Guo, J., Cleland-Huang, J., Berenbach, B.: Foundations for an expert system in domain-specific traceability. In: 2013 21st IEEE International Requirements Engineering Conference (RE), pp. 42–51. IEEE (2013)
24. Hayes, J.H., Dekhtyar, A., Sundaram, S.K.: Advancing candidate link generation for requirements tracing: the study of methods. IEEE Trans. Softw. Eng. **32**(1), 4–19 (2006)
25. Holten, D.: Hierarchical edge bundles: visualization of adjacency relations in hierarchical data. IEEE Trans. Visual Comput. Graph. **12**(5), 741–748 (2006)
26. Shakil Khan, S., Greenwood, P., Garcia, A., Rashid, A.: On the impact of evolving requirements-architecture dependencies: an exploratory study. In: Bellahsène, Z., Léonard, M. (eds.) CAiSE 2008. LNCS, vol. 5074, pp. 243–257. Springer, Heidelberg (2008). https://doi.org/10.1007/978-3-540-69534-9_19
27. Kolovos, D.S., Paige, R.F., Polack, F.A.: On-demand merging of traceability links with models. In: 3rd ECMDA Traceability Workshop, pp. 47–55 (2006)
28. Kolovos, D.S., Paige, R.F., Polack, F.A.C.: The epsilon transformation language. In: Vallecillo, A., Gray, J., Pierantonio, A. (eds.) ICMT 2008. LNCS, vol. 5063, pp. 46–60. Springer, Heidelberg (2008). https://doi.org/10.1007/978-3-540-69927-9_4
29. Laghouaouta, Y., Anwar, A., Nassar, M., Coulette, B.: A dedicated approach for model composition traceability. Inf. Softw. Technol. **91**, 142–159 (2017). https://doi.org/10.1016/j.infsof.2017.07.002
30. Lago, P., Muccini, H., van Vliet, H.: A scoped approach to traceability management. J. Syst. Softw. **82**(1), 168–182 (2009). https://doi.org/10.1016/j.jss.2008.08.026
31. Lambolais, T., Courbis, A.L., Luong, H.V., Percebois, C.: IDF: a framework for the incremental development and conformance verification of UML active primitive components. J. Syst. Softw. **113**, 275–295 (2016). https://doi.org/10.1016/j.jss.2015.11.020
32. Letelier, P.: A framework for requirements traceability in UML-based projects. In: Proceedings of the 1st International Workshop on Traceability in Emerging Forms of Software Engineering, pp. 30–41 (2002)
33. Li, Y., Maalej, W.: Which traceability visualization is suitable in this context? A comparative study. In: Regnell, B., Damian, D. (eds.) REFSQ 2012. LNCS, vol. 7195, pp. 194–210. Springer, Heidelberg (2012). https://doi.org/10.1007/978-3-642-28714-5_17
34. Mäder, P., Gotel, O.: Towards automated traceability maintenance. J. Syst. Softw. **85**(10), 2205–2227 (2012)
35. Mäder, P., Gotel, O., Kuschke, T., Philippow, I.: Tracemaintainer-automated traceability maintenance. In: 2008 16th IEEE International Requirements Engineering Conference. pp. 329–330. IEEE (2008)
36. Meedeniya, D., Rubasinghe, I., Perera, I.: Traceability establishment and visualization of software artefacts in devops practice: a survey. Int. J. Adv. Comput. Sci. Appl. **10**(7), 66–76 (2019)
37. Merten, T., Jüppner, D., Delater, A.: Improved representation of traceability links in requirements engineering knowledge using sunburst and netmap visualizations. In: 2011 4th International Workshop on Managing Requirements Knowledge, pp. 17–21. IEEE (2011)
38. Murta, L.G., Van Der Hoek, A., Werner, C.M.: Archtrace: policy-based support for managing evolving architecture-to-implementation traceability links. In: 21st IEEE/ACM International Conference on Automated Software Engineering (ASE 2006), pp. 135–144. IEEE (2006)
39. OMG: Omg systems modeling language tm version 1.5. An OMG Systems Modeling Language TM Publication, May 2017. http://www.omg.org/spec/SysML/1.5/
40. Pavalkis, S., Nemuraitė, L., Butkienė, R.: Derived properties: a user friendly approach to improving model traceability. Inf. Technol. Control **42**(1), 48–60 (2013)
41. von Pilgrim, J., Vanhooff, B., Schulz-Gerlach, I., Berbers, Y.: Constructing and visualizing transformation chains. In: Schieferdecker, I., Hartman, A. (eds.) ECMDA-FA 2008.

LNCS, vol. 5095, pp. 17–32. Springer, Heidelberg (2008). https://doi.org/10.1007/978-3-540-69100-6_2

42. Ramesh, B., Jarke, M.: Toward reference models for requirements traceability. IEEE Trans. Softw. Eng. **27**(1), 58–93 (2001)

43. Rempel, P., Mäder, P.: Preventing defects: the impact of requirements traceability completeness on software quality. IEEE Trans. Softw. Eng. **43**(8), 777–797 (2016)

44. Santos, W.B., de Almeida, E.S., Meira, S.R.: TIRT: a traceability information retrieval tool for software product lines projects. In: 2012 38th Euromicro Conference on Software Engineering and Advanced Applications, pp. 93–100. IEEE (2012)

45. Silva, R., Pascal, C., Hoang, T.S., Butler, M.: Decomposition tool for event-B. Softw. Pract. Exp. **41**(2), 199–208 (2011)

46. Smith, G., Derrick, J.: Specification, refinement and verification of concurrent systems-an integration of object-Z and CSP. Form. Methods Syst. Des. **18**(3), 249–284 (2001)

47. Spanoudakis, G., Zisman, A., Pérez-Miñana, E., Krause, P.: Rule-based generation of requirements traceability relations. J. Syst. Softw. **72**(2), 105–127 (2004). https://doi.org/10.1016/s0164-1212(03)00242-5

48. Wen, H., Wu, J., Jiang, J., Tang, G., Hong, Z.: A formal approach for consistency management in UML models. Int. J. Softw. Eng. Knowl. Eng. **33**(5), 733–763 (2023)

49. Wen, L., Tuffley, D., Dromey, R.G.: Formalizing the transition from requirements' change to design change using an evolutionary traceability model. Innov. Syst. Softw. Eng. **10**(3), 181–202 (2014). https://doi.org/10.1007/s11334-014-0230-6

50. Wiederseiner, C., Garousi, V., Smith, M.: Tool support for automated traceability of test/code artifacts in embedded software systems. In: 2011 IEEE 10th International Conference on Trust, Security and Privacy in Computing and Communications. IEEE (2011). https://doi.org/10.1109/trustcom.2011.151

51. Winkler, S., von Pilgrim, J.: A survey of traceability in requirements engineering and model-driven development. Softw. Syst. Model. **9**(4), 529–565 (2010). https://doi.org/10.1007/s10270-009-0145-0

Generalized Properties of Generalized Fuzzy Sets GFScom and Its Application

Shengli Zhang[1(✉)] and Jing Chen[2]

[1] School of Information Technology, Minzu Normal University of Xingyi, Xingyi 562400, Guizhou, China
zhangshengli@xynun.edu.cn
[2] College of Economics and Management, Minzu Normal University of Xingyi, Xingyi 562400, Guizhou, China
chenjing@xynun.edu.cn

Abstract. Negative information plays an essential role in knowledge representation and commonsense inference. We further continually develop the theory of a generalized fuzzy set with contradictory, opposite and medium negation (GFScom). The t-norm, s-norm, convexity and concavity properties of GFScom are discussed. By introducing GFScom to Mamdani fuzzy systems, we propose new constructive approaches from any (infinite) input-output data pairs to approximate any continuous function on a compact set to a desired degree of accuracy, and study the first-order and the second-order approximation error bounds for the classes of the constructed fuzzy systems from mathematical viewpoints in details. Furthermore, the new better sufficient conditions for this class of fuzzy systems to be universal approximators are investigated thoroughly. Finally, we illustrate several examples and compare the new results to published error bounds through numerical examples.

Keywords: Mamdani fuzzy systems · negation · universal approximator · three kinds of negations · generalized fuzzy sets GFScom

1 Introduction

Negative information plays an essential role in knowledge representation and commonsense inference(see [2,6,9,24] and references therein). However, the notion of negation is often considered as a poorer form of meaning than affirmation [11]. In the past decades, some researchers suggested that uncertain information processing requires different forms of negations in various fields. Zhu and Xiao [28,36,37] developed Medium Logics (ML) with the contradictory, opposite and fuzzy negation under the view of medium principle (i.e., the principle unconditionally recognizes that for any predicate P and object x it is not always true that either there exists $P(x)$ or the opposite side of $P(x)$, cf. [35]), which has very

S. Zhang and J. Chen—Contributed equally to this work.

© The Author(s), under exclusive license to Springer Nature Singapore Pte Ltd. 2024
Z. Cai et al. (Eds.): NCTCS 2023, CCIS 1944, pp. 36–64, 2024.
https://doi.org/10.1007/978-981-99-7743-7_3

sound, complete syntax and semantics [38,39]. The medium algebra, which may be viewed as a generalization of the well-known De Morgan algebra, developed by Pan [19] is the algebraic abstract of Medium Propositional (MP) logic system in ML, i.e., the medium algebra can be viewed as the algebraic structure of MP. Wagner and Analyti etc. [1,25] pointed out that there are (at least) two types of negation: a weak negation representing non-truth (e.g. "he does not like cat") and a strong negation denoting explicit falsity (e.g. "he dislikes cat"). Esteva and Cintula etc. [3,5] extended the Strict Basic Logic (SBL; an extension of the well-known basic logic) with a unary connective $\sim$. The semantics of $\sim$ is any decreasing involution, i.e., the function $n : [0,1] \to [0,1]$ such that $n(n(x)) = x$ and $n(x) \leq n(y)$ whenever $x \geq y$. The SBL with an involutive negation is only the fuzzy logic with both negations (the other negation is the negation in Basic Logic (BL) proposed by Hájek [8], namely, $\neg x = x \to 0$). Kaneiwa [10] developed the description logic with classical and strong negations, where the classical negation expresses the negation of a statement, while the other is used to depict explicit negative information (or negative facts). Ferré [7] proposed an epistemic extension of the concept of negation in Logical Concept Analysis, i.e., the extensional negation is the classical negation, such as "old/not old" and "pretty/not pretty", and the intentional negation can be interpreted as opposition, such as "big/small" and "fat/thin". Pan [20–22] argued that there are three types of negations, namely, contradictory negation, opposite negation and medium negation, in fuzzy knowledge and its negative relationships, subsequently built up a novel fuzzy set referred to as the fuzzy sets with contradictory negation, opposite negation and medium negation (FScom). In order to provide one logic calculus tool for FScom, Pan [22] and Zhang [32] proposed fuzzy logic with three kinds of negations from the axiomatization and natural calculus reasoning points of view, respectively. Murinova [14] studied the formal theory of generalized Aristotelian square of opposition with intermediate quantifiers(expressions such as *most, many, a lot of, a few, large part of, small part of*), and gave the formal definitions of contradictories, contraries and subcontraries. A first comprehensive research focusing on commonsense implications of negation and contradiction is presented in [9].

In [16] and [18], Novák proposed a formal theory of the trichotomous evaluative expressions which are a subclass of evaluative expressions (expressions such as "very small","quite big","more or less medium", etc.) containing evaluative trichotomy of the type *"small-medium-big"*. On the basis of fuzzy type logic (a higher order fuzzy logic, cf. [17]), Novák presented formal representation of fundamental evaluative trichotomy, i.e., the form of *"small-medium-big"*. In the design procedure of fuzzy systems, on the one hand, the fuzzy distribution needs to be provided which covers the input and output spaces, i.e., the membership function of each fuzzy set must be constructed appropriately. However, in [16] and [18], this concrete constructive approach is not provided. On the other hand, the linguistic variables of the forms are commonly used, such as "positive big", "positive medium", "positive small", "zero", "negative small", "negative medium", "negative big" and so on, to represent the fuzzy sets in the input and output spaces. For such fuzzy sets, the method of how to determine their membership functions is not provided in [16] and [18]. As we stated below, from the logical negations point of view, *big* and *small* are regarded as a pair of opposite negations, while *medium* may be viewed as the medium negation of *small* (or *big*). In general, we are willing to establish the membership function of *small* (or *big*) in a certain context and afterwards infer reasonably membership functions of the others.

In the above stated related works, the classical negation are not satisfied to deal with "negative" information (knowledge). Hence, the different kinds of negations in a variety of fields are needed to be introduced. Most of the above-mentioned works depicted the notions of different negations from logical points. Although Pan [20–22] developed the fuzzy sets FScom, there are some shortcomings in FScom: 1) give any fuzzy set A, the medium negative fuzzy set of A is non-normal; 2) in FScom, the parameter λ is non-trivial, namely, the value of λ is not easy to be determined. In order to sketch the essential and intrinsic relationships between fuzzy knowledge and its different negation forms, Zhang [34] defined a novel type of generalized fu0zzy sets with contradictory, opposite and medium negation GFScom. However, there are still many important issues that have not been addressed. The first issue is to explore the generalized properties of GFScom. Considering the generalized triangular norm operations, namely t-norms and s-norms, what are the prominent properties of GFScom? What is the convexity of GFScom with respect to opposite negative operator, medium negative operator and contradictory negative operator? The second issue is to design the fuzzy systems from any (infinite) input-output data pairs that can approximate continuous function in some optimal fashion based on GFScom. The third issue is to check whether the designed fuzzy system is a universal approximator and what is the approximation bound for the above constructed fuzzy system. The fourth issue is to compare the novel conditions requiring the number of known fuzzy sets with all previously published classical conditions for Mamdani fuzzy systems constructed in this paper. We will give complete study to the above four issues in this paper.

The rest of this paper, one can see that we can readily design the required Mamdani fuzzy systems by means of proposed approaches as long as the fuzzy distribution of only half input-output space is presented. By Theorem 9 stated in the paper, we can see that the novel conditions require a smaller number of known fuzzy sets than all previously published classical conditions. In particular, trichotomous evaluative expressions are given to cover input-output space, we only need to know the membership function of the fuzzy set such as small(or big) and then compute other membership functions according to GFScom. For this especial case, the related works mentioned in this paper cannot deal with it.

The remainder of this paper is organized as follows. In Sect. 2, the notion of generalized fuzzy sets GFScom and its relative algebraic operations are given. In Sect. 3, we further investigate some interesting generalized properties (including convexity and concavity) of GFScom. In Sect. 4, on the basis of GFScom, we propose the design methods of the fuzzy system that can approximate a certain continuous function $g(x)$ in some optimal fashion. In Sect. 5, we build up the approximation bounds for the classes of fuzzy systems constructed by this paper and give approximation accuracy analysis. The demonstrations and comparisons are given to illustrate the methods in Sect. 6 and conclusion and future work end in Sect. 7.

This paper follows the notation of [26] and [23]. The nomenclature in Table 1 is provided for the convenience of the reader.

Table 1. Nomenclature

$A^{\lrcorner}$	Opposite negative set of the fuzzy set A
$A^{\sim}$	Medium negative set of the fuzzy set A
$A^{\neg}$	Contradictory negative set of the fuzzy set A
D	A finite numerical district
$A^j_{i_j}$	i_jth fuzzy set associated with the jth input
$\triangle^j_{i_j}$	i_jth triangular fuzzy set associated with the jth input
h	Interval width for membership functions
N_j	Number of membership functions associated with the jth input
x_j	jth input variable of the fuzzy system
$R_{i_1 i_2 \dots i_n}$	Fuzzy rule with antecedent set $A^j_{i_j}$ for $x_j, j = 1, 2, \dots, n$
U	Input universe of discourse
$\mathcal{F}(U)$	A set of all fuzzy subsets over U
$C_{i_1 i_2 \dots i_n}$	Output fuzzy set associated with antecedent set $A^j_{i_j}$ for $x_j, j = 1, 2, \dots, n$
ϵ	Approximation error bound

2 The Notion of GFScom

On the Necessity of Extending Fuzzy Sets. Fuzzy sets are very applicable for coping with vague and inaccurate phenomena. As we have stated above, from the philosophical point of view, we need to distinguish strictly the notions of contradictory, opposite and medium negation. However, in fuzzy sets, only one negation is considered, i.e., contradictory negation, usually defined by $\neg x = 1 - x$ for all $x \in [0, 1]$. Naturally, in order to deal with three types of negations, we need to extend fuzzy sets by introducing the notions of opposite negation and medium negation.

The Problem of Symmetry. The idea of contradictory negation and opposite negation is, somehow, symmetric. In other words, given two concepts A and B in a certain context, if A is the contradictory negative concept $w.r.t.$ B, in general, we would like to expect that B is the contradictory negative concept $w.r.t.$ A too. The requirement for the opposite negation is identical. However, for the notion of medium negation, such requirement is not necessary since the medium negation only depicts a medium concept (state) negating two opposite sides.

Moreover, further requirement for the opposite negation is as follows: given a pair of opposite negative concepts A and B over the universe of discourse U, we hope the possibility distribution of A looks like the "mirror image" of that of B. For example, we consider a pair of opposite negative concepts "tall stature" and "short stature" in a concrete district. If some person x was viewed as "having tall stature", then there should exist another y with short stature in this district, and vice versa.

In [34], the authors proposed the concept of GFScom, and applied it to construct the table look-up scheme. In what follows, for the integrity and ease of discussion, the notion of GFScom is represented, and $\mathcal{F}(U)$ denotes a set of all the fuzzy subsets in U.

Definition 1. Given any universal discourse U and finite numerical district D, namely, it has the following forms: $[a, b]$, $(a, b]$, $[a, b)$, (a, b), or $\{a = x_1 < x_2 << x_n = b\}$, where $a, b \in \mathbb{R}$, called the left and right end of D, respectively, we call the mapping $f : U \to D$ as (one dimensional) finite quantized district mapping.

Definition 2. Suppose that A belongs to $\mathcal{F}(U)$, a, b are the left and right end of U, respectively, $\forall u \in U$, $\otimes$ be a t-norm, and n be a complement.

(1) If a mapping $A^{\neg} : U \longrightarrow [0, 1]$ satisfying $A^{\neg}(u) = n(A(u))$, the fuzzy subset determined by $A^{\neg}(u)$ is said to be an n contradictory negative set of A. Particularly, the fuzzy subset determined by $A^{\neg}(u) = n(A(u)) = 1 - A(u)$ is referred to as a contradictory negative set of A when n is the linear complement.

(2) If a mapping $A^{\lrcorner} : U \longrightarrow [0, 1]$ satisfying $A^{\lrcorner}(u) = A(a + b - u)$ and $A^{\lrcorner}(u) + A(u) \leq 1$, the fuzzy subset determined by $A^{\lrcorner}$ is referred to as an opposite negative set of A.

(3) If a mapping $A^{\sim} : U \longrightarrow [0, 1]$ satifying $A^{\sim}(u) = A^{\neg}(u) \otimes (A^{\lrcorner})^{\neg}(u) = n(A(u)) \otimes n(A^{\lrcorner}(u)) = n(A(u)) \otimes n(A(a + b - u))$, we call the fuzzy subset determined by $A^{\sim}$ a $\otimes$-n medium negative set of A. Particularly, if t-norm $\otimes$ is a min-operator and n a linear complement, the fuzzy subset satisfying $A^{\sim}(u) = \min\{1 - A(u), 1 - A(a + b - u)\}$ is referred to as a medium negative set of A.

The above defined fuzzy sets are called Generalized Fuzzy Set with Contradictory, Opposite and Medium negation, written as GFScom for short.

Definition 3. In GFScom, the operations such as containment, equivalency, union and intersection between a pair of arbitrary fuzzy subsets are identical to the counterparts in Zadeh fuzzy sets.

3   Properties of GFScom

3.1   Generalized Properties of GFScom

In this subsection, the generalized properties of GFScom will be explored.

Definition 4 [12,13]. Given a universe of discourse U, $A, B, C \in \mathcal{F}(U)$. Let $\otimes, \oplus$ be a t-norm, s-norm, respectively, then

(1) If $C(x) = A(x) \oplus B(x)$, $\forall x \in U$, denoted by $C = A\bigcup_\oplus B$, C is called the module union of A and B;

(2) If $C(x) = A(x) \otimes B(x)$, $\forall x \in U$, written as $C = A\bigcap_\otimes B$, C is called the module intersection of A and B.

Theorem 1. *Let* $\otimes, \oplus, n$ *be a t-norm, s-norm and complement, respectively. For any universal discourse U with the left end a and the right end b, A, B and C are any GFScom on U, we have*

(1) (i) $A^{\neg\neg} = A$ (law of double contradictory), (ii) $A^{\dashv\dashv} = A$ (law of double opposition), (iii) $A^\sim = A^{\dashv\sim}$;

(2) (i) $A\bigcup_\oplus B = B\bigcup_\oplus A$, (ii) $A\bigcap_\oplus B = B\bigcap_\oplus A$;

(3) (i) $(A\bigcup_\oplus B)\bigcup_\oplus C = A\bigcup_\oplus (B\bigcup_\oplus C)$,
(ii) $(A\bigcap_\otimes B)\bigcap_\otimes C = A\bigcap_\otimes (B\bigcap_\otimes C)$;

(4) If $A \subseteq B$, then $\forall C \in \mathcal{F}(U)$, $A\bigcup_\oplus C \subseteq B\bigcup_\oplus C$, $A\bigcap_\otimes C \subseteq B\bigcap_\otimes C$;

(5) $A\bigcup_\oplus \emptyset = A$, $A\bigcap_\otimes \emptyset = \emptyset$, $A\bigcup_\oplus U = U$, $A\bigcap_\otimes U = A$;

(6) If $\otimes, \oplus$ are dual with respect to the complement n, and $(A\bigcup_\oplus B)^\dashv$ and $(A\bigcap_\otimes B)^\dashv$ are defined, i.e., $\forall u \in U$, $(A\bigcup_\oplus B)^\dashv(u) + (A\bigcup_\oplus B)(u) \leq 1$, $(A\bigcap_\otimes B)^\dashv(u) + (A\bigcap_\otimes B)(u) \leq 1$, then we have
(i) $(A\bigcup_\oplus B)^\neg = A^\neg \bigcap_\otimes B^\neg$, $(A\bigcap_\otimes B)^\neg = A^\neg \bigcup_\oplus B^\neg$,
(ii) $(A\bigcup_\oplus B)^\dashv = A^\dashv \bigcup_\oplus B^\dashv$, $(A\bigcap_\otimes B)^\dashv = A^\dashv \bigcap_\otimes B^\dashv$,
(iii) $A^\sim = A^\neg \bigcap_\otimes A^{\dashv\neg}$, $(A\bigcup_\oplus B)^\sim = A^\sim \bigcap_\otimes B^\sim$;

(7) $A\bigcap_\otimes B \subseteq A\bigcap B \subseteq A\bigcup B \subseteq A\bigcup_\oplus B$;

(8) (i) $A\bigcup_\oplus(\bigcup_{k=1}^n A_k) = \bigcup_{k=1}^n(A\bigcup_\oplus A_k)$,
(ii) $A\bigcap_\otimes(\bigcup_{k=1}^n A_k) = \bigcup_{k=1}^n(A\bigcap_\otimes A_k)$,
(iii) $A\bigcup_\oplus(\bigcap_{k=1}^n A_k) = \bigcap_{k=1}^n(A\bigcup_\oplus A_k)$,
(iv) $A\bigcap_\otimes(\bigcap_{k=1}^n A_k) = \bigcap_{k=1}^n(A\bigcap_\otimes A_k)$;

(9) If both $\otimes$ and $\oplus$ are continuous, for any index set T, we have
(i) $A\bigcup_\oplus(\bigcup_{t\in T} A_t) = \bigcup_{t\in T}(A\bigcup_\oplus A_t)$,
(ii) $A\bigcap_\otimes(\bigcup_{t\in T} A_t) = \bigcup_{t\in T}(A\bigcap_\otimes A_t)$,
(iii) $A\bigcup_\oplus(\bigcap_{t\in T} A_t) = \bigcap_{t\in T}(A\bigcup_\oplus A_t)$,
(iv) $A\bigcap_\otimes(\bigcap_{t\in T} A_t) = \bigcap_{t\in T}(A\bigcap_\otimes A_t)$.

Proof. We only prove (1),(6) and (9), while others are analogous.

(1) (i) For arbitrary u in U, by Definition 2, one can see $A^{\neg\neg}(u) = n(n(A(u))) = A(u)$. Hence $A^{\neg\neg} = A$ follows.

(ii) For arbitrary u in U, by Definition 2, we have $A^{\dashv\dashv}(u) = A^\dashv(a+b-u) = A(a + b - (a + b - u)) = A(u)$, where a, b is, respectively, the left and right end of U. Consequently, $A^{\dashv\dashv} = A$ holds.

(iii) $\forall u \in u$, $A^{\dashv\sim}(u) = A^{\dashv\neg}(u) \otimes A^{\dashv\dashv\neg}(u) = A^\neg(u) \otimes A^{\dashv\neg}(u) = A^\sim(u)$ follows from Definition 2 and (1)(ii). Hence, $A^\sim = A^{\dashv\sim}$ holds.

(6) (i) For any u in U, since $\otimes$ and $\oplus$ are mutually dual with respect to n, one can see that $(A\bigcup_\oplus B)^\neg(u) = n((A\bigcup_\oplus B)(u)) = n(\oplus(A(u),B(u))) = n(n(\otimes(n(A(u)),n(B(u))))) = \otimes(n(A(u)),n(B(u))) = A^\neg(u)\bigcap_\otimes B^\neg(u)$ by Definitions 2 and 3. Analogously, we can prove the other.

(ii) For any u in U, by Definition 2 we get $(A\bigcup_\oplus B)^\lrcorner(u) = (A\bigcup_\oplus B)(a+b-u) = \otimes(A(a+b-u),B(a+b-u)) = A^\lrcorner(u)\bigcup_\oplus B^\lrcorner(u)$. Hence, the equality holds. The verification of the other equality is similar.

(iii) The first equality is trivial. Subsequently, we need only to prove the second equality, i.e., $(A\bigcup_\oplus B)^\sim = A^\sim\bigcap_\otimes B^\sim$.

By the above proved outcomes, we have

$$
\begin{aligned}
(A\bigcup_\oplus B)^\sim &= (A\bigcup_\oplus B)^\neg\bigcap_\otimes(A\bigcup_\oplus B)^{\lrcorner\neg} \qquad (1)\\
&= (A^\neg\bigcap_\otimes B^\neg)\bigcap_\otimes(A^\lrcorner\bigcup_\oplus B^\lrcorner)^\neg\\
&= (A^\neg\bigcap_\otimes B^\neg)\bigcap_\otimes(A^{\lrcorner\neg}\bigcap_\otimes B^{\lrcorner\neg})\\
&= (A^\neg\bigcap_\otimes A^{\lrcorner\neg})\bigcap_\otimes(B^\neg\bigcap_\otimes B^{\lrcorner\neg})\\
&= A^\sim\bigcap_\otimes B^\sim.
\end{aligned}
$$

(9) (i) For any u in U, thanks to Definitions 2 and 3 and continuity of $\oplus$, we can get $(A\bigcup_\oplus(\bigcup_{t\in T}A_t))(u) = A(u)\oplus(\vee_{t\in T}A_t(u)) = \vee_{t\in T}A(u)\oplus A_t(u) = (\bigcup_{t\in T}(A\bigcup_\oplus A_t))(u)$. Consequently, the equality follows. The proof for the rest is analogous and omitted.

3.2   Convexity and Concavity of GFScom

It is well known that convexity is an important concept for the quantitative and qualitative analysis in operation research which helps to optimize the solution of problems. The notion of convexity also forms one of the pillars of nonclassical analysis which is a novel branch of fuzzy mathematics. So, many scholars studied some properties of convex fuzzy sets (e.g., see [15] and references therein). Therefore, in the design procedure of fuzzy systems, it is useful for us to analyze the constructed fuzzy system if the convex (or concave) fuzzy sets are used to construct the desired fuzzy system.

In this subsection, we suppose for concreteness that U is a n-dimensional Cartesian product D^n, where D is an interval of the form: $[a,b]$, $(a,b]$, $[a,b)$, (a,b) such that $a,b\in\mathbb{R}$.

Definition 5 *convexity (up convexity).* Let A be any GFScom on U. A is convex if and only if

$$A(\lambda x_1 + (1-\lambda)x_2) \geq A(x_1)\wedge A(x_2) = \min\{A(x_1),A(x_2)\} \qquad (2)$$

for all x_1 and x_2 in U and all λ in $[0,1]$.

In contrast to convexity, one can readily get the following notion.

Definition 6 *concavity (down convexity)*. Let A be any GFScom on U. A is concave if and only if

$$A(\lambda x_1 + (1 - \lambda)x_2) \leq A(x_1) \vee A(x_2) = \max\{A(x_1), A(x_2)\} \qquad (3)$$

for all x_1 and x_2 in U and all λ in $[0, 1]$. Specially, we call A strongly concave if $A(\lambda x_1 + (1 - \lambda)x_2) \leq A(x_1) \wedge A(x_2) = \min\{A(x_1), A(x_2)\}$ holds for all x_1 and x_2 in U and all λ in $[0, 1]$.

Clearly, it is not hard to see that if A is strongly concave, then it is concave; conversely, the result does not follow.

A basic property of convex (strongly-concave) GFScom is expressed by

Theorem 2. *Let A and B be any GFScom on U, $\otimes$, $\oplus$ a t-norm, s-norm, respectively. Then we have*

(1) If A and B are strongly concave, so are their module intersection $A \cap_\otimes B$ and module union $A \cup_\oplus B$;
(2) If A and B are convex, so is their intersection $A \cap B$.

Proof. We only prove (1), (2) is similar.

(1) Let $C = A \cap_\otimes B$ be strongly concave. Then

$$C(\lambda x_1 + (1 - \lambda)x_2) = A(\lambda x_1 + (1 - \lambda)x_2) \cap_\otimes B(\lambda x_1 + (1 - \lambda)x_2). \qquad (4)$$

Now, since A and B are strongly concave, the following inequalities

$$A(\lambda x_1 + (1 - \lambda)x_2) \leq A(x_1) \wedge A(x_2) \qquad (5)$$
$$B(\lambda x_1 + (1 - \lambda)x_2) \leq B(x_1) \wedge B(x_2) \qquad (6)$$

hold, and hence

$$C(\lambda x_1 + (1 - \lambda)x_2) \leq (A(x_1) \wedge A(x_2)) \cap_\otimes (B(x_1) \wedge B(x_2)) \qquad (7)$$

follows from the monotonicity of t-norms. For the right-hand side of the above inequality, one can get

$$
\begin{aligned}
(A(x_1) &\wedge A(x_2)) \cap_\otimes (B(x_1) \wedge B(x_2)) \qquad (8) \\
&= [(A(x_1) \wedge A(x_2)) \cap_\otimes B(x_1)] \wedge [(A(x_1) \\
&\qquad \wedge A(x_2)) \cap_\otimes B(x_2)] \\
&= (A(x_1) \cap_\otimes B(x_1)) \wedge (A(x_2) \cap_\otimes B(x_1)) \\
&\qquad \wedge (A(x_1) \cap_\otimes B(x_2)) \wedge (A(x_2) \cap_\otimes B(x_2)) \\
&\leq (A(x_1) \cap_\otimes B(x_1)) \wedge (A(x_2) \cap_\otimes B(x_2)) \\
&= (A \cap_\otimes B)(x_1) \wedge (A \cap_\otimes B)(x_2)
\end{aligned}
$$

from Definition 6 and Theorem 1(8). Hence,

$$C(\lambda x_1 + (1 - \lambda)x_2) \leq (A \cap_\otimes B)(x_1) \wedge (A \cap_\otimes B)(x_2) \qquad (9)$$

follows. Thus, $C(\lambda x_1 + (1 - \lambda)x_2) \leq C(x_1) \wedge C(x_2)$ holds. That is to say, $A \cap_\otimes B$ is strongly concave. The proof of the other is analogous.

(2) It is immediate from Lemma 1 in [15]. The proof is finished. In the following, we present the convex-concave connections of a fuzzy set and its three types of negative sets.

Theorem 3. *Let A be any GFScom on U. Then we have*

(1) If A is convex, then its opposite negative set $A^{\dashv}$ is also convex, and vice versa.

(2) If A is concave, then its opposite negative set $A^{\dashv}$ is also concave, and vice versa.

Proof. We only prove (1). The proof of (2) is analogous. If A is convex, i.e., the inequality (2) follows, we then have $A(\lambda x_1 + (1 - \lambda)x_2) \geq (A(x_1) \wedge A(x_2))$ for all x_1 and x_2 in U and all λ in $[0, 1]$. In the special case of $a + b - x_1$, $a + b - x_2$ in U , the above inequality follows, too, that is,

$$A(\lambda(a + b - x_1) + (1 - \lambda)(a + b - x_2)) \geq A(a + b - x_1) \wedge A(a + b - x_2) \tag{10}$$

or equivalently

$$A(a + b - (\lambda x_1 + (1 - \lambda)x_2)) \geq A(a + b - x_1) \wedge A(a + b - x_2) \tag{11}$$

and therefore $A^{\dashv}(\lambda x_1 + (1 - \lambda)x_2) \geq A^{\dashv}(x_1) \wedge A^{\dashv}(x_2)$.

Conversely, assume that $A^{\dashv}$ is convex. By the just above-proven procedure, one can readily see $A^{\dashv\dashv}$ is convex. Furthermore, obviously, $A^{\dashv\dashv} = A$ holds by the aforementioned Theorem 1(1). Hence, A is convex. The proof is completed.

Theorem 4. *Let A be any GFScom on U, n any complement. Then we have*

(1) If A is concave, then its n contradictory negative set $A^{\neg}$ is convex, and vice versa.

(2) If A is convex, then its n contradictory negative set $A^{\neg}$ is concave, and vice versa.

Proof.

(1) If A is concave, by inequality (3), we get

$$A(\lambda x_1 + (1 - \lambda)x_2) \leq A(x_1) \vee A(x_2) \tag{12}$$

for all x_1 and x_2 in U and all λ in $[0, 1]$. Furthermore, the following inequality

$$n(A(\lambda x_1 + (1 - \lambda)x_2)) \geq n(A(x_1) \vee A(x_2)) \tag{13}$$

holds, where n is any complement, and therefore,

$$A^{\neg}(\lambda x_1 + (1 - \lambda)x_2) \geq A^{\neg}(x_1) \wedge A^{\neg}(x_2). \tag{14}$$

Consequently, $A^{\neg}$ is convex.

Conversely, the n contradictory negative set $A^{\neg}$ is convex, by inequality (2), we have

$$A^{\neg}(\lambda x_1 + (1 - \lambda)x_2) \geq A^{\neg}(x_1) \wedge A^{\neg}(x_2) \tag{15}$$

for all x_1 and x_2 in U and all λ in $[0,1]$. Moreover, the inequality

$$n(A^\neg(\lambda x_1 + (1-\lambda)x_2)) \leq n(A^\neg(x_1) \wedge A^\neg(x_2)) \tag{16}$$

follows, where n is any complement. The equivalent inequality

$$n(n(A(\lambda x_1 + (1-\lambda)x_2))) \leq n(n(A(x_1))) \vee n(n(A(x_2))) \tag{17}$$

holds. Thus,

$$A(\lambda x_1 + (1-\lambda)x_2) \leq A(x_1) \vee A(x_2). \tag{18}$$

Therefore, A is concave.

(2) It is analogous to the proof of Theorem 4(1).

Theorem 5. *Let A be any GFScom on U. If A is concave, then its medium negative set $A^\sim$ is convex.*

Proof. If A is concave, then $A^\neg$ is convex by Theorem 4(1) and $A^\dashv$ is concave by Theorem 3(2). Moreover, it is immediate that $A^{\dashv\neg}$ is convex from Theorem 4(1). According to Theorems 2(1) and 1(6), one can easily see that $A^\sim = A^\neg \cap A^{\dashv\neg}$ is convex.

Note that the only case is considered in Theorem 5 but two cases in Theorems 3 and 4, the reason is that, in generally, we can not obtain the convex-concave property of intersection of fuzzy sets A and B when A and B are concave. Thus, when A is convex, the convex-concave property of $\otimes$-n medium negative set of A can not been determined according to Definition 6. However, the special case of $\otimes$-n medium negative set, i.e., the t-norm $\otimes$ is a min-operator and n a linear complement, is convex whenever A is concave.

4   Design of Fuzzy Systems Based on GFScom

In this section, we assume that the analytic formula of nonlinear function: $g(x):$ $U \subset \mathbb{R}^n \to \mathbb{R}$ is unknown. But we can determine the input-output pairs $(x; g(x))$ for any $x \in U$. Based on the above GFScom, our task is to design a fuzzy system that can approximate $g(x)$ in an optimal manner.

4.1   Preliminary Concepts and Notations

Definition 7 [26,31]. *Pseudo-Trapezoid-Shaped Membership Functions (PTS).* Let $[a,d] \subseteq U \subset \mathbb{R}$ and $a \leq d$. A continuous function $A(x) = A(x; a, b, c, d, H)$ with $a \leq b \leq c \leq d$ is a PTS function given by

$$A(x; a, b, c, d, H) = \begin{cases} I(x), & \text{when } x \in [a, b) \\ H, & \text{when } x \in [b, c] \\ D(x), & \text{when } x \in (c, d] \\ 0, & \text{when } x \in U - [a, d] \end{cases}, \tag{19}$$

where $0 < H \leq 1$, $0 \leq I(x) \leq 1$ is strictly monotone increasing in $[a, b)$ and $0 \leq D(x) \leq 1$ is strictly monotone decreasing in $(c, d]$. When $H = 1$, it is simply denoted by $A(x) = A(x; a, b, c, d)$.

Remark 1 Pseudo-trapezoid membership functions of the form Eq. (19) contain a number of commonly-employed membership functions as special cases. For instance, if we choose

$$I(x) = \frac{x-a}{b-a} \quad \text{and} \quad D(x) = \frac{x-d}{c-d}, \tag{20}$$

then the pseudo-trapezoid-shaped membership functions change into the *trapezoid membership functions*. If $b = c$, and $I(x)$ and $D(x)$ are defined as in Eq. (20), we can obtain the *triangular membership functions*. For normal triangular membership functions, we often denote them by the simpler notation $\triangle(x; a, b, d)$.

4.2 Design of Fuzzy System with First-Order Approximation Accuracy

Now, based on the above defined GFScom, we are ready to design a particular type of fuzzy systems that have some nice properties. We first specify the problem as follows.

The Problem: Let $g(x)$ be a function on the compact set $U = [\alpha_1, \beta_1] \times [\alpha_2, \beta_2] \times \cdots \times [\alpha_n, \beta_n] \subset \mathbb{R}^n$ and the analytic expression of $g(x)$ be unknown. Assume that for any $x \in U$, we can determine $g(x)$. Our task is to design a fuzzy system that approximates $g(x)$ to any degree of accuracy using GFScom developed by this paper.

We now design such a fuzzy system step-by-step as follows.

Step 1. Define $\lceil \frac{N_i}{2} \rceil$ $(i = 1, 2, 3, \ldots, n;$ $\lceil x \rceil$ denotes the smallest integer which is not less than $x)$ fuzzy sets $A_1^i, A_2^i, \ldots, A_{\lceil \frac{N_i}{2} \rceil}^i$ in $[\alpha_i, \frac{\alpha_i + \beta_i}{2}]$ which are normal, consistent and complete.

Specially, we may, for example, take those fuzzy sets with PTS functions $A_1^i(x; a_i^1, b_i^1, c_i^1, d_i^1), \ldots, A_{\lceil \frac{N_i}{2} \rceil}^i(x; a_i^{\lceil \frac{N_i}{2} \rceil}, b_i^{\lceil \frac{N_i}{2} \rceil}, c_i^{\lceil \frac{N_i}{2} \rceil}, d_i^{\lceil \frac{N_i}{2} \rceil})$, and $A_1^i < A_2^i < \cdots < A_{\lceil \frac{N_i}{2} \rceil}^i$ with $a_i^1 = b_i^1 = \alpha_i$, and the arguments of $A_{\lceil \frac{N_i}{2} \rceil}^i$ on the domain $U_i = [\alpha_i, \beta_i]$ satisfy the following conditions: $c_i^{\lceil \frac{N_i}{2} \rceil} = d_i^{\lceil \frac{N_i}{2} \rceil} = \frac{\alpha_i + \beta_i}{2}$ whenever N_i is odd; otherwise, $c_i^{\lceil \frac{N_i}{2} \rceil} = \alpha_i + \beta_i - d_i^{\lceil \frac{N_i}{2} \rceil} < d_i^{\lceil \frac{N_i}{2} \rceil} \leq \alpha_i + \beta_i - c_i^{\lceil \frac{N_i}{2} \rceil}$ and $A_{\lceil \frac{N_i}{2} \rceil}^i(\frac{\alpha_i + \beta_i}{2}) \leq 0.5$.

Step 2. By Definition 2, 1) compute $(A_{j_i}^i)^{\lrcorner}(j_i = 1, 2, \ldots, \lceil \frac{N_i}{2} \rceil, i = 1, 2, \ldots, n)$ on $U_i = [\alpha_i, \beta_i]$ when N_i is even; 2) when N_i is odd, calculate $(A_{j_i}^i)^{\lrcorner}(j_i = 1, 2, \ldots, \lceil \frac{N_i}{2} \rceil - 1, i = 1, 2, \ldots, n)$ on $U_i = [\alpha_i, \beta_i]$, and $A_{\lceil \frac{N_i}{2} \rceil}^{i'}(x) = A_{\lceil \frac{N_i}{2} \rceil}^i(\alpha_i + \beta_i - x)$ for any $x \in U_i$.

Specifically, whenever N_i is even, let $A_{N_i}^i(x; a_i^{N_i}, b_i^{N_i}, c_i^{N_i}, d_i^{N_i}) = (A_1^i)^{\lrcorner}$, $\ldots, A_{\lceil \frac{N_i}{2} \rceil + 1}^i(x; a_i^{\lceil \frac{N_i}{2} \rceil + 1}, b_i^{\lceil \frac{N_i}{2} \rceil + 1}, c_i^{\lceil \frac{N_i}{2} \rceil + 1}, d_i^{\lceil \frac{N_i}{2} \rceil + 1}) = (A_{\lceil \frac{N_i}{2} \rceil}^i)^{\lrcorner}$, where $a_i^{N_i} = \alpha_i + \beta_i - d_i^1$, $b_i^{N_i} = \alpha_i + \beta_i - c_i^1$, $c_i^{N_i} = \alpha_i + \beta_i - b_i^1$, $d_i^{N_i} = \alpha_i + \beta_i - a_i^1; \ldots;$

$a_i^{\lceil \frac{N_i}{2} \rceil + 1} = \alpha_i + \beta_i - d_i^{\lceil \frac{N_i}{2} \rceil}$, $b_i^{\lceil \frac{N_i}{2} \rceil + 1} = \alpha_i + \beta_i - c_i^{\lceil \frac{N_i}{2} \rceil}$, $c_i^{\lceil \frac{N_i}{2} \rceil + 1} = \alpha_i + \beta_i - b_i^{\lceil \frac{N_i}{2} \rceil}$,

$d_i^{\lceil \frac{N_i}{2} \rceil + 1} = \alpha_i + \beta_i - a_i^{\lceil \frac{N_i}{2} \rceil}$. Whenever N_i is odd, let $A_{N_i}^i = (A_1^i)^{\lrcorner}, \ldots, A_{\lceil \frac{N_i}{2} \rceil + 1}^i = $

$(A_{\lceil \frac{N_i}{2} \rceil - 1}^i)^{\lrcorner}$, $A_{\lceil \frac{N_i}{2} \rceil}^i = A_{\lceil \frac{N_i}{2} \rceil}^i \bigcup A_{\lceil \frac{N_i}{2} \rceil}^{i'}$ (Here $A_{\lceil \frac{N_i}{2} \rceil}^i \bigcup A_{\lceil \frac{N_i}{2} \rceil}^{i'}$ is a new fuzzy set, also

written as $A_{\lceil \frac{N_i}{2} \rceil}^i$ for the sake of simplicity), where $\bigcup$ represents fuzzy union, i.e.,
max operator.

From the following Theorem 6 and the above two steps , one can see that $A_1^i, A_2^i, \ldots, A_{N_i}^i$ are normal, consistent and complete GFScom on $U_i = [\alpha_i, \beta_i]$, and $A_1^i < A_2^i < \ldots < A_{N_i}^i$.

Step 3. Define $e_j^1 = \alpha_j$, $e_j^{N_j} = \beta_j$ and $e_j^{i_j} \in [b_j^{i_j}, c_j^{i_j}]$ (e.g. $e_j^{i_j} = \frac{1}{2}(b_j^{i_j} + c_j^{i_j})$) for $i_j = 2, \ldots, N_j - 1; j = 1, 2, \ldots, n$.

Step 4. Construct $m = N_1 \times N_2 \times \cdots N_n = \prod_{i=1}^n N_i$ fuzzy IF-THEN rules in the following form:

$$R_{i_1 i_2 \ldots i_n} : IF \; x_1 \; is \; A_{i_1}^1 \; and \; \cdots \; and \; x_n \; is \; A_{i_n}^n, \\ THEN \; y \; is \; C_{i_1 i_2 \ldots i_n} \tag{21}$$

where $i_1 = 1, \ldots, N_1$, $\ldots$, $i_n = 1, \ldots, N_n$ and the point in $\mathbb{R}$ at which the fuzzy set $C_{i_1 i_2 \ldots i_n}$ achieves its maximum value, denoted as $\bar{y}_{i_1 i_2 \ldots i_n}$ (when $C_{i_1 i_2 \ldots i_n}$ is a normal fuzzy set, $C_{i_1 i_2 \ldots i_n}(\bar{y}_{i_1 i_2 \ldots i_n}) = 1$; in this paper, we always assume that $C_{i_1 i_2 \ldots i_n}$ is a normal fuzzy set), is chosen as

$$\bar{y}_{i_1 i_2 \ldots i_n} = g(e_1^{i_1}, e_2^{i_2}, \ldots, e_n^{i_n}). \tag{22}$$

Step 5. Construct the fuzzy system $f(x)$ from the $\prod_{i=1}^n N_i$ generated by Step 4 using singleton fuzzifier [26,31], product inference engine [26,31], center average defuzzifier [26,31], i.e., taking "and" as product operator, fuzzy implication as Mamdani product implication (i.e., $a \rightarrow b = ab, \forall a, b \in [0,1]$) as follows:

$$y = f(x) = \frac{\sum_{i_n=1}^{N_n} \cdots \sum_{i_1=1}^{N_1} A_{i_1 i_2 \ldots i_n}(x) \bar{y}_{i_1 i_2 \ldots i_n}}{\sum_{i_n=1}^{N_n} \cdots \sum_{i_1=1}^{N_1} A_{i_1 i_2 \ldots i_n}(x)},$$
$$= \sum_{i_n=1}^{N_n} \cdots \sum_{i_1=1}^{N_1} B_{i_1 i_2 \ldots i_n}(x) \bar{y}_{i_1 i_2 \ldots i_n} \tag{23}$$

where the crisp input value $x = (x_1, x_2, \ldots, x_n) \in U$, $A_{i_1 i_2 \ldots i_n}(x) = A_{i_1}^1(x_1) A_{i_2}^2(x_2) \cdots A_{i_n}^n(x_n)$, and

$$B_{i_1 i_2 \ldots i_n}(x) = \frac{A_{i_1 i_2 \ldots i_n}(x)}{\sum_{i_n=1}^{N_n} \cdots \sum_{i_1=1}^{N_1} A_{i_1 i_2 \ldots i_n}(x)} \\ = \frac{A_{i_1}^1(x_1) A_{i_2}^2(x_2) \cdots A_{i_n}^n(x_n)}{\sum_{i_n=1}^{N_n} \cdots \sum_{i_1=1}^{N_1} A_{i_1}^1(x_1) A_{i_2}^2(x_2) \cdots A_{i_n}^n(x_n)}. \tag{24}$$

Since the fuzzy sets $A_1^i, A_2^i, \ldots, A_{N_i}^i$ are complete GFScom on $U_i = [\alpha_i, \beta_i]$, at every point $x \in U$ there exists $i_1, i_2, \ldots, i_n$ such that $A_{i_1}^1(x_1) A_{i_2}^2(x_2) \cdots A_{i_n}^n(x_n)$

$\neq 0$. Therefore, the fuzzy system (23) is well defined, that is, its denominator is always nonzero.

In the above procedure, we only consider the case of the membership function distribution over $[\alpha_i, \frac{\alpha_i+\beta_i}{2}]$. However, if the membership function distribution on $[\frac{\alpha_i+\beta_i}{2}, \beta_i]$ can be determined, then we may carry out the same work as in Steps 1 through 5 of the above design procedure in terms of Definition 2.

4.3 Design of Fuzzy System with Second-Order Accuracy

The design problem is the same as in Sect. 4.2. Next, on the basis of GFScom, we design the fuzzy system with second-order accuracy in a step-by-step manner.

Step 1. Define $\lceil \frac{N_j}{2} \rceil$ $(j = 1, 2, 3, \ldots, n)$ fuzzy sets $A_1^j, A_2^j, \ldots, A_{\lceil \frac{N_j}{2} \rceil}^j$ in $[\alpha_j, \frac{\alpha_j+\beta_j}{2}]$ which are normal, consistent and complete with the triangular membership functions

$$A_{i_j}^j(x_j) = \triangle_{i_j}^j(x_j; e_{i_j-1}^j, e_{i_j}^j, e_{i_j+1}^j) \tag{25}$$

for $i_j = 1, 2, \ldots, \lceil \frac{N_j}{2} \rceil$, where $e_0^j = e_1^j = \alpha_j$, $e_1^j < e_2^j < \cdots < e_{\lceil \frac{N_j}{2} \rceil}^j \leq e_{\lceil \frac{N_j}{2} \rceil+1}^j$, and $e_{\lceil \frac{N_j}{2} \rceil}^j = e_{\lceil \frac{N_j}{2} \rceil+1}^j = \frac{\alpha_j+\beta_j}{2}$ whenever N_j is odd. Otherwise, $e_{\lceil \frac{N_j}{2} \rceil}^j < \frac{\alpha_j+\beta_j}{2}$, $e_{\lceil \frac{N_j}{2} \rceil}^j + e_{\lceil \frac{N_j}{2} \rceil+1}^j = \alpha_j + \beta_j$ and $A_{\lceil \frac{N_j}{2} \rceil}^j(\frac{\alpha_j+\beta_j}{2}) \leq 0.5$.

Step 2. When N_j is even, calculate $(A_{i_j}^j)^{\lrcorner}$ $(i_j = 1, 2, \ldots, \lceil \frac{N_j}{2} \rceil)$ in $U_j = [\alpha_j, \beta_j]$. When N_j is odd, calculate $(A_{i_j}^j)^{\lrcorner}$ $(i_j = 1, 2, \ldots, \lceil \frac{N_j}{2} \rceil - 1)$ in $U_j = [\alpha_j, \beta_j]$ and $A_{\lceil \frac{N_j}{2} \rceil}^{j'}(x) = A_{\lceil \frac{N_j}{2} \rceil}^j(\alpha_j + \beta_j - x)$ for all $x \in U_j$. Specially, for $j = 1, 2, \ldots, n$, we distinguish one case from the other as follows:

a) When N_j is even, let $A_{N_j}^j(x_j) = \triangle_{N_j}^j(x_j; e_{\lceil \frac{N_j}{2} \rceil-1}^j, e_{\lceil \frac{N_j}{2} \rceil}^j, e_{\lceil \frac{N_j}{2} \rceil+1}^j) = (A_1^j)^{\lrcorner}$, $\ldots$, $A_{\lceil \frac{N_j}{2} \rceil+1}^j(x_j) = \triangle_{\lceil \frac{N_j}{2} \rceil+1}^j(x_j; e_{\lceil \frac{N_j}{2} \rceil}^j, e_{\lceil \frac{N_j}{2} \rceil+1}^j, e_{\lceil \frac{N_j}{2} \rceil+2}^j) = (A_{\lceil \frac{N_j}{2} \rceil}^j)^{\lrcorner}$, where $e_{N_j}^j = e_{N_j+1}^j = \beta_j$, $e_{N_j-1}^j = \alpha_j + \beta_j - e_2^j$; $\ldots$; $e_{\lceil \frac{N_j}{2} \rceil}^j = e_{\lceil \frac{N_j}{2} \rceil}^j$, $e_{\lceil \frac{N_j}{2} \rceil+1}^j = e_{\lceil \frac{N_j}{2} \rceil+1}^j$, $e_{\lceil \frac{N_j}{2} \rceil+2}^j = \alpha_j + \beta_j - e_{\lceil \frac{N_j}{2} \rceil-1}^j$.

b) When N_j is odd, $A_{N_j}^j, A_{N_j-1}^j, \ldots, A_{\lceil \frac{N_j}{2} \rceil+1}^j$ are the same as the above a), and let $A_{\lceil \frac{N_j}{2} \rceil}^j = A_{\lceil \frac{N_j}{2} \rceil}^j \bigcup A_{\lceil \frac{N_j}{2} \rceil}^{j'}$ (Notice that $A_{\lceil \frac{N_j}{2} \rceil}^j \bigcup A_{\lceil \frac{N_j}{2} \rceil}^{j'}$ is a novel fuzzy set, still denoted as $A_{\lceil \frac{N_j}{2} \rceil}^j$ for the sake of simplicity), where $\bigcup$ denotes fuzzy union, i.e., max operator.

Step 3 and Step 4. The same as Steps 4 and 5 of the design procedure in Sect. 4.2. That is, the constructed fuzzy system is given by Eq. (23), where $\bar{y}_{i_1 i_2 \ldots i_n}$ is given by Eq. (22).

In the sequel, we make a few remarks on this above procedure of designing fuzzy systems.

Remark 2. A fundamental difference between the designed fuzzy systems in Sects. 4.2 and 4.3 is the former usually requires a large number of rules to approximate some simple functions. However, using the fuzzy system with second-order accuracy, we may use fewer rules to approximate the same function with the same accuracy. In summary, the difference between the constructed fuzzy systems in this paper is the same as for that between the traditional fuzzy system with first-order accuracy and fuzzy system with second-order accuracy (see [26] for more details).

Remark 3. Although the opposite negative operator ⅃ is only considered in the constructed fuzzy systems in Sects. 4.2 and 4.3, the opposite negative operator ⅃ is not enough for a practical Mamdani fuzzy system, such as Mamdani fuzzy controller. Firstly, for an applied fuzzy system, the classical negative operator "not" (called the contradictory negative operator in this paper) is usually needed to be considered. This is the reason why we use the classical complement to define the proposed contradictory negative operator in this paper. Secondly, for each variable in the input space, if the designed fuzzy system consists of the evaluative trichotomy of the form "big-medium-small" (sometimes, the contradictory negative operator ¬, i.e., the classical negative operator "not", is needed), thus, we only need to obtain the membership function of each fuzzy set "big" ("small") over the domain $U \subset \mathbb{R}^n$, we can then design the desired fuzzy system by using the proposed methods of this paper (e.g., see Case 3 below). Consequently, considering the design of an actual Mamdani fuzzy system, it is necessary to introduce the other two negations ¬ and ∼.

5 Approximation Accuracy Analysis of the Fuzzy System Designed Based on GFScom

In this section, we build up the approximation bounds for the two classes of fuzzy systems constructed in Sect. 4.

We consider the case where the unknown function $g(x)$ is a continuous function on $U = [\alpha_1, \beta_1] \times [\alpha_2, \beta_2] \times \cdots [\alpha_n, \beta_n] \subseteq \mathbb{R}^n$. Before giving the approximation bounds, we first introduce some formal notations and results as follows [31]:

Define the infinite norm for a bounded function g in U to be $\|g\|_\infty = \sup_{x \in U} |g(x)|$ and the modulus of continuity of g in U to be

$$\omega(g, h, U) = \sup\{|g(x) - g(y)| \mid |x_i - y_i| \leq h_i, i = 1, 2, \ldots, n\}, \qquad (26)$$

and let

$$U_{i_1 i_2 \cdots i_n} = [e_1^{i_1}, e_1^{i_1+1}] \times \cdots \times [e_n^{i_n}, e_n^{i_n+1}], \qquad (27)$$

where $h = (h_1, h_2, \ldots, h_n)$ $(h_i \geq 0$ for all $1 \leq i \leq n)$, $e_j^1 = \alpha_j$, $e_j^{N_j} = \beta_j$, and $e_j^{i_j} \in [b_j^{i_j}, c_j^{i_j}]$ $(i_j = 2, \ldots, N_j - 1; j = 1, 2, \ldots, n)$.

Theorem 6 [33]. *Let $A_1, A_2, \ldots, A_N$ be any GFScom in $U = [\alpha, \beta]$. $A_1, A_2, \ldots, A_N$ are complete, consistent and normal fuzzy subsets with PTS functions* *on $U_1 = [\alpha, \frac{\alpha+\beta}{2}]$ if and only if $A_1^{\dashv}, A_2^{\dashv}, \cdots, A_N^{\dashv}$ are complete, consistent and normal fuzzy subsets with PTS functions on $U_2 = [\frac{\alpha+\beta}{2}, \beta]$. Further, if $A_1 < A_2 < \cdots < A_N$, then we have $A_1 < A_2 < \cdots < A_N < A_N^{\dashv} < \cdots < A_2^{\dashv} < A_1^{\dashv}$.*

Theorem 7. *Let $f(x)$ be the fuzzy system in (23) and $g(x)$ be the unknown function in (22). Then*

$$max\{|g(x) - f(x)||x \in U_{i_1 i_2 \cdots i_n}\} \le \omega(g, h_{i_1 i_2 \cdots i_n}, U_{i_1 i_2 \cdots i_n})$$

$$i_1 i_2 \cdots i_n \in \hat{I}, \quad (28)$$

$$\|g - f\|_\infty \le \omega(g, h, U), \quad (29)$$

where $\hat{I} = \{i_1 i_2 \cdots i_n | i_j = 1, \ldots, N_j - 1; j = 1, 2, \ldots, n\}$, $h_{i_1 i_2 \cdots i_n} = (h_{i_1}^1, h_{i_2}^2, \ldots, h_{i_n}^n)$, $h_{i_j}^j = e_j^{i_j+1} - e_j^{i_j}$, $h = (h_1, h_2, \ldots, h_n)$ and $h_j = max\{h_{i_j}^j | i_j = 1, 2, \ldots, N_j - 1\}$.

Further, if g is continuously differentiable on U, then

$$\|g - f\|_\infty \le \sum_{j=1}^n \left\|\frac{\partial g}{\partial x_j}\right\|_\infty h_j \le h \sum_{j=1}^n \left\|\frac{\partial g}{\partial x_j}\right\|_\infty \quad (30)$$

where $h = max\{h_j | j = 1, 2, \ldots, n\}$.

Proof. By assumptions, we can verify the following results:

(a) $U = \bigcup_{i_1 i_2 \cdots i_n \in \hat{I}} U_{i_1 i_2 \cdots i_n}$. In fact, since $[\alpha_i, \beta_i] = [e_i^1, e_i^2] \cup [e_i^2, e_i^3] \cup \cdots \cup [e_i^{N_i-1}, e_i^{N_i}]$, $i = 1, 2, \ldots, n$, we have

$$U = [\alpha_1, \beta_1] \times [\alpha_2, \beta_2] \times \cdots [\alpha_n, \beta_n]$$
$$= \bigcup_{i_1=1}^{N_1-1} \cdots \bigcup_{i_n=1}^{N_n-1} U_{i_1 i_2 \cdots i_n} = \bigcup_{i_1 i_2 \cdots i_n} U_{i_1 i_2 \cdots i_n} \quad (31)$$

which means that for all $x \in U$, there exists $U_{i_1 i_2 \cdots i_n}$ such that $x \in U_{i_1 i_2 \cdots i_n}$.

(b) For any $x \in U_{i_1 i_2 \cdots i_n}$, we have

$$f(x) = \sum_{k_1 k_2 \cdots k_n \in I_{2^n}} B_{i_1+k_1\ i_2+k_2\ \cdots\ i_n+k_n}(x)\bar{y}_{i_1+k_1\ \cdots\ i_n+k_n} \quad (32)$$

where $I_{2^n} = \{k_1 k_2 \cdots k_n | k_j = 0, 1; j = 1, 2, \ldots, n\}$. In fact, suppose $x \in U_{i_1 i_2 \cdots i_n}$, that is $x_1 \in [e_1^{i_1}, e_1^{i_1+1}]$, $x_2 \in [e_2^{i_2}, e_2^{i_2+1}]$, ..., $x_n \in [e_n^{i_n}, e_n^{i_n+1}]$. By Theorem 6 one can see the fuzzy sets $A_1^{(j)}, A_2^{(j)}, \ldots, A_{N_j}^{(j)}$ are normal, consistent and complete on $[\alpha_j, \beta_j]$ for $j = 1, 2, \ldots, n$, at least one and at most two $A_{i_j}^{(j)}(x_j)$ are nonzero for $i_j = 1, 2, \ldots, N_j$. By the definition of $e_j^{i_j} (i_j = 1, 2, \ldots, N_j - 1)$, these two possible nonzero are $A_{i_j}^{(j)}(x_j)$ and $A_{i_j+1}^{(j)}(x_j)$. Hence, the fuzzy system $f(x)$ in (23) is simplified to the equality (32).

Noting that $\sum_{k_1 k_2 \cdots k_n \in I_{2^n}} B_{i_1+k_1 \ i_2+k_2 \ \cdots \ i_n+k_n}(x) = 1$ and the equality (32), for any $x \in U_{i_1 i_2 \cdots i_n}$, we can obtain

$$|g(x) - f(x)|$$

$$\leq \sum_{k_1 k_2 \cdots k_n \in I_{2^n}} B_{i_1+k_1 \ \cdots \ i_n+k_n} |g(x) - \bar{y}_{i_1+k_1 \ \cdots \ i_n+k_n}| \qquad (33)$$

$$\leq \max\{|g(x) - \bar{y}_{i_1+k_1 \ \cdots \ i_n+k_n}| \ \| k_1 k_2 \cdots k_n \in I_{2^n}\}.$$

Noting that $\bar{y}_{i_1+k_1 \ i_2+k_2 \ \cdots \ i_n+k_n} = g(e_1^{i_1+k_1}, \ e_2^{i_2+k_2}, \ \ldots, \ e_n^{i_n+k_n})$ and $(e_1^{i_1+k_1}, e_2^{i_2+k_2}, \ \ldots, \ e_n^{i_n+k_n}) \in U_{i_1 i_2 \ldots i_n} \ (k_1 k_2 \cdots k_n \in I_{2^n})$, we have $|x_j - e_j^{i_j+k_j}| \leq e_j^{i_j+1} - e_j^{i_j} \ (k_j = 0, 1; j = 1, 2, \ldots, n)$. Hence, for any $x \in U_{i_1 i_2 \ldots i_n}$, the following inequality

$$|g(x) - \bar{y}_{i_1+k_1 \ i_2+k_2 \ \cdots \ i_n+k_n}| \leq \omega(g, h_{i_1 i_2 \ldots i_n}, U_{i_1 i_2 \ldots i_n})$$
$$(k_1 k_2 \cdots k_n \in I_{2^n}) \qquad (34)$$

holds. From (33) and (34), we can obtain the inequalities (28) and (29).

Further, if g is continuously differentiable on U, using the Mean Value Theorem, we have

$$\omega(g, h, U) = \sup\{|g(x) - g(y)| \ \| |x_j - y_j| \leq h_j; j = 1, \ldots, n\}$$
$$\leq \sum_{j=1}^{n} \left\|\frac{\partial g}{\partial x_j}\right\|_\infty h_j \leq h \sum_{j=1}^{n} \left\|\frac{\partial g}{\partial x_j}\right\|_\infty \qquad (35)$$

which implies immediately the inequality (30). The proof is complete.

Remark 4. From the proof of Theorem 7 we see that if we change $A_{i_1}^1(x_1) A_{i_2}^2(x_2) \cdots A_{i_n}^n(x_n)$ to $\min\{A_{i_1}^1(x_1), A_{i_2}^2(x_2), \cdots, A_{i_n}^n(x_n)\}$, the proof is still valid. Therefore, if we use minimum inference engine (i.e., take "and" as min operator, implication as Mamdani min implication operator) in the design procedure and keep the others unchange, the designed fuzzy system still has the approximation capability in Theorem 7.

Theorem 8. *Let $f(x)$ be the fuzzy system designed through the above four Steps in Sect. 4.3, that is, the membership functions of fuzzy sets $A_{i_j}^j$ are the triangular-shaped functions $A_{i_j}^j(x_j) = \triangle_{i_j}^j(x_j; e_{i_j-1}^j, e_{i_j}^j, e_{i_j+1}^j) \ (i_j = 1, 2, \ldots, N_j; j = 1, 2, \ldots, n)$ with $e_0^j = e_1^j = \alpha_j, \ e_{N_j}^j = e_{N_j+1}^j = \beta_j$ and $e_1^j < e_2^j < \cdots < e_{N_j}^j$, and the fuzzy system constructed by using singleton fuzzifier, product inference engine and center average defuzzifier. Then*

(1) $\forall x \in U$, we have

$$f(x) = \sum_{i_1 i_2 \cdots i_n \in I} [\prod_{j=1}^{n} A_{i_j}^j(x_j)] \bar{y}_{i_1 i_2 \ldots i_n}, \qquad (36)$$

where $I = \{i_1 i_2 \cdots i_n | i_j = 1, 2, \ldots, N_j; j = 1, 2, \ldots, n\}$.

(2) If g is a continuously differentiable function on U, then

$$\|g - f\|_\infty \leq \sum_{j=1}^{n} \frac{1}{2} h_j \left\| \frac{\partial g}{\partial x_j} \right\|_\infty \leq \frac{1}{2} h \sum_{j=1}^{n} \left\| \frac{\partial g}{\partial x_j} \right\|_\infty, \tag{37}$$

where $h_{i_j}^j = e_{i_j+1}^j - e_{i_j}^j$, $h_j = max\{h_{i_j}^j | i_j = 1, 2, \ldots, N_j - 1; j = 1, 2, \ldots, n\}$, $h = max\{h_j | j = 1, 2, \ldots, n\}$.

(3) If g is a twice continuously differentiable function on U, then

$$\|g - f\|_\infty \leq \sum_{j=1}^{n} \frac{1}{8} (h_j)^2 \left\| \frac{\partial^2 g}{\partial (x_j)^2} \right\|_\infty \leq \frac{1}{8} h^2 \sum_{j=1}^{n} \left\| \frac{\partial^2 g}{\partial (x_j)^2} \right\|_\infty, \tag{38}$$

where $h_{i_j}^j = e_{i_j+1}^j - e_{i_j}^j$, $h_j = max\{h_{i_j}^j | i_j = 1, 2, \ldots, N_j - 1; j = 1, 2, \ldots, n\}$, $h = max\{h_j | j = 1, 2, \ldots, n\}$.

Proof. (1) By Theorem 6, we see that A_1^j, A_2^j, ..., $A_{N_j}^j$ are normal, complete and consistent fuzzy sets on $U_j = [\alpha_j, \beta_j]$, and $A_1^j < A_2^j < \cdots < A_{N_j}^j$. Moreover, the membership function of fuzzy set $A_{i_j}^j$ ($i_j = 1, 2, \ldots, N_j; j = 1, 2, \ldots, n$) is a triangular-shaped function. Therefore, we can obtain $\sum_{i_j=1}^{N_j} A_{i_j}^j (x_j) = 1$ for any $x_j \in [\alpha_j, \beta_j]$. Hence, it is not difficult to see $\sum_{i_1 i_2 \cdots i_n \in I} \prod_{j=1}^{n} A_{i_j}^j (x_j) = 1$. As a result, it follows that $B_{i_1 i_2 \cdots i_n}(x) = \prod_{j=1}^{n} A_{i_j}^j (x_j)$ which implies that the equality (36) from (23).
(2) By Theorem 6 and the constructed procedure of $f(x)$, i.e., Steps 1 through 4 in Sect. 4.3, we can see the fuzzy sets A_1^j, A_2^j, ..., A_n^j ($j = 1, 2, \ldots, n$) are consistent, complete and normal on $U_j = [\alpha_j, \beta_j]$. For consistent and complete fuzzy sets, we have

$$f(x) = \sum_{k_1=0}^{1} \sum_{k_2=0}^{1} \cdots \sum_{k_n=0}^{1} \bar{y}_{i_1+k_1 \ i_2+k_2 \ \cdots \ i_n+k_n} \prod_{j=1}^{n} A_{i_j+k_j}^j (x_j)$$
$$= \sum_{j=1}^{n} \sum_{k_j=0}^{1} \bar{y}_{i_1+k_1 \ \cdots \ i_n+k_n} A_{i_j+k_j}^j (x_j) \prod_{m=1, m\neq j}^{n} A_{i_m+k_m}^m (x_m) \tag{39}$$

where $\bar{y}_{i_1+k_1 \ i_2+k_2 \ \cdots \ i_n+k_n} = g(e_{i_1+k_1}^1, e_{i_2+k_2}^2, \ldots, e_{i_n+k_n}^n)$ for $i_j = 1, 2, \ldots, N_j - 1; j = 1, 2, \ldots, n$.
Hence,

$$|g(x) - f(x)| \leq \sum_{j=1}^{n} \sum_{k_j=0}^{1} \left(|g(x) - \bar{y}_{i_1+k_1 \ \cdots \ i_n+k_n}| A_{i_j+k_j}^j (x_j) \right)$$
$$\times \prod_{m=1, m\neq j}^{n} A_{i_m+k_m}^m (x_m). \tag{40}$$

For the normal fuzzy sets,

$$|g(x) - f(x)| \leq \sum_{j=1}^{n} \sum_{k_j=0}^{1} |g(x) - \bar{y}_{i_1+k_1 \ i_2+k_2 \ \cdots \ i_n+k_n}| A_{i_j+k_j}^j (x_j). \tag{41}$$

Using the Mean Value Theorem, then

$$|g(x) - f(x)| \leq \sum_{j=1}^{n} \sum_{k_j=0}^{1} \left| \frac{\partial g(x)}{\partial x_j} \right|_{x=\xi} |x_j - e_{i_j+k_j}^j| A_{i_j+k_j}^j(x_j). \qquad (42)$$

Let $g'_{x_j}(x_j) = \bigvee_{x_i \in [\alpha_j, \beta_j], i \neq j} \left| \frac{\partial g}{\partial x_j} \right|$. Noting that $A_{i_j}^j(x_j) + A_{i_j+1}^j(x_j) = 1$ for any $x_j \in [e_{i_j}^j, e_{i_j+1}^j]$ $(j = 1, 2, \ldots, n)$ and $A_{i_j}^j$ is a triangular-shaped function, we have

$$|g(x) - f(x)|$$
$$\leq \sum_{j=1}^{n} \max_{e_{i_j}^j \leq x_j \leq e_{i_j+1}^j} |g'_{x_j}(x_j)| \frac{2(e_{i_j+1}^j - x_j)(x_j - e_{i_j}^j)}{h_{i_j}^j}, \qquad (43)$$

where $h_{i_j}^j = e_{i_j+1}^j - e_{i_j}^j$.
Furthermore, it is easy to verify the identity

$$\max_{e_{i_j}^j \leq x_j \leq e_{i_j+1}^j} \{|x_j - e_{i_j}^j||x_j - e_{i_j+1}^j|\} = \frac{(h_{i_j}^j)^2}{4} \qquad (44)$$

follows. Substituting (44) into (43), we obtain

$$|g(x) - f(x)| \leq \frac{1}{2} \sum_{j=1}^{n} h_{i_j}^j (\max_{e_{i_j}^j \leq x_j \leq e_{i_j+1}^j} |g'_{x_j}(x_j)|). \qquad (45)$$

Therefore, we have

$$\|g(x) - f(x)\|_\infty \leq \frac{1}{2} \sum_{j=1}^{n} h_j \left\| \frac{\partial g}{\partial x_j} \right\|_\infty \leq \frac{1}{2} h \sum_{j=1}^{n} \left\| \frac{\partial g}{\partial x_j} \right\|_\infty, \qquad (46)$$

where $h_j = \max\{h_{i_j}^j | i_j = 1, 2, \ldots, N_j - 1\}$, $h = \max\{h_j | j = 1, 2, \ldots, n\}$. That is, the inequality (37) follows.
(3) Clearly, $f(x)$ is equal to $g(x)$ at points $x^* = (e_{i_1+k_1}^1, e_{i_2+k_2}^2, \ldots, e_{i_n+k_n}^n)$, where $i_j = 1, 2, \ldots, N_j - 1$, $k_j = 0, 1$ for $j = 1, 2, \ldots, n$, namely $g(x^*) - f(x^*) = 0$. Let $x \neq x^*$ be fixed, and without loss of generality, the approximation error can be expressed as

$$g(x) - f(x) = [(x_j - e_{i_j}^j)(x_j - e_{i_j+1}^j)]_j^T P(x). \qquad (47)$$

Consider the following function of s, where $s = (s_1, s_2, \ldots, s_n)$:

$$W(s) = g(s) - f(s) - [(x_j - e_{i_j}^j)(x_j - e_{i_j+1}^j)]_j^T P(x). \qquad (48)$$

Obviously, the above constructed function $W(s) = 0$ at points $s = (e_{i_1+k_1}^1, e_{i_2+k_2}^2, \ldots, e_{i_n+k_n}^n)$ with $k_j = 0, 1$, and at the additional $s = x$. As a result, according to the well known generalized Rolle's Theorem [4], the function $\frac{\partial^2 W(s)}{\partial s_i^2}$ for $i = 1, 2, \ldots, n$ must vanish at points including $\xi = (\xi_1, \xi_2, \ldots, \xi_n)$. The vector of second-order derivatives of $W(s)$ is attained as

$$\begin{pmatrix} \frac{\partial^2 W(s)}{\partial s_1^2} \\ \vdots \\ \frac{\partial^2 W(s)}{\partial s_n^2} \end{pmatrix} = \begin{pmatrix} \frac{\partial^2 g(s)}{\partial s_1^2} \\ \vdots \\ \frac{\partial^2 g(s)}{\partial s_n^2} \end{pmatrix} - 2P(x). \tag{49}$$

Therefore, at arbitrary fixed point x, we have

$$P(x) = \frac{1}{2} \left[\frac{\partial^2 g(\xi)}{\partial x_1^2}, \cdots, \frac{\partial^2 g(\xi)}{\partial x_n^2} \right]^T. \tag{50}$$

Substituting (50) into (47), we can obtain

$$g(x) - f(x) = \frac{1}{2} \sum_{j=1}^{n} (x_j - e_{i_j}^j)(x_j - e_{i_j+1}^j) \frac{\partial^2 g(\xi)}{\partial x_j^2}. \tag{51}$$

So the following inequality

$$\|g(x) - f(x)\|_\infty$$
$$\leq \frac{1}{2} \sum_{j=1}^{n} \vee_{e_{i_j}^j \leq x_j \leq e_{i_j+1}^j} |x_j - e_{i_j}^j| |x_j - e_{i_j+1}^j| \left\| \frac{\partial^2 g(x)}{\partial x_j^2} \right\|_\infty \tag{52}$$

holds. Therefore, we have

$$\|g(x) - f(x)\|_\infty \leq \frac{1}{8} \sum_{j=1}^{n} h_j^2 \left\| \frac{\partial^2 g(x)}{\partial x_j^2} \right\|_\infty \leq \frac{1}{8} h^2 \sum_{j=1}^{n} \left\| \frac{\partial^2 g(x)}{\partial x_j^2} \right\|_\infty \tag{53}$$

by using (44), where $h_j = \max\{h_{i_j}^j | i_j = 1, 2, \ldots, N_j - 1\}$, $h = \max\{h_j | j = 1, 2, \ldots, n\}$. That is, the inequality (38) holds. The proof is completed.

Theorem 8 implies immediately the following corollary which shows the fuzzy systems constructed by Sect. 4.3 can duplicate any linear (or affine) function and multilinear (or mutliaffine) function.

Corollary 1. *Suppose that the following two conditions holds:*

1) $g_1(x)$ is any affine function on $U = [\alpha_1, \beta_1] \times [\alpha_2, \beta_2] \times \cdots \times [\alpha_n, \beta_n]$ given by

$$g_1(x_1, x_2, \ldots, x_n) = a_0 + a_1 x_1 + a_2 x_2 + \cdots + a_n x_n \tag{54}$$

and $g_2(x)$ is any multiaffine function on U defined by

$$g_2(x_1, x_2, \ldots, x_n)$$
$$= a_0 + \sum_{(k_1, k_2, \ldots, k_n) \in K} a_{i_1 i_2 \cdots i_n} (x_1)^{k_1} (x_2)^{k_2} \cdots (x_n)^{k_n}, \tag{55}$$

where $K = \{(k_1, k_2, \ldots, k_n) | k_j = 0, 1; j = 1, 2, \ldots, n$ and $\sum_{j=1}^{n} k_j > 0\}$, $i_1 i_2 \cdots i_n \in I = \{i_1 i_2 \cdots i_n | i_j = 1, 2, \ldots, N_j; j = 1, 2, \ldots, n\}$;

2) fuzzy system $f(x)$ is constructed by Sect. 4.3. For a given $k \in K$, thus, we have $f(x) = g_k(x)$ for any $x \in U$, i.e., $f \equiv g_k$ on U.

Remark 5. If we consider the error bound of Theorem 2 in [31] for a second-order approximator, we can see that the error bounds of Theorem 8 uses the identical number of membership functions with those of [31] for the same approximation accuracy degree. However, providing only fewer membership functions than those of [31], we can construct the desired fuzzy system by using the developed approach in this paper.

In Sect. 4.3, if $\lceil \frac{N_j}{2} \rceil$ $(j = 1, 2, 3, \ldots, n)$ fuzzy sets $A_1^j, A_2^j, \ldots, A_{\lceil \frac{N_j}{2} \rceil}^j$ in the interval $[\alpha_j, \frac{\alpha_j + \beta_j}{2}]$ are determined by the proposed approach in [23], we can obtain the new better claim as follows.

Firstly, we start with some notations. If a function is continuous, with all of its partial derivatives up to the lth-order continuity, we say that the function is C^l. Let the function $g(x)$ be C^{l-1} on $U = [\alpha_1, \beta_1] \times [\alpha_2, \beta_2] \times \cdots [\alpha_n, \beta_n] \subseteq \mathbb{R}^n$ and define

$$g_{x_j}^{(l)}(x_j) = \max_{\substack{x_i \in [\alpha_i, \beta_i] \\ i=1,2,\ldots,n \\ i \neq j}} \left| \frac{\partial^l g(x)}{\partial x_j^l} \right|, \tag{56}$$

$$\alpha_j = e_1^j < e_2^j < \cdots < e_{N_j}^j = \beta_j, \tag{57}$$

and

$$\varepsilon_{i_j,l}^j = \min_{e_{i_j}^j \leq a_{i_j}^j \leq e_{i_j+1}^j} \max_{e_{i_j}^j \leq x_j \leq e_{i_j+1}^j} \left| g_{x_j}^{(l)}(x_j) - g_{x_j}^{(l)}(a_{i_j}^j) \right|, \tag{58}$$

where N_j is odd, $e_{\lceil \frac{N_j}{2} \rceil}^j = \frac{\alpha_j + \beta_j}{2}$, $j = 1, 2, \ldots, n$, $i_j = 1, 2, \ldots, N_j - 1$, and $a_{i_j}^j \in [e_{i_j}^j, e_{i_j+1}^j]$.

In addition, we refer to $U' = [u_1, v_1] \times \cdots \times [u_n, v_n]$, where $u_i \in \{\alpha_i, \frac{\alpha_i + \beta_i}{2}\}$, $v_i \in \{\frac{\alpha_i + \beta_i}{2}, \beta_i\}$, $u_i \neq v_i$ for all $i = 1, 2, \ldots, n$, as the half-input space of U.

Now, we give the another claim as follows.

Theorem 9. *Let U' be a half-input space of U, N_j odd for every $j = 1, 2, \ldots, n$. If the $\lceil \frac{N_j}{2} \rceil$ fuzzy sets over U' are obtained by means of the proposed approach in [23], then the constructed fuzzy system $f(x)$ built from Sect. 4.3 has the following:*

(1) If g is a continuously differentiable function on U, then

$$\|g - f\|_\infty \leq \frac{1}{2} \sum_{j=1}^n h_j^{i_j} \left(\left| g_{x_j}^{(1)}(a_{i_j}^j) \right| + \varepsilon_{i_j,1}^j \right), \tag{59}$$

where $h_{i_j}^j = e_{i_j+1}^j - e_{i_j}^j$ and $a_{i_j}^j \in [e_{i_j}^j, e_{i_j+1}^j]$.
(2) If g is a twice continuously differentiable function on U, then

$$\|g - f\|_\infty \leq \frac{1}{8} \sum_{j=1}^n \left(h_j^{i_j} \right)^2 \left(\left| g_{x_j}^{(2)}(a_{i_j}^j) \right| + \varepsilon_{i_j,2}^j \right), \tag{60}$$

where $h^j_{i_j} = e^j_{i_j+1} - e^j_{i_j}$ and $a^j_{i_j} \in [e^j_{i_j}, e^j_{i_j+1}].$

Proof. It follows from Lemma 1 of [23] and Theorem 6. Also, we refer the reader to the proof of the above Theorem 8, since the proving methods of both these claims are similar. The proof is completed.

Furthermore, compared with the Theorems 1 and 2 in [23], we have the following corollary.

Corollary 2. *The fuzzy system $f(x)$ constructed from Theorem 9 requires a smaller number of known membership functions than the counterparts of [23] for the same guaranteed error bound.*

Proof. From Theorem 9, we only verify that it follows whenever N_j is even for some $j \in \{1, 2, \ldots, n\}$. Indeed, when N_j is even for some $j \in \{1, 2, \ldots, n\}$, it is trivial that $N_j \geq \left\lceil \frac{N_j+1}{2} \right\rceil$.

Remark 6. From [23], the constructed Mamdani fuzzy system requires a smaller number of membership functions than all previously published fuzzy systems. By Corollary 2, we can get that the sufficient conditions in Theorem 9 require a smaller number of known membership functions than all previously published conditions. Furthermore, the computation cost of the developed approach in this paper is smaller than that of the Mamdani fuzzy systems developed in [23] for the same guaranteed error bound.

6   Illustrative Cases

Case 1 [23,31]. Based on GFScom, design a fuzzy system $f(x)$ to approximate the continuous function $g(x) = \sin(x)/x$ defined on $U = [-3, 3]$ with a given accuracy of $\epsilon = 0.2$.

First, we use the error bound of Eq. (38) and obtain 9 fuzzy sets to approximate the function $g(x) = \sin(x)/x$ with the desired degree. So it is sufficient that the membership functions of only $\lceil \frac{9}{2} \rceil = 5$ fuzzy sets are defined appropriately in the interval $[-3, 0]$ (or $[0, 3]$).

Next, we use the error bound of Eq. (59) and obtain the results in the interval $[-3, 0]$ listed in Table 2.

Table 2. Approximation results over the interval $[-3, 0]$ for Case 1 using the error bound of Eq. (59)

i_1	1	2	3
$h^{i_1}_1$	0.918	0.918	1.164

Finally, since $g(x) = \sin(x)/x$ is a second-order differential function, we can use the error bound of Eq. (60) and obtain the results in the interval $[-3, 0]$ listed

Table 3. Approximation results over the interval $[-3, 0]$ for Case 1 using the error bound of Eq. (60)

i_1	1	2
$h_1^{i_1}$	2.305	0.695

in Table 3. Although in this case fewer known fuzzy sets are required when using the bound of Eq. (60) than the bound of Eq. (59), in general, this is not true.

Table 4 compares our results with the results in [23, 31] and [29] for approximation accuracy $\epsilon = 0.2$.

Table 4. Comparison of the number of known fuzzy sets needed to achieve the error bound $\epsilon = 0.2$

Method	No. of Known Fuzzy Sets for Input Variable
(3) of Theorem 8	5
(1) of Theorem 9	4
(2) of Theorem 9	3
Theorem 1 of [23]	7
Theorem 2 of [23] (Second order approximation)	4
Theorem 2 of [31] (Second order approximation)	9
Theorem 3.4 of [29]	207

Case 2. Assume $g(x_1, x_2) = e^{x_1 + x_2}$ (unknown) is defined on $U = [-0.5, 0.5]^2$. If two of membership functions of fuzzy sets in the designed fuzzy system $f(x_1, x_2)$ with a desired degree of accuracy $\epsilon = 0.2$ to approximate $g(x_1, x_2)$ is, respectively, given by

$$A_1^1(x_1) = \begin{cases} -2x_1, & x_1 \in [-0.5, 0] \\ 0, & x_1 \in [0, 0.5] \end{cases} \tag{61}$$

and

$$A_1^2(x_2) = \begin{cases} -2x_2, & x_2 \in [-0.5, 0] \\ 0, & x_2 \in [0, 0.5] \end{cases} \tag{62}$$

thus, how can we design a fuzzy system to roughly approximate $g(x_1, x_2)$?

Obviously, in terms of the traditional design methods of fuzzy systems (see [26] and therein references for more details), it is not feasible to construct the fuzzy system under the above conditions. However, using the method developed in this paper, i.e., the design procedure in Sect. 4.3, we can do it.

First, from the Eq. (61) and Definition 2, we can compute the opposite negative set $A_1^{1\lrcorner}$ and medium negative set $A_1^{1\sim}$ of A_1^1 as follows:

$$A_3^1(x_1) = A_1^{1\lrcorner}(x_1) = \begin{cases} 2x_1, & x_1 \in [0, 0.5] \\ 0, & x_1 \in [-0.5, 0] \end{cases} \quad \text{and}$$

$$A_2^1(x_1) = A_1^{1\sim}(x_1) = \begin{cases} 2x_1 + 1, & x_1 \in [-0.5, 0) \\ 1, & x_1 = 0 \\ 1 - 2x_1, & x_1 \in (0, 0.5] \end{cases}$$

By symmetry and the Eq. (62), the same applies to the opposite negative set
$A_3^2 = A_1^{2\lrcorner}$ and medium negative set $A_2^2 = A_1^{2\sim}$ of A_1^2.

If we choose $t_1^1 = t_1^2 = -0.5$, $t_2^1 = t_2^2 = 0$, $t_3^1 = t_3^2 = 0.5$, then we can construct
the following fuzzy system:

$$f(x_1, x_2) = \sum_{i_1=1}^{3} \sum_{i_2=1}^{3} A_{i_1}^1(x_1) A_{i_2}^2(x_2) e^{t_{i_1}^1 + t_{i_2}^2}$$

which approximates $g(x_1, x_2)$ with the accuracy degree $\epsilon = 0.2$. The figure of
system function $f(x_1, x_2)$ is depicted as follows (Fig. 1). A comparison of the
figure of $g(x_1, x_2)$ and the figure of the errors of the system function (or approximation function) and the origin function $g(x_1, x_2)$ are also described in Figs. 2
and 3.

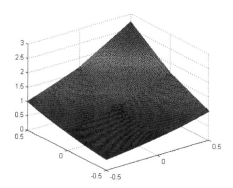

Fig. 1. The system function $y = f(x_1, x_2)$ of the fuzzy system in Case 2

For Case 2, Table 5 compares our result with the results in [23, 30] and [29]
for approximation accuracy $\epsilon = 0.2$.

Case 3. Consider a simple two-input-single-output liquid level control problem:
in some liquid level control system, the fluid mass in the container often changes
randomly. By adjusting the opening degree of the valve, we can control the liquid

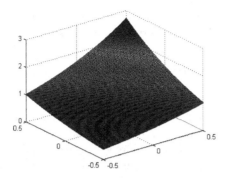

Fig. 2. The origin function $y = g(x_1, x_2)$ in Case 2

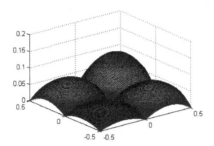

Fig. 3. The errors of the system function $y = f(x_1, x_2)$ and the origin function $y = g(x_1, x_2)$ in Case 2

Table 5. Comparison of the number of known fuzzy sets needed to achieve the error bound $\epsilon = 0.2$

Method	No. of Known Fuzzy Sets for Each Input Variable
GFScom	1
Theorem 2 of [23]	4
Theorem 2 of [30]	6
Theorem 3.4 of [29]	309

level in the container such that the level keeps the steady state error small. Both input variables, named *level* (denoted l) and *rate* (denoted r), represents the liquid level and the flow input rate, respectively. The output variable, named *valve* (denoted v), denotes the opening degree of the valve. Suppose that the range of the *level* be $[-1, 1]$, *rate* be $[-0.1, 0.1]$ and *valve* be $[-1, 1]$.

By inquiring skilled experts in the field, we get that the range of the input variable l is covered by 3 fuzzy sets, named *High*, *Okay* and *Low*, and the membership function of *High* is expressed as follows:

$$High(l) = \exp\left(-\frac{(l+1)^2}{2 \cdot (0.3)^2}\right)$$

where $l \in [-1, 1]$.

60   S. Zhang and J. Chen

Also, the range of the other input r is covered by 3 fuzzy sets, termed *Negative*, *Zero* and *Positive*, and the membership function of *Negative* is defined as follows

$$Negative(r) = \exp\left(-\frac{(r+0.1)^2}{2\cdot(0.03)^2}\right)$$

where $r \in [-0.1, 0.1]$.

In the sequel, we simulate the above liquid level control procedure by using the well-known *sltank* in Matlab 7.10.0 (R2010a).

First, for simplicity, we use the square wave with amplitude 0.5 and frequency 0.1 rad/s to imitate change of the liquid level in the container. Moreover, the mathematical model of the controlled object in *sltank* is directly used as that in our system.

Considering the definition of GFScom and the above simulation conditions, we design the following five fuzzy sets (named *close_fast*, *close_slow*, *no_change*, *open_slow* and *open_fast*) over the output interval $[-1, 1]$, shown in Fig. 4.

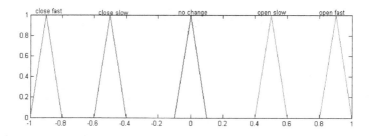

Fig. 4. The distribution of membership functions over the output space in Case 3

Next, from previous operating experiences, we conclude the following control rules listed in Table 6. Note that the fuzzy rule base is small and incomplete, but these fuzzy rules are sufficient for our simulation.

Table 6. Fuzzy rule base for the liquid level control problem in Case 3

l	r			
	None	*Negative*	*Zero*	*Positive*
None				
High	*close_fast*			
Okay	*no_change*	*open_slow*		*close_slow*
Low	*open_fast*			

Finally, by using the proposed method in this paper, we can obtain the results shown in Figs. 5 and 6. From the resulting simulation, one can see that the constructed fuzzy controller in this paper successfully resolves the liquid level control problem in Case 3. Note that the model of the controlled plant in *sltank* is nonlinear, so this demonstration illustrates that the proposed fuzzy controller in this paper can implement the control of nonlinear systems effectively.

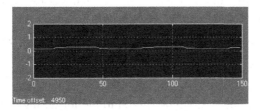

Fig. 5. The change of liquid level in Case 3

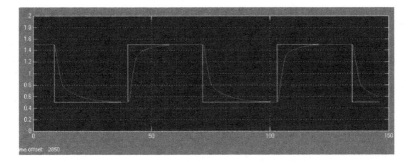

Fig. 6. Comparison of the square wave (yellow) and its response curve (red) in Case 3 (Color figure online)

7   Conclusion and Future Work

In this paper, we have continually developed the theory of GFScom introduced in [34]. By considering triangular norm operations, we exploited the generalized properties of GFScom. The important specification of our generalized fuzzy sets is that opposite negation and medium negation are added to the ordinary fuzzy sets developed by Zadeh and the law of the classical double contradiction, i.e., $A^{\neg\neg} = A$, and the law of the new double opposition, that is, $A^{\dashv\dashv} = A$, hold for GFScom. In the sequel, we studied the convexity and concavity properties of GFScom. On the basis of GFScom, the constructive approaches of the Mamdani-type fuzzy system that can approximate any continuous function on a compact set to a given degree of accuracy have been presented. We established the approximation bounds for the classes of the constructed fuzzy systems. Illustrative cases and numerical comparisons are provided to show the effectiveness and advantage of the developed approaches. At last, we need further to point out that the developed model in this paper can not give the one-to-one relationship of fuzzy sets between the input and output variables.

This is the first step of GFScom. There are many issues that can be done in the future. We list several suggestions as follows.

- What is the detailed structure of GFScom? For example, what are the relations of opposite negative operator, medium negative operator and other connectives such as conjunction, disjunction, implication? How should they be depicted in fuzzy logic? Although our work is based upon the medium logic ML system, we think ML is not very suitable for acting as the structure of GFScom. Therefore, how to construct the logic structure of GFScom should be studied.
- How can we design other types of fuzzy systems, such as T-S type fuzzy systems and Boolean type fuzzy systems by using GFScom.
- In [6], when N is a continuous function the characterization of (S, N)-implications is explored, and also a first characterization of this family of implications is illustrated. Analogously, when the contradictory, opposite and medium negation in fuzzy logic and reasoning are distinguished, what is the characterization of (S, N)-implications? This is interesting and next work.
- In [27], the authors presented the so-called a generalized momentum method compatible with single latent factor-dependent, non-negative and multiplicative update(SLF-NMU). Similarly, regarding information processing and feature extraction, on the basis of GFScom, is it possible to construct the corresponding SLF-NMU?

We will address these issues in subsequent papers.

Acknowledgments. This work is supported by the Guizhou Provincial Science and Technology Foundation, Grant No. 1458 [2019] Contract Foundation of the Science and Technology department of Guizhou Province.

Compliance with Ethical Standards
Conflicts of Interest. Shengli Zhang and Jing Chen declare that they have no conflict of interest.

Human and Animal Rights. This article does not contain any studies with human participants or animals performed by any of the authors.

References

1. Analyti, A., Antoniou, G., Damásio, C.V., et al.: Extended RDF as a semantic foundation of rule markup languages. J. Artif. Intell. Res. **32**(1), 37–94 (2008). https://doi.org/10.1613/jair.2425
2. Bustince, H., Campión, M., Miguel, L.D., et al.: Strong negations and restricted equivalence functions revisited: an analytical and topological approach. Fuzzy Sets Syst. **441**, 110–129 (2022). https://doi.org/10.1016/j.fss.2021.10.013

3. Cintula, P., Klement, E.P., Mesiar, R., et al.: Fuzzy logics with an additional involutive negation. Fuzzy Sets Syst. **161**(3), 390–411 (2010). https://doi.org/10.1016/j.fss.2009.09.003

4. Davis, P.J.: Interpolation and Approximation. Blaisdell, New York (1963)

5. Esteva, F., Godo, L., Hájek, P., et al.: Residuated fuzzy logics with an involutive negation. Arch. Math. Logic **39**(2), 103–124 (2000). https://doi.org/10.1007/s001530050006

6. Fernandez-Peralta, R., Massanet, S., Mesiarová-Zemánková, A., et al.: A general framework for the characterization of (S, N)-implications with a non-continuous negation based on completions of t-conorms. Fuzzy Sets Syst. **441**, 1–32 (2022). https://doi.org/10.1016/j.fss.2021.06.009

7. Ferré, S.: Negation, opposition, and possibility in logical concept analysis. In: Missaoui, R., Schmidt, J. (eds.) ICFCA 2006. LNCS (LNAI), vol. 3874, pp. 130–145. Springer, Heidelberg (2006). https://doi.org/10.1007/11671404_9

8. Hájek, P.: Metamathematics of Fuzzy Logic. Kluwer Academic Publishers, Dordrecht (1998)

9. Jiang, L., Bosselut, A., Bhagavatula, C., et al.: "I'm not mad": Commonsense implications of negation and contradiction (2021). https://arxiv.org/abs/2104.06511

10. Kaneiwa, K.: Description logics with contraries, contradictories, and subcontraries. N. Gener. Comput. **25**(4), 443–468 (2007). https://doi.org/10.1007/s00354-007-0028-2

11. Kassner, N., Schütze, H.: Negated and misprimed probes for pretrained language models: birds can talk, but cannot fly. In: Proceedings of the 58th Annual Meeting of the Association for Computational Linguistics, pp. 7811–7818. Association for Computational Linguistics (2020). https://doi.org/10.18653/v1/2020.acl-main.698

12. Klement, E.P., Mesiar, R., Pap, E.: Triangular Norms. Kluwer, Dordrrecht (2000)

13. Klir, G.J., Yuan, B.: Fuzzy Sets and Fuzzy Logic: Theory and Applications. Prantice-Hall, Upper Saddle River (1995)

14. Murinová, P., Novák, V.: Analysis of generalized square of opposition with intermediate quantifiers. Fuzzy Sets Syst. **242**, 89–113 (2014). https://doi.org/10.1016/j.fss.2013.05.006

15. Nourouzi, K., Aghajani, A.: Convexity in triangular norm of fuzzy sets. Chaos Solit. Fract. **36**(4), 883–889 (2008). https://doi.org/10.1016/j.chaos.2006.07.006

16. Novák, V.: Antonyms and linguistic quantifers in fuzzy logic. Fuzzy Sets Syst. **124**(3), 335–351 (2001). https://doi.org/10.1016/S0165-0114(01)00104-X

17. Novák, V.: On fuzzy type theory. Fuzzy Sets Syst. **149**(2), 235–273 (2005). https://doi.org/10.1016/j.fss.2004.03.027

18. Novák, V.: A comprehensive theory of trichotomous evaluative linguistic expressions. Fuzzy Sets Syst. **159**(22), 2939–2969 (2008). https://doi.org/10.1016/j.fss.2008.02.023

19. Pan, Y., Wu, W.M.: Medium algebras. J. Math. Res. Exposition **10**(2), 265–270 (1990)

20. Pan, Z.H.: Fuzzy set with three kinds of negations in fuzzy knowledge processing. In: Proceedings of The Ninth International Conference on Machine Learning and Cybernatics, Piscataway, USA, vol. 5, pp. 2730–2735. IEEE Computer Society Press (2010). https://doi.org/10.1109/ICMLC.2010.5580945

21. Pan, Z.H.: Three kinds of fuzzy knowledge and their base of set. Chin. J. Comput. **35**(7), 1421–1428 (2012). https://doi.org/10.3724/SP.J.1016.2012.01421. (in Chinese)

22. Pan, Z.: Three kinds of negation of fuzzy knowledge and their base of logic. In: Huang, D.-S., Jo, K.-H., Zhou, Y.-Q., Han, K. (eds.) ICIC 2013. LNCS (LNAI), vol. 7996, pp. 83–93. Springer, Heidelberg (2013). https://doi.org/10.1007/978-3-642-39482-9_10

23. Sonbol, A.H., Fadali, M.S., Jafarzadeh, S.: TSK fuzzy approximators: design and accuracy analysis. IEEE Trans. Syst. Man Cybern. Part B (Cybern.) **42**(3), 702–712 (2012). https://doi.org/10.1109/TSMCB.2011.2174151

24. Torres-Blanc, C., Cubillo, S., Hernndez-Varela, P.: New negations on the membership functions of type-2 fuzzy sets. IEEE Trans. Fuzzy Syst. **27**(7), 1397–1406 (2019). https://doi.org/10.1109/TFUZZ.2018.2879033

25. Wagner, G.: Web Rules Need Two Kinds of Negation. In: Bry, F., Henze, N., Małuszyński, J. (eds.) PPSWR 2003. LNCS, vol. 2901, pp. 33–50. Springer, Heidelberg (2003). https://doi.org/10.1007/978-3-540-24572-8_3

26. Wang, L.X.: A Course in Fuzzy Systems and Control. Prentice Hall PTR, Englewood Cliff (1997)

27. Luo, X., Liu, S.G.: A fast non-negative latent factor model based on generalized momentum method. IEEE Trans. Syst. Man Cybern.-Syst. **51**(1), 610–620 (2021). https://doi.org/10.1109/tsmc.2018.2875452

28. Xiao, X.A., Zhu, W.J.: Propositional calculus system of medium logic(I). J. Math. Res. Exp. **8**(2), 327–331 (1988)

29. Ying, H.: Sufficient conditions on general fuzzy systems as function approximators. Automatica **30**(3), 521–525 (1994). https://doi.org/10.1016/0005-1098(94)90130-9

30. Zeng, K., Zhang, N.Y., Xu, W.L.: A comparative study on sufficient conditions for Takagi-Sugeno fuzzy systems as universal approximators. IEEE Trans. Fuzzy Syst. **8**(6), 773–780 (2000). https://doi.org/10.1109/91.890337

31. Zeng, X.J., Singh, M.G.: Approximation accuracy analysis of fuzzy systems as function approximators. IEEE Trans. Fuzzy Syst. **4**(1), 44–63 (1996). https://doi.org/10.1109/91.481844

32. Zhang, S.L.: Formal deductive system of fuzzy propositional logic with different negations. J. Front. Comput. Sci. Technol. **8**(4), 494–505 (2014). https://doi.org/10.3778/j.issn.1673-9418.1306006. (in Chinese)

33. Zhang, S.L., Li, Y.M.: Algebraic representation of negative knowledge and its application to design of fuzzy systems. Chin. J. Comput. **39**(12), 2527–2546 (2016). https://doi.org/10.11897/SP.J.1016.2016.02527

34. Zhang, S., Li, Y.: A novel table look-up scheme based on GFScom and its application. Soft. Comput. **21**(22), 6767–6781 (2016). https://doi.org/10.1007/s00500-016-2226-7

35. Zhu, W.J., Xiao, X.A.: On the Naive mathematical models of medium mathematical system MM. J. Math. Res. Exposition **8**(1), 139–151 (1988)

36. Zhu, W.J., Xiao, X.A.: Predicate calculus system of medium logic(II). J of Nanjing University **24**(4), 583–596 (1988)

37. Zhu, W.J., Xiao, X.A.: Propositional calculus system of medium logic(II). J. Math. Res. Exposition **8**(3), 457–466 (1988)

38. Zou, J.: Semantic interpretation of propositional calculus system MP^* of medium logic and its soundness and completeness. J. Math. Res. Exposition **8**(3), 467–468 (1988). (in Chinese)

39. Zou, J.: Semantic interpretation of predicate calculus system of medium logic ME^* and its soundness and completeness. Chin. Sci. Bulletin **34**(6), 448–451 (1989)

A Novel Method for Signal Sequence Classification Based on Markov Reward Models

Dongliang Zhou[ID] and Lihui Lei[(✉)][ID]

Shaanxi Normal University, Xi'an 710119, China
`leilihui@snnu.edu.cn`

Abstract. The efficiency and accuracy of signal sequence classification have always been the ultimate goals of researchers. However, it is difficult for existing methods to meet both requirements at the same time. This paper proposes a new signal sequence classification method based on Markov Reward Model (MRM) to solve the above problem. Firstly, a deterministic probabilistic finite automaton, learned from training sequence dataset, is transformed into a discrete time Markov Chain; then, leveraging JS divergence, a MRM is constructed; and finally, sequence classification is achieved on MRM efficiently and accurately. This method can be applied to many practical signal processing applications.

Keywords: Markov Reward Model · Deterministic probabilistic finite automaton · Sequence classification · JS divergence

1 Introduction

The research of sequence classification has a long history. Nowadays, with the rapid development of artificial intelligence technologies, sequence classification has been successfully applied in various research fields, such as genomic analysis [1], information retrieval [2], finance analysis [3], anomaly detection [4], etc. .

Generally, a sequence represents an ordered list of events and the events are described by symbols, numbers, vectors, or other complex data. In practical, all sequences can be categorized into 5 types, i.e., simple symbol sequences, complex symbol sequences, univariate time series, multivariate time series, and complex event sequences [5]. In this paper, through encoding and other data pre-processing means, signals are translated into simple sequences, i.e., ordered lists of symbols, and a new signal sequence classification method is introduced.

As far as we know, existing sequence classification methods can be divided into two types, i.e., statistical model based classification methods and neural network based classification methods [6]. Both methods need extracting features from sequences, and then employ a classifier to achieve sequence classification, according to the extracted features. We have noted that the latter have stronger generalization and adaptive abilities, and can handle high-dimensional and non-linear data; while the former are easier to explain and understand, and usually

Supported by organization 11671244.

have higher efficiency. Therefore, in this paper, we try to find a method that has the advantages of two methods.

Hidden Markov Model (HMM) is a probability graph model that can model sequences [7,8]. It assumes that each element in the sequence has a corresponding hidden state; and the transitions between these hidden states satisfy Markov properties, that is, the current state is only related to the previous state and not to other states. For a testing sequence, its probability can be calculated under HMM model, and then be classified into the category corresponding to the probability. However, HMM has a limitation on the number of elements in a sequence. When the number of elements is too large, the training speed of the model will slow down, and may even be unable to process.

Recurrent Neural Network (RNN) [9] and its cousins, such as Long Short-Term Memory (LSTM) [10] and Gated Recurrent Unit (GRU) [11], are neural network models and are effective in sequence classification, because it considers the temporal relationships in data. Compared with the statistical model based classification methods requiring manual feature design, they adaptively learn features from sequences, thereby achieving better classification results. However, they have lower computational efficiency when dealing with long sequences.

CNN extract and integrate local features of sequences through convolution operations and has high computational efficiency [12], so that it often be used to achieve large-scale sequence classification. However, CNN must to face the issue that the convolutional kernel size need to be design manually [13].

Deterministic Probabilistic Finite Automaton (DPFA) is a statistical model. It can model the probability distribution of sequence [14–16]. Thus, the testing sequence can be classified into the category corresponding to the probability. What's more important, the modelling of DPFA is more efficient than natural networks. However, the existing DPFA based sequence classification methods cannot solve two problems: 1) for a testing sequence, if its probabilities are the same on different DPFA models, how do we complete the classification; 2) if the test sequence contains a sub-sequence that does not be considered in the training phase, how to complete the classification.

In this paper, we propose a novel method for sequence classification based on Markov Reward Model (MRM). Firstly, a DPFA learned from training sequence dataset is transformed into a Discrete Time Markov Chain; then, leveraging JS divergence, a MRM is constructed; and finally, sequence classification is achieved on MRM efficiently and accurately. Compared with the classification methods based on natural networks, there is less time cost for this classification process, since the construction of MRM is based on DPFA and DPFA modeling is more efficient. The main contributions are following:

1) the MRM constructing method is proposed;
2) with our method, the sequence with the same probabilities on different DFPA models can be classified;
3) with our method, the sequence containing some sub-sequences do not be described by the DPFA model can be classified;
4) this method improves the efficiency and accuracy of sequence classification.

2   Mathematical Preliminaries

In this section, we recall the concepts of automata and Discrete Time Markov Chain (DTMC) [17]. The former is the underlying structure of the learning model, and the latter is an important technology to complete sequence classification.

Definition 1 *(DPFA [14]). A tuple $A = (\Sigma, Q, I, F, \delta_P)$ is a DPFA, where*

- *Σ is a finite alphabet;*
- *Q is a finite set of states;*
- *The initial probability function $I : Q \rightarrow [0,1]$, there is only one initial state q_λ and $I(q_\lambda) = 1$;*
- *The final probability function $F : Q \rightarrow [0,1]$;*
- *The state transition probability function $\delta_P : Q \times (\Sigma \cup \{\lambda\}) \times Q \rightarrow [0,1]$, $\forall q \in Q, \forall a \in \Sigma, |\{q'|P(q,a,q') > 0\}| = 1$ and $F(q) + \sum\limits_{a \in \Sigma, q' \in Q} P(q,a,q') = 1$.*

Definition 2 *(DTMC [17]). A tuple $M = (S, P, \ell, AP, L)$ is a DTMC, where*

- *S is a countable, nonempty set of states,*
- *$P : S \times S \rightarrow [0,1]$ is the transition probability function such that for all states s: $\sum\limits_{s' \in S} P(s, s') = 1$,*
- *$\ell : S \rightarrow [0,1]$ is the initial distribution, such that $\sum\limits_{s \in S} \ell(s) = 1$,*
- *AP is a set of atomic propositions,*
- *$L : S \rightarrow 2^{AP}$ is labeling functions.*

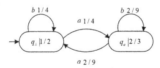

Fig. 1. DPFA Example

Figure 1 gives a simple DFPA. $\Sigma = \{a, b\}$, $Q = \{q_\lambda, q_a\}$, $I(q_\lambda) = 1$, $F(q_\lambda) = 1/2$, $F(q_a) = 2/3$, $\delta_p(q_\lambda, b, q_\lambda) = 1/4$, $\delta_p(q_\lambda, a, q_a) = 1/4$, $\delta_p(q_a, b, q_a) = 2/9$, $\delta_p(q_a, a, q_\lambda) = 2/9$.

Definition 3 *((DFFA [14]). A tuple $A = (\Sigma, Q, I_{fr}, F_{fr}, \delta_{fr})$ is a DFFA, where*

- *Σ is a finite symbol set;*
- *$Q = \{q_w | w \in \Sigma^*\}$ is a finite states set;*
- *$I_{fr} : Q \rightarrow \mathbb{N}^+$, and there is only one initial state $q_\lambda \in Q$;*
- *$F_{fr} : Q \rightarrow \mathbb{N}^+ \cup \{0\}$;*

- $\delta_{fr}: Q \times (\Sigma \cup \{\lambda\}) \times Q \to \mathbb{N}^+ \cup \{0\}$, and
  $\forall q \in Q, \forall a \in \Sigma, |\{q'|\delta_{fr}(q,a,q') > 0\}| = 1$.

Definition 4 *(Finite path on DTMC [17]). A finite path on DTMC is a finite sequence of states, denoted by π, $\pi = s_1 s_2 \cdots s_n$, i.e., starting from state s_1, passing through $s_2, \cdots, s_{n-1}$, and finally arriving at s_n.*

Definition 5 *(Probability of a finite path on DTMC [17]). The probability of the finite path $\pi = s_1 s_2 \cdots s_n$ on DTMC is*

$$P(\pi) = \ell(s_1) \prod_{i=1}^{n-1} P(s_i, s_{i+1}).$$

Definition 6 *(Reachability on DTMC). For a DTMC $M = (S, \mathrm{P}, \ell, AP, L)$, a state $s \in S$ can reach the state set $B \subseteq S$, denoted as $s \xrightarrow{\pi} B$, if there exist a finite path $\pi = s_1 s_2 \cdots s_n$ in the DTMC such that*

- $|\pi| = 1$ and $s_1 \in B$, or
- $|\pi| > 1$, $s_1 = s$, $s_n \in B$ and $\{s_i | s_i \notin B, 1 \leq i < n-1\}$,

the reachable set $R(s \to B) = \{\pi_i | s \xrightarrow{\pi_i} B\}$.

Definition 7 *(Reachability Probabilities). If state s can reach state set B on a DTMC, the reachability probability of $s \to B$ is defined as follows:*

$$\mathrm{Pr}(s \to B) = \sum_{\pi \in \{\pi\}_{s \to B}} P(\pi) \tag{1}$$

3   MRM-Based Sequence Classification

In this section, we firstly describe how to constructing MRM model [17], and then illustrate how to complete sequence classification on MRM.

3.1   Constructing the Model

Constructing MRM consists of three phases, i.e., getting DPFA with learning from sequences, transforming DPFA into DTMC, and appending rewards to DTMC.

3.1.1   Getting DFPA with Learning from Sequence
The main steps for constructing a DPFA using algorithm ALERGIA [14] are as follows. Firstly, a set of sequences with the same category labels are statistically analyzed and a DFFA is constructed based on the statistical results; and then, iteratively trying to merge states with a recursive folding process, the underlying structure of the DPFA is obtained; and finally, by translating the frequency into the probability through normalization, the DPFA is obtained.

For example, supposing the alphabet is $\Sigma = \{a, b\}$, the statistical results of sequences and the obtained DPFA are shown in Fig. 2. The details can refer to the work [14].

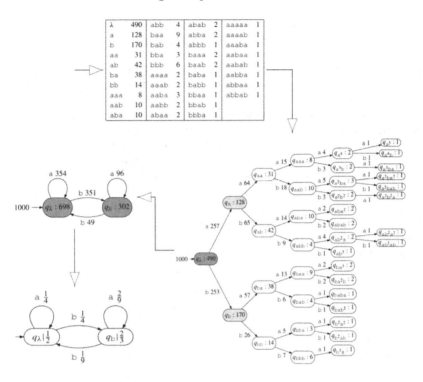

Fig. 2. The process of obtaining a DPFA using the algorithm ALERGIA.

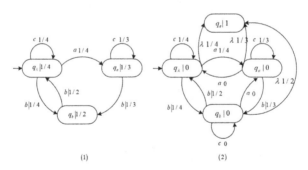

(1)   (2)

Fig. 3. Equivalent transformation of DPFA.

3.1.2 Transforming DPFA into DTMC

Definition 8 *(Fully connected DPFA with termination state) For a DPFA $A = (\Sigma, Q, I, F, \delta_P)$, an equivalent fully connected DPFA is $A' = (\Sigma', Q', I', F', \delta_P')$,*

- $\Sigma' = \Sigma \cup \{\lambda\}$ and $I' = I$;
- $Q' = Q \cup \{q_e\}$;
- $F'(q_e) = 1$, $F'(q_i) = 0$ and $q_i \in Q - \{q_e\}$;
- $\delta_P' = \delta_P \cup \{(q, \lambda, q_e, F(q))| \forall q \in Q - \{q_e\}\} \cup \{(q, b, q', 0)|\delta_P(q, b, q') = 0\}$.

For example, Fig. 3(2) shows the equivalent fully connected DPFA of the DPFA in Fig. 3(1). Algorithm 1 described the transformation process.

Definition 9 *(DPFA Equivalent Conversion of DTMC) For a DPFA $A = (\Sigma, Q, I, F, \delta_P)$, it can be equivalently converted to DTMC $M = (S, P, \ell, AP, L)$.*

- $S = S_0 \cup S_1 \cup S_2 \cup S_3 \cup S_4$ and $S_i \cap S_j = \emptyset$ $(1 \le i \ne j \le 4)$, where
  $S_0 = \{Q - q_\lambda\}, S_1 = \{s_{init}, q_e\}, S_2 = \{q_a | \delta_P(q_\lambda, a, q_\lambda) > 0\},$
  $S_3 = \{q_a' | \delta_P(q, a, q_\lambda) > 0\}, S_4 = \{q_\omega'' | \delta_P(q_\omega, a, q_\omega) > 0\};$
  $P = \{P(s_{init}, q, \delta_P(q_\lambda, a, q_a)) | q \in S_0, q_a \in Q - \{q_\lambda\}, q_\lambda \in Q\}$
  $\cup \{P(q, q', \delta_P(q_a, b, q_b)) | q, q' \in S_0, q \ne q', q_a, q_b \in Q - \{q_\lambda\}, q_a \ne q_b\}$
  $\cup \{P(q, q', \delta_P(q_a, a, q_\lambda)) | q \in S_0, q' \in S_3, q_a \in Q - \{q_\lambda\}, q_\lambda \in Q\}$
  $\cup \{P(q, q', \delta_P(q_a, a, q_a)) | q \in S_0, q' \in S_4, q_a \in Q - \{q_\lambda\}\}$
  $\cup \{P(s_{init}, q, \delta_P(q_\lambda, a, q_\lambda)) | q \in S_2, q_\lambda \in Q\}$
  $\cup \{P(q, q, \delta_P(q_\lambda, a, q_\lambda)) | q \in S_2, q_\lambda \in Q\}$
  $\cup \{P(q, q', \delta_P(q_\lambda, a, q_a)) | q \in S_2, q' \in S_0, q_a \in Q - \{q_\lambda\}\}$
  $\cup \{P(q, q', \delta_P(q_\lambda, a, q_a)) | q \in S_3, q' \in S_0, q_a \in Q - \{q_\lambda\}, q_\lambda \in Q\}$
  $\cup \{P(q, q', \delta_P(q_\lambda, a, q_\lambda)) | q \in S_3, q' \in S_2, q_\lambda \in Q\}$
  $\cup \{P(q, q, \delta_P(q_a, a, q_a)) | q \in S_4, q_a \in Q - \{q_\lambda\}\}$
  $\cup \{P(q, q', \delta_P(q_a, a, q_\lambda)) | q \in S_4, q' \in S_3, q_a \in Q - \{q_\lambda\}, q_\lambda \in Q\}$
  $\cup \{P(q, q', \delta_P(q_a, b, q_b)) | q \in S_4, q' \in S_0, q_a, q_b \in Q - \{q_\lambda\}, q_a \ne q_b\}$
  $\cup \{P(q, q_e, F(q_a)) | q \in S - S_1, q_a \in Q - \{q_\lambda\}\}$
  $\cup \{P(q_e, q_e, 1)\}$
- $\ell(s_{init}) = 1;$
- $AP = \Sigma \cup \{\lambda\};$
- $L(q) = a(q \in S - S_1, a \in \Sigma), L(q) = \lambda(q \in S_1);$

For example, leveraging the Algorithm 1, the DPFA shown in Fig. 1 are transformed into the DTMC shown in Fig. 4.

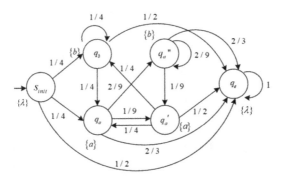

Fig. 4. The MC obtained by the DPFA according to Algorithm 1 in Fig. 1.

Algorithm 1: Transforming DPFA into DTMC

Input : A DPFA $A = (\Sigma, Q, I, F, \delta_P)$
Output: DTMC $M = (S, P, \ell, AP, L)$

Initialization;
The DPFA $A = (\Sigma, Q, I, F, \delta_P)$ is transformed into an equivalent fully connected DPFA with termination states, denoted as
$A' = (\Sigma', Q', I, F', \delta_P')$;
$S \leftarrow \{s_{init}, q_e\}$;
foreach $a \in \Sigma$ **do**
  $\quad\lfloor \; S = S \cup \{q_a\}$;
foreach $q_a \in Q (a \in \Sigma)$ **do**
  $\quad\lfloor \; S = S \cup \{q_a'\}$;
foreach $\delta_P(q, a, q) \geq 0 (a \in \Sigma, q \in Q)$ **do**
  $\quad\lfloor \; S = S \cup \{q_a''\}$;
foreach $a \in \Sigma$ **do**
  $\quad P(s_{init}, q_a) = \delta_P(q_\lambda, a, q_a), L(q_a) = a$;
  $\quad P(q_a, q_a') = \delta_P(q_a, a, q_\lambda), L(q_a') = a$;
  $\quad P(q_a', q_a) = \delta_P(q_\lambda, a, q_a)$;
  $\quad$**if** $\delta_P(q_a, b, q_a) \geq 0$ **then**
  $\quad\quad\lfloor \begin{array}{l} P(q_a, q_a'') = \delta_P(q_a, b, q_a), L(q_a'') = b; \\ P(q_a'', q_a'') = \delta_P(q_a, b, q_a); \end{array}$
  $\quad$**foreach** $c \in \Sigma$ **do**
  $\quad\quad\lfloor \; P(q_a', q_c) = \delta_P(q_\lambda, c, q_c)$;
  $\quad P(q_a'', q_a') = \delta_P(q_a, a, q_\lambda)$;
  $\quad P(q_a, q_e) = F(q_a)$;
  $\quad P(q_a', q_e) = F(q_\lambda)$;
  $\quad P(q_a'', q_e) = F(q_a)$;
  $\quad P(s_{init}, q_e) = F(q_\lambda)$;
  $\quad P(q_e, q_e) = 1$;
Termination;

3.1.3 Appending Rewards to DTMC

Definition 10 *(MRM [17]). A Markov reward model is a tuple (M, rew), where M is a DTMC with state set S, and a reward function $rew : S \rightarrow \mathbb{R}^+ \cup \{0\}$.*

Definition 11 *(Jensen-Shannon divergence [18]). JS divergence is a measure used to quantify the difference between two probability distributions. It is defined as the average of the Kullback-Leibler divergence between the two probability distributions. It is defined as follows:*

$$JSD(P||Q) = \tfrac{1}{2} \sum p(x) \log(\tfrac{p(x)}{p(x)+q(x)}) + \tfrac{1}{2} \sum q(x) \log(\tfrac{q(x)}{p(x)+q(x)}) + \log 2.$$

During the MRM constructing process, we specifically focus on capturing the level of model variation. To quantify the variation, we utilized JS divergence as a tool to iteratively measure the distance between probability distributions, which can effectively and accurately describe the variation of the model.

Definition 12 *(The mapping function). For a DPFA $A = (\Sigma, Q, I, F, \delta_P)$, the mapping function $l(a) = \{(q, q')|\delta_P(q, a, q') > 0, a \in \Sigma, q, q' \in Q\}$ (Figs. 5 and 6).*

Algorithm 2: Constructing a DPFA with the same structure of the given DPFA

Input : $x = a_1 a_2 \cdots a_n, A = (\Sigma, Q, I, F, \delta_P)$
Output: DPFA $A_x = (\Sigma, Q, I, F_x, \delta_{Px})$

Initialization;
Set all probabilities on the DPFA to zero and convert them to an FPTA
  $A = (\Sigma, Q, I_{fr}, F_{fr}, \delta_{fr})$ with all frequencies being zero.;
Run the string sequence x on the converted FPTA.;
for $i \leftarrow 1$ **to** n **do**
  if a_i *causes state transfer or self-loop.* **then**
   $\lfloor$ $\delta_{fr}(q, a, q') = \delta_{fr}(q, a, q') + 1$;
  if $i = n$ **then**
   $\lfloor$ $F_{fr}(q) = F_{fr}(q) + 1$
Convert the obtained FPTA into a DPFA $A_x = (\Sigma, Q, I, F_x, \delta_{Px})$ by
  performing normalization.;
Termination;

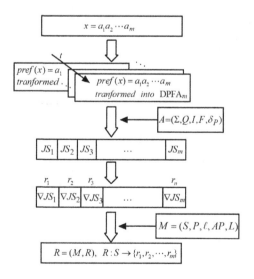

Fig. 5. Algorithm 3 framework.

Algorithm 3: Constructing the MRM based on JS divergence

Input : The set of string sequences $Sample = \{x_1, x_2 \cdots x_n\}$ and $x_i = a_1 a_2 \cdots a_m$,the DPFA $A = (\Sigma, Q, I, F, \delta_P)$ constructed from $Sample$ using the ALERGIA algorithm, and the MC obtained from the transformation of this DPFA,mapping function l.

Output: MRM M $= (M, rew)$

Initialization;
$rew(s_{init}) = 0, rew(q_e) = 0$;
def S_a, S_a', S_a'', $count_S = 0$;
foreach $s \in S$ **do**
  if $s = q_a, a \in \Sigma$ **then**
    $S_a \leftarrow \{q_a\}$;
  if $s = q_a', a \in \Sigma$ **then**
    $S_a' \leftarrow \{q_a'\}$;
  if $s = q_a'', a \in \Sigma$ **then**
    $S_a'' \leftarrow \{q_a''\}$;

for $i \leftarrow 1$ **to** n **do**
  for $j \leftarrow 1$ **to** m **do**
    Apply algorithm 2 with input $a_1 a_2 \cdots a_j$ to obtain the DPFA $A_j = (\Sigma, Q, I, F, \delta_{P_j})$;
    Apply definition 8 with input A_j and A to obtain the fully connected DPFA with termination states $A_j = (\Sigma, Q', I', F', \delta_P')$ and $A = (\Sigma, Q, I, F, \delta_P)$;
    def $sum = 0, q_{pre}, q_{suf} = l(a_i)$;
    foreach $q' \in Q'$ **do**
      def $sum(j-1) = sum$;
      $sum = sum + JSD(P(q')|P(q))$ //P(q) represents the probability distribution of state q, where q corresponds to the same state in automaton A as q'. ;
    if $q_{pre} = q_{suf}$ **then**
      $count_{q''} = sum - sum(j-1)$;
    if $q_{pre} = q_\lambda$ **then**
      $count_q = sum - sum(j-1)$;
    if $q_{suf} = q_\lambda$ **then**
      $count_{q'} = sum - sum(j-1)$;

foreach $s \in S$ **do**
  $rew(s) = count_s/n$;
Termination;

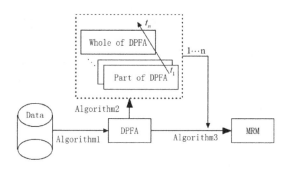

Fig. 6. Relationship of Algorithms 1–3

3.2   Classification Method

Definition 13 *(Expected Reward for reachability Probabilities* [17]*). For a DPFA $A = (\Sigma, Q, I, F, \delta_P)$, $s \in S$ and $B \subseteq S$, the expected reward of $s \to B$ is defined as follows.*

$$ExpRew(s \to B) = \begin{cases} \infty & \Pr(s \to B) < 1 \\ \sum_{\pi \in R(s \to B)} P(\pi) \cdot rew(\pi) & \Pr(s \to B) = 1 \end{cases}$$

Definition 14 *(Path Accumulation Reward)* [17]. *For a path $\pi = s_1 \cdots s_n$ on the MRM, the cumulative reward of the path is $rew(\pi) = \sum_{i=1}^{n-1} rew(s_i)$.*

Definition 15 *(Sequence classification on MRM)For the sequences of classes $C_1, C_2, \cdots, C_n$, there are MRM models $M_1, M_2, \cdots, M_n$. A given sequence $x = a_1, a_2, \cdots, a_m$ has corresponding state sequences respectively on $M_i (1 \le i \le n)$, which is denoted as $s_{init} s_0^i s_1^i \cdots s_m^i q_e^i$, the category of sequence x is determined by selecting the minimum value,*

$$C_i = \min_i \left(|rew(s_0^i s_1^i \cdots s_m{}^i) - Expre(\pi)_i| \right)(1 \le i \le n)$$

During the process of classification, if the testing sequence contains some sub-sequences that do not be described by the MRM model, then we deal with the sequence by the on-the-fly method as follows. Let the subsequence cannot be find on MRM is ω,

1) $\pi' = \pi\omega$, $rew(\pi') = rew(\pi) + rew(\omega)$, $P(\pi') = P(\pi) \cdot \prod_{|w|} 10^{-6}$;

2) $\pi' = \omega\pi$, $rew(\pi') = rew(\omega) + rew(\pi)$, $P(\pi') = P(\pi) \cdot \prod_{|w|} 10^{-6}$;

3 $\pi' = \pi\omega\pi''$, $rew(\pi') = rew(\pi) + rew(w) + rew(\pi'')$, $P(\pi') = P(\pi) \cdot P(\pi'') \cdot \prod_{|w|} 10^{-6}$

We connect the states corresponding to the sequence of atomic propositions represented by ω by a very small amount (10^{-6}), which does not affect the calculation of the cumulative reward of π'.

4   Experiment

4.1   Dataset

The data set was exemplary segmented EEG time series recordings of 10 epilepsy patients collected at the Neurology and Sleep Centre, Hauz Khas, New Delhi [19]. The data were acquired using a Grass Telefactor Comet AS40 amplification system at a sampling rate of 200 Hz. During the acquisition, gold-plated scalp EEG electrodes were placed according to a 10–20 electrode placement system. The signal is filtered between 0.5 and 70 Hz and then segmented into pre-ictal, interictal and seizure phases. Each downloadable folder contains 50 MAT files of EEG time series signals. The folder name corresponds to the seizure phase. Each MAT file consisted of 1024 samples of one EEG time series data with a duration of 5.12 s.

4.2   Data Processing

The first 40 files in preictal, ictal, and interictal are taken as the training set and 41 to 50 as the test set, respectively. Since the modeling and classification methods utilized in this paper prioritize the issue of character order in sequences rather than the semantics of the characters themselves, the coding method of equal frequency binning is used for the training set, and the data were coded as A, B, C, D, E, F, G, and H. Thus, each MAT file was coded as a sequence of strings in ascending order according to the timestamp, and three DPFAs that would absorb the character F were constructed using the ALERGIA algorithm as A_{pre}, A_{itc}, and A_{int}, respectively, for the preictal model, the itcal model, and the interictal model, and the above three DPFAs were quasi-switched to M_{pre}, M_{itc}, and M_{int} using Algorithm 3 (Fig. 7).

4.3   Experimental Results

MRM's Expected Rewards. The expected rewards of the three MRMs obtained from the experiment are shown in Table 1.

Table 1. Expected rewards for the three models

model	expected rewards
M_{pre}	43068.048383552646271
M_{itc}	55387.602797140784881
M_{int}	34563.045367978487064

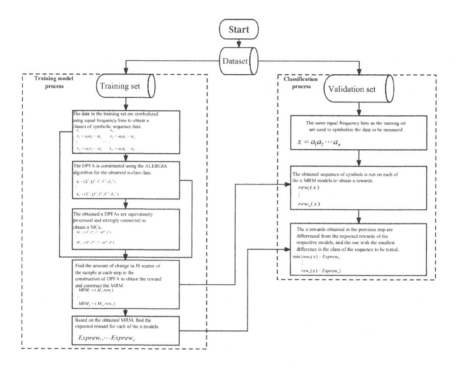

Fig. 7. Experimental process.

Classification Results. The three types of validation set data are encoded by the results of the equal frequency binning box at the time of modeling, and the obtained character sequences are run on the three MRMs respectively, and the values of the three types of sequences on the three models are obtained according to the above definition of the sequence classification problem on MRM as shown in the following three tables.

Table 2 represents the difference between the accumulated rewards obtained from running the ten preItcal data on three models and the expected rewards of these three models. The data marked in bold indicate the minimum values. According to the classification definition based on the aforementioned MRM, all ten data points are correctly classified.

Table 3 represents the difference between the accumulated rewards obtained from running the ten itcal data on three models and the expected rewards of these three models. The data marked in bold indicate the minimum values. According to the classification definition based on the aforementioned MRM, 9 data points are correctly classified, while one data point is misclassified as preItcal.

Table 4 represents the difference between the accumulated rewards obtained from running the ten interItcal data on three models and the expected rewards of these three models. The data marked in bold indicate the minimum values. According to the classification definition based on the aforementioned MRM,

Table 2. The results of preTest calculations on the three models

M_{pre}	M_{itc}	M_{int}
6701.084221	201987.7905	8851.87539
9545.957999	231703.8429	10559.96894
9886.3244	214825.1311	10602.26156
2976.112542	183870.8487	5852.228679
7563.152986	223039.4242	9144.410688
8610.342403	93144.06132	11678.28693
7565.895927	217314.1513	9167.954336
10911.12302	108495.8964	23787.29924
426.3387312	193768.1902	3577.651131
7039.764421	219103.111	8309.540848

Table 3. The results of itcTest calculations on the three models

M_{pre}	M_{itc}	M_{int}
20152.93923	**14769.54592**	89984.97568
18857.89253	**6185.127503**	83272.04511
18746.16351	**4146.383672**	82623.2543
19943.87872	**9060.858413**	87641.88905
19380.01459	**5246.990987**	83323.22556
4861.417311	74149.32926	33417.30443
20717.38858	**8756.918582**	86928.42242
16379.15102	**6077.359055**	79824.2292
23783.15436	**12634.43799**	93771.45523
20764.44541	**3717.519109**	85512.11688

Table 4. The results of intTest calculations on the three models

M_{pre}	M_{itc}	M_{int}
467.9740809	151907.4654	1411.564514
1976.498247	148745.4461	5564.912906
4562.939409	158078.2663	**3884.322461**
575.1236663	159817.6127	1341.42754
2567.241381	151848.2913	4258.433138
4192.94763	176220.6194	5276.550599
13210.03697	111868.9635	**5757.523198**
2081.539692	112588.7868	**548.9658646**
825.809125	134535.0135	**633.6976618**
687.0810661	136134.695	**413.5319749**

5 data points are correctly classified, while 5 data points are misclassified as preItcal.

4.4 Performance Analysis

Performance is quantified using standard measures, namely, sensitivity, specificity, and accuracy (Table 5).

$$\text{Precision} = \frac{TP}{TP + FP} \times 100\% \tag{2}$$

$$\text{Recall} = \frac{TP}{TP + FN} \times 100\% \tag{3}$$

$$\text{Accuracy} = \frac{TP + TN}{TP + FN + FP + FN} \times 100\% \tag{4}$$

Table 5. Overall performance of the based MRM classifier on three test datasets

dataSet	Precision	Recall	Accuracy
preTest	0.625	1.0	0.8
itcTest	1.0	0.9	0.967
intTest	1.0	0.5	0.833

The following is the experimental performance of epilepsy classification using the plain Bayesian classification method (Table 6 and 7).

Table 6. Overall performance of the plain Bayesian classifier on the three test datasets

dataSet	Precision	Recall	Accuracy
preTest	0.421	0.8	0.567
itcTest	1.0	0.4	0.8
intTest	0.429	0.3	0.63

When doing classification experiments with DPFA, one piece of data in the preTest sample set could not be classified, and two pieces of data in each of itcTest and intTest could not be classified, i.e., the probability of these five pieces of data on all three models is 0. This is due to the fact that some of the samples of transferring between the states are missing in the training sample set, and such state transferring occurs in the test set, which leads to the fact that the test set The probability of the data cannot be calculated, and we can also consider the unclassifiable due to the equal probability of these 5 data.

Table 7. Overall performance of the DPFA classifier on the three test datasets

dataSet	Precision	Recall	Accuracy
preTest	0.8	0.889	0.88
itcTest	1.0	1.0	1.0
intTest	0.857	0.75	0.64

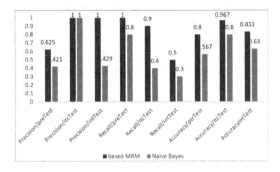

Fig. 8. Performance comparison of three types of validation sets on two classification models.

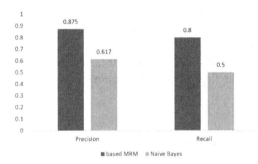

Fig. 9. Comparison of the performance of the two classification models on the entire validation set.

Since only 25 data were actually involved in the DPFA classification experiments, an overall performance comparison with plain Bayesian classification and MRM classification is not done.

It is easy to see from Fig. 8 that the MRM-based classifier achieves higher precision, accuracy and recall than the plain Bayesian classifier on the validation set for different classes.

Since the sample sizes of the three different types of validation sets are equal, the macro-averaging method is directly used here to calculate the precision and recall of the two classifiers over the entire validation set, and the results are shown in Fig. 9, where the MRM-based classifier is much higher than the plain Bayesian classifier in both metrics.

5   Conclusion

In this paper, we propose a novel approach to sequence classification that uses the difference between the expected reward of a Markov reward model (MRM) and the cumulative reward obtained by running a character sequence on the MRM as an indicator for classification. In addition, we propose an algorithm for converting deterministic probabilistic finite automata (DPFA) to Markov chains (MC) equivalent. This conversion process consists of transforming a part of the edges in DPFA into states in MC. In constructing the DPFA using the ALERGIA algorithm, we use JS divergence to quantify the degree of variation of the model assigning a reward function to the states in the MC to obtain the MRM. A significant advantage of our approach over DPFA-based sequence classification methods is that it is able to handle the case where the probability of a sequence running on the model is zero due to missing samples. Compared with Bayesian-based sequence classification methods, our approach significantly improves the classification accuracy while maintaining an acceptable level of computational efficiency. Regarding future research directions, we aim to extend the application of our method from single-dimensional features to multidimensional features, which involves considering automata combinations in the modeling process. In addition, we intend to expand the scope of our method to address sequence prediction problems based on our original modeling. In summary, the work presented in this paper introduces a completely new perspective for sequence modeling and analysis. It not only enhances our understanding of sequence structure and behavior, but also caters to the practical needs of various applications. We expect that our research will have a substantial impact on the future development of the field of sequence analysis.

References

1. Lee, P.S., Lee, K.H.: Genomic analysis. Curr. Opin. Biotechnol. **11**(2), 171–175 (2000)
2. Singhal, A., et al.: Modern information retrieval: a brief overview. IEEE Data Eng. Bull. **24**(4), 35–43 (2001)
3. Loughran, T., McDonald, B.: Textual analysis in accounting and finance: a survey. J. Acc. Res. **54**(4), 1187–1230 (2016)
4. Chandola, V., Banerjee, A., Kumar, V.: Anomaly detection: a survey. ACM Comput. Surv. (CSUR) **41**(3), 1–58 (2009)
5. Aghabozorgi, S., Shirkhorshidi, A.S., Wah, T.Y.: Time-series clustering-a decade review. Inf. Syst. **53**, 16–38 (2015)
6. Xing, Z., Pei, J., Keogh, E.: A brief survey on sequence classification. ACM SIGKDD Explor. Newsl. **12**(1), 40–48 (2010)
7. Dwivedi, S.K., Sengupta, S.: Classification of HIV-1 sequences using profile Hidden Markov models. PLoS ONE **7**(5), e36566 (2012)
8. Li, B., et al.: Research on location algorithm of mobile network based on hidden Markov model. In: Wang, Y., Liu, Y., Zou, J., Huo, M. (eds.) International Conference On Signal And Information Processing, Networking And Computers, pp. 938–946. Springer Nature Singapore, Singapore (2022). https://doi.org/10.1007/978-981-19-9968-0_113

9. Lipton, Z.C., Berkowitz, J., Elkan, C.: A critical review of recurrent neural networks for sequence learning. arXiv preprint arXiv:1506.00019 (2015)
10. Yildirim, Ö.: A novel wavelet sequence based on deep bidirectional LSTM network model for ECG signal classification. Comput. Biol. Med. **96**, 189–202 (2018)
11. Zulqarnain, M., Ghazali, R., Ghouse, M.G., Mushtaq, M.F.: Efficient processing of GRU based on word embedding for text classification. JOIV Int. J. Inform. Visual. **3**(4), 377–383 (201)
12. Câmara, G.B.M., et al.: Convolutional neural network applied to SARS-CoV-2 sequence classification. Sensors **22**(15), 5730 (2022)
13. Ferreira, M.D., Corrêa, D.C., Nonato, L.G., de Mello, R.F.: Designing architectures of convolutional neural networks to solve practical problems. Expert Syst. Appl. **94**, 205–217 (2018)
14. De la Higuera, C.: Grammatical Inference: Learning Automata and Grammars. Cambridge University Press, Cambridge (2010)
15. Adenis, P., Mukherjee, K., Ray, A.: State splitting and state merging in probabilistic finite state automata. In: Proceedings of the 2011 American Control Conference, pp. 5145–5150. IEEE, San Francisco, CA, USA (2011)
16. Segala, R.: Modeling and verification of randomized distributed real-time systems. Massachusetts Institute of Technology (1996)
17. Baier, C., Katoen, J.-P.: Principles of Model Checking. MIT Press, Cambridge (2008)
18. Kumari, R., Sharma, D.K.: Generalized 'useful'AG and 'useful'JS-divergence measures and their bounds. Int. J. Eng. Sci. Math. **7**(1), 441–450 (2018)
19. Swami, P., Panigrahi, B., Nara, S., Bhatia, M., Gandhi, T.: EEG epilepsy datasets. **2**(14280.32006) (2016). https://doi.org/10.13140/RG

Approximation Algorithms

An Optimal Algorithm Based on Fairness of Resource Allocation in Wireless Mesh Networks

Jiadong Peng and Zhanmao Cao[✉]

School of Computer, South China Normal University, Tianhe District, Guangzhou 510631, China
{20162180043,caozhanmao}@m.scnu.edu.cn

Abstract. Wireless Mesh Networks (WMNs) are popular due to their adaptability, easy-setup, and transmission efficiency, etc. The fair multiple concurrent flows in WMNs are quite challenging to arrange the simultaneous transmission with the interference nature of wireless media. Due to the limited resources like the number of orthogonal channels and interfaces, interference between channels affects the fair distribution of bandwidth among mesh routers. It is deserving to combine sub-paths in sub-blocks by DC for more candidate routes. To eliminate the conflicts and competition, we propose an optimal algorithm based on resource fairness to ensure performance and minimize resource waste. The performance of the algorithm is efficient, which is verified with various simulations.

Keywords: Wireless Mesh Network · Resource fairness · Block processing · Interference avoidance · Routing

1 Introduction

Multiple-radio multiple-channel Wireless mesh networks (MRMC WMNs) have its position for smart society. In broadband access or everything connection, WMNs support the current development. The popularity is from the advantages of high capacity, easy access, self-healing, and extendable coverage to rural areas [1].

WMNs are composed of many wireless nodes that communicate with each other. There are two types of nodes: Mesh Routers and Mesh Clients, which work together to create a wireless mesh network with multiple hops, using Gateways to connect to the Internet. Router nodes can be static or mobile, depending on the application.

Mesh mode is one of the important characteristics that makes WMNs different from traditional wireless networks [2]. The WMN routers are generally stationary, hence, no power problem like that in sensor. WMNs are suitable for a wide range of applications in emergencies [3]. The mesh is able to find the alternate routes for data transmission when one of the routes breaks down. Therefore, the network has the capability of survivability in case of unexpected failures. However, there are still challenges to improve overall network performance such as more choices for routing, more fairness for resource usage.

When there are multiple traffic requests from multiple pair of sender-destination, the QoS is dependent to no conflict path. Notice a learning scheme can find CA to deduce

Z. Cai et al. (Eds.): NCTCS 2023, CCIS 1944, pp. 85–95, 2024.
https://doi.org/10.1007/978-981-99-7743-7_5

the confliction [4]. At any time slot, only interference-free links from local area can be merged together to form a global route. As overlapping channels will interfere with each other, resulting in the decline of network capacity [5], we just assign orthogonal channels. Link nodes within the interference range are screened with an interference-free condition as given in [6], which introduce a CPG model to simplify CA scheme for concurrent transmitting.

Fair resource allocation can effectively release the resource contention issue in multiple concurrent flow (MCF), thereby improving WMNs performance. In MCF traffic situations, different flows may compete on channels, interfaces, network bandwidth, etc. Due to unfair resource allocation among nodes, network performance may be decreased by node starvation or path blocked.

Due to the NP-hard nature of find optimal fair resource allocation [10], it makes sense to find a solution based on merging that of the known smaller mesh. F. A. Ghaleb et al. proposes a fairness-oriented genetic algorithm to solve the node starvation problem [7]. Unfortunately, the heuristic algorithm may result in low efficiency as they may get stuck in local minima, leading to unfair channel distribution in the mesh. Consequently, it may not find a suitable solution within a reasonable time cost.

To design optimization algorithms for fair resource allocation makes significant meaning for exploring potential capacity. This paper proposes a strategy model for fair resource allocation. Henceforth, developing an optimal combination algorithm. This algorithm can minimize the node starvation while considering network resource utilization. The performance of the algorithm is verified with various simulations.

The rest is organized as follows: Sect. 2 is a short review of recent related work. Section 3 aims to set up a model and propose an optimal combination algorithm based on resource fairness (OCA). Section 4 shows the performance evaluation and necessary comparison. Section 5 is a short conclusion.

2 Related Work

To transmit multiple concurrent flows, optimal fair resource allocation is still worth further explore. Firstly, multiple traffic flows from different source-destination pairs may cause confliction without perfect routing and scheduling scheme. Secondly, the complexity of routing multiple flows is very complex, because many constraints must be considered for scheduling, routing, channel allocation, and interference avoidance. Thirdly, the routing and packet scheduling problem is generally NP-complete [8]. CA problem is NP-hard, because it can be mapped to a coloring problem [9]. It is really challenging to find optimal fair resource usage scheme, because one sub-problem to determine an optimal link schedule has been shown to be NP-hard [10].

Fairness is defined as the equal distribution of resources on the mesh nodes [9]. The fair resource allocation leads to many open challenges that need to be addressed in algorithms, such as fair bandwidth, channel access and load balancing [11]. Furthermore, interference of wireless media hinders equitable utilization of WMNs resources. When a node attempts to use a link of not interference-free, node starvation occurs [12]. To get rid of these cases, it is necessary to design an optimization algorithm for fair resource allocation.

By allocating resources fairly, each flow obtains the appropriate resources under the same priority. This can avoid issues such as deadlock and hunger caused by resource competition. Up to now, research on the fairness of resource allocation is still scarce. To improve the stability and reliability, we will tackle the fair resource allocation in MRMC WMNs.

Some schemes have been proposed for the MCF problem, focusing on different aspects such as routing, scheduling, or channel allocation. The primary object is to improve capacity, throughput, etc., or to reduce delay by reducing global network interference. However, fairness has not been considered as an important aspect. For example, Liu *et al.* propose a gateway selection algorithm on both the gateway deployment cost and the link collision domain [13]. In the case of ensuring full coverage of the network, the bottleneck collision domain is used to calculate the maximum throughput to optimize the throughput. Shi *et al.* proposes a scheme to obtain optimal solutions to routing and channel assignment [14]. To reduce computational complexity of joint routing and channel assignment, routing and channel assignment are regarded as two separate problems and solved sequentially in their research.

Anita *et al.* proposed a multiple disjoint path determination mechanism based on-demand routing in WMN to formulate path discovery and data transmission delays [15]. By optimizing the neighbor list of nodes, they reduce the unnecessary delay in route discovery process. The routing can obtain multiple disjoint communication routes with high capacity and reduce the communication delay in the proposed work. The aforementioned studies explore solutions to the problems posed by MCF from different perspectives. Most of them aim to mitigate the MCF problem by minimizing global network interference. However, we focus on researching the fairness of resource allocation, aiming to explore a new direction in addressing the issue.

To simplify CA, Cao et al. introduced the Cartesian Product of Graph (CPG) model is to WMN, which decomposes the complex layered structure [6]. CPG is useful to reduce the complexity of CA, especially to the cases of path selection for the multiple concurrent flows. It can intuitively help to deal with channel conflictions. Cao provides a combinatorial optimization algorithm called COSS [16]. It uses heuristic methods to find many compatible paths to realize the combinatorial optimization of compatible paths. From their experimental results, we can see that the combination algorithm has indeed achieved good network performance. Our algorithm will be compared with it in the simulation.

As discussed above, the fairness in MCF problem is a challenge and leaves research space. In this paper, we propose an algorithm by dividing the mesh into smaller blocks, in order to make more effective fair use of resources.

3   Model and Algorithm

We consider an almost static network topology since routers are always pre-deployed and almost fixed during their operation. To facilitate the discussion, we provide below some preliminaries and notations for the WMNs.

$\Gamma = \{G, I, C, R\}$ is the structure of a given MRMC WMN. G is the mesh graph, and I is the interference conditions. Each router has multiple radio interfaces, the number is $|R|$.

The link of neighbor routers u and v is represented by $l_{(u,v)}$. When the link is activated, it can be used to transfer data from u to v. A link between two adjacent routers is active on one channel c_i. C is the set of available orthogonal channels, $C = \{c_1, c_2 \dots c_i \dots c_k\}$.

We consider a set of traffic requests $\Delta = \{\lambda_1, \lambda_2 \dots, \lambda_i, \dots \lambda_t\}$, where $\lambda_i = \{(s_i, d_i), z_i\}$ gives the ith pair of source node s_i and destination node d_i with the data size z_i. To such λ_i, we aim to search the routing path p_i, which can transfer data packets from s_i to d_i. t is the number of traffic requests.

In a wireless mesh network, multiple radio interfaces support a node works on different channels. i.e., a node can send or receive data at the same time slot by using different interface over different channels. What we manage to encourage is to let a node send or receive data from multiple nodes concurrently. As CPG model help to assign channels, our work takes its advantages.

If the transmitting links interfere with each other by inappropriate channels and time slots, the transmission will result in the decline of network throughput. The orthogonal channels are allocated to links in order to reduce computational complexity. Hence, the interference relation can be verified in each channel topology of CPG.

Supporting concurrent transmission is essential for reliable wireless networks. If and only if multiple links satisfy all the following link interference free conditions, the multiple links can coexist without interruption with each other. For the sender, the distance between any two different senders is not less than two hops. For the receiver, the distance between any two different receivers shall not be less than one hop. For the sender and receiver, the distance exceeds one hop.

We also use link ranking for processing. In the link ranking step, the following four criteria are used to rank nodes: their degree, interface, channel resources and usage frequency. The node level is normalized and the score for each node is given. The link ranking is obtained by summing the scores of the nodes that form the link. After the consistency processing of indicators, each indicator is converted into a very large indicator that is as large as possible. However, there is also a problem that different indicator units and orders of magnitude are different, so we need to perform dimensionless processing on these indicator data.

In order to achieve fair allocation of resources, we have designed the following formula to implement. γ_l is a parameter for estimating the free channel and interface resources that link l may use. Let k is the number of all links activated within the interference range of link l. The bigger γ_l means the link has more possibility to be activated. $|R_l|$ is the number of interfaces of the two end nodes on l, and $|C_l|$ is the number of channels of that. We use $|R_l|$ and $|C_l|$ to predict the resources of l. We search for the number of links that meet the criteria according to the interference avoidance conditions. It is clear the available resources are inverse relation with k, i.e. The higher k is, the more likely l may be interfered. We put k in the denominator part in (1).

$$\gamma_l = \frac{|C_l| \times |R_l|}{k} \tag{1}$$

Q_l can be viewed as the relatively free resources for l. β_l is the sum number of the accessible nodes to link l. The m_l affects the number of paths that may pass through the node. The bigger Q_l means the link may be heavily loaded in multiple concurrent flows.

The number of interfaces can represent the bearing capacity of the node. If m_l is large, it means the mesh near link will be dense.

$$Q_l = \frac{k \times \beta_l}{|R_l|} \tag{2}$$

Our evaluation is composed of two values of γ_l and Q_l, as shown in (3). Let L be a sub path of the current block, $F(L)$ is the interference value of L. For the influence degree of these two values on $F(L)$, we use parameter α to control.

l may be interfered. We put k in the denominator part in (1).

$$F(L) = \alpha \sum_{l \in L} \frac{1}{\gamma_l} + (1 - \alpha) \cdot \sum_{l \in L} Q_l \tag{3}$$

When our algorithm is executed to the part of path evaluation, we evaluate the path p through the interference factor $F(p)$ of P. K_P is the sum number of these links activated within the interference range of p. The lower $F(p)$ means the better performance of the path. The $F(p)$ of the whole path P is calculated as (4). It is the sum of the interference values $F(L)$ of all blocks after calculating the weight. We evaluate the whole path through $F(p)$ to judge whether the performance will degrade after being combined.

$$F(p) = \sum_{L \subseteq p} \frac{\sum_{k \in L} k}{K_p} \times F(L) \tag{4}$$

In this study, we maximize link fairness to avoid the interference problems. We propose an optimal combination algorithm to solve such a problem. The algorithm promises the performance and the least waste of resources by dividing the mesh into smaller blocks. Our proposed algorithm aims to find the most effective solution to achieve node fairness and alleviate the MCF problem.

We use Floyd scheme to obtain the number of the shortest path between any two nodes in the early precomputing stage. At the same time, we get the shortest hop path of any pair node of the multiple traffic request pairs. h_i is the shortest hop number of pair (s_i, d_i).

After precomputing stage, we divide the mesh network according to each traffic request pair. As long as there is a new traffic request (s_{i+1}, d_{i+1}), Algorithm 1 will be executed to find a routing scheme for (s_{i+1}, d_{i+1}). After the whole topology is divided into several blocks, the global routing for (s_{i+1}, d_{i+1}) can be realized by intra block routing and inter block combination. It greatly reduces time cost and complexity.

Our algorithm divides the mesh according to the hop number of a traffic pair. The number 3 of hop is set as a threshold of a block. i.e., if a block size is bigger than 3, continue the dividing process. The algorithm can effectively handle data transmissions between nodes within 3 hops. In the dividing process, we try to split a block into two parts of almost the same size.

Algorithm 1. Resource fairness optimal algorithm

Algorithm Resource fairness optimal algorithm

Input: network topology, nodes position, traffics set
Output: paths set P
1.   **for** each node pair s and d in network topology **do**
2.   use Floyd Algorithm to search the shortest-hop path
3.   add to set P'
4.   **end for**
5.   **for** each traffic(s_i, d_i) in traffics set **do**
6. $P \leftarrow \emptyset$
7.   **subpart**(s_i, d_i)
8. $P \leftarrow P \cup \{p\}$
9.   **end for**
10.   **process** subpart(s_i, d_i)
11.   get the minimum hops k of this node pair from P'
12.   **if** $k \leq 3$ **then**
13.   get the shortest-hop path p' from P'
14.   **if** $F(p')$ is the largest in P' **then**
15. $p \leftarrow p \cup p'$
16.   **end if**
17.   return
18.   **end if**
19.   make a split line
20.   take cross-border node pair(n_1, n_2) on the split line
21.   subpart (s_i, n_1)
22.   subpart (n_2, d_i)
23.   **end function**

For a given pair (s_i, d_i), we have s_i, d_i location coordinates. Based the location information, we can divide the topology. We first connect s_i and d_i to get a line. Then we make the middle vertical line of it. Therefore, we divide the topology into two sub-blocks. We repeat the above steps for the sub-blocks until the size threshold of direct conquer is reached.

The topology is divided by several splitting lines. We need to select some candidate node pairs near these lines so that we can combine route between the two neighbor blocks. We use the sliding window to obtain the nodes near the splitting lines. The window will first move along a splitting line. Nodes near the splitting line will be captured by the sliding window. Then we can select the link candidate nodes from the neighbor blocks. The link end nodes should be in two different neighbor blocks. After obtaining these candidate links, we use them to merge the local paths to a longer one.

We need to combine the routing between the sub-blocks. In a block, we transmit data to other blocks through candidate nodes. It is necessary to weigh which candidate node to select during routing, because there are multiple candidate nodes. If we search all the possible sub-paths, the number of paths will be a large number. We select candidate nodes according to the hop distances. We obtain several candidate sub-paths to avoid interference.

After all blocks completes the routing, the task comes to combine local paths. Through the formula (4), we expect that the path can be more effective due to the fair allocation of resources. Because the path is evaluated for resources and interference, it can be optimized in the next several steps like scheduling.

Before scheduling, we collect the global information of the network, including nodes, transmission requests, network topology, etc. Based on this information, we can update the status of all nodes and make a reasonable plan for all transmission requests.

In each time slot, we check whether the unscheduled paths are compatible. If the conditions are met, the appropriate channel and the current time slot is allocated to the path for scheduling. Repeatedly check the unscheduled paths until all paths are scheduled.

The algorithm finds as many compatible paths as possible under each slot. It can maximize the number of compatible paths in the same time slot. More data can be transmitted in the same time slot. It effectively improving the utilization of network resources.

4 Performance

In order to evaluate the performance of our algorithm, we do a series of simulations. We use a randomly generated topology model to verify the efficiency of our algorithm. All simulations were carried out with random 64 nodes mesh, as shown in Fig. 1.

In different simulation experiments, in order to study the performance of the algorithm under different conditions, we will change the deployment of interface and channel for the routers, as well as the traffic modes. The traffic modes are 40 pairs to 200 pairs with interval of 40.

The parameters and values are listed in following. Time duration is set to be 5ms, packet size is set to be 1MB, and each link capacity is set to be 200 MB/s. In general, the computing time depends on both the topology and t. The topology has two aspects: the size, and the special local distribution.

The Fig. 2 shows the transmit time of our algorithm under different traffic requests. It can be seen from the figure that when there are few numbers of traffic requests like 40 or 80, the use of resources such as channel interface is still relatively surplus. The transmit time is almost the same. Above 80, with the increase of traffic requests, insufficient network resources, channel conflict and excessive node load will appear. Our algorithm can reduce the corresponding problems through the evaluation mechanism of interference factors.

At the same time, the transmission time varies with different resource combinations. In the case of $|C| \wedge |R| = 8 \wedge 16$, the transmission time of the curve as a whole is higher than that of $12 \wedge 24$ and $16 \wedge 32$. When the resources are insufficient, the interference and conflict phenomenon will obviously increase the network transmission time. Optimizing resource allocation and reducing conflicts are the focus of our algorithm.

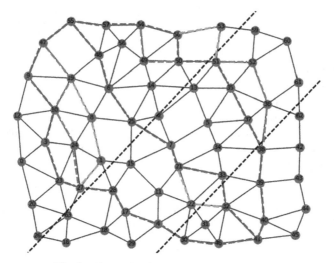

Fig. 1. The randomly generated mesh topology

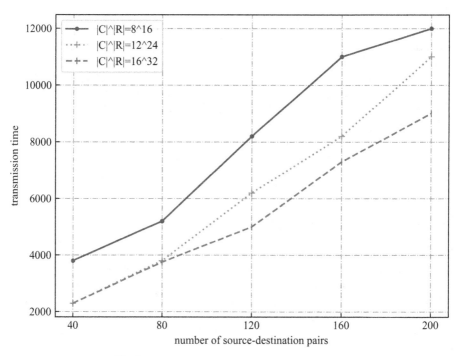

Fig. 2. Transmit time with different combination

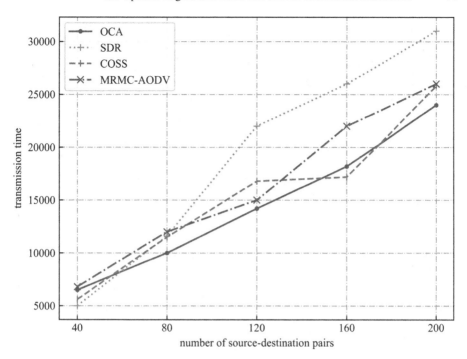

Fig. 3. Transmission time comparison

The Fig. 3 is a comparison with OCA, SDR, MRMC-AODV and COSS in transmission time. Given a certain network resource combination 8 ∧ 16, the transmission time of OCA algorithm is faster than SDR and MRMC-AODV algorithm on the whole, and slower than COSS only in the case of 160 pairs. As t increases, our transmission time does not increase dramatically.

It is not suitable to consider only the shortest path in WMNs. SDR is an algorithm to obtain the shortest path. Because of interference and resource allocation, only considering the shortest path can easily lead to overload, which makes the network performance worse. The path selection criteria of the OCA can intelligently select the path with the largest available resources in the current network state, and can effectively reduce the overlap between multiple paths. Through resource intelligence, the algorithm realizes node load balancing and improves network performance.

The Fig. 4 is a comparison with OCA, SDR, MRMC-AODV and COSS in terms of maximum throughput. In order to realize multi-path simultaneous optimization, we propose a blocking algorithm for wireless mesh networks, which is based on the idea of block computing. It can improve the performance of the network and balance the load of nodes and channels. When the t is 40 or 80, the throughput of the four algorithms is very similar. As t increases to 120, 160 or 200, the advantages of our algorithm gradually manifest. Through throughput performance comparison, given a certain resource, it is slightly better than SDR, MRMC-AODV and COSS algorithms with the increase of pairs.

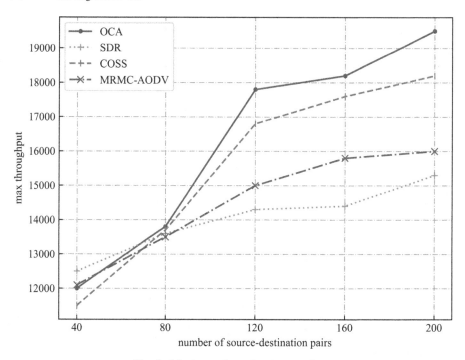

Fig. 4. Maximum throughput comparison

5 Conclusion

This study solves the problem of network performance degradation caused by unfair resource allocation in existing research. The main drawback of unfair allocation of network resources is that interference leads to unfair allocation of network resources. This restriction leads to unfair resource distribution in WMN, which affects network performance. We conducted extensive experimental evaluations to measure the performance of the proposed technology and compare it with existing solutions. The results show that the algorithm improves link fairness and network capacity utilization while reducing interference, which is outperformed to existing solutions.

References

1. Mogaibel, H.A., Othman, M., Subramaniam, S., Hamid, N.A.W.A.: Review of channel assignment approaches in multi-radio multi-channel wireless mesh network. J. Netw. Comput. Appl. **72**, 113–139 (2016)
2. Roh, H., Lee, J.: Channel assignment, link scheduling, routing, and rate control for multichannel wireless mesh networks with directional antennas. J. Commun. Netw. **18**(6), 884–890 (2016)
3. Fujinaka, H., Ohta, T., Kakuda, Y.: Evacuation route guidance scheme for building evacuation using wireless mesh network systems, In: 2020 Eighth International Symposium on Computing and Networking Workshops (CANDARW) (2020)

4. Kumar, N., Lee, J.: Collaborative-learning-automata-based channel assignment with topology preservation for wireless mesh networks under QoS constraints. IEEE Syst. J. **9**(3), 675–685 (2015)
5. Farooq, M.U., Zeeshan, M.: Connected dominating set enabled on-demand routing (CDS-OR) for wireless mesh networks. IEEE Wirel. Commun. Lett. **10**(11), 2393–2399 (2021)
6. Cao, Z., Wu, C.Q., Zhang, Y., et al.: On modeling and analysis of mimo wireless mesh networks with triangular overlay topology, Math. Prob. Eng. 1–11 (2015)
7. Ghaleb, F.A., Al-Rimy, B.A.S., Boulila, W., et al.: Fairness-oriented semichaotic genetic algorithm-based channel assignment technique for node starvation problem in wireless mesh networks. Comput. Intell. Neurosci. **2021**, 2977954 (2021)
8. Islam, A., Nurain, N.: Channel assignment techniques for multi-radio wireless mesh networks: a survey, IEEE Commun. Surv. Tutorials. **18**(2), 988–1017 (2016)
9. Khan, U.U., Dilshad, N., Rehmani, M.H., Umer, T.: Fairness in cognitive radio networks: models, measurement methods, applications, and future research directions. J. Netw. Comput. Appl. **73**, 12–26 (2016)
10. Rattal, S., Reyouchi, E.M.: An effective practical method for narrowband wireless mesh networks performance. SN Appl. Sci. **12**(1), 1532–1540 (2019)
11. Zhang, D., Li, G., Zheng, K., Ming, X., Pan, Z.-H.: An energy-balanced routing method based on forward-aware factor for wireless sensor networks. IEEE Trans. Industr. Inf. **10**(1), 766–773 (2014)
12. Wei, Z.H., Hu, B.J.: A fair multi-channel assignment algorithm with practical implementation in distributed cognitive radio networks. IEEE Access **6**, 14255–14267 (2018)
13. W. Liu, C. Xu and T. Zhao et al., "Research on gateway deployment for throughput optimization in wireless mesh networks. In: 2019 International Conference on Computer, Information and Telecommunication Systems(CITS) IEEE (2019)
14. Shi, W., Cui, K., Chai, Y.: Routing and channel assignment for multicast in multi-channel multi-radio wireless mesh networks, J. Commun. **11**(11) (2016)
15. Anita, C.S., Sasikumar, R.: Neighbor Coverage and Bandwidth Aware Multiple Disjoint Path Discovery in Wireless Mesh Networks, Wireless Personal Communications. **126**(4), 2949–2968 (2022)
16. Cao, Z., Huang, Q., Wu, C.: Maximize concurrent data flows in multi-radio multi-channel wireless mesh networks. Comput. Sci. Inf. Syst. **17**(3), 759–777 (2020)

An Approximation Algorithm
for Stochastic Power Cover Problem

Menghan Cao[(✉)]

School of Mathematics and Statistics, Yunnan University, Kunming 650500, China
Cao-MH@outlook.com

Abstract. In this paper, we introduce the stochastic power cover (SPC) problem, which aims to determine the two-stage power assignment and minimize the total expected power consumption. For this problem, we are given a set U of n users, a set S of m sensors on the plane and k possible scenarios, where k is a polynomial and each consists of a probability of occurrence. Each sensor $s \in S$ can adjust the power it produces by changing its radius and the relationship between them satisfies the following power equation $p(s) = c \cdot r(s)^\alpha$. The objective is to identify the radius of each sensor in the first stage and augment the first-stage solution in order to cover all users and minimize the expected power over both stages. Our main result is to present an $O(\alpha)$-approximation algorithm by using the primal-dual technique.

Keywords: Power cover · Stochastic optimization · Approximation algorithm · Primal dual

1   Introduction

The minimum power cover (MPC) problem is a classical combinatorial optimization problem that can be defined as follows. Given a set U of n users and a set S of m sensors on the plane. Each sensor $s \in S$ can adjust the power it produces by changing its radius and the relationship between the radio and its power satisfies the following power equation

$$p(s) = c \cdot r(s)^\alpha, \qquad (*)$$

where the coefficient $c > 0$ and the attenuation coefficient $\alpha \geq 1$ are constants. We call a user $u \in U$ is covered by a sensor $s \in S$ if the distance between u and s is no more than $r(s)$, where $r(s)$ is the radius of $Disk(s, r(s))$ which is the disk centered at s with radius $r(s)$. A user is covered by a power assignment $p : S \mapsto \mathbb{R}^+$ if it belongs to some disk supported by p. The minimum power cover problem is to find a power assignment p covering all users such that the total power $\sum_{s \in S} p(s)$ is as small as possible. Here, we assume that there is no limit on the power at a sensor. For the MPC problem, when $\alpha > 1$, Alt et al. [20] proved that this problem is NP-hard. Charikar and Panigrahy [1] presented a primal-dual algorithm to obtain a constant approximation. Bilò et al. [2] presented a

Z. Cai et al. (Eds.): NCTCS 2023, CCIS 1944, pp. 96–106, 2024.
https://doi.org/10.1007/978-981-99-7743-7_6

polynomial time approximation scheme (PTAS) based on a plane subdivision and shifted the quad-tree technique.

By applying relevant constraints to MPC problem, we can obtain some variational problems, such as the prize-collecting cover problem [7,21], which needs to pay the penalty if a user is not covered; the cover problem with submodular/linear penalties [9–11,13,14]; the capacitated cover problem [12,22,23] in which each sensor has a capacity; the partial cover problem [8,16], which requires covering a specified number of elements and the stochastic cover problem etc. Among them, the stochastic power cover problem is an important problem in stochastic optimization problem and deserves careful study.

In recent years, an increasing number of people have focused on the stochastic optimization problem [17], which is a basic method of dealing with uncertainty for combinatorial optimization problems by building models of uncertainty using the probability distributions of the input instances. The two-stage stochastic optimization model is a popular stochastic model that can solve many combinatorial optimization problems such as stochastic matching [15], stochastic facility location [17], and stochastic set cover problem [18] etc. Additionally, there are many useful techniques for designing approximation algorithms for stochastic combinatorial optimization problems, including the linear programming relaxation approach, boosted sampling [24,25], contention resolution schemes [26], Poisson approximation [4,19] etc.

In the field of stochastic optimization problem, there are many studies on stochastic set cover problems. In this problem, we do not know the points we need to cover at first, but the scenarios of uncertainty go with known probability distributions. It is possible for us to anticipate possible scenarios and purchase some subsets in advance in the first stage. In the second stage, we obtain the probability distribution for all the scenarios. The goal is to optimize the first-stage decision variables to minimize the expected cost over both stages. Ravic and Sinhac [3] proposed the stochastic set cover problem and showed that there exists an $O(\log mn)$ approximation algorithm by analyzing the relationship between the minimum power cover and stochastic set cover problem. Furthermore, Li et al. [4] designed an approximation algorithm with a ratio of $2(\ln n+1)$, in which n is the cardinality of the universe. Parthasarathy [5] designed an adaptive greedy algorithm with ratio $H(n)$ for the stochastic set cover problem. For the stochastic set cover problem with submodular penalty, Sun et al. [6] proposed a 2η-approximation algorithm using the primal-dual technique, where η is the maximum frequency of the element of the ground set in the set cover problem.

Inspired by the above problems, we consider the two-stage, finite-scenario stochastic version of the minimum power cover problem, which generalizes the minimum power cover problem and the stochastic minimum set cover problem. For this problem, we are given a set U of n users, a set S of m sensors on the plane and k possible scenarios, where k is a polynomial and each consists of a probability of occurrence. Each sensor $s \in S$ can adjust the power it produces by changing its radius and the relationship between them satisfies the following power equation $p(s) = c \cdot r(s)^\alpha$, where $c > 0$ and the attenuation coefficient

$\alpha \geq 1$ are some constants. The objective is to identify the radius of each sensor in the first stage and augment the first-stage solution to cover all users and minimize the expected power over both stages. The remainder of this paper is organized as follows. We introduce the stochastic set cover problem in Sect. 2. In Sect. 3, we design a polynomial-time algorithm with an approximate ratio of $O(\alpha)$ by using the primal-dual technique and present the proof. In Sect. 4, we give a brief conclusion.

2 Stochastic Power Cover Problem

Based on the definition of the minimum power cover problem, the two-stage finite-scenario stochastic power cover problem can be defined as follows. The input in our version of the stochastic power cover problem consists of a set U of n users, a first-stage set $U_0 \subseteq U$, a set S of m sensors on the plane and k possible scenarios where k is a polynomial. As with the definition in MPC problem introduced above, the relationship between the radius of a sensor and the power it consumes also satisfies the power equation $(*)$ where c and α are some constants. However, $c > 0$ will change as the scenario changes and we usually call $\alpha \geq 1$ the attenuation coefficient. For a scenario $j \in \{1, 2, \ldots, k\}$, we use p_j to define its probability, $U_j \subseteq U$ is the set of users that need to be covered, which may or may not be subsets of the first-stage set U_0 and the coefficient in the power equation is denoted by c_j in scenario j. In the first stage, the coefficient in the power equation is c_0. We need to anticipate possible scenarios and determine the radius of the sensors in advance in the first stage. In the second stage, when the coverage requirements in all the scenarios appear in the form of the probability distribution, we need to expand the radius of the disks or pick more disks to complement the decision of the first stage. The objective for this problem is to find a power assignment that covers all the users and minimizes the total power of the first stage and the expected power consumption of the second stage.

For convenience, we use a set $\mathcal{F}$ of disks whose centers are sensors to represent a power assignment for the sensor set S. If $\mathcal{F}^*$ is an optimal assignment for this problem, then for any disk $Disk(s, r(s)) \in \mathcal{F}^*$, there is at least one user $u \in U$ that lies on the boundary of disk $Disk(s, r(s))$; otherwise, we may reduce the radius of the disks to cover the same set of users and find a feasible assignment with a lower value. Since in every scenario there are at most n points of users, each sensor can generate up to n disks with different radius and all sensors have a maximum of mn disks that need to be considered. For all scenarios, there are at most kmn disks that need to be considered, so in the following, we use $\mathcal{D}$ to denote such a set of all disks, $(U, \mathcal{D}, k)$ denotes an instance of the SPC problem. For any $D \in \mathcal{D}$, let $c(D)$ represent the center sensor of D, and $r(D, j)$ is the radius of disk D in scenario $j \in \{1, 2, \ldots, k\}$, $U(D)$ denotes the users covered by D and $U_j(D)$ denotes the users covered by D in U_j for all $j = 0, 1, \ldots, k$.

Based on an analysis similar to [7], in order to control the approximation ratio, we need to guess the disk with the maximum radius denoted by $D_{j,max}$ in an optimal solution $\mathcal{F}^* = \bigcup_{j=0}^{k} \mathcal{F}_j^*$ for $j \in \{0, 1, \ldots, k\}$, that is $r(D_{j,max}, j) = \max_{D:D \in \mathcal{F}_j^*} r(D, j)$.

Let $\mathcal{D}_{max} = \bigcup_{j=0}^{k} D_{j,max}$, OPT' is the optimal value of the residual instance about $\mathcal{D}_{max}$, OPT is the optimal value of the original instance $(U, \mathcal{D}, k)$. Similar to the analysis in [7], we have the following lemma:

Lemma 1. $OPT = OPT' + \sum_{j=0}^{k} p_j c_j r(D_{j,max}, j)^\alpha$.

In the guessing technique, each disk $D_{j,max}$ is guessed as the disk with the maximum radius of $\mathcal{F}_j^*$ for all $j = 0, 1, \ldots, k$ in the optimal solution $\mathcal{F}^*$; therefore, by looping $(k + 1)mn$ times, we can assume that $\mathcal{D}_{max}$ is known. Later, we will present a three-phase primal-dual approximation algorithm for the residual instance. And for simplicity of notation, we still use $(U, \mathcal{D}, k)$ to denote the residual instance.

$$\min \sum_{D \in \mathcal{D}} c_0 r(D, 0)^\alpha x_{D,0} + \sum_{j=1}^{k} \sum_{D \in \mathcal{D}} p_j c_j r(D, j)^\alpha x_{D,j} \qquad \text{(IP)}$$

$$\text{s.t.} \sum_{\substack{D \in \mathcal{D} \\ u \in U_0(D)}} x_{D,0} + \sum_{\substack{D \in \mathcal{D} \\ u \in U_j(D)}} x_{D,j} \geq 1, \ \forall j \in \{1, 2, \ldots, k\}, \forall u \in U_0 \cap U_j, \qquad (1)$$

$$\sum_{\substack{D \in \mathcal{D} \\ u \in U_j(D)}} x_{D,j} \geq 1, \ \forall j \in \{1, 2, \ldots, k\}, \forall u \in U_j \setminus U_0, \qquad (2)$$

$$x_{D,0}, x_{D,j} \in \{0, 1\}, \ \forall j \in \{1, 2, \ldots, k\}, \forall D \in \mathcal{D}. \qquad (3)$$

In this formulation, the variable $x_{D,j}$ indicates in scenario j whether we select the disk D. That is:

$$x_{D,j} = \begin{cases} 1, & \text{if disk } D \text{ is selected in scenario } j \text{ to cover some users,} \\ 0, & \text{otherwise.} \end{cases}$$

The first set of constraints of (1) guarantees that each user $u \in U_0 \cap U_j$ is covered in either the first or second stage, and constraint (2) forces the users in $U_j \setminus U_0$ must be covered in the second stage. We can obtain the linear program by replacing constraint (3). Its LP relaxation and corresponding dual program of the linear relaxation are as shown below:

$$\min \sum_{D \in \mathcal{D}} c_0 r(D, 0)^\alpha x_{D,0} + \sum_{j=1}^{k} \sum_{D \in \mathcal{D}} p_j c_j r(D, j)^\alpha x_{D,j} \qquad \text{(LP)}$$

$$\text{s.t.} \sum_{\substack{D \in \mathcal{D} \\ u \in U_0(D)}} x_{D,0} + \sum_{\substack{D \in \mathcal{D} \\ u \in U_j(D)}} x_{D,j} \geq 1, \ \forall j \in \{1, 2, \ldots, k\}, \forall u \in U_0 \cap U_j,$$

$$\sum_{\substack{D \in \mathcal{D} \\ u \in U_j(D)}} x_{D,j} \geq 1, \ \forall j \in \{1, 2, \ldots, k\}, \forall u \in U_j \setminus U_0,$$

$$x_{D,0}, x_{D,j} \geq 0, \ \forall j \in \{1, 2, \ldots, k\}, \forall D \in \mathcal{D}.$$

$$\max \quad \sum_{j=1}^{k} \sum_{u \in U_j} y_{u,j} \tag{DP}$$

$$\text{s.t.} \quad \sum_{j=1}^{k} \sum_{u \in U_0(D) \cap U_j(D)} y_{u,j} \leq c_0 r(D,0)^{\alpha}, \qquad \forall D \in \mathcal{D},$$

$$\sum_{u \in U_j(D)} y_{u,j} \leq p_j c_j r(D,j)^{\alpha}, \qquad \forall D \in \mathcal{D}, j \in \{1,2,\ldots,k\},$$

$$y_{u,j} \geq 0, \qquad \forall u \in U_j, j \in \{1,2,\ldots,k\}$$

Next, we recall the definition and some geometric properties of the ρ-relaxed independent set that have been introduced in [8], where $\rho \in [0,2]$ is a given constant. Given a set U of users and a set $\mathcal{D}$ of disks on the plane, for any two disks $D_1, D_2 \in \mathcal{D}$, if $U(D_1) \cap U(D_2) = \emptyset$ or $d(c(D_1), c(D_2)) > \rho \max\{r(D_1), r(D_2)\}$, we call that $\mathcal{D}$ is a ρ-relaxed independent set, where $d(a,b)$ is the Euclidean distance between points a and b.

According to the above definition, we can obtain the following lemma, and its proof process is the same as in [8]. This lemma will be used in the later proof of the approximate ratio of the primal-dual algorithm.

Lemma 2. *For any* $t \in \{2,3,\ldots\}$, *we have* $\max_{u \in U} |\{D | u \in U(D), D \in \mathcal{D}\}| \leq t-1$, *where* $\mathcal{D}$ *is a ρ-relaxed independent set with* $\rho = 2\sin\frac{\pi}{t}$.

3   Algorithm for the SPC Problem

The algorithm is a three-phase primal-dual approximation algorithm consisting of four steps. For ease of description and modeling, we now present some more notations as follows: for a disk D, $U(D)$ denotes the users covered by D, and $P(D)$ denotes the expected power it consumes, that is,

$$P(D) = c_0 r(D,0)^{\alpha} + \sum_{j=1}^{k} p_j c_j r(D,j)^{\alpha} = \sum_{j=0}^{k} p_j c_j r(D,j)^{\alpha},$$

here $p_0 = 1$. For a set of disks $\mathcal{D}$, we also use $U(\mathcal{D})$ to denote the set of users covered by disks in $\mathcal{D}$; for a solution $\mathcal{F}$, let $P(\mathcal{F})$ denote the expected power it consumes, that is,

$$P(\mathcal{F}) = \sum_{D:D\in\mathcal{F}} P(D) = \sum_{j=0}^{k} \sum_{D:D\in\mathcal{F}} p_j c_j r(D,j)^\alpha.$$

We say a disk $D \in \mathcal{D}$ is tight if it satisfies either

$$\sum_{j=1}^{k} \sum_{u\in U_0(D)\cap U_j(D)} y_{u,j} = c_0 r(D,0)^\alpha, \tag{5}$$

or

$$\sum_{u\in U_j(D)} y_{u,j} = p_j c_j r(D,j)^\alpha. \tag{6}$$

The basic framework of the algorithm is shown as follows:

- **Step1:** In the first step, we raise the dual variables $y_{u,j}$ uniformly for all users in $U_j \setminus U_0$, separately for each j. All disks that become tight (satisfy Eq. (5)) have $x_{D,j}$ set to 1. In this way, we can find a disk set $\mathcal{D}_j^{tight}$, where $\mathcal{D}_j^{tight}$ can cover all users in $U_j \setminus U_0$.
- **Step2:** In the second step, we do a greedy dual-ascent on all uncovered users of U_j. These users are contained in $U_0 \cap U_j$. We also raise the dual variables $y_{u,j}$ for these uncovered users, if a disk is tight (satisfy Eq. (5)), then we select it in the stage one solution by setting $x_{D,0} = 1$, and if it is not tight for $x_{D,0}$ but is tight for $x_{D,j}$, then we select it in the resource solution and set $x_{D,j} = 1$. In this way, we can find a disk set $\mathcal{D}_0^{tight}$ and extend the disk set $\mathcal{D}_j^{tight}$, where $\mathcal{D}_0^{tight} \cup \mathcal{D}_j^{tight}$ can cover all users in U_j.
- **Step3:** Before going into the fourth step, remove the disk $D_{j,last}$ which is the last disk added into $\mathcal{D}_j^{tight}(j = 0, 1, \ldots, k)$. Then, a maximal ρ-relaxed independent set of disks $\mathcal{I}_j$ is computed in a greedy manner.
- **Step4:** Finally, every disk in $\mathcal{I}_j$ has its radius enlarged $1 + \rho$ times. Such set of disks together with $D_{j,last}(j = 0, 1, \ldots, k)$ are the output of the algorithm.

We propose the detailed three-phase primal-dual algorithm in Algorithm 1 below.

Algorithm 1: *Three − phase primal − dual algorithm*

Input: A set U of n users, a disk set $\mathcal{D}$, a power function $P : \mathcal{D} \mapsto \mathbb{R}^+$, k possible scenarios and its probability, a set of users $U_j \subseteq U, j = 0, 1, \ldots, k$, an interger $t \in \{2, 3, \ldots\}$.

Output: A subset of disks $\mathcal{F}$.

1 Initially, let $\mathcal{D}_j^{tight} = \emptyset$ $(j = 0, 1, \ldots, k)$, $y_{u,j} = 0$ $(j = 1, \ldots, k, u \in U_j)$, $X_j = U_j \setminus U_0$ $(j = 1, \ldots, k)$, $R_j^{temp} = \emptyset$ $(j = 1, \ldots, k)$.

2 **for** $j = 1, \ldots, k$ **do**

3   **while** $R_j^{temp} \neq U_j \setminus U_0$ **do**

4   Increase $y_{u,j}$ $(u \in X_j)$ simultaneously until some disks D become tight.

5   **if** $\sum_{u \in U_j(D)} y_{u,j} = p_j c_j r(D, j)^\alpha$ **then**

6          $\mathcal{D}_j^{tight} := \mathcal{D}_j^{tight} \cup \{D\}, x_{D,j} := 1, R_j^{temp} := R_j^{temp} \cup U_j(D)$, $X_j := X_j \setminus U_j(D)$.

7   **end**

8   **end**

9 **end**

10 Set $T_j := U_j \setminus R_j^{temp}$ $(j = 1, \ldots, k)$.

11 **while** $R_j^{temp} \neq U_j, j = 1, \ldots, k$ **do**

12   Increase $y_{u,j}$ $(j = 1, \ldots, k, u \in T_j)$ simultaneously until some disks D become tight.

13   **if** $\sum_{j=1}^{k} \sum_{u \in U_0(D) \cap U_j(D)} y_{u,j} = c_0 r(D, 0)^\alpha$ **then**

14        $\mathcal{D}_0^{tight} := \mathcal{D}_0^{tight} \cup \{D\}, x_{D,0} := 1, R_j^{temp} := R_j^{temp} \cup U_j(D), T_j := T_j \setminus U_j(D)$.

15   **end**

16   **else if** $\sum_{u \in U_j(D)} y_{u,j} = p_j c_j r(D, j)^\alpha$ **then**

17        $\mathcal{D}_j^{tight} := \mathcal{D}_j^{tight} \cup \{D\}, x_{D,j} := 1, R_j^{temp} := R_j^{temp} \cup U_j(D), T_j := T_j \setminus U_j(D)$.

18   **end**

19 **end**

20 **for** $j = 0, \ldots, k$ **do**

21   Let $D_{j,last}$ be the last disk added into $\mathcal{D}_j^{tight}$.

22   Set $l_j := |\mathcal{D}_j^{tight} \setminus \{D_{j,last}\}|, \mathcal{I}_j := \mathcal{D}_j^{tight} \setminus \{D_{j,last}\}, \rho := 2 \sin \frac{\pi}{t}$. Sort the disks in $\mathcal{D}_j^{tight} \setminus \{D_{j,last}\}$ such that $r(D_1, j) \geq r(D_2, j) \geq \cdots r(D_{l_j}, j)$.

23   **for** $l_j' = 1$ to l_j **do**

24   **if** *there exists a disk* $D_{l_j''} \in \mathcal{I}_j$ *with* $l_j'' < l_j'$ *such that* $U(D_{l_j''}) \cap U(D_{l_j'}) \neq \emptyset$ *and* $d(c(D_{l_j''}), c(D_{l_j'})) \leq \rho r(D_{l_j''}, j)$ **then**

25   Delete $D_{l_j'}$ from $\mathcal{I}_j$.

26   **end**

27   **end**

28     $\mathcal{F}_j := \{D(c(D), (1 + \rho)r(D)) | D \in \mathcal{I}_j\} \cup D_{j,last}$.

29 **end**

30 $\mathcal{I} := \bigcup_{j=0}^{k} \mathcal{I}_j, \mathcal{F} := \bigcup_{j=0}^{k} \mathcal{F}_j$. Output $\mathcal{F}$.

Lemma 3. $\mathcal{F}$ *is a feasible solution.*

Proof. Consider a user in scenario $j = 1, \ldots, k$, by definition of the algorithm, it will be either covered by disks in $\mathcal{D}_j^{tight}$, or disks in $\mathcal{D}_0^{tight}$ (or both), so that $\bigcup_{j=0}^{k} \mathcal{D}_j^{tight}$ is a feasible solution for $(U, \mathcal{D}, k)$. Next, we will prove that $\mathcal{F}$ is also a feasible solution. For any user $u \in U(\mathcal{D}_j^{tight}), j = 0, \ldots, k$, if u is not covered by $\mathcal{F}_j$, then it must be covered by a disk $D_{l'_j} \in \mathcal{D}_j^{tight} \setminus \mathcal{F}_j$. Following from the definition of ρ-relaxed independent set, there is a disk $D_{l''_j} \in \mathcal{I}_j$ satisfying that $r(D_{l''_j}, j) \geq r(D_{l'_j}, j)$ and $d(c(D_{l''_j}), c(D_{l'_j})) \leq \rho r(D_{l''_j}, j)$. Therefore, we have

$$
\begin{aligned}
d(u, c(D_{l''_j})) &\leq d(u, c(D_{l'_j})) + d(c(D_{l''_j}), c(D_{l'_j})) \\
&\leq r(D_{l'_j}, j) + \rho r(D_{l''_j}, j) \\
&\leq (1 + \rho) r(D_{l''_j}, j).
\end{aligned}
$$

That implies that u is covered by disk $D(c(D_{l''_j}), (1 + \rho) r(D_{l''_j}, j)) \in \mathcal{F}_j$ contradicting previous assumption. Therefore, $\mathcal{F}$ is a feasible solution.

Lemma 4. *For any integer $t \in \{2, 3, 4, \ldots\}$, the objective value of $\mathcal{F}$ is no more than $2(t-1)(1 + 2\sin\frac{\pi}{t})^\alpha OPT' + P(\mathcal{D}^{max})$.*

Proof.

$$
\begin{aligned}
P(\mathcal{I}) &= \sum_{j=0}^{k} p_j \sum_{D:D\in\mathcal{I}_j} c_j r(D, j)^\alpha \\
&= \sum_{D:D\in\mathcal{I}_0} c_0 r(D, 0)^\alpha + \sum_{j=1}^{k} p_j \sum_{D:D\in\mathcal{I}_j} c_j r(D, j)^\alpha \\
&= \sum_{D:D\in\mathcal{I}_0} \sum_{j=1}^{k} \sum_{u:u\in U_0(D)\cap U_j(D)} y_{u,j} + \sum_{j=1}^{k} \sum_{D:D\in\mathcal{I}_j} \sum_{u:u\in U_j(D)} y_{u,j} \\
&= \sum_{j=1}^{k} \sum_{D:D\in\mathcal{I}_0} \sum_{u:u\in U_0(D)\cap U_j(D)} y_{u,j} + \sum_{j=1}^{k} \sum_{D:D\in\mathcal{I}_j} \sum_{u:u\in U_j(D)} y_{u,j} \\
&\leq \sum_{j=1}^{k} \sum_{u:u\in U(\mathcal{I}_0)} y_{u,j} \cdot |\{D_0|D_0 \in \mathcal{I}_0, u \in U(D_0)\}| \\
&\quad + \sum_{j=1}^{k} \sum_{u:u\in U(\mathcal{I}_j)} y_{u,j} \cdot |\{D_j|D_j \in \mathcal{I}_j, u \in U(D_j)\}| \\
&\leq (t-1) \sum_{j=1}^{k} \sum_{u:u\in U(\mathcal{I}_0)} y_{u,j} + (t-1) \sum_{j=1}^{k} \sum_{u:u\in U(\mathcal{I}_j)} y_{u,j} \\
&\leq (t-1) \sum_{j=1}^{k} \sum_{u:u\in U(\mathcal{D}_0^{tight}\setminus\{D_{0,last}\})} y_{u,j} + (t-1) \sum_{j=1}^{k} \sum_{u:u\in U(\mathcal{D}_j^{tight}\setminus\{D_{j,last}\})} y_{u,j} \\
&\leq 2(t-1) \sum_{j=1}^{k} \sum_{u:u\in U_j} y_{u,j} \\
&\leq 2(t-1)OPT'' \\
&\leq 2(t-1)OPT',
\end{aligned}
$$

where OPT'' is the optimal value of the dual program. The third equation follows from Eq. (5) and (6), the second inequation follows from Lemma 2 and $\mathcal{I}_j$ is a ρ-relaxed independent set, and the third inequation follows from $\mathcal{I}_j \subseteq \mathcal{D}_j^{tight} \setminus \{D_{j,last}\}, j = 0, 1, \ldots, k$ and the last inequation follows from the well-known strong duality theorem. From the inequations above, we have

$$P(\mathcal{F}) = (1+\rho)^\alpha P(\mathcal{I}) + \sum_{j=0}^{k} p_j c_j r(D_{j,last}, j)^\alpha$$

$$\leq 2(t-1)(1+\rho)^\alpha OPT' + \sum_{j=0}^{k} p_j c_j r(D_{j,last}, j)^\alpha$$

$$\leq 2(t-1)(1+2\sin\frac{\pi}{t})^\alpha OPT' + P(\mathcal{D}^{max}).$$

The first equality follows from $\mathcal{F}_j = \{D(c(D), (1+\rho)r(D, j)) | D \in \mathcal{I}_j\} \cup D_{j,last}$, the second inequality follows from $r(D_{j,last}, j) \leq r(D_{j,max}, j), \mathcal{D}_{max} = \bigcup_{j=0}^{k} D_{j,max}$. Therefore, the lemma holds.

Theorem 1. *There is an $O(\alpha)$-approximation algorithm for the MinSPC problem.*

Proof.

$$P(\mathcal{F} \cup \mathcal{D}_{max}) = P(\mathcal{F}) + P(\mathcal{D}_{max})$$

$$\leq 2(t-1)(1+2\sin\frac{\pi}{t})^\alpha OPT' + 2P(\mathcal{D}^{max})$$

$$\leq 2(t-1)(1+2\sin\frac{\pi}{t})^\alpha(OPT' + P(\mathcal{D}^{max}))$$

$$= 2(t-1)(1+2\sin\frac{\pi}{t})^\alpha OPT,$$

where the first inequality follows from Lemma 4, and the second inequality follows from $\alpha \geq 1, t \in \{2, 3, 4, \ldots\}$, and the last equality follows from Lemma 1. Furthermore, as in the analysis in [8], the approximation of Algorithm 1 is $O(\alpha)$.

4   Conclusions

In this paper, we introduce the stochastic minimum power cover problem, which generalizes the minimum power cover problem and the stochastic minimum set cover problem. We prove an $O(\alpha)$-approximation algorithm for this problem, which can be implemented in polynomial time.

For the stochastic optimization problems, we now consider only the two-stage finite-scenario version for the stochastic power cover problem. In the future, there is substantial potential for us to design some algorithms for this problem with multi-stage, exponential scenarios and more constraints which comes with great challenges.

References

1. Charikar, M., Panigrahy, R.: Clustering to minimize the sum of cluster diameters. J. Comput. Syst. Sci. **68**(2), 417–441 (2004)
2. Bilò, V., Caragiannis, I., Kaklamanis, C., Kanellopoulos, P.: Geometric clustering to minimize the sum of cluster sizes. In: Brodal, G.S., Leonardi, S. (eds.) ESA 2005. LNCS, vol. 3669, pp. 460–471. Springer, Heidelberg (2005). https://doi.org/10.1007/11561071_42
3. Ravi, R., Sinha, A.: Hedging uncertainty: approximation algorithms for stochastic optimization problems. Math. Program. **108**(1), 97–114 (2006)
4. Li, J., Liu, Y.: Approximation algorithms for stochastic combinatorial optimization problems. J. Oper. Res. Soc. China **4**(1), 1–47 (2016)
5. Parthasarathy, S.: Adaptive greedy algorithms for stochastic set cover problems. arXiv preprint arXiv:1803.07639 (2018)
6. Sun, J., Sheng, H., Sun, Y., et al.: Approximation algorithms for stochastic set cover and single sink rent-or-buy with submodular penalty. J. Comb. Optim. **44**(4), 2626–2641 (2022)
7. Liu, X., Li, W., Xie, R.: A primal-dual approximation algorithm for the k-prize-collecting minimum power cover problem. Optim. Lett. **16**(8), 2373–2385 (2022)
8. Dai, H., Deng, B., Li, W., Liu, X.: A note on the minimum power partial cover problem on the plane. J. Comb. Optim. **44**(2), 970–978 (2022)
9. Liu, X., Li, W., Dai, H.: Approximation algorithms for the minimum power cover problem with submodular/linear penalties. Theoret. Comput. Sci. **923**, 256–270 (2022)
10. Dai, H.: An improved approximation algorithm for the minimum power cover problem with submodular penalty. Computation **10**(10), 189 (2022)
11. Liu, X., Dai, H., Li, S., Li, W.: The k-prize-collecting minimum power cover problem with submodular penalties on a plane. Sci. Sin. Inform **52**(6), 947–959 (2022)
12. Zhang, Q., Li, W., Su, Q., Zhang, X.: A primal-dual-based power control approach for capacitated edge servers. Sensors **22**(19), 7582 (2022)
13. Liu, X., Li, W.: Combinatorial approximation algorithms for the submodular multi-cut problem in trees with submodular penalties. J. Comb. Optim. **44**(3), 1964–1976 (2020)
14. Liu, X., Li, W., Yang, J.: A primal-dual approximation algorithm for the k-prize-collecting minimum vertex cover problem with submodular penalties. Front. Comp. Sci. **17**(3), 1–8 (2023)
15. Kong, N., Schaefer, A.J.: A factor 12 approximation algorithm for two-stage stochastic matching problems. Eur. J. Oper. Res. **172**(3), 740–746 (2006)
16. Li, M., Ran, Y., Zhang, Z.: A primal-dual algorithm for the minimum power partial cover problem. J. Combi. Optim. **44**(3), 1913–1923 (2020)
17. Louveaux, F.V., Peeters, D.: A dual-based procedure for stochastic facility location. Oper. Res. **40**(3), 564–573 (1992)
18. Takazawa, Y.: Approximation algorithm for the stochastic prize-collecting set multicover problem. Oper. Res. Lett. **50**(2), 224–228 (2022)
19. Le Cam, L.: An approximation theorem for the poisson binomial distribution. Pac. J. Math. **10**(4), 1181–1197 (1960)
20. Alt, H., Arkin, E M, Brönnimann H, et al. Minimum-cost coverage of point sets by disks. In: Proceedings of the Twenty-Second Annual Symposium on Computational Geometry, pp. 449–458 (2006)

21. Dai, H., Li, W., Liu, X.: An approximation algorithm for the h-prize-collecting power cover problem. In: Li, M., Sun, X. (eds.) Frontiers of Algorithmic Wisdom. IJTCS-FAW 2022. LNCS, vol. 13461, pp. 89–98. Springer, Cham (2022). https://doi.org/10.1007/978-3-031-20796-9_7

22. Dai, H.: An Approximation Algorithm for the Minimum Soft Capacitated Disk Multi-coverage Problem. In: 40th National Conference of Theoretical Computer Science, pp. 96–104. Springer, Changchun (2022)

23. Zhang, Q., Li, W., Su, Q., Zhang, X.: A local-ratio-based power control approach for capacitated access points in mobile edge computing. In: Proceedings of the 6th International Conference on High Performance Compilation, Computing and Communications, pp. 175–182 (2022)

24. Gupta, A., Pál, M., Ravi, R., Sinha, A.: Boosted sampling: approximation algorithms for stochastic optimization. In: Proceedings of the Thirty-Sixth Annual ACM Symposium on Theory of Computing, pp. 417–426 (2004)

25. Charikar, M., Chekuri, C., Pal, M.: Sampling bounds for stochastic optimization. In: 8th International Workshop on Approximation Algorithms for Combinatorial Optimization Problems, pp. 257–269. Springer, Berkeley (2005)

26. Feldman, M., Svensson, O., Zenklusen R.: Online contention resolution schemes. In: Proceedings of the twenty-seventh annual ACM-SIAM symposium on Discrete algorithms, pp. 1014–1033 (2016)

ϵ-Approximate Bisimulations for Nondeterministic Fuzzy Kripke Structures

Yucheng Liu$^{(\boxtimes)}$

College of Information Engineering, Yangzhou University, Yangzhou 225127, China
cqlyc1117@163.com

Abstract. Bisimulation is a famous behavioral equivalence relation for discrete event systems and has developed rapidly in model checking. Inspired by the bisimulations theory of nondeterministic fuzzy Kripke structures($NFKSs$) proposed by Deng [26], in this paper, we define the concept of ϵ-approximate bisimulations for $NFKSs$. Next, we introduce the notion of the set of traces. On above basis, we propose a new mapping which is used to compare the behaviors of two $NFKSs$ under ϵ-approximate bisimulation. Meanwhile, we investigate the property of finite paths. This property lays the groundwork for exploring the behaviors of two $NFKSs$ under the ϵ-approximate bisimulation. Fortunately, we demonstrate that if two $NFKSs$ equipped with an ϵ-approximate bisimulation between them, then their behaviors are ϵ-approximate each other. Furthermore, we discover that there might not exist the greatest ϵ-approximate bisimulation for a given $NFKS$. At last, in order to complish approximate minimization operation for a given $NFKS$ under ϵ-approximate bisimulation, we elaborate three algorithms to generate all maximal ϵ-approximate bisimulations. Surprisingly, with help of the maximal ϵ-approximate bisimulations, the quotient $NFKSs$ obtained through the Definition 24 not only have minimum number of states, but also the behavior of quotient $NFKS$ differs by ϵ from the behavior of initial $NFKS$.

Keywords: nondeterministic fuzzy Kripke structure $\cdot$ ϵ-approximate bisimulations $\cdot$ finite paths and traces $\cdot$ algorithm for constructing quotient $NFKSs$

1 Introduction

In daily life, people's lives are influenced by delicated computers and software systems. With the continuous development of technology, a common phenomenon is that the increasing complexity of systems will lead to an upward trend in the number of defects. Therefore, the main challenge in the field of computer science is to provide formal technologies and tools that can effectively detect the correctness of the system's operation despite their intricacy. In the past twenty years, the most attractive method for verifying computer system attributes is model checking. After decades of research and accumulation, model checking has produced many verification techniques [1–7].

© The Author(s), under exclusive license to Springer Nature Singapore Pte Ltd. 2024
Z. Cai et al. (Eds.): NCTCS 2023, CCIS 1944, pp. 107–132, 2024.
https://doi.org/10.1007/978-981-99-7743-7_7

It is worth noting that when modeling actual systems, there are systems where the choice of the successor state at a certain state is based on nondeterministic fuzzy choices. As a consequence, Pan and Fan [27] proposed nondeterministic fuzzy Kripke structure($NFKS$), which abstracts a system into five common parts: states, operations, atomic propositions, transition functions and label functions. However, the actual models established by the five common parts vary from person to person, and there is the same situation in automata theories. When modeling a discrete event system by nondeterministic fuzzy automata, it is generally possible to build different models for the same system. In order to compare these models, a straightfoword method is to employ the concept of fuzzy language equivalence. However, although this equivalence has been widely used to solve problems, it is sometimes considered too rough. With rapid development of formal verification, bisimulation be supposed to be one of the accurate mean to solve this difficulty. Here, we enumerate some works on bisimulations for readers of interest [8,10,12–18]. Unofficially, bisimulation is a binary relation between two discrete event systems, which describes systems that behave in the same way. In other words, one system simulates the other in any steps and vice versa. This step-by-step calculation leads to its becoming one of core methods in process calculation [9,11]. As mentioned above, although $NFKS$ is regarded as kind of satisfactory mathematical model for building nondeterministic fuzzy discrete event systems, how to solve the state explosion by simplifying the model structures is still one of focuses of research on nondeterministic fuzzy model checking. In model checking theory, bisimulations can reduce the state of a structure by aggregating equivalent states, so that the quotient structure has equivalent behavior and fewer states. Based on this, Deng [26] extends ideas of bisimulations for $NFKS$. As we thought, bisimulations ensure the complete fragments of $NFKS$, even if the number of states and nondeterministic fuzzy transition functions are different, the quotient $NFKS$ with fewer states also has same behavior.

Nevertheless, bisimulations have limitations in comparing two system with different behaviors. Most of the time, we often encounter two systems that have different behaviors, but there is a situation where although two systems behave differently, their behaviors are similar. In order to describe this kind of approximate bisimulation, Ying and Martin [24] introduced the concept of λ-bisimulation as the criteria to measure this similarity. With the development of the approximate bisimulations, experts renamed it as ϵ-bisimulation [25].

Based on the above description, this paper first introduces the ϵ-approximate bisimulations for $NFKSs$. In fact, a crucial theoretical idea to consider in ϵ-approximate bisimulation is whether the two systems behave similarly. As a result, referring to paper [28,30], we define the new mapping which is used to describe the behavior of $NFKSs$ in Definition 16. Next, we discussed the relationship between the finite paths of two $NFKSs$ under the ϵ-approximate bisimulations in Theorem 17. As we all known, when constructing a $NFKS$ to model a nondeterministic fuzzy discrete event system, the state explosion of $NFKS$ becomes the main problem that weakens the performance of the system. In many cases, it is enough to construct a $NFKS$ with fewer states whose behavior approximates the behavior of initial $NFKS$. For purpose of reducing the number of states of system and constructing required $NFKS$, it is necessary for us to study the method of constructing quotient $NFKS$. However, as we know, there exists greatest bisimulation for a $NFKS$. Contrary to this fact, we give an example to show that might not exist the greatest ε-approximate bisimulation for a $NFKS$ in Example 21. Under the circumstances, with reference to the paper [19–23,29,31], we design a series of algorithms to build all maximal ε-approximate bisimulations for a $NFKS$ and take advantage of these relations to construct quotient $NFKS$.

The paper structure is organized in the following ways. In the Sect. 2, we review some basic notions. In the Sect. 3, we define the ε-approximate bisimulations for $NFKSs$(see Definition 8 and Definition 10), and prove that the behavior of two $NFKSs$ are also ε-approximate each other under the ε-approximate bisimulation(see Theorem 20). Then we discuss the relationship between the finite paths of two $NFKSs$ under the ε-approximate bisimulation(see Theorem 17). In the Sect. 4, based on the three conditions of ε-approximate bisimulation in Definition 10, all maximal ε-approximate bisimulations can be obtained through three algorithms, and on this basis, the quotient $NKFS$ can be constructed in Definition 24. In addition, whether the behaviors of quotient $NFKS$ obtained with help of maximal ε-approximate bisimulations are ε-approximate to initial $NFKS$ is also discussed.

2   Preliminaries

At first, we mention some operation symbols for use in the following. The mathematical symbol $\bigvee$ and $\bigwedge$ are interpreted as the supremum and the infimum of the subset contained in $[0,1]$.

Suppose A is a non-empty set, A fuzzy subset of A is a mapping $f : A \longrightarrow [0,1]$. We use $\mathcal{F}(A)$ to denote the set of all fuzzy subsets of A that is $\mathcal{F}(A) = \{f|f : A \to [0,1]\}$. If $f(a) \in \{0,1\}$ for any $a \in A$, then the fuzzy subset f degrades into the crisp one. The support set for a fuzzy subset of f is defined as follows:

$$supp(f) = \{a \in A|f(a) > 0\} \tag{1}$$

Whenever $supp(f)$ is finite, for example, $supp(f) = \{a_1, a_2, \ldots, a_n\}$, then we denote f in Zadeh's notation as

$$f = \frac{f(a_1)}{a_1} + \frac{f(a_2)}{a_2} + \cdots + \frac{f(a_n)}{a_n} \tag{2}$$

Definition 1 *(see [27]). A nondeterministic fuzzy Kripke structure(NFKS) $T = (S, Act, \delta, AP, L)$ is a 5-tuple, where*

1) S represents a finite number of nonempty state set,
2) Act is a set of actions,
3) $\delta : S \times Act \to \mathcal{F}(S)$ is nondeterministic fuzzy transition function,

4) AP represents a set of finite atomic propositions,
5) $L : S \longrightarrow \mathcal{F}(AP)$ *is fuzzy label function.*

For a nondeterministic fuzzy transition function $\delta : S \times Act \to \mathcal{F}(S)$, $\delta(s,c)(s')$ represents a membership value of the transition that state s to state s' through action c. $L(s)(p)$ shows a membership value that label p belongs to state s.

On the basis, we will introduce the concept of paths in $NFKSs$.

Definition 2 *(see [27,32]). Let* $T = (S, Act, \delta, AP, L)$ *be a NFKS. A finite path* θ *of NFKS starting from s is defined as follows:*

$$\theta = s_0 a_0 s_1 a_1 \ldots s_n \tag{3}$$

where $s_0 = s$, $n \in \mathbb{N}$, $s_n \in S$, $a_n \in Act$.

Definition 3 *(see [27,32]). Let* $T = (S, Act, \delta, AP, L)$ *be a NFKS. An infinite path* ϑ *of NFKS starting from s is defined as follows:*

$$\vartheta = s_0 a_0 s_1 a_1 s_2 \ldots \tag{4}$$

where $s_0 = s$, $s_0, s_1, s_2 \cdots \in S$, $a_0, a_1, \cdots \in Act$.

Let $T = (S, Act, \delta, AP, L)$ be a $NFKS$. For $s \in S$, $Paths(T,s)$ represents the set of all paths starting from s in T, and $Paths(T)$ represents the set of all paths in T, where $Paths(T) = \bigcup_{s \in S} Paths(T,s)$. Specifically, for the set of finite paths starting from s in T, we denote it as $Paths_{fin}(T,s)$, where $s \in S$. Similarly, for the set of all finite paths in T, we denote it as $Paths_{fin}(T)$, where $Paths_{fin}(T) = \bigcup_{s \in S} Paths_{fin}(T,s)$.

Next, we will introduce the concept of bisimulations for $NFKSs$.

Definition 4 *(see [26]). Let* $T_i = (S_i, Act, \delta_i, AP, L_i)$, $i = 1, 2$ *be two NFKSs. A bisimulation for* (T_1, T_2) *is a binary relation* $R_\mu \subseteq S_1 \times S_2$: $\forall (s_1, s_2) \in R_\mu$ *satisfies*

$$L_1(s_1)(p) = L_2(s_2)(p), \tag{5}$$
$$\{\forall s_1' | \delta_1(s_1, c)(s_1') = e\} \Rightarrow \{\exists s_2' | \delta_2(s_2, c)(s_2') = e \wedge R_\mu(s_1', s_2')\}, \tag{6}$$
$$\{\forall s_2' | \delta_2(s_2, c)(s_2') = e\} \Rightarrow \{\exists s_1' | \delta_1(s_1, c)(s_1') = e \wedge R_\mu(s_1', s_2')\}. \tag{7}$$

where $s_1' \in S_1, s_2' \in S_2, c \in Act, p \in AP, e \in [0,1]$. T_1 *is bisimular to* T_2 *if there exists a bisimulation* R_μ *for* (T_1, T_2), *denoted* $T_1 \sim_{R_\mu} T_2$.

Definition 5 *(see [26]). Let* $T = (S, Act, \delta, AP, L)$ *be a NFKS. A bisimulation for T is a equivalence relation* $R_\zeta \subseteq S \times S$: $\forall (s_1, s_2) \in R_\zeta$ *satisfies*

$$L(s_1)(p) = L(s_2)(p), \tag{8}$$
$$\{\forall s_1' | \delta(s_1, c)(s_1') = e\} \Rightarrow \{\exists s_2' | \delta(s_2, c)(s_2') = e \wedge R_\zeta(s_1', s_2')\}, \tag{9}$$
$$\{\forall s_2' | \delta(s_2, c)(s_2') = e\} \Rightarrow \{\exists s_1' | \delta(s_1, c)(s_1') = e \wedge R_\zeta(s_1', s_2')\}. \tag{10}$$

where $s'_1, s'_2 \in S, c \in Act, p \in AP, e \in [0,1]$. s_1 is bisimular to s_2 if there exists equivalence relation R_ζ in T, and $(s_1, s_2) \in R_\zeta$ satisfies the above conditions, which is denoted as $s_1 \sim_{R_\zeta} s_2$.

As mentioned in the introduction, the problem of state explosion in the systems is an important issue. According to [26], we know that bisimulations satisfy reflexivity, symmetry, and transitivity. Taking advantage of bisimulation, we aggregate the equivalent states to acquire the quotient $NFKSs$, which becomes a new $NFKSs$ with fewer states.

In the last definition of the preliminaries, we will introduce quotient calculation, which is used to reduce the number of states in the system.

Definition 6 *(see* [26, 32]*). Let* $T = (S, Act, \delta, AP, L)$ *be a NFKS. R_ζ is a bisimulation for T. The quotient NFKS with respect to T is defined by:* $T/_{R_\zeta} = (S/_{R_\zeta}, Act, \delta_{R_\zeta}, AP, L_{R_\zeta})$,

$$S/_{R_\zeta} = \{[s]_{R_\zeta} | s \in S\}, \text{where } [s]_{R_\zeta} = \{s' \in S | (s, s') \in R_\zeta\}, \tag{11}$$

$$\delta_{R_\zeta}([s_1]_{R_\zeta}, c)([s'_1]_{R_\zeta}) = \delta(t_1, c)(t'_1), \text{where } t_1 \in [s_1]_{R_\zeta}, t'_1 \in [s'_1]_{R_\zeta}, \tag{12}$$

$$L_{R_\zeta}([s]_{R_\zeta})(p) = L(t)(p), \text{where } p \in AP, t \in [s]_{R_\zeta}. \tag{13}$$

Fortunately, according to the bisimulation R_ζ, the quotient $NFKS$ obtained by the quotient calculation not only has fewer states, but also has bisimulation with the initial $NFKS$. Here is an example to explain the generation process of quotient $NFKS$.

Example 7. Given a $NFKS$ $T = (S, Act, \delta, AP, L)$, where $S = \{s_0, s_1, s_2, s_3\}$, $Act = \{a, b\}$, $AP = \{p, q\}$. T is depicted in Fig. 1.

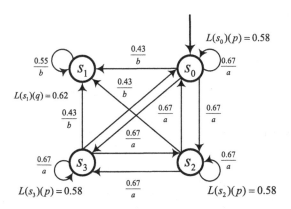

Fig. 1. $NFKS$ T

$R_\zeta = \{(s_0, s_0), (s_1, s_1), (s_2, s_2), (s_3, s_3), (s_0, s_2), (s_2, s_0), (s_2, s_3), (s_3, s_2), (s_0, s_3),$ $(s_3, s_0)\}$

is bisimulation for T, where

$$\delta(s_0, b)(s_1) = 0.43, \delta(s_2, b)(s_1) = 0.43, \delta(s_3, b)(s_1) = 0.43,$$
$$\delta(s_0, a)(s_2) = 0.67, \delta(s_2, a)(s_0) = 0.67, \delta(s_2, a)(s_3) = 0.67,$$
$$\delta(s_3, a)(s_2) = 0.67, \delta(s_0, a)(s_3) = 0.67, \delta(s_3, a)(s_0) = 0.67,$$
$$\delta(s_1, b)(s_1) = 0.55, \delta(s_0, a)(s_0) = 0.67, \delta(s_2, a)(s_2) = 0.67,$$
$$\delta(s_3, a)(s_3) = 0.67$$

According Definition 6, we can obtain the aggregated state sets, aggregated nondeterministic fuzzy transition functions and the aggregated fuzzy label functions as follows:

$$S/_{R_\varsigma} = \{[s_1]_{R_\varsigma}, [s_0]_{R_\varsigma}\}, \quad \text{where } [s_1]_{R_\varsigma} = \{s_1\}, [s_0]_{R_\varsigma} = \{s_0, s_2, s_3\}$$
$$\delta_{R_\varsigma}([s_0]_{R_\varsigma}, b)([s_1]_{R_\varsigma}) = 0.43, \delta_{R_\varsigma}([s_1]_{R_\varsigma}, b)([s_1]_{R_\varsigma}) = 0.55,$$
$$\delta_{R_\varsigma}([s_0]_{R_\varsigma}, a)([s_0]_{R_\varsigma}) = 0.67, L_{R_\varsigma}([s_0]_{R_\varsigma})(p) = 0.58,$$
$$L_{R_\varsigma}([s_1]_{R_\varsigma})(q) = 0.62$$

$NFKS \ T/_{R_\varsigma}$ is shown in the following Fig. 2 .

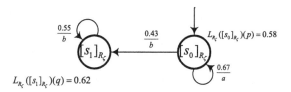

Fig. 2. $NFKS \ T/_{R_\varsigma}$

A bisimulation for $(T, T/_{R_\varsigma})$ is a binary relation $R_\mu \subseteq S \times S/_{R_\varsigma}$:

$$R_\mu = \{(s_0, [s_0]_{R_\varsigma}), (s_2, [s_0]_{R_\varsigma}), (s_3, [s_0]_{R_\varsigma}), (s_1, [s_1]_{R_\varsigma})\}$$

3 ϵ-Approximate Bisimulations for $NFKSs$

In this section, we first prepare to define the concept of ϵ-approximate bisimulations for $NFKSs$ in Definition 8 and Definition 10. Next, we introduce the definition of the sets of traces in Definition 15. We then use this definition to construct the mapping FV_T which expresses the behaviors of $NFKSs$ in Definition 16. In Theorem 20, we exploit ϵ-approximate bisimulations to study relationship between the behaviors of two $NFKSs$.

Now, we introduce ϵ-approximate bisimulations for $NFKSs$.

In the following, if not noted otherwise, we always assume that $\epsilon \in [0, 1]$.

Definition 8. *Let $T_i = (S_i, Act, \delta_i, AP, L_i)$, $i = 1, 2$, be two NFKSs. An ϵ-approximate bisimulation for (T_1, T_2) is a binary relation $R_\mu^\epsilon \subseteq S_1 \times S_2$ satisfying: for any $(s_1, s_2) \in R_\mu^\epsilon$*

$$|L_1(s_1)(p) - L_2(s_2)(p)| \leq \epsilon,$$
$$\{\forall s_1' | \delta_1(s_1, c)(s_1') = e_1\} \Rightarrow \{\exists s_2' | \delta_2(s_2, c)(s_2') = e_2 \wedge |e_1 - e_2| \leq \epsilon \wedge R_\mu^\epsilon(s_1', s_2')\},$$
$$\{\forall s_2' | \delta_2(s_2, c)(s_2') = e_3\} \Rightarrow \{\exists s_1' | \delta_1(s_1, c)(s_1') = e_4 \wedge |e_3 - e_4| \leq \epsilon \wedge R_\mu^\epsilon(s_1', s_2')\}.$$

where $s_1' \in S_1$, $s_2' \in S_2$, $c \in Act$, $p \in AP$, $j = 1,2,3,4$, $e_j \in [0,1]$. T_1 is ϵ-approximate bisimular to T_2 if there exists an ϵ-approximate bisimulation R_μ^ϵ for (T_1, T_2), denoted $T_1 \sim_{R_\mu^\epsilon} T_2$.

Example 9. We give an example to illustrate the ϵ-approximate bisimulation for (T_1, T_2) in Fig. 3, where $S_1 = \{h_0, h_1, h_2, h_3, h_4, h_5, h_6\}$, $S_2 = \{t_0, t_1, t_2, t_3\}$, $AP = \{slot, select, beer, juice\}$, $Act = \{insert, select\_juice, select\_beer, get\}$.

$$\delta_1(h_0, insert)(h_1) = 0.92, \delta_1(h_0, insert)(h_2) = 0.88,$$
$$\delta_1(h_1, select\_beer)(h_3) = 0.56, \delta_1(h_2, select\_beer)(h_5) = 0.58,$$
$$\delta_1(h_1, select\_juice)(h_4) = 0.62, \delta_1(h_2, select\_juice)(h_6) = 0.64,$$
$$\delta_1(h_3, get)(h_3) = 0.81, \delta_1(h_4, get)(h_4) = 0.71, \delta_1(h_5, get)(h_5) = 0.83,$$
$$\delta_1(h_6, get)(h_6) = 0.73, \delta_2(t_0, insert)(t_1) = 0.89,$$
$$\delta_2(t_1, select\_beer)(t_2) = 0.55, \delta_2(t_1, select\_juice)(t_3) = 0.65,$$
$$\delta_2(t_2, get)(t_2) = 0.82, \delta_2(t_3, get)(t_3) = 0.72$$

The small positive real number is chosen as $\epsilon = 0.04$.

$$R_\mu^\epsilon = \{(h_0, t_0), (h_1, t_1), (h_2, t_1), (h_3, t_2), (h_4, t_3), (h_5, t_2), (h_6, t_3)\}$$

is an ϵ-approximate bisimulation for (T_1, T_2).

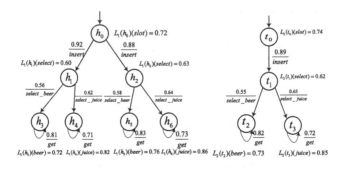

Fig. 3. *NFKS* T_1(left) and *NFKS* T_2(right)

Definition 10. *Let* $T = (S, Act, \delta, AP, L)$ *be a NFKS. An ϵ-approximate bisimulation for T is an equivalence relation $R_\zeta^\epsilon \subseteq S \times S$ satisfying: for any* $(s_1, s_2) \in R_\zeta^\epsilon$

$$|L(s_1)(p) - L(s_2)(p)| \leq \epsilon,$$
$$\{\forall s_1' | \delta(s_1, c)(s_1') = e_1\} \Rightarrow \{\exists s_2' | \delta(s_2, c)(s_2') = e_2 \wedge |e_1 - e_2| \leq \epsilon \wedge R_\zeta^\epsilon(s_1', s_2')\},$$
$$\{\forall s_2' | \delta(s_2, c)(s_2') = e_3\} \Rightarrow \{\exists s_1' | \delta(s_1, c)(s_1') = e_4 \wedge |e_3 - e_4| \leq \epsilon \wedge R_\zeta^\epsilon(s_1', s_2')\}.$$

where $s_1', s_2' \in S$, $p \in AP$, $j = 1, 2, 3, 4$, $e_j \in [0, 1]$. s_1 *is ϵ-approximate bisimular to s_2 if there exists an ϵ-approximate bisimulation R_ζ^ϵ for T, and $(s_1, s_2) \in R_\zeta^\epsilon$, denoted* $s_1 \sim_{R_\zeta^\epsilon} s_2$.

Furthermore, the equivalence relation in Definition 10 is also a binary relation.

Example 11. Following the logic above, We give an example to illustrate the ϵ-approximate bisimulation for T in Fig. 4, where $S = \{t_1, t_2, t_3, t_4, t_5, t_6, t_7, t_8, t_9, t_{10}, t_{11}\}$, $AP = \{a, b, c, d, e\}$, $Act = \{a_1, a_2, a_3\}$.

$$\delta(t_1, a_1)(t_2) = 0.48, \delta(t_1, a_1)(t_3) = 0.5,$$
$$\delta(t_2, a_2)(t_4) = 0.2, \delta(t_3, a_2)(t_5) = 0.17,$$
$$\delta(t_4, a_3)(t_6) = 0.55, \delta(t_5, a_3)(t_{10}) = 0.57,$$
$$\delta(t_4, a_3)(t_7) = 0.61, \delta(t_5, a_3)(t_{11}) = 0.63,$$
$$\delta(t_2, a_2)(t_8) = 0.48, \delta(t_3, a_2)(t_9) = 0.45$$

The small positive real number is chosen as $\epsilon = 0.04$.

$$R_\zeta^\epsilon = \{(t_1, t_1), (t_2, t_2), (t_3, t_3), (t_4, t_4), (t_5, t_5), (t_6, t_6), (t_7, t_7), (t_8, t_8),$$
$$(t_9, t_9), (t_{10}, t_{10}), (t_{11}, t_{11}), (t_2, t_3), (t_3, t_2), (t_4, t_5), (t_5, t_4), (t_6, t_{10}),$$
$$(t_{10}, t_6), (t_7, t_{11}), (t_{11}, t_7), (t_8, t_9), (t_9, t_8)\}$$

is an ϵ-approximate bisimulation for T.

Definition 12. *Let $T = (S, Act, \delta, AP, L)$ be a NFKS. Based on the finite path $\theta = s_0 a_0 s_1 a_1 s_2 \ldots s_n$, we introduce the trace of θ as follows:*

$$trace(\theta) = L(s_0) a_0 L(s_1) a_1 L(s_2) \ldots L(s_n) \tag{14}$$

where $\theta \in Paths_{fin}(T)$, $n \in \mathbb{N}$, $s_n \in S$, $a_n \in Act$.

Definition 13. *Let $T = (S, Act, \delta, AP, L)$ be a NFKS. Based on the infinite path $\vartheta = s_0 a_0 s_1 a_1 s_2 \ldots$, we introduce the trace of ϑ as follows:*

$$trace(\vartheta) = L(s_0) a_0 L(s_1) a_1 L(s_2) \ldots \tag{15}$$

where $\vartheta \in Paths(T)$, $s_0, s_1, \cdots \in S$, $a_0, a_1 \cdots \in Act$.

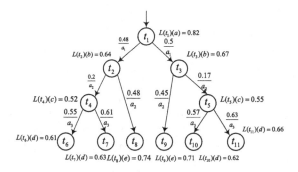

Fig. 4. *NFKS T*

Definition 14. *Let $T = (S, Act, \delta, AP, L)$ be a NFKS. We define that the set of traces of all finite paths starting with s in T is called $trace(Paths_{fin}(T, s))$.*

Definition 15. *Let $T = (S, Act, \delta, AP, L)$ be a NFKS. For convenience, the set of traces of finite paths starting from s in T is defined as follows:*

$$Traces(s) = trace(Paths_{fin}(T, s)) \tag{16}$$

where $s \in S$.

Definition 16. *Given $T = (S, Act, \delta, AP, L)$ as a NFKS. For any $s_0 \in S$, we define the mapping $FV_T : Traces(s_0) \longrightarrow [0, 1]$, for any $\theta = s_0 a_0 s_1 a_1 s_2 \ldots s_n \in Paths_{fin}(T, s_0)$, $trace(\theta) \in Traces(s_0)$,*

$$FV_T(trace(\theta))$$

$$= \bigvee_{p_0, p_1, \cdots \in AP} \left\{ L(s_0)(p_0) \wedge \left\{ \bigwedge_{i=0}^{n-1} [\delta(s_i, a_i)(s_{i+1}) \wedge L(s_{i+1})(p_{i+1})] \right\} \right\}$$

where $i \in \mathbb{N}$, $s_i \in S$, $a_i \in Act$, $p_i \in AP$.

Theorem 17. *Let $T_i = (S_i, Act, \delta_i, AP, L_i)$, $i = 1, 2$, be two NFKSs, R_μ^ϵ is an ϵ-approximate bisimulation for (T_1, T_2). For each finite path $\theta_1 = s_{0,1}a_{0,1} \ldots s_{n,1} \in Paths_{fin}(T_1, s_{0,1})$ there exists a path $\theta_2 = s_{0,2}a_{0,2} \ldots s_{n,2} \in Paths_{fin}(T_2, s_{0,2})$, where $(s_{n,1}, s_{n,2}) \in R_\mu^\epsilon$, $n \in \mathbb{N}$. Meanwhile, θ_1 and θ_2 have same length.*

Proof. Let $\theta_1 = s_{0,1}a_{0,1}s_{1,1}a_{1,1}s_{2,1} \ldots s_{n,1} \in Paths_{fin}(T_1, s_{0,1})$ be a finite path starting from $s_{0,1}$ in T_1. Correspondingly, we define $\theta_2 = s_{0,2}a_{0,2}s_{1,2} \ldots s_{n,2} \in Paths_{fin}(T_2, s_{0,2})$ be a finite path starting from $s_{0,2}$ in T_2, where the transitions $s_{i,1}a_{i,1}s_{i+1,1}$ are matched by transition $s_{i,2}a_{i,2}s_{i+1,2}$ such that $(s_{i+1,1}, s_{i+1,2}) \in R_\mu^\epsilon$, $i \in \mathbb{N}$, $0 \leqslant i \leqslant n - 1$. This is done by induction on i, see Fig. 5.

(1) Induction of foundation: $i = 0$:
    When $s_{0,1}$ is the terminal state, we can conclude that $s_{0,2}$ must also be the terminal state by $(s_{0,1}, s_{0,2}) \in R_\mu^\epsilon$. Therefore, $\theta_1 = s_{0,1}$ and $\theta_2 = s_{0,2}$

are finite paths in T_1 and T_2 respectively. Otherwise, if $s_{0,1}$ is not terminal state, the transition $s_{0,1}a_{0,1}s_{1,1}$ can match by a transition $s_{0,2}a_{0,2}s_{1,2}$ such that $(s_{1,1}, s_{1,2}) \in R_{\mu}^{\epsilon}$. This yields $\theta_1 = s_{0,1}a_{0,1}s_{1,1}$ and $\theta_2 = s_{0,2}a_{0,2}s_{1,2}$ in T_1 and T_2 respectively.

(2) Step of inclusion: $0 \leqslant i \leqslant n - 1$:

If θ_1 has length i, then $\theta_1 = s_{0,1}a_{0,1}s_{1,1} \ldots s_{i,1} \in Paths_{fin}(T_1, s_{0,1})$ is finite path and $s_{i,1}$ is a terminal state. By the ϵ-approximate bisimulation R_{μ}^{ϵ}, there is a state $s_{i,2} \in S_2$ and $s_{i,2}$ is a terminal state. Therefore, $\theta_2 = s_{0,2}a_{0,2}s_{1,2} \ldots s_{i,2} \in Paths_{fin}(T_2, s_{0,2})$ be a finite path starting from $s_{0,2}$ in T_2, and θ_2 matches θ_1.

Assume that $s_{i,1}$ is not terminal state. The transition $s_{i,1}a_{i,1}s_{i+1,1}$ can match by a transition $s_{i,2}a_{i,2}s_{i+1,2}$ such that $(s_{i+1,1}, s_{i+1,2}) \in R_{\mu}^{\epsilon}$. This yields $\theta_1 = s_{0,1}a_{0,1}s_{1,1} \ldots s_{i+1,1}$ and $\theta_2 = s_{0,2}a_{0,2}s_{1,2} \ldots s_{i+1,2}$ in T_1 and T_2 respectively, and θ_2 matches θ_1.

By inducing the length of finite paths, we can obtain that Theorem 17 holds. □

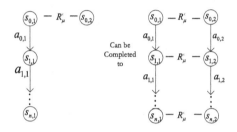

Fig. 5. Construction of statewise ϵ-bisimilar paths.

Definition 18. *Let $T_i = (S_i, Act, \delta_i, AP, L_i)$, $i = 1, 2$, be two NFKSs. R_{μ}^{ϵ} is an ϵ-approximate bisimulation for (T_1, T_2). Two finite paths $\theta_1 = s_{0,1}a_{0,1} \ldots s_{n,1}$, $\theta_2 = s_{0,2}a_{0,2} \ldots s_{n,2}$, $\theta_1 \in Paths_{fin}(T_1, s_{0,1})$, $\theta_2 \in Paths_{fin}(T_2, s_{0,2})$. If $i \in \mathbb{N}$, $0 \leqslant i \leqslant n$, $\forall(s_{i,1}, s_{i,2}) \in R_{\mu}^{\epsilon}$, we denote $\theta_1 \sim_{R_{\mu}^{\epsilon}} \theta_2$.*

Definition 19. *Let $T_i = (S_i, Act, \delta_i, AP, L_i)$, $i = 1, 2$, be two NFKSs. R_{μ}^{ϵ} is an ϵ-approximate bisimulation for (T_1, T_2). Given two infinite paths $\vartheta_1 = s_{0,1}a_{0,1}s_{1,1}a_{1,1}s_{2,1} \ldots$, $\vartheta_2 = s_{0,2}a_{0,2}s_{1,2}a_{1,2}s_{2,2} \ldots$, $\vartheta_1 \in Paths(T_1, s_{0,1})$, $\vartheta_2 \in Paths(T_2, s_{0,2})$. If $i \in \mathbb{N}$, $i \geqslant 0$, $\forall(s_{i,1}, s_{i,2}) \in R_{\mu}^{\epsilon}$, we denote $\vartheta_1 \sim_{R_{\mu}^{\epsilon}} \vartheta_2$.*

Given T_1 and T_2 as two NFKSs. R_{μ}^{ϵ} is an ϵ-approximate bisimulation for (T_1, T_2). The following theorem shows that the behaviors of T_1 and T_2.

Theorem 20. *Let $T_i = (S_i, Act, \delta_i, AP, L_i)$, $i = 1, 2$, be two NFKSs. R_{μ}^{ϵ} is an ϵ-approximate bisimulation for (T_1, T_2), if $\theta_1 \in Paths_{fin}(T_1, s_{0,1})$, $\theta_2 \in Paths_{fin}(T_2, s_{0,2})$, $\theta_1 \sim_{R_{\mu}^{\epsilon}} \theta_2$, then $|FV_{T_1}(trace(\theta_1)) - FV_{T_2}(trace(\theta_2))| \leq \epsilon$. We denote $FV_{T_1}(trace(\theta_1)) \sim_{R_{\mu}^{\epsilon}} FV_{T_2}(trace(\theta_2))$.*

Proof. By mapping $trace(\theta_1)$ and $trace(\theta_2)$ respectively, we can obtain the following equalities:

$$FV_{T_1}(trace(\theta_1)) = \bigvee_{p_{0,1},p_{1,1}\cdots\in AP} \{L_1(s_{0,1})(p_{0,1})\wedge$$

$$\{\bigwedge_{i=0}^{n-1}[\delta_1(s_{i,1},a_{i,1})(s_{i+1,1})\wedge L_1(s_{i+1,1})(p_{i+1,1})]\}\}$$

$$FV_{T_2}(trace(\theta_2)) = \bigvee_{p_{0,2},p_{1,2}\cdots\in AP} \{L_2(s_{0,2})(p_{0,2})\wedge$$

$$\{\bigwedge_{i=0}^{n-1}[\delta_2(s_{i,2},a_{i,2})(s_{i+1,2})\wedge L_2(s_{i+1,2})(p_{i+1,2})]\}\}$$

Since $(s_{0,1},s_{0,2})\in R_\mu^\epsilon$, then

$$|\bigvee_{p_{0,1}\in AP} L_1(s_{0,1})(p_{0,1}) - \bigvee_{p_{0,2}\in AP} L_2(s_{0,2})(p_{0,2})| \le \epsilon$$

Therefore, $p_{0,1} = p_{0,2}$, Then

$$\bigvee_{p_{0,1},p_{1,2}\cdots\in AP} \{[L_1(s_{0,1})(p_{0,1}) - \epsilon]\wedge$$

$$\{\bigwedge_{i=0}^{n-1}[\delta_2(s_{i,2},a_{i,2})(s_{i+1,2})\wedge L_2(s_{i+1,2})(p_{i+1,2})]\}\}$$

$$\le FV_{T_2}(trace(\vartheta_2)) \le$$

$$\bigvee_{p_{0,1},p_{1,2}\cdots\in AP} \{[L_1(s_{0,1})(p_{0,1}) + \epsilon]\wedge$$

$$\{\bigwedge_{i=0}^{n-1}[\delta_2(s_{i,2},a_{i,2})(s_{i+1,2})\wedge L_2(s_{i+1,2})(p_{i+1,2})]\}\}$$

Since R_μ^ϵ is an ϵ-approximate bisimulation for (T_1,T_2), there exists

$$|\bigvee_{p_{1,1},p_{2,1}\cdots\in AP} \{\bigwedge_{i=0}^{n-1}[\delta_1(s_{i,1},a_{i,1})(s_{i+1,1})\wedge L_1(s_{i+1,1})(p_{i+1,1})]\}$$

$$-\bigvee_{p_{1,2},p_{2,2}\cdots\in AP} \{\bigwedge_{i=0}^{n-1}[\delta_2(s_{i,2},a_{i,2})(s_{i+1,2})\wedge L_2(s_{i+1,2})(p_{i+1,2})]\}| \le \epsilon$$

Therefore, $i \in \mathbb{N}$, for all $0 \le i \le n - 1$, $p_{i,1} = p_{i,2}$, we can obtain:

$$\bigvee_{p_{0,1},p_{1,1}\cdots\in AP} \{[L_1(s_{0,1})(p_{0,1}) - \epsilon]\wedge$$

$$\{\bigwedge_{i=0}^{n-1}[\delta_1(s_{i,1},a_{i,1})(s_{i+1,1}) \wedge L_1(s_{i+1,1})(p_{i+1,1})] - \epsilon\}\}$$

$$\leqslant FV_{T_2}(trace(\vartheta_2)) \leqslant$$

$$\bigvee_{p_{0,1},p_{1,1}\cdots\in AP} \{[L_1(s_{0,1})(p_{0,1}) + \epsilon]\wedge$$

$$\{\bigwedge_{i=0}^{n-1}[\delta_1(s_{i,1},a_{i,1})(s_{i+1,1}) \wedge L_1(s_{i+1,1})(p_{i+1,1})] + \epsilon\}\}$$

Hence, if $\theta_1 \sim_{R_\mu^\epsilon} \theta_2$, then

$$|FV_{T_1}(trace(\theta_1)) - FV_{T_2}(trace(\theta_2))| \leq \epsilon$$

To sum up, if $\theta_1 \in Paths_{fin}(T_1, s_{0,1})$, $\theta_2 \in Paths_{fin}(T_2, s_{0,2})$, $\theta_1 \sim_{R_\mu^\epsilon} \theta_2$, then

$$FV_{T_1}(trace(\theta_1)) \sim_{R_\mu^\epsilon} FV_{T_2}(trace(\theta_2))$$

$\square$

Thus, for all $\theta_1 \in Paths_{fin}(T_1, s_{0,1})$, $\theta_2 \in Paths_{fin}(T_2, s_{0,2})$, $\theta_1 \sim_{R_\mu^\epsilon} \theta_2$, the Theorem 20 holds. Based on Theorem 20, we draw a conclusion that if there is an ϵ-approximate bisimulation for (T_1, T_2), then the behaviors of T_1 and T_2 is also ϵ-approximate. Conveniently, using mapping FV_T, we can easily compare the similarities and differences between two $NFKSs$.

4   Algorithms for Constructing Quotient $NFKSs$

As well known, bisimulations as the abstraction and equivalent technologies have been applied to model structures simplification. Researchers were able to use this equivalence relation to construct quotient $NFKSs$(see [26]). This can reduce the resource consumption caused by the number of states in the system. Fortunately, quotient $NFKSs$ not only exist bisimulations with initial $NFKSs$, but also have minimum states. However, there might not exist greatest ϵ-approximate bisimulation for a $NFKS$. In this section, we explore methods to construct all maximal ϵ-approximate bisimulations in polynomial time. We first provide an example to illustrate the significance of following three algorithms.

Example 21. Let $T = (S, Act, \delta, AP, L)$ be a $NFKS$,where $S = \{s_0, s_1, s_2, s_3\}$, $Act = \{a, b\}$, $AP = \{p, q\}$. The structure of T is shown in Fig. 6:

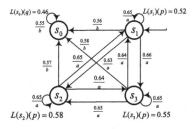

Fig. 6. nondeterministic fuzzy Kripke Structure T

where

$L(s_0)(q) = 0.46, L(s_1)(p) = 0.52, L(s_2)(p) = 0.58, L(s_3)(p) = 0.55,$
$\delta(s_1, a)(s_3) = 0.66, \delta(s_1, b)(s_0) = 0.56, \delta(s_1, a)(s_2) = 0.63,$
$\delta(s_3, a)(s_1) = 0.64, \delta(s_3, b)(s_0) = 0.58, \delta(s_3, a)(s_2) = 0.65,$
$\delta(s_2, a)(s_1) = 0.65, \delta(s_2, b)(s_0) = 0.57, \delta(s_2, a)(s_3) = 0.64.$
$\delta(s_0, b)(s_0) = 0.55, \delta(s_1, a)(s_1) = 0.65, \delta(s_2, a)(s_2) = 0.65, \delta(s_3, a)(s_3) = 0.65$

The small positive real number is $\epsilon = 0.03$.
Obviously,

$$R_1 = \{(s_0, s_0), (s_1, s_1), (s_2, s_2), (s_3, s_3), (s_2, s_3), (s_3, s_2)\},$$
$$R_2 = \{(s_0, s_0), (s_1, s_1), (s_2, s_2), (s_3, s_3), (s_1, s_3), (s_3, s_1)\}.$$

are ϵ-approximate bisimulations for T. R_1 and R_2 are equivalence relations. But, R_1 and R_2 are incomparable. Hence, based on equivalence relation R_1 and R_2, we do quotient calculation respectively

$$S/_{R_1} = \{[s_1]_{R_1}, [s_0]_{R_1}, [s_2]_{R_1}\},$$
$$\text{where } [s_1]_{R_1} = \{s_1\}, [s_0]_{R_1} = \{s_0\}, [s_2]_{R_1} = \{s_2, s_3\},$$
$$S/_{R_2} = \{[s_1]_{R_2}, [s_0]_{R_2}, [s_2]_{R_2}\},$$
$$\text{where}[s_1]_{R_2} = \{s_1, s_3\}, [s_0]_{R_2} = \{s_0\}, [s_2]_{R_2} = \{s_2\}.$$

Therefore, R_1 and R_2 can be regarded as maximal ϵ-approximate bisimulations. Apparently, with the help of maximal ϵ-approximate bisimulations, the number of states of quotient $NFKSs$ obtained by R_1 and R_2 respectively reach the minimum. As we know, for a complex $NFKS$, there might not exist the greatest ϵ-approximate bisimulation. Hence, we use following three algorithms to construct all maximal ϵ-approximate bisimulations to pave way for the quotient calculation in Definition 24. Given $T = (S, Act, \delta, AP, L)$ as a $NFKS$. Algorithm 1 and Algorithm 2 is used to compute all maximal equivalence relations on L which satisfy the first condition of Definition 10. And then, based on those equivalence relations, Algorithm 3 is used to compute all maximal ϵ-approximate bisimulations for T.

In Algorithm 1, the first step is to partition states based on atomic propositions. This results in the formation of decision tree, where different leaf nodes represent set of states. More precisely, we consider all the states in the set of S separately and improve the decision tree formed by AP step by step. The initial decision tree consists only of the root r_0. The entire formation of the decision tree is mainly in a top-down manner. When s is the first state where the membership value of the fuzzy label function is $L(s)(p) \in [0,1]$, we will insert it as a new vertex. The insertion position of state s is after traversing the decision tree to reach leaf node v, the state set of v is extended with s.

Algorithm 1. Computing the initial partition on AP

Input: $NFKS\ T = (S, Act, \delta, AP, L)$
Output: G_{hash}
1: createRootNode(r_0)
2: $AP = \{b_1, b_2, \ldots, b_m\}$
3: **for** all $s \in S$ **do**
4:     r $= r_0$
5:     **for** i=1,......, m-1 **do**
6:         **if** $L(s)(b_i) \in [0,1]$ **then**
7:             **if** TreeRight(r) = nil **then**
8:                 new(TreeRight(r))
9:             **end if**
10:             r := TreeRight(r)
11:         **else**
12:             **if** TreeLeft(r) = nil **then**
13:                 new(TreeLeft(r))
14:             **end if**
15:             r := TreeLeft(r)
16:         **end if**
17:     **end for**
18:     **if** $L(s)(b_m) \in [0,1]$ **then**
19:         **if** TreeRight(r) = nil **then**
20:             new(TreeRight(r))
21:         **end if**
22:         states(TreeRight(r)) := states(TreeRight(r)) $\cup \{s\}$
23:     **else**
24:         **if** TreeLeft(r) = nil **then**
25:             new(TreeLeft(r))
26:         **end if**
27:         states(TreeLeft(r)) := states(TreeLeft(r)) $\cup \{s\}$
28:     **end if**
29: **end for**

Algorithm 2 as the important step in aggregating states that match the equivalence of label function. In this step, we will divide state sets in more detail based on the membership values that label p belongs to state s on the basis of Algorithm 1. The fifth step of Algorithm 2 is the most important step, which selectively removes state pairs that do not satisfy the equivalence of the label function on the basis of Algorithm 1.

Algorithm 2. compute the all maximal equivalence relations on L

Input: $R_{(ini)} := \{(s, s')||L(s)(p) - L(s')(p)| \leq \epsilon\}$
Output: $R_{(maxequ)}$
1: $R_{(i)} := R_{(ini)}$ and $i := 1$
2: **while** $flag = true$ **do**
3:     $R_{temp} := R_{(i)}$
4:     **if** $(s, s') \in R_{temp}, (s', s'') \in R_{temp}$ and $(s, s'') \notin R_{temp}$ **then**
5:         $R_{temp} := \{R_{temp} - \{(s, s'), (s', s)\}\}$ or $\{R_{temp} - \{(s', s''), (s'', s')\}\}$
6:     **end if**
7:     $R_{(i+1)} := R_{temp}$
8:     **if** $R_{(i+1)} = R_{(i)}$ **then**
9:         $R_{maxequ} := R_{maxequ} \cup R_{(i+1)}$ and $flag := false$
10:     **else**
11:         $i := i + 1$
12:     **end if**
13: **end while**
14: **if** $\exists R' \subset R''$ **then**
15:     $R_{maxequ} := R_{maxequ} - R'$
16: **end if**

Algorithm 3 is based on Algorithm 1 and combined with the results of the Algorithm 2 to obtain the all maximal ε-approximate bisimulations.

Algorithm 3. compute the all maximal ε-approximate bisimulations

---

Input: $R_{(maxequ)}$
Output: R_f
1: $R_f := \{\}$
2: **for all** $R_{maxequ(i)} \in R_{(maxequ)}$ **do**
3:     $R_1 := R_{maxequ(i)}$ and $i := 1$
4:     **while** $flag = true$ **do**
5:         $R_t := R_{(i)}$
6:         **if** $(s, s') \in R_{maxequ(i)}, (s_1, s_1') \in R_{maxequ(i)}$ and $|\delta(s, a)(s_1) - \delta(s', a)(s_1')| \geqslant \epsilon$
        then
7:             $R_t := \{R_t - \{(s, s'), (s', s)\}\}$
8:         **end if**
9:         $R_{(i+1)} := R_{temp}$
10:         **if** $R_{(i+1)} = R_{(i)}$ **then**
11:             $R_f := R_f \cup R_{(i+1)}$ and $flag := false$
12:         **else**
13:             $i := i + 1$
14:         **end if**
15:     **end while**
16: **end for**
17: **if** $\exists R' \subset R''$ **then**
18:     $R_f := R_f - R'$
19: **end if**

The following propositions make sure that the set of $R_{(maxequ)}$ we obtain in Algorithm 2 is set of all maximal equivalence relations on L which satisfy the first condition of Definition 10 and the set of R_f we obtain from Algorithm 3 is the set of maximal ϵ-approximate bisimulations for $NFKS$.

Proposition 22. *In Algorithm 2, R_{maxequ} is the set of all maximal equivalence relations on L which satisfy the first condition of Definition 10.*

Proof. Let R_{max} be a maximal equivalence relation on L which satisfy the first condition of Definition 10. Apparently, $R_{max} \subseteq R_{(ini)}$.
(1) If $R_{max} = R_{(ini)}$, then $R_{(ini)}$ is the only maximal equivalence relation L which satisfies the first condition of Definition 10. Meanwhile, $R_{maxequ} = R_{(ini)} = \{R_1\}$. Hence, the conclusion is valid.
(2) If $R_{max} \subset R_{(ini)}$. then $R_{(ini)}$ is not equivalence relation on L. Therefore, we need to demonstrate if there exist $i \in \mathbb{N}$ and $R \in R_{(i)}$ such that $R_{max} \subset R$, then there exists $R_{new} \in R_{(i+1)}$ such that $R_{max} \subseteq R_{new}$.
Obviously, if the above statement holds, then R is not equivalence relation on L. At the same time, it shows that there exist $(s, s') \in R$, $(s', s'') \in R$, but $(s, s'') \notin R$. So it follows that $(s, s'), (s', s)$ and $(s', s''), (s'', s')$ cannot exist in R_{max} simultaneously. Hence, we must to execute the fifth step of Algorithm 2, which gives the result $R_{max} \subseteq R - \{(s, s'), (s', s)\}$ or $R_{max} \subseteq R - \{(s', s''), (s'', s')\}$. To sum up, there exist $R_{new} \in R_{i+1}$ such that $R_{max} \subseteq R_{new}$.
Since R_{max} is maximal, then we cannot delete fourteen to sixteen steps of Algorithm 2. From the above proofs, we can easily conclude that R_{maxequ} just contains all maximal equivalence relations on L which satisfy first condition of Definition 10. □

Proposition 23. *In Algorithm 3, R_f is the set of all maximal ϵ-approximate bisimulations for T. Meanwhile, for any $R \in R_f$, R is an ϵ-approximate bisimulation for T.*

Proof. Let R_{max} be a maximal ϵ-approximate bisimulation for T. Apparently, Since the result of Algorithm 3 is based on Algorithm 2, then R_{max} is an equivalence relation which satisfies the first condition of Definition 10. So there exists $R \in R_f$ such that $R_{max} \subseteq R$.
(1) If $R_{max} = R$, then $R_{max} \in R_f$ and R_{max} cannot be removed in seventeen to nineteen steps of Algorithm 3. Hence, the conclusion is valid.
(2) If $R_{max} \subset R$. then R does not satisfy second and third condition of Definition 10. Therefore, we need to demonstrate if there exist $i \in \mathbb{N}$ and $R \in R_{(i)}$ such that $R_{max} \subset R$, then there exists $R_{new} \in R_{(i+1)}$ such that $R_{max} \subseteq R_{new}$.
Obviously, if the above statement holds, then R does not satisfy second and third condition of Definition 10. At the same time, it shows that there exist $(s, s') \in R$, $(s_1, s'_1) \in R$, but $|\delta(s, a)(s_1) - \delta(s', a)(s'_1)| \geqslant \epsilon$. So it follows that $\{(s, s'), (s', s)\}$ cannot exist in R_{max}. Hence, we must to execute the seventh step of Algorithm 3, which gives the result $R_{max} \subseteq R - \{(s, s'), (s', s)\}$. To sum up, there exist $R_{new} \in R_{i+1}$ such that $R_{max} \subseteq R_{new}$.
What's more, R_{maxequ} is set of maximal equivalence relations which satisfy first condition of Definition 10, and Algorithm 3 deletes the state pairs that do not satisfy ϵ-approximation of the nondeterministic fuzzy transition function on the

basis of Algorithm 2 in every $R_{maxequ(i)} \in R_{maxequ}$. Since R_{max} is maximal, then we cannot delete seventeen to nineteen step of Algorithm 3. we can easily conclude that R_f just contains all maximal ϵ-approximate bisimulations for $NFKS$.

(3) Furthermore, for any $R \in R_f$, we can easily demonstrate that any state pairs $(s, s') \in R$ satisfy all condition of Definition 10, then R is an ϵ-approximate bisimulation for $NFKS$.

In summary, the proposition is valid.   □

Based on the above three algorithms, we can construct the quotient $NFKSs$.

Definition 24. *Let* $T = (S, Act, \delta, AP, L)$ *be a* $NFKS$. *R is an* ϵ*-approximate bisimulation for* T. *The quotient* $NFKS$ *for* T *is defined by:*

$$T/R = (S/R, Act, \delta_R, AP, L_R)$$

where

(1)$S/R = \{[s]_R | s \in S\}$ is the quotient space, where $[s]_R = \{s' \in S | (s, s') \in R\}$,

(2)δ_R is a quotient nondeterministic fuzzy transition function,

$$\delta_R([s]_R, a)([s']_R) = [\bigwedge_{\substack{s_1 \in [s]_R \\ s_2 \in [s']_R}} \delta(s_1, a)(s_2) + \bigvee_{\substack{s_3 \in [s]_R \\ s_4 \in [s']_R}} \delta(s_3, a)(s_4)]/2,$$

(3)$L_R([s]_R)(p) = [\bigwedge_{s_1 \in [s]_R} L(s_1)(p) + \bigvee_{s_2 \in [s]_R} L(s_2)(p)]/2.$

Next, we will give an example to introduce the use of the above three algorithms.

Example 25. Let $T = (S, Act, \delta, AP, L)$ be a $NFKS$,where $S = \{s_0, s_1, s_2, s_3, s_4, s_5\}$, $Act = \{\sigma_1, \sigma_2, \sigma_3\}$, $AP = \{p_1, p_2\}$. The structure of T is shown in Fig. 7:

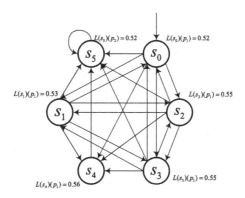

Fig. 7. nondeterministic fuzzy Kripke Structure T

where

$$\delta(s_0,\sigma_3)(s_5) = 0.48, \delta(s_0,\sigma_1)(s_1) = 0.55, \delta(s_0,\sigma_1)(s_2) = 0.55,$$
$$\delta(s_0,\sigma_2)(s_4) = 0.75, \delta(s_0,\sigma_1)(s_3) = 0.57, \delta(s_1,\sigma_3)(s_5) = 0.45,$$
$$\delta(s_1,\sigma_1)(s_0) = 0.54, \delta(s_1,\sigma_1)(s_2) = 0.54, \delta(s_1,\sigma_1)(s_3) = 0.56,$$
$$\delta(s_1,\sigma_2)(s_4) = 0.76, \delta(s_2,\sigma_3)(s_5) = 0.46, \delta(s_2,\sigma_1)(s_0) = 0.55,$$
$$\delta(s_2,\sigma_1)(s_1) = 0.54, \delta(s_2,\sigma_1)(s_3) = 0.57, \delta(s_2,\sigma_2)(s_4) = 0.73,$$
$$\delta(s_3,\sigma_3)(s_5) = 0.43, \delta(s_3,\sigma_1)(s_0) = 0.56, \delta(s_3,\sigma_1)(s_1) = 0.55,$$
$$\delta(s_3,\sigma_1)(s_2) = 0.55, \delta(s_3,\sigma_2)(s_4) = 0.75, \delta(s_4,\sigma_3)(s_5) = 0.48,$$
$$\delta(s_5,\sigma_2)(s_5) = 0.62$$

The small positive real number is chosen as $\epsilon = 0.03$.

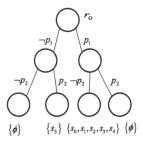

Fig. 8. Decision Tree for AP

By executing Algorithm 1, we can obtain a decision tree for AP, where the decision tree is shown in Fig. 8. By executing the initial input of the Algorithm 2, we can obtain the initial result set:

$$R_{(ini)} = \{(s_0, s_0), (s_0, s_1), (s_0, s_2), (s_0, s_3), (s_1, s_0), (s_1, s_1), (s_1, s_2), (s_1, s_3),$$
$$(s_1, s_4), (s_2, s_0), (s_2, s_1), (s_2, s_2), (s_2, s_3), (s_2, s_4), (s_3, s_0), (s_3, s_1),$$
$$(s_3, s_2), (s_3, s_3), (s_3, s_4), (s_4, s_1), (s_4, s_2), (s_4, s_3), (s_4, s_4), (s_5, s_5)\}$$

In Algorithm 2, we only provide the general idea of the algorithm briefly, where the fifth step of Algorithm 2 will generate different results due to different deleted state pairs. We provide the following representation of the state pairs that can be deleted in the above example.

$$R_{(del)} = \{(s_0, s_1), (s_0, s_2), (s_0, s_3), (s_1, s_0), (s_2, s_0), (s_3, s_0),$$
$$(s_1, s_4), (s_2, s_4), (s_3, s_4), (s_4, s_1), (s_4, s_2), (s_4, s_3)\}$$

For the state pairs available for deletion in $R_{(del)}$, if we choose to delete $\{(s_1, s_4), (s_2, s_4), (s_3, s_4), (s_4, s_1), (s_4, s_2), (s_4, s_3)\}$, we can obtain $R_{(maximal1)}$.

Similarly, if we choose to delete $\{(s_0, s_1), (s_0, s_2), (s_0, s_3), (s_1, s_0), (s_2, s_0), (s_3, s_0)\}$, we can obtain $R_{(maximal2)}$. The representation of $R_{(maximal1)}$ and $R_{(maximal2)}$ are as follows

$$R_{(maximal1)} = \{(s_0, s_0), (s_0, s_1), (s_0, s_2), (s_0, s_3), (s_1, s_0), (s_1, s_1), (s_1, s_2), (s_1, s_3),$$
$$(s_2, s_0), (s_2, s_1), (s_2, s_2), (s_2, s_3), (s_3, s_0), (s_3, s_1), (s_3, s_2), (s_3, s_3),$$
$$(s_4, s_4), (s_5, s_5)\}$$

$$R_{(maximal2)} = \{(s_0, s_0), (s_1, s_1), (s_1, s_2), (s_1, s_3), (s_1, s_4), (s_2, s_1), (s_2, s_2), (s_2, s_3),$$
$$(s_2, s_4), (s_3, s_1), (s_3, s_2), (s_3, s_3), (s_3, s_4), (s_4, s_1), (s_4, s_2), (s_4, s_3),$$
$$(s_4, s_4), (s_5, s_5)\}$$

By executing Algorithm 3, we can summarize that the set $R_f = \{R_{f_1}, R_{f_2}\}$ composed of all maximal ε-approximate bisimulations for T, where

$$R_{f_1} = \{(s_0, s_0), (s_0, s_1), (s_0, s_2), (s_1, s_0), (s_1, s_1), (s_1, s_2),$$
$$(s_2, s_0), (s_2, s_1), (s_2, s_2), (s_3, s_3), (s_4, s_4), (s_5, s_5)\}$$
$$R_{f_2} = \{(s_0, s_0), (s_1, s_1), (s_1, s_2), (s_1, s_3), (s_2, s_1), (s_2, s_2),$$
$$(s_2, s_3), (s_3, s_1), (s_3, s_2), (s_3, s_3), (s_4, s_4), (s_5, s_5)\}$$

If we choose R_{f_1} as the maximal ε-approximate bisimulation, we can get the new quotient $NFKS$ $T/_{R_{f_1}} = (S/_{R_{f_1}}, Act, \delta_{R_{f_1}}, AP, L_{R_{f_1}})$, where

$S/_{R_{f_1}} = \{[s_0]_{R_{f_1}}, [s_3]_{R_{f_1}}, [s_4]_{R_{f_1}}, [s_5]_{R_{f_1}}\}$,

where $[s_0]_{R_{f_1}} = \{s_0, s_1, s_2\}, [s_3]_{R_{f_1}} = \{s_3\}, [s_4]_{R_{f_1}} = \{s_4\}, [s_5]_{R_{f_1}} = \{s_5\}$,

$L_{R_{f_1}}([s_0]_{R_{f_1}})(p_1) = (0.52 + 0.55)/2 = 0.535, L_{R_{f_1}}([s_3]_{R_{f_1}})(p_1) = 0.55$,

$L_{R_{f_1}}([s_4]_{R_{f_1}})(p_1) = L(s_4)(p_1) = 0.56, L_{R_{f_1}}([s_5]_{R_{f_1}})(p_2) = L(s_5)(p_2) = 0.52$,

$\delta_{R_{f_1}}([s_0]_{R_{f_1}}, \sigma_3)([s_5]_{R_{f_1}}) = [\delta(s_1, \sigma_3)(s_5) + \delta(s_0, \sigma_3)(s_5)]/2 = 0.465$,

$\delta_{R_{f_1}}([s_0]_{R_{f_1}}, \sigma_1)([s_3]_{R_{f_1}}) = [\delta(s_1, \sigma_1)(s_3) + \delta(s_0, \sigma_1)(s_3)]/2 = 0.565$,

$\delta_{R_{f_1}}([s_3]_{R_{f_1}}, \sigma_1)([s_0]_{R_{f_1}}) = [\delta(s_3, \sigma_1)(s_2) + \delta(s_3, \sigma_1)(s_0)]/2 = 0.555$,

$\delta_{R_{f_1}}([s_0]_{R_{f_1}}, \sigma_1)([s_0]_{R_{f_1}}) = [\delta(s_2, \sigma_1)(s_1) + \delta(s_0, \sigma_1)(s_1)]/2 = 0.545$,

$\delta_{R_{f_1}}([s_0]_{R_{f_1}}, \sigma_2)([s_4]_{R_{f_1}}) = [\delta(s_2, \sigma_2)(s_4) + \delta(s_1, \sigma_2)(s_4)]/2 = 0.745$,

$\delta_{R_{f_1}}([s_3]_{R_{f_1}}, \sigma_2)([s_4]_{R_{f_1}}) = \delta(s_3, \sigma_2)(s_4) = 0.75$,

$\delta_{R_{f_1}}([s_3]_{R_{f_1}}, \sigma_3)([s_5]_{R_{f_1}}) = \delta(s_3, \sigma_3)(s_5) = 0.43$,

$\delta_{R_{f_1}}([s_4]_{R_{f_1}}, \sigma_3)([s_5]_{R_{f_1}}) = \delta(s_4, \sigma_3)(s_5) = 0.48$,

$\delta_{R_{f_1}}([s_5]_{R_{f_1}}, \sigma_2)([s_5]_{R_{f_1}}) = \delta(s_5, \sigma_2)(s_5) = 0.62$.

Similarly, if we choose R_{f_2} as the maximal ϵ-approximate bisimulation, we can get the new quotient $NFKS$ $T/R_{f_2} = (S/R_{f_2}, Act, \delta_{R_{f_2}}, AP, L_{R_{f_2}})$, where

$$S/R_{f_2} = \{[s_1]_{R_{f_2}}, [s_0]_{R_{f_2}}, [s_4]_{R_{f_2}}, [s_5]_{R_{f_2}}\},$$

where $[s_1]_{R_{f_2}} = \{s_1, s_2, s_3\}, [s_0]_{R_{f_2}} = \{s_0\}, [s_4]_{R_{f_2}} = \{s_4\}, [s_5]_{R_{f_2}} = \{s_5\},$

$L_{R_{f_2}}([s_1]_{R_{f_2}})(p_1) = (0.53 + 0.55)/2 = 0.54, L_{R_{f_2}}([s_0]_{R_{f_2}})(p_1) = 0.52,$

$L_{R_{f_2}}([s_5]_{R_{f_2}})(p_2) = L(s_5)(p_2) = 0.52, L_{R_{f_2}}([s_4]_{R_{f_2}})(p_1) = L(s_4)(p_1) = 0.56,$

$\delta_{R_{f_2}}([s_0]_{R_{f_2}}, \sigma_1)([s_1]_{R_{f_2}}) = [\delta(s_0, \sigma_1)(s_3) + \delta(s_0, \sigma_1)(s_2)]/2 = 0.56,$

$\delta_{R_{f_2}}([s_1]_{R_{f_2}}, \sigma_1)([s_0]_{R_{f_2}}) = [\delta(s_1, \sigma_1)(s_0) + \delta(s_3, \sigma_1)(s_0)]/2 = 0.55,$

$\delta_{R_{f_2}}([s_1]_{R_{f_2}}, \sigma_1)([s_1]_{R_{f_2}}) = [\delta(s_2, \sigma_1)(s_1) + \delta(s_2, \sigma_1)(s_3)]/2 = 0.555,$

$\delta_{R_{f_2}}([s_1]_{R_{f_2}}, \sigma_2)([s_4]_{R_{f_2}}) = [\delta(s_2, \sigma_2)(s_4) + \delta(s_1, \sigma_2)(s_4)]/2 = 0.745,$

$\delta_{R_{f_2}}([s_1]_{R_{f_2}}, \sigma_3)([s_5]_{R_{f_2}}) = [\delta(s_3, \sigma_3)(s_5) + \delta(s_2, \sigma_3)(s_5)]/2 = 0.445,$

$\delta_{R_{f_2}}([s_0]_{R_{f_2}}, \sigma_3)([s_5]_{R_{f_2}}) = \delta(s_0, \sigma_3)(s_5) = 0.48,$

$\delta_{R_{f_2}}([s_4]_{R_{f_2}}, \sigma_3)([s_5]_{R_{f_2}}) = \delta(s_4, \sigma_3)(s_5) = 0.48,$

$\delta_{R_{f_2}}([s_0]_{R_{f_2}}, \sigma_2)([s_4]_{R_{f_2}}) = \delta(s_0, \sigma_2)(s_4) = 0.75,$

$\delta_{R_{f_2}}([s_5]_{R_{f_2}}, \sigma_2)([s_5]_{R_{f_2}}) = \delta(s_5, \sigma_2)(s_5) = 0.62.$

We finally conclude the two quotient $NFKS$ as shown in Fig. 10.

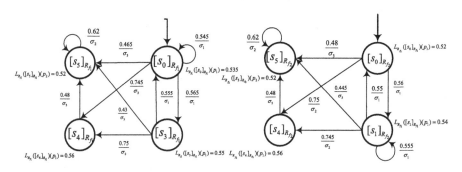

Fig. 9. $NFKS$ T/R_{f_1} (left) and $NFKS$ T/R_{f_2} (right)

Apparently, with the help of the maximal ϵ-approximate bisimulations, we gain the quotient $NFKSs$ with minimum numbers of states. Meanwhile, it is more noteworthy that the new quotient $NFKSs$ with the initial $NFKS$ exist ϵ-approximate bisimulations, where ϵ is the same. For example, ϵ-approximate bisimulation for $(T, T/R_{f_1})$ is a binary relation $R_\mu^\epsilon \subseteq S \times S/R_{f_1}$, which is expressed as follows

$$R_\mu^\epsilon = \{(s_0, [s_0]_{R_{f_1}}), (s_1, [s_0]_{R_{f_1}}), (s_2, [s_0]_{R_{f_1}}),$$
$$(s_3, [s_3]_{R_{f_1}}), (s_4, [s_4]_{R_{f_1}}), (s_5, [s_5]_{R_{f_1}})\}$$

where $\epsilon = 0.03$.

Similarly, ϵ-approximate bisimulation for $(T, T/_{R_{f_2}})$ is a binary relation $R_\mu^\epsilon \subseteq S \times S/_{R_{f_2}}$, which is represents as follows

$$R_\mu^\epsilon = \{(s_0, [s_0]_{R_{f_2}}), (s_1, [s_1]_{R_{f_2}}), (s_2, [s_1]_{R_{f_2}}),$$
$$(s_3, [s_1]_{R_{f_2}}), (s_4, [s_4]_{R_{f_2}}), (s_5, [s_5]_{R_{f_2}})\}$$

where $\epsilon = 0.03$.

Theorem 26. *Let $T = (S, Act, \delta, AP, L)$ be a $NFKS$. If R is a maximal ϵ-approximate bisimulation for T, then the behavior of T differs by ϵ from the behavior of quotient $NFKS$ $T/_R$.*

Proof. Assume R is a maximal ϵ-approximate bisimulation for T.

According to Algorithm 1,2,3 and Definition 24, we conclude that there exists an ϵ-approximate bisimulation R_μ^ϵ for $(T, T/_R)$. Therefore, based on Theorem 20, for any $s_{0,1} \in S$, $s_{0,2} \in S/_R$, we obtain that for all $\theta_1 \in Paths_{fin}(T, s_{0,1})$, $\theta_2 \in Paths_{fin}(T/_R, s_{0,2})$, $\theta_1 \sim_{R_\mu^\epsilon} \theta_2$, the following inequality holds:

$$|FV_T(trace(\theta_1)) - FV_{T/_R}(trace(\theta_2))| \le \epsilon$$

In summary, Theorem 26 holds. $\square$

Next, an actual discrete event will be given to explain the significance of the quotient $NFKS$ in solving practical problems. We cite example from paper [30].

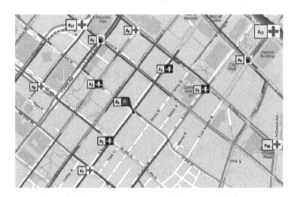

Fig. 10. Urban real-time traffic network

Example 27. Considering the real-time traffic flow information of the city in Fig. 10, the quotient structure of $NFKS$ can provide an intuitive result to help the ambulance center to make optimal vehicle dispatching.

As shown in Fig. 10. s_0 represents the current location of the ambulance, s_1, s_2, s_3, s_4 represent the patients who currently need ambulance to be taken to the hospital, s_5, s_9 represent two gas stations, s_6, s_7, s_8, s_{10}, s_{11}, s_{12} represent the distribution map of the current hospital. The road sections marked in dark color represent that the current road is very crowded. Let's consider the reality that the ambulance needs to be refueled during a relatively long journey. In addition, we assign corresponding membership degrees to different road sections according to the real-time traffic flow of the road sections. The more crowded the road, the greater the degree of membership, and the smaller the degree of membership, the smoother the current road.

In Fig. 11. $T = (S, Act, \delta, AP, L)$ is a $NFKS$. $S = \{S_0, S_1, \ldots, S_{12}\}$, $AP = \{p_1, p_2, p_3, p_4\}$. p_1 stands for ambulance, p_2 stands for patients, p_3 stands for gas stations, p_4 stands for hospitals. Moreover, $Act = \{t\}$. t represents transportation.

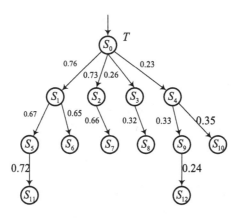

Fig. 11. nondeterministic fuzzy Kripke structure T

where

$L(s_0)(p_1) = 0.98, L(s_1)(p_2) = 0.67, L(s_2)(p_2) = 0.66, L(s_3)(p_2) = 0.68,$
$L(s_4)(p_2) = 0.69, L(s_5)(p_3) = 0.72, L(s_6)(p_4) = 0.82, L(s_7)(p_4) = 0.82,$
$L(s_8)(p_4) = 0.82, L(s_9)(p_3) = 0.72, L(s_{10})(p_4) = 0.82, L(s_{11})(p_4) = 0.83,$
$L(s_{12})(p_4) = 0.83,$
$\delta(s_0, t)(s_1) = 0.76, \delta(s_0, t)(s_2) = 0.73, \delta(s_0, t)(s_3) = 0.26, \delta(s_0, t)(s_4) = 0.23,$
$\delta(s_1, t)(s_5) = 0.67, \delta(s_1, t)(s_6) = 0.65, \delta(s_2, t)(s_7) = 0.66, \delta(s_3, t)(s_8) = 0.32,$
$\delta(s_4, t)(s_9) = 0.33, \delta(s_4, t)(s_{10}) = 0.35, \delta(s_9, t)(s_{12}) = 0.24, \delta(s_5, t)(s_{11}) = 0.72.$

Obviously,

$$R_\zeta^\epsilon = \{(S_0, S_0), (S_1, S_1), (S_2, S_2), (S_3, S_3), (S_4, S_4), (S_5, S_5), (S_6, S_6),$$
$$(S_7, S_7), (S_8, S_8), (S_9, S_9), (S_{10}, S_{10}), (S_{11}, S_{11}), (S_{12}, S_{12}),$$
$$(S_1, S_2), (S_2, S_1), (S_3, S_4), (S_4, S_3), (S_6, S_7), (S_7, S_6), (S_8, S_{10}), (S_{10}, S_8)\}$$

is an ϵ-approximate bisimulation for T.

$T/_{R_\zeta^\epsilon} = \{S/_{R_\zeta^\epsilon}, Act, \delta_{R_\zeta^\epsilon}, AP, L_{R_\zeta^\epsilon}\}$ in Fig. 12 is the quotient $NFKS$ of T, it simplifies decision and provides an optimal scheduling strategy. $S/_{R_\zeta^\epsilon} = \{[S_0]_{R_\zeta^\epsilon},$
$[S_1]_{R_\zeta^\epsilon}, [S_3]_{R_\zeta^\epsilon}, [S_5]_{R_\zeta^\epsilon}, [S_6]_{R_\zeta^\epsilon}, [S_{11}]_{R_\zeta^\epsilon}, [S_9]_{R_\zeta^\epsilon}, [S_8]_{R_\zeta^\epsilon}, [S_{12}]_{R_\zeta^\epsilon}\}$, where $[S_0]_{R_\zeta^\epsilon} = \{S_0\}, [S_1]_{R_\zeta^\epsilon} = \{S_1, S_2\}, [S_3]_{R_\zeta^\epsilon} = \{S_3, S_4\}, [S_5]_{R_\zeta^\epsilon} = \{S_5\}, [S_6]_{R_\zeta^\epsilon} = \{S_6, S_7\},$
$[S_{11}]_{R_\zeta^\epsilon} = \{S_{11}\}, [S_9]_{R_\zeta^\epsilon} = \{S_9\}, [S_8]_{R_\zeta^\epsilon} = \{S_8, S_{10}\}, [S_{12}]_{R_\zeta^\epsilon} = \{S_{12}\}.$

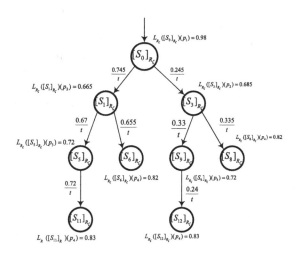

Fig. 12. nondeterministic fuzzy Kripke structure $T/_{R_\zeta^\epsilon}$

where

$$L_{R_\zeta^\epsilon}([S_0]_{R_\zeta^\epsilon})(p_1) = 0.98, L_{R_\zeta^\epsilon}([S_1]_{R_\zeta^\epsilon})(p_2) = (0.67 + 0.66)/2 = 0.65,$$
$$L_{R_\zeta^\epsilon}([S_3]_{R_\zeta^\epsilon})(p_2) = (0.68 + 0.69)/2 = 0.685, L_{R_\zeta^\epsilon}([S_5]_{R_\zeta^\epsilon})(p_3) = 0.72,$$
$$L_{R_\zeta^\epsilon}([S_6]_{R_\zeta^\epsilon})(p_4) = (0.82 + 0.82)/2 = 0.82, L_{R_\zeta^\epsilon}([S_{11}]_{R_\zeta^\epsilon})(p_4) = 0.83,$$
$$L_{R_\zeta^\epsilon}([S_9]_{R_\zeta^\epsilon})(p_3) = 0.72, L_{R_\zeta^\epsilon}([S_8]_{R_\zeta^\epsilon})(p_4) = (0.82 + 0.82)/2 = 0.82,$$
$$L_{R_\zeta^\epsilon}([S_{12}]_{R_\zeta^\epsilon})(p_4) = 0.83,$$
$$\delta_{R_\zeta^\epsilon}([S_0]_{R_\zeta^\epsilon}, t)([S_1]_{R_\zeta^\epsilon}) = 0.745, \delta_{R_\zeta^\epsilon}([S_0]_{R_\zeta^\epsilon}, t)([S_3]_{R_\zeta^\epsilon}) = 0.245,$$
$$\delta_{R_\zeta^\epsilon}([S_1]_{R_\zeta^\epsilon}, t)([S_5]_{R_\zeta^\epsilon}) = 0.67, \delta_{R_\zeta^\epsilon}([S_1]_{R_\zeta^\epsilon}, t)([S_6]_{R_\zeta^\epsilon}) = 0.655,$$
$$\delta_{R_\zeta^\epsilon}([S_5]_{R_\zeta^\epsilon}, t)([S_{11}]_{R_\zeta^\epsilon}) = 0.72, \delta_{R_\zeta^\epsilon}([S_3]_{R_\zeta^\epsilon}, t)([S_9]_{R_\zeta^\epsilon}) = 0.33,$$
$$\delta_{R_\zeta^\epsilon}([S_3]_{R_\zeta^\epsilon}, t)([S_8]_{R_\zeta^\epsilon}) = 0.335, \delta_{R_\zeta^\epsilon}([S_9]_{R_\zeta^\epsilon}, t)([S_{12}]_{R_\zeta^\epsilon}) = 0.24.$$

5   Conclusions

This paper defines the new kind of approximate bisimulation for nondeterministic fuzzy Kripke structures that called ϵ-approximate bisimulations as shown in Definition 8 and Definition 10. Compared with [33–38], this paper propose a more widely used concept of approximate bisimulation on nondeterministic fuzzy Kripke structure in model checking. For the sake of comparing the behaviors of two $NFKSs$, we propose a new mapping based on the set of traces in Definition 16. Interestingly, the behaviors of two $NFKSs$ under our proposed new approximate bisimulations are also ϵ-approximate. Therefore, the definition of new mapping provides a more general means for us to compare the behavior of different $NFKSs$. In addition, we point out that there might not exist the greatest ϵ-approximate bisimulation for a $NFKS$. For purpose of reducing the number of states of $NFKS$ and enabling the quotient $NFKS$ to satisfy the ϵ-approximate bisimulations with the initial $NFKS$, we design three algorithms inspired by paper [29] to construct all maximal ϵ-approximate bisimulations. This step lays the groundwork for us to execute quotient operations in Definition 24. However, algorithms only provides us with a feasible idea for generating all maximal ϵ-approximate bisimulations. The optimizations of the algorithms and the study of a more generalized simplification technique to solve quotient calculation for different models are an unresolved issue.

References

1. Li, Y., Droste, M., Lei, L.: Model checking of linear-time properties in multi-valued systems. Inf. Sci. **377**, 51–74 (2017)
2. Chechilk, M., Devereux, B., Gurfinkel, A., Easterbrook, S.: Multi-valued symbolic model-checking. ACM Trans. Softw. Eng. Methodol. **12**(4), 371–408 (2003). https://dl.acm.org/doi/abs/10.1145/990010.990011
3. Li, Y., Li, L.: Model checking of linear-time properties based on possibility measures. IEEE Trans. Fuzzy Syst. **21**(5), 842–854 (2013)
4. Li, Y.: Quantitative Model checking of linear-time properties based on generalized possibility measures. Fuzzy Sets Syst. **320**, 17–39 (2017). https://www.sciencedirect.com/science/article/pii/S0165011417301318
5. Li, Y., Li, Y., Ma, Z.: Computation tree logic model checking based on possibility measures. Fuzzy Sets Syst. **262**, 44–59 (2015). https://www.sciencedirect.com/science/article/pii/S0165011414001134
6. Li, Y., Li, Y., Ma, Z.: Quantitative computation tree logic model checking based on generalized possibility measures. IEEE Trans. Fuzzy Systems. **23**(6), 2034–2047 (2015). https://ieeexplore.ieee.org/abstract/document/7024119
7. Liang, C.J., Li, Y.M.: The model checking problem of computing tree logic base on generalized possibility measures. Acta Electronica Sinica. **45**(11), 2641–2648 (2017), (in Chinese)
8. Deng, W., Qiu, D.: Supervisory control of fuzzy discrete-event systems for simulation equivalence. IEEE Trans. Fuzzy Systems. **23**(1), 178–192 (2015). https://ieeexplore.ieee.org/abstract/document/6763108
9. Milner, R.: A Calculus of Communicating Systems. Springer-Verlag, Berlin (1980). https://doi.org/10.1007/3-540-10235-3

10. Ćirić, M., Ignjatović, J., Jančić, I., Damljanović, N.: Computation of the greatest simulations and bisimulations between fuzzy automata. Fuzzy Sets Syst. **208**, 22–42 (2012). https://www.sciencedirect.com/science/article/pii/S0165011412002254
11. Milner, R.: Communication and Concurrency. Prentice Hall, New York (1980)
12. Ćirić, M., Ignjatović, J., Damljanović, N., Bašić, M.: Bisimulations for fuzzy automata. Fuzzy Sets Syst. **186**(1), 100–139 (2011). https://www.sciencedirect.com/science/article/pii/S0165011411003198
13. Nguyen, L.A.: Logical characterizations of fuzzy bisimulations in fuzzy modal logics over residuated lattices. Fuzzy Sets Syst. **431**, 70–93 (2022). https://www.sciencedirect.com/science/article/pii/S016501142100289X
14. Cao, Y., Chen, G., Kerre, E.: Bisimulations for fuzzy-transition systems. IEEE Trans. Fuzzy Syst. **19**(3), 540–552 (2011). https://ieeexplore.ieee.org/abstract/document/5716670
15. Damljanović, N., Ćirić, M., Ignjatović, J.: Bisimulations for weighted automata over an additively idempotent semiring. Theor. Comput. Sci. **534**, 86–100 (2014). https://www.sciencedirect.com/science/article/pii/S0304397514001583
16. Fan, T.: Fuzzy bisimulation for Gödel logic. IEEE Trans. Fuzzy Syst. **23**(6), 2387–2396 (2015). https://ieeexplore.ieee.org/abstract/document/7095540/
17. Kupferman, O., Lustig, Y.: Latticed simulation relations and games. Int. J. Found. Comput. Sci. **21**(2), 167–189 (2010). https://www.worldscientific.com/doi/abs/10.1142/S0129054110007192
18. Xing, H., Zhang, Q., Huang, K.: Analysis and control of fuzzy discrete event systems using bisimulation equivalence. Theor. Comput. Sci. **456**, 100–111 (2012). https://www.sciencedirect.com/science/article/pii/S0304397512005312
19. Ćirić, M., Stamenković, A., Ignjatović, J., Petković, T.: Fuzzy relation equations and reduction of fuzzy automata. J. Comput. Syst. Sci. **76**(7), 609–633 (2010). https://www.sciencedirect.com/science/article/pii/S0022000009001044
20. Jančić, I.: Weak bisimulations for fuzzy automata. Fuzzy Sets Syst. **249**, 49–72 (2014). https://www.sciencedirect.com/science/article/pii/S0165011413004181
21. Högberg, J., MaLetti, A., May, J.: Backward and forward bisimulation minimisation of tree automata. Theor. Comput. Sci. **410**(37), 3539–3552 (2009)
22. Li, L., Qiu, D.: On the state minimization of fuzzy automata. IEEE Trans. Fuzzy Syst. **23**(2), 434–443 (2015). https://ieeexplore.ieee.org/abstract/document/6783686
23. Ćirić, M., Ignjatović, J., Basic, M., Jančić, I.: Nondeterministic automata: equivalence, bisimulations, and uniform relations. Inf. Sci. **261**, 185–218 (2014). https://www.sciencedirect.com/science/article/pii/S0020025513005409
24. Ying, M., Wirsing, M.: Approximate bisimilarity. In: International Conference Algebraic Methodology Software Technology, vol. 1816, pp. 309–322 (2000)
25. Ma, Y., Zhang, M.: The infinite evolution mechnism of ε-bisimularity. J. Comput. Sci. Technol. **6**, 1097–1105 (2013)
26. Deng, H., Li, Z.: Nondeterministic fuzzy simulation and bisimulation. Chin. J. Elect. **29**(2), 297–303 (2020).https://ietresearch.onlinelibrary.wiley.com/doi/abs/10.1049/cje.2020.01.007
27. Fan, Y., Li, Y., Ma, Z.: Computation tree logic model checking for nondeterministic fuzzy kripke structure. Acta Electronica Sinica. **46**(1), 152–159 (2018). (in Chinese)
28. Sharma, A.: The linear time-branching time spectrum of equivalences for stochastic systems with non-determinism. Theor. Comput. Sci. **850**, 148–167 (2021). https://www.sciencedirect.com/science/article/pii/S0304397520306356

29. Yang, C., Li, Y.: Fuzzy ϵ-approximate regular languages and minimal deterministic fuzzy automata ϵ-accepting them. Fuzzy Sets Syst. **420**, 72–86 (2021). https://www.sciencedirect.com/science/article/pii/S016501142030316X

30. Deng, H., Li, Z.: Multi-valued bisimulation quotienting algorithm. J Intell Fuzzy Syst. **36**(1), 37–45 (2019)

31. Yang, C., Li, Y.: ϵ-Bisimulation relations for fuzzy automata. IEEE Trans. Fuzzy Systems. **26**(4), 2017–2029 (2018). https://ieeexplore.ieee.org/abstract/document/8061033/

32. Baier, C., Katoen, J.P.: Principles of Model checking. The MIT Press, Cambridge (2008)

33. Sotudeh, G., Movaghar, A.: Abstraction and approximation in fuzzy temporal logics and models. Formal Aspects Comput. **27**(2), 309–334 (2015). https://link.springer.com/article/10.1007/s00165-014-0318-7

34. Cao, Y., Ezawa, Y., Chen, G., Pan, H.: Modeling and specification of nondeterministic fuzzy discrete-event systems. In: Decision Making under Constraints, pp. 45–58(2020)

35. Cao, Y., Sun, S., Wang, H., Chen, G.: A behavioral distance for fuzzy-transition systems. IEEE Trans. Fuzzy Syst. **21**(4), 735–747 (2013). https://ieeexplore.ieee.org/abstract/document/6362199

36. Cao, Y., Ezawa, Y.: Nondeterministic fuzzy automata. Inf. Sci. **191**, 86–97 (2012). https://www.sciencedirect.com/science/article/pii/S0020025511006736

37. Wu, H., Chen, Y., Bu, T., Deng, Y.: Algorithmic and logical characterizations of bisimulations for non-deterministic fuzzy transition systems. Fuzzy Sets Syst. **333**, 106–123 (2018). https://www.sciencedirect.com/science/article/pii/S0165011417300842

38. Wu, H., Chen, T., Han, T., Chen, Y.: Bisimulations for fuzzy transition systems revisited. Int. J. Approx. Reason. **99**, 1–11 (2018). https://www.sciencedirect.com/science/article/pii/S0888613X17306291

Scheduling with Hierarchies and Overload Cost

Yaru Yang, Wuyun Fu, and Honglin Ding[✉]

School of Mathematics and Statistics, Yunnan University, Kunming 650504,
China
Ding-HL@outlook.com

Abstract. In this paper, we consider the problem of scheduling with hierarchies and overload cost (SHOC). Given a set of jobs $\mathcal{J} = \{J_1, \ldots, J_n\}$, a set of two hierarchical identical parallel machines $\mathcal{M} = \{M_1, M_2\}$, a processing time function p and a hierarchy function g on the job set $\mathcal{J}$, a regular working time L_0 of the machines, a start-up cost c_0 and a cost c_1 of per unit overload, and the hierarchies of the machines M_1 and M_2 are 1 and 2 respectively. Each machine can only process the jobs whose hierarchies are no less than the hierarchy of this machine. We are asked to assign all jobs of $\mathcal{J}$ to the machines M_1 and M_2, and if the total processing time L_i $(i = 1, 2)$ of any machine is more than L_0, a charge of c_1 should be paid for per unit overload. The objective is to minimize the total cost of processing all the jobs. We design a $1 + \frac{1}{20}c_1/c_0$-approximation algorithm to solve our problem by using the LPT method. And based on four characteristics of optimal solutions and two dynamic programmings, we give a pseudo-polynomial time algorithm to find an optimal solution in $\mathcal{O}(nL_0)$ time.

Keywords: Hierarchy · Overload cost · Approximation guarantee · Dynamic programming · Pseudo-polynomial time algorithm

1 Introduction

In the machine manufacturing industries, when workers need to use a fixed number of machines to process some workpieces, they first need to start the machines. There is a fixed start-up cost for each machine from start-up to normal operation. After each machine is started, it can work continuously for a fixed period of time. And the workpiece with higher precision should be arranged on the machine with better performance as far as possible. Sometimes, there are too many workpieces waiting to be processed, and machines have to work overtime, which needs to pay extra.

Motivated by such a practical application, we study the problem of scheduling with hierarchies and overload cost (SHOC, in short) and its details as following. Given a set of jobs $\mathcal{J} = \{J_1, \ldots, J_n\}$ and two identical parallel machines $\mathcal{M} = \{M_1, M_2\}$, each job J_j $(1 \leq j \leq n)$ is associated with a processing time p_j and a hierarchy $g_j \in \{1, 2\}$, and the hierarchies of machines M_1 and M_2 are 1 and 2 respectively. The start-up cost of each machine is c_0, and after starting,

© The Author(s), under exclusive license to Springer Nature Singapore Pte Ltd. 2024
Z. Cai et al. (Eds.): NCTCS 2023, CCIS 1944, pp. 133–147, 2024.
https://doi.org/10.1007/978-981-99-7743-7_8

each machine can work continuously for L_0 time. If any machine works continuously for more than L_0 time, a charge of c_1 shall be paid for per unit overload. Each machine can only process the jobs whose hierarchies are no less than the hierarchy of this machine. We are asked to to assign all the jobs to machines, and the objective is to minimize the total cost of processing all the jobs.

Before we present the literature and provide our main results, we first define the notion of competitive ratio. The basic character of online problem (such as scheduling or bin packing) is lack of information, and the off-line problem is known all information. For an online problem, the performance of the online algorithm is measured by the competitive ratio. In particular, for a minimization problem, the competitive ratio of an online algorithm A is defined as the minimum value ρ satisfying $C^A(\mathcal{I}) \leq \rho \cdot C^*(\mathcal{I})$ for any instance $\mathcal{I}$, where $C^A(\mathcal{I})$ denotes the output value obtained by executing algorithm A for the instance $\mathcal{I}$, and $C^*(\mathcal{I})$ denotes the offline optimal value. On the other hand, if there is no online algorithm for the online problem which has a competitive ratio strictly less than ρ, then ρ is referred as a lower bound of this online problem. Furthermore, if there is an online algorithm with a competitive ratio exactly matching the problem's lower bound, we call this algorithm is an optimal online algorithm, and the problem has a tight bound ρ.

The scheduling and bin packing are two classical discrete optimization problems that are closely related. The problems related to them have been studied extensively and deeply by many scholars, and some classical results have been obtained. For the classical problem of minimum makespan scheduling which is to assign n independent jobs to m identical parallel machines to minimize the makespan, Graham presented [10] the longest processing time (LPT) algorithm in 1969, which can yield a schedule with makespan no more than $4/3 - 1/3m$. Hochbaum and Shmoys [12] designed a polynomial time approximation scheme (PTAS) for it in 1987.

The study on problems related to scheduling with extendable working time and bin packing with extendable bins originates from research work of Dell'Olmo et al. [7] in 1998. They first introduced the online extensible bin packing problem and designed a 13/12 approximation algorithm to solve it. In this problem, the number of available bins is fixed but the size of each bin is extendable, if necessary, and the objective is to minimize the total size of the bins. In 1999, Dell'Olmo et al. [8] then studied a generalization of this problem, where the bins have different sizes. They proved that the approximation ratio of the longest processing time (LPT) algorithm is $4 - 2\sqrt{2}$, and the competitive ratio of the list scheduling (LS) algorithm is $5/4$, which is improved slightly by Ye et al. [27]. Epstein et al. [9] considered the vector scheduling problem in asymmetric settings. They presented a PTAS for the problem by using the dynamic programming techniques, where the state space is a vector that depends on the dimension of $1/\epsilon$. In 1999, Speranza et al. [20] studied the problem of scheduling tasks on identical machines with extendable working time. They proved the lower bound of this problem is $7/6$ and designed a $5/4$-approximation algorithm to solve it. In fact, this problem is the off-line version of Dell'Olmo's problem provided in 1998. Alon et al. [1] presented a unify EPTAS for scheduling on parallel machines which is also suitable for the problem in 1998.

Woeginger [22] proved that if the number m of bins is fixed, there is a FPTAS for the problem in 2000. It's worth noting that Coffman et al. [5] presented an asymptotic FPTAS for the extensible bin packing problem in 2006. Most recently, Levin [16] designed an efficient PTAS (EPTAS) for a new generalization of the extensible bin packing with unequal bin sizes problem, where the cost of exceeding the size of each bin depends on the index of the bin and not only on the amount in which the size of the bin is exceeded. In 2016, Chen et al. [3] investigated the problem of scheduling on parallel identical machines with late work criterion. They proved this problem is binary NP-hard in the case of $m = 2$ and unary NP-hard when the number of machines is arbitrary. Also, they presented an optimal online algorithm with a competitive ratio of $\sqrt{5} - 1$ for the problem of scheduling on two identical machines with a common due date in order to maximize the total early work. In 2021, Chen et al. [4] studied the scheduling with the goal of early work maximization and designed an optimal online algorithm with a competitive ratio of $6/5$ when the total size of all the jobs is known in advance.

In recent years, many scholars start considering scheduling problems with a grade of service (or hierarchies) [11]. In 2001, Bar-Noy et al. [2] first studied the online hierarchical scheduling problems on m parallel identical machines under the hierarchial constraint. They proposed an online algorithm with competitive ratio of $e + 1 \approx 3.718$ for the non-preemptive version. In 2004, Hwang et al. [13] considered the problem of parallel machine scheduling under a grade of service (GoS) provision, denoted as $P_m|GoS|C_{max}$. They presented the lowest grade-longest processing times first (LG-LPT) algorithm, and proved that the approximation guarantee of LG-LPT algorithm is $5/4$ in the case of $m = 2$ and is $2 - 1/(m-1)$ in the case of $m \geq 3$. In 2008, Ou et al. [18] developed a polynomial time approximation scheme (PTAS) for this problem. In the same year, Ji et al. [14] designed a fully polynomial time approximation scheme (FPTAS) to solve it. Park et al. [19] and Jiang et al. [15] are also investigated the online and semi-online versions for the problem $P_m|GoS|C_{max}$. Zhang et al. [28] presented an online algorithm TLS with a competitive ratio of $1 + \frac{m^2-m}{m^2-km+k^2} < \frac{7}{3}$, which improves the result in [15]. In 2009, Li et al. [17] developed an EPTAS with running time $\mathcal{O}(nlogn)$ for $P|GoS|C_{max}$ and a simple FPTAS with running time $\mathcal{O}(n)$ in the case of m is fixed, improving the results in [22]. In 2018, Dai et al. [6] divided each job J_j into a_j identical tasks and studied the scheduling problem for bag-of-tasks on two parallel machines with hierarchical constraints, they designed two semi-online algorithms. In 2022, Wei et al. [21] considered the online scheduling in shared manufacturing, where each item has a unit-size. In the same year, Xiao et al. [24] studied the problem of online and semi-online scheduling on two hierarchical machines with a common due date with the goal of the total early work maximization. They presented an optimal online algorithm with a competitive ratio of $\sqrt{2}$, and designed an optimal online algorithm with a competitive ratio of $4/3$ when the total size of all the jobs is known in advance. For the problem on three hierarchical machines with a common due date, Xiao et al. [25] designed an optimal online algorithm with a competitive ratio of 1.302. For the machine covering problem with the goal of maximizing the minimum machine load, Wu et al. [23] considered the semi-online case on two hierarchical machines where the processing times are discrete by $\{1, 2, 2^2, \cdots, 2^k\}$ with $k \geq 2$, and designed an optimal online algorithm with a competitive ratio of 2^k. Xiao et al. [26] considered the semi-online case on three hierarchical machines where the size of all the jobs is bounded by an interval $[1 + \alpha]$, they presented two optimal online algorithms with competitive ratios of $1 + \alpha$ and $1 + 2\alpha$, when there is only one machine of hierarchy 1 and there are two machines of hierarchy 1, respectively.

The rest of this paper is organized as follows. In Sect. 2, we provide some related definitions and notations, lemmas and assumptions. In Sect. 3, we design an $1 + \frac{1}{20}c_1/c_0$-approximation algorithm to solve our problem. In Sect. 4, according to the characteristcs of optimal solutions, we propose two dynamic programmings, and then design a pseudo-polynomial time algorithm to find an optimal schedule in $\mathcal{O}(nL_0)$ time. Finally, a conclusion is made in Sect. 5.

2 Preliminaries

2.1 Definitions and Notations

The definition of the SHOC problem is shown in Sect. 1. We use the notation $\mathcal{I} = (\mathcal{J}, \mathcal{M}, p, g, L_0, c_0, c_1)$ to denote an instance of the SHOC problem, which is constituted by a set of n jobs $\mathcal{J} = \{J_1, \ldots, J_n\}$, a set of two hierarchical identical parallel machines $\mathcal{M} = \{M_1, M_2\}$, a processing time function p and a hierarchy function g on the job set $\mathcal{J}$, a regular working time L_0 of the machines, a start-up cost c_0 and a cost c_1 of per unit overload. And stipulate that the hierarchies of machines M_1 and M_2 are 1 and 2 respectively. For each job J_j $(1 \leq j \leq n)$, use $J_j = (p_j, g_j)$ to represent this job, where p_j and g_j are the processing time (also called size) and the hierarchy of the job J_j respectively. If $g_j = 1$, we refer to J_j as a job of hierarchy 1 or low-hierarchy job, otherwise, call J_j a job of hierarchy 2 or high-hierarchy job. Let $\mathcal{J}_l$ and $\mathcal{J}_h$ represent all of the low-hierarchy jobs and all of the high-hierarchy jobs, respectively, i.e., $\mathcal{J}_l = \{J_j \in \mathcal{J} \mid g_j = 1\}$, $\mathcal{J}_h = \{J_j \in \mathcal{J} \mid g_j = 2\}$. According to the definition of the SHOC problem, each job J_j can be processed by machine M_i $(i = 1, 2)$ if and only if the hierarchy g_j of this job is no less than the hierarchy of the machine M_i. So, M_1 can process all jobs, and M_2 can only process the high-hierarchy jobs. A feasible solution (named schedule) of the SHOC problem is a partition $\mathcal{S} = (S_1, S_2)$ of the job set $\mathcal{J}$, such that $S_1 \cup S_2 = \mathcal{J}$, $S_1 \cap S_2 = \emptyset$, $\mathcal{J}_l \subset S_1$, and the jobs of S_1 and S_2 are assigned to M_1 and M_2, respectively. For each schedule $\mathcal{S}$, let $L_i^{\mathcal{S}} = \sum_{J_j \in S_i} p_j$ to denote the load of M_i, and use $C_i^{\mathcal{S}}$ to denote the cost incurred by machine M_i in processing assigned jobs (also called the cost of M_i) and can be accurately expressed as

$$C_i^{\mathcal{S}} = \begin{cases} 0 & \text{if } L_i^{\mathcal{S}} = 0, \\ c_0 & \text{if } 0 < L_i^{\mathcal{S}} \leq L_0, \\ c_0 + (L_i^{\mathcal{S}} - L_0)c_1 & \text{if } L_i^{\mathcal{S}} > L_0, \end{cases}$$

where $L_i^S - L_0$ and $(L_i^S - L_0)c_1$ are called overload and overload cost of M_i, respectively, and $i = 1, 2$. The objective of the SHOC problem is to find a schedule S such that the total cost $C^S = \sum_{i=1}^{2} C_i^S$ is minimized.

Obviously, if the total processing time of all jobs $\sum_{J_j \in J} p_j$ is no more than L_0, or $c_1 \leq c_0/L_0$ is true, then assigning all jobs to the machine M_1 will be an optimal schedule. It is a trivail conclusion. However, in real life, the cost c_1 of per unit overtime working hours is usually not less than the cost c_0/L_0 of per unit working time. Hence, we only consider such instance $\mathcal{I}$ of the SHOC problem later in this paper, which satisfies that $c_0/L_0 < c_1$ and $\sum_{J_j \in J} p_j > L_0$.

For convenience, let P, T_1 and T_2 denote the total processing time of all the jobs in $\mathcal{J}$, $\mathcal{J}_l$ and $\mathcal{J}_h$ respectively, i.e., $P = \sum_{j=1}^{n} p_j, T_1 = \sum_{J_j \in \mathcal{J}_l} p_j$ and $T_2 = \sum_{J_j \in \mathcal{J}_h} p_j$. Clearly, for each schedule S, we have

$$P = L_1^S + L_2^S = T_1 + T_2.$$

2.2   Lemmas and Assumptions

Based on the definition of the SHOC problem and related notations, we give two lemmas and one assumption which are useful for later analysis and proofs.

Given an instance $\mathcal{I} = (\mathcal{J}, \mathcal{M}, p, g, L_0, c_0, c_1)$ of the SHOC problem, assume that $S = (S_1, S_2)$ is a schedule for $\mathcal{I}$. If these two machines have no any overload cost, then the total cost of the machines will be equal to the total start-up cost $2c_0$. Otherwise, the total cost of machines include not only the total start-up cost $2c_0$, but also the overload cost $(L_1^S - L_0)c_1$ or/and $(L_2^S - L_0)c_1$. Note that $(L_1^S - L_0)c_1 + (L_2^S - L_0)c_1 = (P - 2L_0)c_1$, we can obtain the following lower bound.

Lemma 1. *The total cost C^S of any schedule S (especially optimal schedule) for the instance $\mathcal{I}$ of the SHOC problem satisfies that*

$$C^S \geq \max\{2c_0, 2c_0 + (P - 2L_0)c_1\}.$$

According to the definition of the SHOC problem, all the low-hierarchy jobs must be assigned to the machine M_1 which has hierarchy 1. Hence, we can regard to all of the low-hierarchy jobs as one special job whose processing time is the total processing time of all low-hierarchy jobs and the hierarchy remains 1. Therefore, the following lemma is true.

Lemma 2. *The SHOC problem is polynomially equivalent to the SHOC problem with only one low-hierarchy job.*

For simplicity of description, we only consider the SHOC problem with one low-hierarchy job in the subsequent parts, and still use SHOC to represent such an equivalent subproblem.

Obviously, if the processing time of the only low-hierarchy job is no less than L_0, then $S = (S_1, S_2) = (\mathcal{J}_l, \mathcal{J}_h)$ will be an optimal schedule. In addition, if there exists a high-hierarchy job J_t of which the processing time is no less than L_0, it will be an optimal schedule that assigning J_t alone to M_2 and all remaining jobs to M_1. Thus, to simplify our problem further, let's assume the following.

Assumption 1. *For the given instance $\mathcal{I}$ of the SHOC problem, assume the processing time of each job is less than L_0, i.e., $p_j < L_0$ holds for each $J_j \in \mathcal{J}$.*

3   A $(1 + \frac{1}{20}c_1/c_0)$-Approximation Algorithm

In 2016, Chen *et al.* [3] considerd scheduling on two parallel identical machines with the late work criterion. In this problem, besides two machines, n jobs and the processing time of each job, a common due date is also given. The objective is to minimize the total late work. They proved this problem is NP-complete by polynomially reducing the partition problem to it. In 2022, Levin [16] studied the generalized extensible bin packing problem, of which the objective is to find a partition of the jobs to m machines such that the total cost of the machines is minimized. They proved that there exists a PTAS to solve this problem. The SHOC problem considered in this paper can be regarded as a generalization of these two problems. We will design a strongly polynomial time approximation algorithm to solve it in this section. First, as a generalization, the SHOC problem is naturally NP-complete. In fact, we can also similarly prove it is NP-complete from the partition problem.

Inspired by the LPT algorithm proposed by Graham [10], we design an approximation algorithm to solve the SHOC problem. Our strategy is as follows.

(1) Sort all the jobs in non-increasing order of their processing times.
(2) Assign all jobs to these two machines by using the LPT method.
(3) Swap all the jobs assigned to the two machines, if necessary.

We call this algorithm modified longest processing time (MLPT, in short) and its details are shown in Algorithm 1 below.

Algorithm 1: MLPT

---

1 For the given instance $\mathcal{I} = (\mathcal{J}, \mathcal{M}, p, g, L_0, c_0, c_1)$ of the SHOC problem, sort all the jobs in non-increasing order of their processing times. Assume that $p_1 \geq p_2 \geq \cdots \geq p_n$ and J_r $(1 \leq r \leq n)$ is the only low-hierarchy job.
2 Let $\bar{S}_1 := \emptyset$ and $\bar{S}_2 := \emptyset$.
3 **for** $j = 1$ *to* n **do**
4   Assume that the total processing time of the assigned jobs on machine M_i $(i = 1$ or $2)$ is minimum right now, then assign the job J_j to the machine M_i, i.e., let $\bar{S}_i := \bar{S}_i \cup \{J_j\}$.
5 If $J_r \in \bar{S}_1$, let $S_1 := \bar{S}_1$ and $S_2 := \bar{S}_2$; Otherwise, let $S_1 := \bar{S}_2$ and $S_2 := \bar{S}_1$.
6 Output the schedule $\mathcal{S} = (S_1, S_2)$.

For any instance $\mathcal{I}$ of the SHOC problem, the MLPT algorithm can produce a schedule $\mathcal{S} = (S_1, S_2)$ in the Step 6, which is obviously a feasible solution of $\mathcal{I}$. Furthermore, if the corresponding loads of the machines satisfy $\max\{L_1^{\mathcal{S}}, L_2^{\mathcal{S}}\} \leq$

L_0, then its total cost $C^S = 2c_0$ is the optimal value of the instance $\mathcal{I}$ by the Lemma 1. Moreover, if the loads satisfy $\min\{L_1^S, L_2^S\} \geq L_0$, then its total cost is $C^S = 2c_0 + (L_1^S - L_0)c_1 + (L_2^S - L_0)c_1 = 2c_0 + (P - 2L_0)c_1$, which is also the optimal value of the given instance $\mathcal{I}$. Hence, we have the following lemma.

Lemma 3. *Assume the MLPT algorithm produce a schedule $\mathcal{S} = (S_1, S_2)$. If the corresponding loads of the machines satisfy $\max\{L_1^S, L_2^S\} \leq L_0$ or $\min\{L_1^S, L_2^S\} \geq L_0$, then $\mathcal{S} = (S_1, S_2)$ is an optimal schedule of the instance $\mathcal{I}$.*

By the Lemma 3, in order to analyze the MLPT algorithm more conveniently, we assume the following.

Assumption 2. *For the schedule $\mathcal{S} = (S_1, S_2)$ produced by the MLPT algorithm, assume that the corresponding loads of the machines satisfy*

$$\min\{L_1^S, L_2^S\} < L_0 < \max\{L_1^S, L_2^S\}.$$

Based on the Assumptions 1 and 2, we can prove that the MLPT algorithm can also produce an optimal schedule, if the instance $\mathcal{I}$ includes at most 4 jobs.

Lemma 4. *If the instance $\mathcal{I}$ contains at most 4 jobs, i.e., $n \leq 4$, then the MLPT algorithm can produce an optimal schedule for it.*

Proof. When the number of jobs n is no more than the number of machines, i.e., $n \leq 2$, the conclusion is obviously true. And then, we will prove it is still true when $n = 3$ or $n = 4$.

Case 1: The number of the jobs is $n = 3$, i.e., the instance $\mathcal{I}$ contains 3 jobs J_1, J_2, J_3, which satisfy $p_1 \geq p_2 \geq p_3$. In the Steps 3 and 4 of the MLPT algorithm, these 3 jobs will be assigned to M_1 and M_2, and obtain a schedule, denoted as $\bar{\mathcal{S}} = (\bar{S}_1, \bar{S}_2)$, where $\bar{S}_1 = \{J_1\}, \bar{S}_2 = \{J_2, J_3\}$. We have $L_1^{\bar{S}} = p_1 < L_0 < p_2 + p_3 = L_2^{\bar{S}}$ by the Assumption 2. Let $\mathcal{S}^* = (S_1^*, S_2^*)$ be an optimal schedule of the instance $\mathcal{I}$. Then, either S_1^* or S_2^* contains exactly two jobs. Without loss of generality, assume S_2^* contains two jobs. Because J_2 and J_3 are the two smaller jobs of all the three jobs, we have $L_0 < L_2^{\bar{S}} \leq L_2^{S^*}, L_1^{\bar{S}} < L_0$ and $L_1^{S^*} < L_0$. Therefore, $C^{\bar{S}} = 2c_0 + (L_2^{\bar{S}} - L_0)c_1 \leq 2c_0 + (L_2^{S^*} - L_0)c_1 = C^{\mathcal{S}^*}$ holds.

Case 2: The number of the jobs is $n = 4$, i.e., the instance $\mathcal{I}$ contains 4 jobs J_1, J_2, J_3, J_4, which satisfy $p_1 \geq p_2 \geq p_3 \geq p_4$. Let $\mathcal{S}^* = (S_1^*, S_2^*)$ be an optimal schedule of the instance $\mathcal{I}$. Similarly, a schedule $\bar{\mathcal{S}} = (\bar{S}_1, \bar{S}_2)$ can be obtained in the Steps 3 and 4 of the MLPT algorithm. And there are two types of partitioning of jobs in $\bar{\mathcal{S}}$.

Case 2.1: If $p_1 \leq p_2 + p_3$, then we have $\bar{S}_1 = \{J_1, J_4\}$ and $\bar{S}_2 = \{J_2, J_3\}$. There are two cases by the Assumption 2.

Case 2.1.1: When $L_1^{\bar{S}} = p_1 + p_4 > L_0$ and $L_2^{\bar{S}} = p_2 + p_3 < L_0$ hold, the total cost of the schedule $\bar{\mathcal{S}}$ is $C^{\bar{S}} = 2c_0 + (L_1^{\bar{S}} - L_0)c_1$. And the optimal schedule $\mathcal{S}^* = (S_1^*, S_2^*)$ may also have two types.

(1) Both S_1^* and S_2^* contain exactly 2 jobs. Without loss of generality, assume $S_1^* = \{J_1, J_t\}$, where $t \in \{2, 3, 4\}$. Because $p_4 \leq p_t$, we have $L_0 < L_1^{\bar{S}} = p_1 + p_4 \leq p_1 + p_t = L_1^{S^*}$. Thus, $C^{\bar{S}} = 2c_0 + (L_1^{\bar{S}} - L_0)c_1 \leq 2c_0 + (L_1^{S^*} - L_0)c_1 \leq C^{S^*}$ holds.

(2) Either S_1^* or S_2^* contains exactly 3 jobs. Without loss of generality, assume S_1^* contains 3 jobs. Then $S_1^* = \{J_1, J_s, J_t\}$ or $S_1^* = \{J_2, J_3, J_4\}$ holds, where $s, t \in \{2, 3, 4\}$ and $s \neq t$. Because $p_s \geq p_4$ and $p_1 \leq p_2 + p_3$ hold, so both $p_1 + p_4 \leq p_1 + p_s + p_t$ and $p_1 + p_4 \leq p_2 + p_3 + p_4$ are true. Thus, we have $L_1^{\bar{S}} \leq L_1^{S^*}$. It implies that $C^{\bar{S}} \leq 2c_0 + (L_1^{S^*} - L_0)c_1 \leq C^{S^*}$ holds.

Case 2.1.2: When $L_1^{\bar{S}} = p_1 + p_4 < L_0$ and $L_2^{\bar{S}} = p_2 + p_3 > L_0$ hold, similarly, we can prove $C^{\bar{S}} \leq C^{S^*}$ from the Case 2.1.1.

Case 2.2: If $p_1 > p_2 + p_3$, then we have $\bar{S}_1 = \{J_1\}$ and $\bar{S}_2 = \{J_2, J_3, J_4\}$. By the Assumptions 1 and 2, $L_1^{\bar{S}} = p_1 < L_0$ and $L_2^{\bar{S}} = p_2 + p_3 + p_4 > L_0$ hold. Thus the total cost of the schedule $\bar{S}$ is $C^{\bar{S}} = 2c_0 + (L_2^{\bar{S}} - L_0)c_1$. And the optimal schedule $S^* = (S_1^*, S_2^*)$ still has two types.

(1) Both S_1^* and S_2^* contain exactly 2 jobs. Without loss of generality, assume $S_2^* = \{J_1, J_t\}$ ($t = 2, 3$ or 4). Because $p_4 \leq p_t$, we have $L_0 < L_2^{\bar{S}} = p_2 + p_3 + p_4 < p_1 + p_4 \leq p_1 + p_t = L_2^{S^*}$. Thus $C^{\bar{S}} = 2c_0 + (L_2^{\bar{S}} - L_0)c_1 < 2c_0 + (L_2^{S^*} - L_0)c_1 \leq C^{S^*}$.

(2) Either S_1^* or S_2^* contains exactly 3 jobs. Without loss of generality, assume S_2^* contains 3 jobs. Obviously, we have $L_2^{\bar{S}} \leq L_2^{S^*}$. It implies that $C^{\bar{S}} = 2c_0 + (L_2^{\bar{S}} - L_0)c_1 \leq 2c_0 + (L_2^{S^*} - L_0)c_1 \leq C^{S^*}$ holds.

Combining Case 1, Case 2.1 and Case 2.2, we can obtain that $C^{\bar{S}} \leq C^{S^*}$ is true when the number of the jobs is either 3 or 4. In the Step 5, only the swap operation is performed (if necessary) and the total cost does not change, i.e., $C^{\bar{S}} = C^S$. Hence, $C^S \leq C^{S^*}$ is true, that is, the schedule $S = (S_1, S_2)$ produced by the MLPT algorithm is an optimal schedule of the instance $\mathcal{I}$.   □

Theorem 1. *The MLPT algorithm can find a schedule* $S = (S_1, S_2)$ *in* $\mathcal{O}(n \log n)$ *time, which satisfies*

$$\frac{C^S}{C^{S^*}} \leq 1 + \frac{1}{20}c_1/c_0.$$

Proof. For the given instance $\mathcal{I}$ of the SHOC problem, suppose the MLPT algorithm can produce a schedule $S = (S_1, S_2)$ and its total cost is C^S. Moreover, let $S^* = (S_1^*, S_2^*)$ be an optimal schedule of the instance $\mathcal{I}$, of which the total cost is C^{S^*}. By the Lemmas 3 and 4, we know that the MLPT algorithm can produce an optimal schedule when the loads of the machines satisfy $\max\{L_1^S, L_2^S\} \leq L_0$ or $\min\{L_1^S, L_2^S\} \geq L_0$, or the number of the jobs satisfies $n \leq 4$. Therefore, we only need to prove the conclusion in cases $n \geq 5$ and $\min\{L_1^S, L_2^S\} < L_0 < \max\{L_1^S, L_2^S\}$.

Without loss of generality, assume that $L_1^S < L_0 < L_2^S$. In fact, if $L_2^S < L_0 < L_1^S$, then the conclusion can be proved by exchanging L_1^S and L_2^S in the following proof. Furthermore, we can assume the last job J_n of the instance $\mathcal{I}$ is the last comleted job. Otherwise, let J_t ($2 \leq t \leq n$) be the last completed job and suppose $J_t \in S_i$ in the schedule S. Then, we can construct a new instance $\mathcal{I}'$ of the SHOC problem by deleting the jobs after the job J_t in the instance $\mathcal{I}$. And we can also obtain a schedule $S_{\mathcal{I}'} = (S_1^{\mathcal{I}'}, S_2^{\mathcal{I}'})$ of the instance $\mathcal{I}'$ by deleting the jobs after the job J_t in the schedule $\mathcal{S} = (S_1, S_2)$. It's easy to verify that their total costs are equal, i.e., $C^{\mathcal{S}} = C^{\mathcal{S}_{\mathcal{I}'}}$. And then, we can prove $C^{\mathcal{S}_{\mathcal{I}'}}/C^{\mathcal{S}^*_{\mathcal{I}'}} \leq 1 + \frac{1}{20}c_1/c_0$ by the following proof. Obviously, $C^{\mathcal{S}^*_{\mathcal{I}'}} \leq C^{\mathcal{S}^*}$ is true, it implies $C^{\mathcal{S}}/C^{\mathcal{S}^*} \leq C^{\mathcal{S}_{\mathcal{I}'}}/C^{\mathcal{S}^*_{\mathcal{I}'}}$. So, the conclusion is also true for the given instance $\mathcal{I}$.

So to sum up, we can assume $n \geq 5$, $L_1^{\mathcal{S}} < L_0 < L_2^{\mathcal{S}}$ and the job J_n is the last completed job. According to the MLPT algorithm, J_n must be assigned to the machine M_2 and $L_2^{\mathcal{S}} - p_n \leq L_1^{\mathcal{S}}$ is true. Therefore, we have $P \geq np_n$, implying that $p_n \leq P/n \leq P/5$. Thus $L_1^{\mathcal{S}} + L_2^{\mathcal{S}} \geq L_1^{\mathcal{S}} + L_2^{\mathcal{S}} - p_n = P - p_n \geq 4P/5$ holds, i.e., $L_1^{\mathcal{S}} \geq 2P/5$, it indicates $L_2^{\mathcal{S}} \leq 3P/5$ is true. According to the relationship between L_0 and $P/2$, the conclusion will be proved in two cases.

Case 1: If $L_0 \leq P/2$, then

$$
\begin{aligned}
\frac{C^{\mathcal{S}}}{C^{\mathcal{S}^*}} &\leq \frac{2c_0 + (L_2^{\mathcal{S}} - L_0)c_1}{\max\{2c_0, 2c_0 + (P - 2L_0)c_1\}} \\
&= \frac{2c_0 + (P - 2L_0)c_1 + (L_0 - L_1^{\mathcal{S}})c_1}{2c_0 + (P - 2L_0)c_1} \\
&= 1 + \frac{(L_0 - L_1^{\mathcal{S}})c_1}{2c_0 + (P - 2L_0)c_1} \\
&\leq 1 + \frac{(L_0 - L_1^{\mathcal{S}})c_1}{2c_0} \\
&\leq 1 + \frac{(P/2 - 2P/5)c_1}{2c_0} = 1 + \frac{1}{20}c_1/c_0.
\end{aligned}
$$

Case 2: If $L_0 \geq P/2$, then

$$
\begin{aligned}
\frac{C^{\mathcal{S}}}{C^{\mathcal{S}^*}} &\leq \frac{2c_0 + (L_2^{\mathcal{S}} - L_0)c_1}{\max\{2c_0, 2c_0 + (P - 2L_0)c_1\}} \\
&= \frac{2c_0 + (L_2^{\mathcal{S}} - L_0)c_1}{2c_0} = 1 + \frac{(L_2^{\mathcal{S}} - L_0)c_1}{2c_0} \\
&\leq 1 + \frac{(3P/5 - P/2)c_1}{2c_0} = 1 + \frac{1}{20}c_1/c_0.
\end{aligned}
$$

Obviously, the running time of the MLPT algorithm depends on the sorting of n jobs in the Step 1, which can be done by calling the binary insertion sort algorithm and its running time is $\mathcal{O}(n \log n)$. $\square$

Note that the approximation guarantee of the MLPT algorithm $\frac{1}{20}c_1/c_0$ is not a constant and may increase as the ratio c_1/c_0 increases. It seems to indicate that our algorithm does not find a good approximate solution. However, in real life, the ration c_1/c_0 is usually a small number, such as 2, 3 and so on. When the ratios c_1/c_0 are 2 and 3, the approximation guarantees are $11/10$ and $23/20$, respectively, which are almost optimal. And we can prove that there is no any constant approximation algorithm to solve the SHOC problem from the partition problem.

4 A Pseudo-polynomial Time Algorithm

In this section, we first give 4 characteristics that an optimal schedule of any instance $\mathcal{I}$ of the SHOC problem may have. And then, design two dynamic programmings to find an optimal schedule by the four characteristics. Based on these two dynamic programmings, we present a pseudo-polynomial time algorithm to solve the SHOC problem in $\mathcal{O}(nL_0)$ time.

According to the analysis in the previous sections, each schedule (especially optimal schedule) $\mathcal{S} = (S_1, S_2)$ of the instance $\mathcal{I}$ must satisfy one of the following four characteristics.

(1) $L_1^{\mathcal{S}} \leq L_0$ and $L_2^{\mathcal{S}} \leq L_0$;
(2) $L_1^{\mathcal{S}} \leq L_0$ and $L_2^{\mathcal{S}} > L_0$;
(3) $L_1^{\mathcal{S}} > L_0$ and $L_2^{\mathcal{S}} \leq L_0$;
(4) $L_1^{\mathcal{S}} > L_0$ and $L_2^{\mathcal{S}} > L_0$.

For an optimal schedule of the instance $\mathcal{I}$, which satisfies the first 3 characteristics, there exists one machine M_i ($i = 1$ or 2) such that its load $L_i^{\mathcal{S}}$ is no more than L_0. For convenience, use $p(S)$ to denote the total processing time of any job set S, i.e., $p(S) = \sum_{J_j \in S} p_j$. In order to find such an optimal schedule, We can use the following strategy, denoted as ST_I.

(1) First, find a job set $S_I \subset \mathcal{J}$ such that the total processing time $p(S_I)$ is no more than L_0 and $p(S_I)$ is maximum.
(2) Let a job set $CS_I = \mathcal{J} \setminus S_I$. If the only low-hierarchy job is in S_I, then assign the all jobs of S_I to the machine M_1, otherwise, to M_2. And then, assign the other jobs, i.e., the jobs of CS_I, to the other machine.

Consequently, we can obtain a schedule, denoted as $\mathcal{S}_I = (S_1^I, S_2^I)$. In fact, it's an optimal schedule of the instance $\mathcal{I}$. Because as long as S_I satisfies the conditions in the strategy ST_I, the total processing time of the job set CS_I must be minimum. Thus, the overload $p(CS_I) - L_0$ is also minimum, if any.

In order to find the job set S_I satisfying the conditions in the strategy ST_I, let $U(j, L) = \max\{p(S) \mid S \subset \{J_1, J_2, \cdots, J_j\}, p(S) \leq L\}$ for $j = 1, 2, \cdots, n$ and $0 \leq L \leq L_0$. And let $U(j, L) = 0$ if $\min\{p(J_k) \mid 1 \leq k \leq j\} > L$, i.e., such a job set S not exists. Without loss of generality, assume that all of the processing times $p_1, p_2, \cdots, p_n$ and the regular working time L_0 are integers. Then, we can obtain the job set S_I by solving the following dynamic programming, denoted as DP_I,

$$U(j+1, L) = \begin{cases} U(j, L) & \text{if } p_{j+1} > L; \\ \max\{U(j, L), U(j, L - p_{j+1}) + p_{j+1}\} & \text{otherwise.} \end{cases}$$

Lemma 5. *For the instance $\mathcal{I}$ of the SHOC problem, we can find the job set S_I satisfying the conditions in the strategy ST_I in $\mathcal{O}(nL_0)$ time by solving the dynamic programming DP_I.*

Proof. Recall the definitions of the notations $U(j, L)$ where $j = 1, 2, \cdots, n$ and $0 \le L \le L_0$, that is each notation $U(j, L)$ denotes the total processing time of a job set S which satisfies that $S \subset \{J_1, J_2, \cdots, J_j\}$, $p(S) \le L$ and $p(S)$ is maximum, and let $U(j, L) = 0$ if such a job set S not exists. Initially, set $U(0, L) = 0$ for $L = 0, 1, \cdots, L_0$.

By induction for the iteration variable j, we can prove that each value $U(j, L)$ calculated by the dynamic programming DP_I conforms to the definition of this notaion $U(j, L)$. Obviously, when $j = 0$, each initial value $U(0, L)$ conforms to the definition of the notation $U(0, L)$, where $L = 0, 1, \cdots, L_0$. When $j = k$, assume that each value $U(k, L)$ calculated by dynamic programming DP_I conforms to the definition of this notaion $U(k, L)$, where $L = 0, 1, \cdots, L_0$. When $j = k + 1$ and $L = 0, 1, \cdots, L_0$, if $p_{k+1} > L$, then the job J_{k+1} can't be in S, which implies that $U(k+1, L) = U(k, L)$ holds. Otherwise, the job J_{k+1} may or may not in the S. By the assumptions for the notations $U(k, L)$ and $U(k, L - p_{k+1})$, we have $U(k+1, L) = \max\{U(k, L), U(k, L - p_{k+1}) + p_{k+1}\}$ is true. Therefore, each value $U(k+1, L)$ calculated by the dynamic programming DP_I does conform to the definition of the notaion $U(k+1, L)$, where $0 \le L \le L_0$.

When $U(n, L_0)$ is computed iteratively, the iterative calculation performed on the dynamic programming DP_I will stop. The set S corresponding to $U(n, L_0)$ is the job set S_I that this lemma needs. Obviously, the calculation of the dynamic programming DP_I is completed in $\mathcal{O}(nL_0)$ time. □

By the dynamic programming DP_I, we design an algorithm to find the job set S_I satisfying the conditions in the strategy ST_I in $\mathcal{O}(nL_0)$ time, and its details are described in the following Algorithm 2.

Algorithm 2: OPT-S_I

---

1 **Input** an instance $\mathcal{I} = (\mathcal{J}, \mathcal{M}, p, g, L_0, c_0, c_1)$ of the SHOC problem. Note that the following steps do not require the weight function g and the costs c_0, c_1.

2 Set $U(0, L) := 0$ for $L = 0, 1, \cdots, L_0$, let $S(j, L) := \emptyset$ for all values of j and L.

3 **for** $j = 1$ *to* n **do**

4   **for** $L = 0$ *to* L_0 **do**

5   Set $U(j, L) := U(j - 1, L)$ and $S(j, L) := S(j - 1, L)$.

6   **if** $p_j \le L$ *and* $U(j - 1, L) < U(j - 1, L - p_j) + p_j$ **then**

7   Set $U(j, L) := U(j - 1, L - p_j) + p_j$ and $S(j, L) := S(j - 1, L - p_j) \cup \{J_j\}$.

8 **return** $S(n, L_0)$.

Now, we consider another optimal schedule satisfying the last characteristic, that is the loads L_1^S and L_2^S of the machines are both greater than L_0. Similarly, in order to find such an optimal schedule, We use the following strategy, denoted as ST_{II}.

(1) First, find a job set $S_{II} \subset \mathcal{J}$ such that the total processing time $p(S_{II})$ is greater than L_0 and $p(S_{II})$ is minimum.

(2) Let a job set $CS_{II} = \mathcal{J}\backslash S_{II}$. If the only low-hierarchy job is in S_{II}, then assign the all jobs of S_{II} to the machine M_1, otherwise, to M_2. And then, assign the other jobs, i.e., the jobs of CS_{II}, to the other machine.

Consequently, we can obtain a schedule $\mathcal{S}_{II} = (S_1^{II}, S_2^{II})$. If the instance $\mathcal{I}$ has an optimal schedule $\mathcal{S}^* = (S_1^*, S_2^*)$ satisfying the last characteristic, then, the total processing time $p(S_{II})$ of the job set S_{II} must satisfy $p(S_{II}) \leq p(S_1^*)$ and $p(S_{II}) \leq p(S_2^*)$. Hence, the total processing of the job set CS_{II} must be greater than L_0. Otherwise, it contradicts with the optimality of the shedule $\mathcal{S}^* = (S_1^*, S_2^*)$. It indicates that $p(S_{II}) > L_0$ and $p(CS_{II}) > L_0$ are both true. By Lemma 3, the shedule $\mathcal{S}_{II} = (S_1^{II}, S_2^{II})$ does be an optimal schedule, which is obtained by using the job set S_{II} and following the strategy ST_{II}.

In order to find the job set S_{II} satisfying the conditions in the strategy ST_{II}, let $Q(j, L) = \min\{p(S) \mid S \subset \{J_1, J_2, \cdots, J_j\}, p(S) > L\}$ for $j = 1, 2, \cdots, n$ and $0 \leq L \leq L_0$. And let $Q(j, L) = \infty$ if $\sum_{k=1}^{j} p_k \leq L$. Then, we can obtain the job set S_{II} by solving the following dynamic programming, denoted as DP_{II},

$$Q(j+1, L) = \begin{cases} \min\{Q(j, L), p_{j+1}\} & \text{if } p_{j+1} > L; \\ \min\{Q(j, L), Q(j, L - p_{j+1}) + p_{j+1}\} & \text{otherwise.} \end{cases}$$

Lemma 6. *For the instance $\mathcal{I}$ of the SHOC problem, we can find the job set S_{II} satisfying the conditions in the strategy ST_{II} in $\mathcal{O}(nL_0)$ time by solving the dynamic programming DP_{II}.*

By initializing $Q(0, L) = \infty$ for $L = 0, 1, \cdots, L_0$, we can prove by mathematical induction that for all $0 \leq j \leq n$, each value $Q(j, L)$ calculated by the dynamic programming DP_{II} conforms to the definition of this notaion $Q(j, L)$, where $0 \leq L \leq L_0$. Its proof is similar to the proof of Lemma 5 and we omit here. Finally, by the dynamic programming DP_{II} and the Lemma 6, we give an algorithm to find the job set S_{II} satisfying the conditions in the strategy ST_{II} in $\mathcal{O}(nL_0)$ time, and its details are described in the following Algorithm 3.

Finally, based on above analysis, lemmas and strategies, we can design a pseudo-polynomial time algorithm to solve the SHOC problem. For an instance $\mathcal{I}$ of the SHOC problem, each optimal schedule of $\mathcal{I}$ must satisfy one of the above 4 characteristics. By the strategy ST_I and the Lemma 5, if there exists an optimal schedule satisfing one of the first 3 characteristics, the schedule $\mathcal{S}_I = (S_1^I, S_2^I)$ is also an optimal schedule. And then, by the strategy ST_{II} and the Lemma 6, if there exists an optimal schedule satisfing the last characteristic, the schedule $\mathcal{S}_{II} = (S_1^{II}, S_2^{II})$ is also an optimal schedule. Therefore, we can design algorithm to find an optimal schedule of the instance $\mathcal{I}$ according to the following strategy.

(1) Call the Algorithm OPT-S_{II} to find the job set S_{II}.
(2) If the total processing time $p(\mathcal{J}\backslash S_{II})$ is no less than L_0, then the schedule $\mathcal{S}_{II} = (S_1^{II}, S_2^{II})$ obtained by using the strategy ST_{II} is an optimal schedule. Otherwise, continue to execute the next step.
(3) Call the Algorithm OPT-S_I to find the job set S_I, and the schedule $\mathcal{S}_I = (S_1^{II}, S_2^{II})$ obtained by using the strategy ST_I must be an optimal schedule.

Algorithm 3: OPT-S_{II}

---

1 **Input** an instance $\mathcal{I} = (\mathcal{J}, \mathcal{M}, p, g, L_0, c_0, c_1)$ of the SHOC problem. Note that the following steps do not require the weight function g and the costs c_0, c_1.

2 Set $Q(0, L) = \infty$ for $L = 0, 1, \cdots, L_0$, let $S(j, L) := \emptyset$ for all values of j and L.

3 **for** $j = 1$ *to* n **do**

4   **for** $L = 0$ *to* L_0 **do**

5   Set $Q(j, L) := Q(j - 1, L)$ and $S(j, L) := S(j - 1, L)$.

6   **if** $p_j > L$ *and* $p_j < Q(j - 1, L)$ **then**

7   Set $Q(j, L) := p_j$ and $S(j, L) := \{J_j\}$.

8   **if** $p_j \leq L$ *and* $Q(j - 1, L - p_j) + p_j < Q(j - 1, L)$ **then**

9   Set $Q(j, L) := Q(j - 1, L - p_j) + p_j$ and
          $S(j, L) := S(j - 1, L - p_j) \cup \{J_j\}$.

10 **return** $S(n, L_0)$.

By the strategy above, we can design a pseudo-polynomial time algorithm to solve the SHOC problem and its details can be described as follows.

Algorithm 4: OPT

---

1 For instance $\mathcal{I} = (\mathcal{J}, \mathcal{M}, p, g, L_0, c_0, c_1)$ of the SHOC problem, call the Algorithm OPT-S_{II} to find the job set S_{II} and let $S := S_{II}$.

2 **if** $p(\mathcal{J} \backslash S) \geq L_0$ **then**

3   go to **step 5**.

4 Call the Algorithm OPT-S_I to find the job set S_I and let $S := S_I$.

5 **if** *the only low-hierarchy job is in* S **then**

6   Let $S_1 := S$ and $S_2 := \mathcal{J} \backslash S$;

7 **else**

8   Let $S_1 := \mathcal{J} \backslash S$ and $S_2 := S$.

9 Output an optimal schedule $\mathcal{S} = (S_1, S_2)$.

Theorem 2. *For any instance $\mathcal{I}$ of the SHOC problem, the Algorithm OPT can find an optimal schedule of $\mathcal{I}$ in $\mathcal{O}(nL_0)$ time.*

The correctness of Theorem 2 can be obtained from the Lemmas 5 and 6, the strategies ST_I and ST_{II}.

5 Conclusion

In this paper, we consider the problem of scheduling with hierarchies and overload cost (SHOC, in short) on two identical parallel machines. In this problem, we are given a set of jobs, two machines, a regular working time L_0 of machines, a start-up cost c_0 and a cost c_1 of per unit overload, where each job and machine are labeled with hierarchies. We design a modified longest processing time (MLPT) algorithm to solve this problem, and proved that its approximation guarantee is $1 + \frac{1}{20}c_1/c_0$ and the running time is $\mathcal{O}(nlogn)$. And then, according to the characteristics of optimal solutions, we give a pseudo-polynomial time algorithm by using two dynamic programmings. We can find an optimal schedule in $\mathcal{O}(nL_0)$ time by using this algorithm.

Acknowledgements. The work is supported by the General Program of Yunnan Province Science and Technology Department [No. 202001BB050062], and the Postgraduate Research and Innovation Foundation of Yunnan University under Grant KC-22221129.

References

1. Alon, N., Azar, Y., Woeginger, G.J., Yadid, T.: Approximation schemes for scheduling on parallel machines. J. Sched. **1**(1), 55–66 (1998)
2. Bar-Noy, A., Freund, A., Naor, J.: On-line load balancing in a hierarchical server topology. SIAM J. Comput. **31**(2), 527–549 (2001)
3. Chen, X., Sterna, M., Han, X., Blazewicz, J.: Scheduling on parallel identical machines with late work criterion: offline and online cases. Int. J. Sched. **19**(6), 729–736 (2016)
4. Chen, X., Kovalev, S., Liu, Y., Sterna, M., Chalamon, I., Blazewicz, J.: Semi-online scheduling on two identical machines with a common due date to maximize total early work. Discret. Appl. Math. **290**, 71–78 (2021)
5. Coffman, E.G., Jr., Lueker, G.S.: Approximation algorithms for extensible bin packing. J. Sched. **9**(1), 63–69 (2006)
6. Dai, B., Li, J., Li, W.: Semi-online hierarchical scheduling for bag-of-tasks on two machines. In: 2nd International Conference on Computer Science and Artificial Intelligence Proceedings, pp. 609–614. Association for Computing Machinery, New York, United States (2018)
7. Dell'Olmo, P., Kellerer, H., Speranza, M.G., Tuza, Z.: A 13/12 approximation algorithm for bin packing with extendable bins. Inf. Process. Lett. **65**(5), 229–233 (1998)
8. Dell'Olmo, P., Speranza, M.G.: Approximation algorithms for partitioning small items in unequal bins to minimize the total size. Discret. Appl. Math. **4**(1–3), 181–191 (1999)
9. Epstein, L., Tassa, T.: Vector assignment schemes for asymmetric settings. Acta Informatica **42**, 501–514 (2006)
10. Graham, R.L.: Bounds on multiprocessor timing anomalies. SIAM J. Appl. Math. **17**(2), 416–29 (1969)
11. Graham, R.L., Lawler, E.L., Lenstra, J.K., Kan, A.R.: Optimization and approximation in deterministic sequencing and scheduling: a survey. Ann. Discrete Math. **5**, 287–326 (1979)
12. Hochbaum, D.S., Shmoys, D.B.: Using dual approximation algorithms for scheduling problems theoretical and practical results. J. ACM **34**(1), 144–162 (1987)
13. Hwang, H.C., Chang, S.Y., Lee, K.: Parallel machine scheduling under a grade of service provision. Comput. Oper. Res. **31**(12), 2055–2061 (2004)

14. Ji, M., Cheng, T.C.E.: An FPTAS for parallel-machine scheduling under a grade of service provision to minimize makespan. Inf. Process. Lett. **108**(4), 171–174 (2008)
15. Jiang, Y.: Online scheduling on parallel machines with two GoS levels. J. Comb. Optim. **16**(1), 28–38 (2008)
16. Levin, A.: Approximation schemes for the generalized extensible bin packing problem. Algorithmica **84**(2), 325–343 (2022)
17. Li, J., Li, W., Li, J.: Polynomial approximation schemes for the max-min allocation problem under a grade of service provision. Discrete Math. Algorithms Appl. **1**(03), 355–368 (2009)
18. Ou, J., Leung, J.Y.T., Li, C.L.: Scheduling parallel machines with inclusive processing set restrictions. Nav. Res. Logist. **55**(4), 328–338 (2008)
19. Park, J., Chang, S.Y., Lee, K.: Online and semi-online scheduling of two machines under a grade of service provision. Oper. Res. Lett. **34**(6), 692–696 (2006)
20. Speranza, M.G., Tuza, Z.: On-line approximation algorithms for scheduling tasks on identical machines withextendable working time. Ann. Oper. Res. **86**, 491–506 (1999)
21. Wei, Q., Wu, Y., Cheng, T.C.E., Sun, F., Jiang, Y.: Online hierarchical parallel-machine scheduling in shared manufacturing to minimize the total completion time. J. Oper. Res. Soc. **74**, 1–23 (2022)
22. Woeginger, G.: When does a dynamic programming formulation guarantee the existence of a fully polynomial time approximation scheme (FPTAS)? INFORMS J. Comput. **12**(1), 57–74 (2000)
23. Wu, G., Li, W.: Semi-online machine covering on two hierarchical machines with discrete processing times. In: Li, L., Lu, P., He, K. (eds.) NCTCS 2018. CCIS, vol. 882, pp. 1–7. Springer, Singapore (2018). https://doi.org/10.1007/978-981-13-2712-4_1
24. Xiao, M., Liu, X., Li, W., Chen, X., Sterna, M., Blazewicz, J.: Online and semi-online scheduling on two hierarchical machines with a common due date to maximize the total early work. arXiv preprint arXiv:2209.08704, https://doi.org/10.48550/arXiv.2209.08704 (2022)
25. Xiao, M., Li, W.: Online early work maximization on three hierarchical machines with a common due date. In: Li, M., Sun, X. (eds.) Frontiers of Algorithmic Wisdom. IJTCS-FAW 2022. LNCS, vol. 13461, pp. 99–109. Springer, Cham (2022). https://doi.org/10.1007/978-3-031-20796-9_8
26. Xiao, M., Du, Y., Li, W., Yang, J.: Semi-online machine covering problem on three hierarchical machines with bounded processing times. J. Oper. Res. Soc. China 1–13 (2023). https://doi.org/10.1007/s40305-023-00477-1
27. Ye, D., Zhang, G.: On-line extensible bin packing with unequal bin sizes. Discrete Math. Theor. Comput. Sci. **11**(1), 141–152 (2009)
28. Zhang, A., Jiang, Y., Tan, Z.: Online parallel machines scheduling with two hierarchies. Theoret. Comput. Sci. **410**(38–40), 3597–3605 (2009)

Artificial Intelligence

Region-SMOTE: A New Over-Sampling Method in Imbalanced Data Sets Learning

Wencheng Sun[1], Zhiping Cai[2(✉)], and Xiaoyong Chen[1]

[1] National University of Defense Technology, Nanjing 210039, China
[2] College of Computer, National University of Defense Technology, Changsha 410073, China
zpcai@nudt.edu.cn

Abstract. Learning from imbalanced data sets usually produces biased classifiers that have a higher predictive accuracy over the majority class, but poorer predictive accuracy over the minority class. In this paper, we present a new over-sampling method, Region-SMOTE, to improve class imbalance and classification accuracy. In order to combine the boundary distribution information, the vote rule is formulated, which divides the minority samples into safety samples, intermediate samples and dangerous samples, and adopts different processing strategies for different samples. We evaluate Region-SMOTE method from two aspects, F-value and G-mean. We conduct extensive experiments on four data sets, including Diabetes, which is extracted from real-world physical examination database, and another three data sets, which are extracted from UCI, to verify the method. The evaluation results demonstrate that our proposed over-sampling method has better performance.

Keywords: imbalanced data set · over-sampling method · SMOTE

1 Introduction

Recently, the problem of imbalance receives more and more attentions from both theoretical and practical aspects. Unbalanced data is still considered a significant challenge for contemporary machine learning models, such as tourism recommendation [1], medical diagnostics [2,3], software defect prediction [4], and image learning [5] and so on.

In these domains, what really deserves attention is the minority class other than the majority class. The correct classification for the minority class samples is more valuable than that for the majority class samples. However, the traditional classification algorithms fail to achieve good results due to the data imbalance.

The solutions to class imbalance problems include algorithmic level and data level. The algorithm-level methods modify the existing data mining algorithms or propose new algorithms to solve imbalances. The data-level approaches change the distribution of unbalanced data sets, and then provide the balanced data sets to classifiers to improve the classification accuracy of minority classes.

Z. Cai et al. (Eds.): NCTCS 2023, CCIS 1944, pp. 151–160, 2024.
https://doi.org/10.1007/978-981-99-7743-7_9

The data-level solutions are independent of algorithms. Data sampling technology balances the class distribution of data by adding some minority class samples (over-sampling) or deleting some majority class samples (under-sampling). For under-sampling technology [6–8], its advantage is that it can reduce the time of training model, but its disadvantage is that it causes information loss. Over-sampling technology [9–12] can reduce class imbalance by generating a few class samples, which may produce more marginal or noise samples.

The rest of this paper is organized as follows: Related work will be reviewed in Sect. 2. We will elaborate our method in detail in Sect. 3, followed by evaluation reports in Sect. 4. We conclude the paper in Sect. 5.

2   Related Works

The SMOTE algorithm, proposed by Chawla et al. [13] in 2002, is by far the most classical over-sampling algorithm. SMOTE algorithm generates new minority class samples by feature space similarity. As shown in Fig. 1, its algorithm idea is as follows:

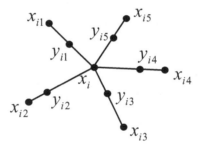

Fig. 1: Sample synthesis of SMOTE algorithm

In an unbalanced data set, all the minority class samples are defined as P. For each data sample x_i in P, k nearest neighbors of the sample in P are searched. Assuming the upper sampling rate of the data set is n, n samples $x_{ij}(j = 1, 2, ..., n)$ are extracted from k nearest neighbor samples, and then n new minority samples $y_{ij}(j = 1, 2, ..., n)$ are generated according to formula (1). The function rand (0,1) function produces a random number between intervals (0,1), and the sampling rate n is determined by the imbalance of the data set.

$$y_{ij} = x_i + rand(0, 1) * (x_i - x_{ij}), j = 1, 2, ..., n \qquad (1)$$

The SMOTE algorithm generates interpolation samples according to predetermined rules, changes the sample distribution, avoids blindness, and reduces the phenomenon of over-fitting. However, SMOTE itself also has some shortcomings, such as the validity of interpolation samples and the fuzzy problem of class boundaries.

The Borderline-SMOTE algorithm is proposed by Han et al. [14], which combines the boundary information to generate new samples. By this way, the blindness of SMOTE method in selecting the minority samples is reduced, thus reducing redundant samples and improving data quality. There are two versions of the Borderline-SMOTE algorithm, Borderline-SMOTE-1 and Borderline-SMOTE-2.

Define the unbalanced data set as D, the minority class sample set as P, the majority class sample set as Q, then $D = P \cup Q$. For each data sample x_i in P, k nearest neighbors of the sample in D are searched, including k_{i1} minority nearest neighbor samples. If $k_{i1} = 0$, the k nearest neighbor samples of the sample x_i are all majority class samples, then the sample x_i will be considered as a noise point without any operation. If $k_{i1} > \frac{k}{2}$, the sample x_i will be considered as a safety sample without any processing. If $0 < k_{i1} \leq \frac{k}{2}$, the sample x_i id located at the boundary of the minority classes, which is added to the dangerous set. Dangerous samples will be oversampled and amplified according to the SMOTE method.

It should be pointed out that the Borderline-SMOTE method is too simple for the classification of three minority samples. In addition, this method does not over-sample the more informative safety samples and reduces the overall effectiveness.

Based on the SMOTE algorithm, Chawla et al. [15] put forward the SMOTE-Boost algorithm. The algorithm combines AdaBoost. M2 algorithm to enhance the learning ability and improves the overall prediction performance of the minority classes. However, the algorithm still generates samples by interpolation, so that the newly generated samples are still distributed on the line of the original samples, which can not well reflect the data distribution.

Based on the SMOTEBoost algorithm, Hu S et al. [16] proposed MSMOT-Boost, which was over-sampled using optimized synthetic samples during the iteration process. According to the distance distribution, the minority samples are divided into the safety sample, the boundary sample and the noise sample. Different strategies are adopted for the three different samples. The boundary samples are selected according to the distance. The selected boundary samples and the safety samples will be over-sampled by SMOTE method. Experiments show that this method is superior to the SMOTEBoost algorithm in terms of accuracy and F-value of two indicators.

3   Methodology

In order to get better prediction results, most classification algorithms try to learn the boundaries of each class as accurately as possible during the training process. The samples near the boundary are easier to be misclassified than the samples far away from the boundary, so it is more important for classification.

The data set shown in Fig. 2 has clear class boundaries, which belongs to relatively simple data sets. However, in most complex data sets, the distribution of data samples is not the same. There are not absolute boundaries between the majority class samples and the minority class samples, and there are a small

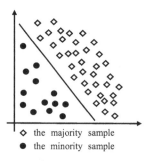

◇ the majority sample
● the minority sample

Fig. 2: Simple data set

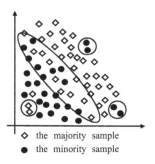

◇ the majority sample
● the minority sample

Fig. 3: Complex data set

Algorithm 1. Region-SMOTE Algorithm

Require:

the imbalanced data set, D;the minority sample set, P;

the safety sample set, S;the intermediate sample set, M; the dangerous sample set, W;

the over-sampling rate, n;

Ensure:

the balanced data set after over-sampling, O;

1: for $x_i \in P$, search its k nearest neighbors from D, including k_{i1} neighbors from the minority class and k_{i2} neighbors from the majority class;

2: according to the vote rule, classify the minority sample x_i;

3: if $x_i \in S$, then generate y_{ij} and $z_{ij}(j = 1, 2, ..., n)$;

4: if $x_i \in M$, then SMOTE (x_i);

5: if $x_i \in W$, then ignore (x_i);

6: **return** O.

---

number of majority samples and minority samples distributed in the main distribution areas of the other samples, as shown in Fig. 3.

First let's introduce the vote rule used in the Region-SMOTE method. Define the unbalanced data set as D, the minority class sample set as P, the majority class sample set as Q, then $D = P \cup Q$. For each data sample x_i in P, we search its k nearest neighbors from D, including k_{i1} neighbors from the minority class and k_{i2} neighbors from the majority class, $k = k_{i1} + k_{i2}$. If $k_{i1} \leq \lceil \frac{k}{5} \rceil$, the sample x_i is a noise point and belongs to W; if $k_{i2} \leq \lfloor \frac{2k}{5} \rfloor$, the sample x_i belongs to S; otherwise, the sample x_i belongs to M.

As shown in Algorithm 1, for intermediate samples, we use SMOTE method for over-sampling; for dangerous samples, we ignore the sampling process.

For safety samples, we do not use the method of generating interpolation points on the line of sample points, but use the method of generating new samples in the whole region. The advantage of this is that it can reflect the characteristics of the minority samples more comprehensively.

$$y_{ij} = x_{i(j+1)} + rand(0, 1) * (x_{i(j+1)} - x_{ij}), j = 1, 2, ..., n \qquad (2)$$

$$z_{ij} = x_i + rand(0,1) * (x_i - y_{ij}), j = 1, 2, ..., n \qquad (3)$$

For each safety sample x_i in S, we search its k nearest neighbors from P. Assuming the upper sampling rate is n, n samples $x_{ij}(j = 1, 2, ..., n)$ are extracted from k nearest neighbor samples, and then n temporary samples $y_{ij}(j = 1, 2, ..., n)$ are generated according to formula (2). Then according to formula (3), n new minority samples $z_{ij}(j = 1, 2, ..., n)$ are generated. As shown in Fig. 4.

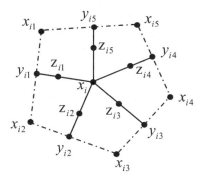

Fig. 4: Safety sample synthesis of Region-SMOTE algorithm

4   Experiments

4.1   Datasets

Table 1: Summary of data sets in experiments

Dataset	Number of samples	Number of attributes	Number of minority class samples/P	Number of majority class instances/Q	IR
Diabetes	5731	41	1017	4714	4.64
cmc	1473	9	333	1140	3.42
ecoli	336	7	77	259	3.36
yeast	1484	8	244	1240	5.08

Our experiments were performed on four data sets summarized in Table 1. Diabetes is extracted from real-world physical examination database [17], and another three data sets are extracted from UCI. It should be noted that we only consider the case of binary classification, and label transformation is carried out for multi-classification data sets. IR (Imbalanced Rate) refers to the ratio of the majority class to the minority class, and the over-sampling rate n is usually determined by the IR value. In order to compare the effects of various over sampling methods, we use the random forest algorithm and the reported values are obtained by performing 5-fold cross-validation.

4.2 Evaluation Criteria

Table 2: Confusion matrix of a two-class problem

	Predicted Positive	Predicted Negative
Actual Positive	True Positives/TP	False Negatives/FN
Actual Negative	False Positives/FP	True Negatives/TN

The evaluation of the classification performance in imbalanced domains generally focuses on two-class problem and the multi-class problem can be simplified to two-class problem. According to convention, the label of the minority class is positive, and the label of the majority class is negative. Table 2 describes a confusion matrix of a two-class problem. The first column of the table is the actual class label for the samples, and the first row represents their predicted class label. TP and TN represent the number of positive and negative samples of correct classification, and FN and FP respectively indicate the number of positive and negative samples of misclassification.

Table 3: Basic evaluation indexes for a two-class problem

Basic evaluation index	Expression
Overall classification accuracy	Accuracy = (TP + TN)/(TP + TN + FP + FN)
Classification accuracy of positive classes	acc^+ = TP/(TP + FN)
Classification accuracy of negatives classes	acc^- = TN/(TN + FP)
TP Rate	TP Rate = TP/(TP + FN)
FP Rate	FP Rate = FP/(FP + TN)
Recall	Recall = TP/(TP + FN) = TP Rate
Precision	Precision = TP/(TP + FP)

Table 3 illustrates the basic evaluation indexes of a two-class problem. Based on these basic indexes, several other important indexes are derived, such as F-value, G-mean and ROC(Receiver Operating Characteristic) curve.

$$F - value = \frac{(1 + \beta^2) * Recall * Precision}{\beta^2 * Recall + Precision} \tag{4}$$

In Eq. (4), β is used to reflect the relative importance of Recall and Precision. When β is greater than 1, it means that Precision is more important. When β is less than 1, Recall is more important. In general, β will be set to 1, which means that both Recall and Precision are just as important. F-value is the result of considering the two Recall and Precision, which is more comprehensive. When

F-value gets a higher value, it means that the performance of the classifier is excellent.

$$G - mean = \sqrt{acc^+ * acc^-} \tag{5}$$

G-mean (Geometric Mean) is another index used to evaluate classification performance and is widely used. G-mean is independent of the class distribution of data sets and is very robust to the data imbalance. G-mean maintains the classification accuracy while maintaining the balance of the two classifications. For example, when the classification accuracy of the majority class is high, and the classification accuracy of the minority class is low, G-mean will not be ideal. Only when both are maintained at a certain level, the value of G-mean is not too bad.

In addition, the ROC curve is also a very common classification performance evaluation index. The vertical axis of the graph is TP Rate and the horizontal axis is FP Rate. In this curve, FP Rate and TP Rate are mutually constrained. For more intuitive and quantitative analysis performance, AUC (Area Under the ROC Curve) is used instead of ROC curve. The larger the value of AUC, the better the classification performance.

In practical applications, the above-mentioned several indexes are generally selected to evaluate the classification effect of the unbalanced data sets. After comprehensive consideration, this paper decided to use the F-value and G-means indexes to measure the experimental results.

4.3   Results and Evaluation

Table 4: Distribution of minority samples in different data sets

Dataset	Diabetes	cmc	ecoli	yeast
Number of safety samples	63	173	77	244
Number of intermediate samples	521	126	0	0
Number of dangerous samples	344	34	0	0

According to the vote rule, the sample distribution of the minority classes in each data set is shown in Tables 4, 5 and 6 refer to the classification results using random forest models after different over-sampling algorithms.

It can be seen that the F-value and G-mean values basically correspond to each other, and can reflect the overall effect of classification. When the F-value is poor, the G-mean value is also poor; when the F-value effect rises, the G-mean effect also rises.

The performance gap between the original data set and the over-sampled data set is very large, especially in the Diabetes data set. The F-value of the original Diabetes data set is only 0.122, and the G-mean value is only 0.259, but

Table 5: F-value of the random forest model after over-sampling

Algorithm	Diabetes	cmc	ecoli	yeast
Original data	0.122	0.352	0.771	0.566
SMOTE	0.896	0.847	0.951	0.931
Borderline-SMOTE-1	0.899	0.850	0.936	0.935
Borderline-SMOTE-2	0.893	0.847	0.927	0.897
Region-SMOTE	0.903	0.890	0.942	0.941

Table 6: G-mean of the random forest model after over-sampling

Algorithm	Diabetes	cmc	ecoli	yeast
Original data	0.259	0.506	0.846	0.664
SMOTE	0.892	0.851	0.950	0.931
Borderline-SMOTE-1	0.895	0.856	0.934	0.933
Borderline-SMOTE-2	0.889	0.851	0.924	0.896
Region-SMOTE	0.901	0.890	0.946	0.938

the effect is greatly improved after over-sampling. For example, after SMOTE over-sampling, the F-value of the original Diabetes data set rises to 0.896, and the G-mean value rises to 0.892. In addition, although the classification effect of different original data sets differ widely, for example, the F-value value of cmc is 0.352 and the F-value value of ecoli is 0.771, the effect of different over-sampled data sets is not obvious. This shows that after the over-sampling processing, the classification effect of each data set has reached the upper limit.

It can be seen that the classifier performs very well in the ecoli and yeast data sets compared to the Diabetes and cmc data sets. Combining Table 4, we can find that the number of intermediate and dangerous samples of the ecoli and yeast data sets are 0, indicating that the class boundaries in the two data sets are relatively clear. In the Diabetes data set, the number of safe samples is the least, and obviously less than the number of intermediate samples and dangerous samples. In addition, the number of intermediate samples is the largest, accounting for 56.1% of the minority class samples, which means that the class boundaries of the Diabetes data set are blurred. Dangerous samples (noise samples) account for 37.1% of the minority class samples, indicating that the data distribution is rather mixed. Compared with the other three data sets with less than 10 attributes, this data set has 41 attributes. In summary, the performance of the classifier in Diabetes is relatively poor, especially in the original data set.

Finally, SMOTE algorithm performs better on small data sets with clear boundaries, such as the ecoli data set. The region-SMOTE method presented in this paper has a slight advantage over the Diabetes, cmc and yeast data sets. It shows that the reliability of the region-SMOTE method is superior to the other three over-sampling algorithms.

5   Conclusions

In this paper we present Region-SMOTE, a new over-sampling method, to over-sample the minority samples and solve the problem of data imbalance. We design the vote rule to make full use of class boundary information, which is more reasonable to divide the minority samples into safety samples, intermediate samples and dangerous samples, and adopts different processing strategies for different samples. We use random forests as classifiers. Data sets used in our work are extracted from real-world physical examination database and UCI. Experimental results indicate that Region-SMOTE is able to achieve better performance.

In our future work, we will considerate the differences of importance features. The approach we propose can be successful for learning from imbalanced data sets, and the related experiments will be conducted.

References

1. Fernández-Muñoz, J.J., Moguerza, M., Duque, C.M., Bruna, D.G.: A study on the effect of imbalanced data in tourism recommendation models. Int. J. Q. Serv. Sci. **3**, 346–356 (2019)
2. Ren, Z., Lin, T., Feng, K., Zhu, Y., Liu, Z., Yan, K.: A systematic review on imbalanced learning methods in intelligent fault diagnosis. IEEE Trans. Instr. Meas. **72**, 1–35 (2023)
3. Blanchard, A.E., et al.: A keyword-enhanced approach to handle class imbalance in clinical text classification. IEEE J. Biomed. Health Inform. **6**, 2796–2803 (2022)
4. Feng, S., Keung, J., Zhang, P., Xiao, Y., Zhang, M.,: The impact of the distance metric and measure on SMOTE-based techniques in software defect prediction. Inf. Softw. Technol. **142**(No.C), 1–14 (2022)
5. Dablain, D., Krawczyk, B., DeepSMOTE, N.C.: DeepSMOTE: fusing deep learning and SMOTE for imbalanced data. IEEE Trans. Neural Netw. Learn. Syst. **99**, 1–15 (2022)
6. Gong, P., Gao, J., Wang, L.: A hybrid evolutionary under-sampling method for handling the class imbalance problem with overlap in credit classification. J. Syst. Sci. Syst. Eng. **6**, 728–752 (2022)
7. Liu, S.M., Chen, J.H., Liu, Z.: An empirical study of dynamic selection and random under-sampling for the class imbalance problem. Expert Syst. Appl. **221**, 119703 (2023)
8. Guzmán-Ponce, A., Valdovinos, R.M., Sánchez, J.S., Marcial-Romero, J.R.: A new under-sampling method to face class overlap and imbalance. Appl. Sci. **10**, 5164 (2020)
9. Kim, M., Hwang, K.B.: An empirical evaluation of sampling methods for the classification of imbalanced data. PLoS one **17**(7), e0271260 (2022)
10. Duan, Y., et al.: SORAG: synthetic data over-sampling strategy on multi-label graphs. Remote Sens. **14**, 4479 (2022)

160 W. Sun et al.

11. Din, N.U., Zhang, L., Yang, Y.: Automated battery making fault classification using over-sampled image data CNN features. Sensors **23**, 1927 (2023)
12. Xiaolong, X.U., Wen, C.H.E.N., Yanfei, S.U.N.: Over-sampling algorithm for imbalanced data classification. J. Syst. Eng. Electron. **30**(6), 1182–1191 (2019)
13. Chawla, N.V., Bowyer, K.W., Hall, L.O.: SMOTE: synthetic minority over-sampling technique. J. Artif. Intell. Res. **16**(1), 321–357 (2002)
14. Han, H., Wang, W.-Y., Mao, B.-H.: Borderline-SMOTE: a new over-sampling method in imbalanced data sets learning. In: Huang, D.-S., Zhang, X.-P., Huang, G.-B. (eds.) ICIC 2005. LNCS, vol. 3644, pp. 878–887. Springer, Heidelberg (2005). https://doi.org/10.1007/11538059_91
15. Chawla, N.V., Lazarevic, A., Hall, L.O., Bowyer, K.W.: SMOTEBoost: improving prediction of the minority class in boosting. In: Lavrač, N., Gamberger, D., Todorovski, L., Blockeel, H. (eds.) PKDD 2003. LNCS (LNAI), vol. 2838, pp. 107–119. Springer, Heidelberg (2003). https://doi.org/10.1007/978-3-540-39804-2_12
16. Hu, S., Liang, Y., Ma, L., He, Y.: MSMOTE: improving classification performance when training data is imbalanced. Int. Workshop Comput. Sci. Eng. **2**, 13–17 (2010)
17. Aliyun: TIANCHI. https://tianchi.aliyun.com/dataset/3964?t=1689217278709

Intelligent Decision Making for Tanker Air Control Conflict Deployment

Yipeng Wang[1](✉), Boyu Chen[2], Yujian Song[1], and Deyue Zhang[1]

[1] PLA Unit, Cangzhou 95939, China
598123703@qq.com
[2] Air Force Engineering University Air Traffic Control Pilotage College,
Xian, China

Abstract. Flight conflict, as the highest level of safety in air traffic control operation, has always been the focus of air control work. The research of air traffic control conflict deployment intelligence technology is the current hot direction. In this paper, we propose a control conflict deployment strategy solving method based on deep Q network (DQN). The value of action value function Q in Q learning algorithm is used as a criterion to evaluate the goodness of the strategy, and the multilayer perceptron is used as a neural network to approximate the Q value; stochastic gradient descent algorithm is used to update the parameters of the neural network; the contradiction arising from the combination of neural network and Q learning is solved by the way of experience playback and establishment of dual network structure. A large amount of sample data of conflict scenes is generated through simulation data for the training solution of the model to obtain the optimal strategy. The experimental results show that the tanker control conflict deployment strategy obtained by the deep Q-network algorithm training in this paper can play a good effect in the designed multiple conflict scenarios, and also can better take into account the control rules and the overall airspace operation situation; it lays the foundation for the future control operation of the conflict deployment auxiliary decision-making technology.

Keywords: Air traffic control · Flight conflict resolution · Deep Q network

1 Introduction

With limited resources available in the airspace, the increasing flight traffic will lead to more serious flight conflicts, and the controller's workload to deploy conflicts will increase greatly, and the safety of control operations will be affected dramatically. In the control operation, the basic unit of controller's work is a control sector, and its workload is mainly reflected in two aspects of air-to-air command and inter-sector transfer, of which air-to-air command deployment of flight conflicts is a very critical work. In the case of continuously increasing

© The Author(s), under exclusive license to Springer Nature Singapore Pte Ltd. 2024
Z. Cai et al. (Eds.): NCTCS 2023, CCIS 1944, pp. 161–169, 2024.
https://doi.org/10.1007/978-981-99-7743-7_10

traffic, the operation of aircraft in the control sector will inevitably generate many flight conflicts [1]. When the traffic volume increases to or exceeds the capacity of the control sector, the control sector is saturated and the controller's load to deploy conflicts in the sector has reached its limit.

The controller's excessive deployment load will bring potential risks to the control operation. The traditional solution to this problem is to divide more sectors and add more control seats to reduce the controller's load of flight conflicts. However, the solution of dividing multiple sectors is a limited solution strategy, and the number of sectors cannot be increased indefinitely. When the number of sectors is too large, the control efficiency will be reduced, the number of control handovers between sectors will be increased, and the handover load between sectors will be increased, so the traditional solution can no longer effectively reduce the controller's conflict deployment load at the current development rate [4]. Therefore, it is an effective way to solve this problem by exploring an intelligent conflict deployment aid method that can adapt to the future traffic growth, which is the subject of this paper.

In machine learning, there is a method with superb decision making ability, namely reinforcement learning, and the process of flight conflict deployment in control operation is essentially a decision making process: the controller obtains aircraft flight status information in the sector by observing the ATC radar screen, analyzes the overall operation situation in the sector and predicts the possibility of conflict in the future, determines the possibility of conflict and then makes a decision on the conflicting aircraft according to the control operation rules and control experience. After determining the possibility of conflict, we issue deployment instructions to the conflicting aircraft according to the control operation rules and control experience. Therefore, the capability of machine learning can be fully used to solve the problem of intelligent decision making of conflict deployment in control operation. The powerful decision-making ability of machine learning can be used to solve the problem of control conflict deployment, which will help to reduce the controller's load of deploying flight conflicts and improve the efficiency of control operation.

In this paper, we propose an artificial intelligence-based approach to air traffic control conflict deployment; the goal is to use deep reinforcement learning theory to train a "controller" that can autonomously perceive the current airspace situation and deploy flight conflicts generated in the environment based on the airspace environment information. Then, we analyze the characteristics of flight conflict deployment and the process of conflict deployment by controllers from the perspective of control operation, model the Markov decision process of the whole flight conflict deployment process in control operation, and design a deep Q-network algorithm for the flight conflict deployment strategy problem to the model is trained. Finally, several conflict scenarios are designed to test the effectiveness of the instructions given by the strategy model.

2   Deep Q-Network Based Control Conflict Deployment Strategy Solving

Among the machine learning methods, reinforcement learning methods are effective means to solve Markov decision process (MDP) models. The dimensionality of operational data information generated in ATC operations is high, and the method of deep Q-network, which can handle high-dimensional input information, is selected for solving the conflict deployment MDP model; a multilayer perceptual neural network is designed to replace the original convolutional neural network, and a deep Q-network-based method for solving the control conflict deployment strategy is proposed; a large amount of conflict scenario data is generated using flight plans to train the MDP model [2].

2.1   Reinforcement Learning

Reinforcement Learning (RL), also known as evaluation learning, is an important branch in the field of machine learning. Unlike other machine learning methods, reinforcement learning outperforms other types of learning in problem decision making, and is widely used in industrial control, unmanned vehicles, video games, robot obstacle avoidance, and other fields.

Reinforcement learning is based on a Markovian decision process, in which an intelligent body (Agent) selects an action based on a strategy without prior knowledge in a "trial-and-error" manner, and the current state and the selected action are changed by a state function, so that the intelligent body enters the next state; it takes different actions to interact with the environment, and the environment gives feedback to the actions taken. The environment gives feedback rewards for the actions taken, and the rewards are used to guide the behavior of the intelligent body. If the task environment gives positive feedback rewards to an action strategy of the intelligence (Agent), then the tendency of the intelligence (Agent) to produce this action strategy in the future will be strengthened; conversely, the tendency will be weakened. The goal of the intelligent body is to find the optimal action strategy at each moment of the state that maximizes the expected cumulative reward value [3].

The learning process of reinforcement learning is as follows:

1. the intelligent body acquires the state S_t at the current moment.
2. According to the current state S_t, the intelligence selects an action a_t, from the set of actions, and executes it.
3. According to the mapping relationship between state and action the state changes to the next moment's state S_{t+1}, while the intelligence gets the reward R_t from the environment feedback.
4. update the mapping relation between state and action according to the reward value R_t.

Commonly used reinforcement learning algorithms include: policy iteration, value iteration, Monte Carlo, instantaneous difference, Q-learning, SARSA, and so on. For example, instantaneous difference and Q-learning are model-independent algorithms, while strategy iteration and value iteration are model-related algorithms; according to the action strategy used to update the value function, they can be divided into in-strategy and out-of-strategy categories, for example, Q-learning algorithms are out-of-strategy algorithms, while SARSA algorithms are in-strategy algorithms.

In ordinary reinforcement learning, the Q-value of each state action pair is generally stored in the form of Q-Table because the dimensionality of the state and action space in most of its task forms is not high; however, the task forms in practical engineering are often complex and have a large dimensional state and action space, in which case the Q-Table form cannot store a large number of Q-values; and deep Learning is more capable of handling high-dimensional inputs, and introducing deep learning models into reinforcement learning can play a good effect on solving complex engineering tasks; thus, Deep Reinforcement Learning (DRL) was born. It not only has the ability of deep learning to propose features from high-dimensional raw data, which can achieve the approximation of complex nonlinear functions; but also has the policy decision capability of reinforcement learning, which can adjust the parameters to achieve the optimal policy by sensing the feedback from the environment through continuous trial and error of the intelligent body. Deep reinforcement learning combines the strong perceptual ability of deep learning and the strong decision making ability of reinforcement learning, but still belongs to the category of reinforcement learning in essence [5].

Currently, there are Deep Q Network (DQN) based on value function and Deep Deterministic Policy Gradient (DDPG) based on policy, and so on. In this paper, the Deep Q Network (DQN) algorithm is applied to the solution of the conflict deployment policy problem.

2.2   Deep Q Network

The Deep Q network (DQN) proposed by Google's DeepMind team in 2015 brought the research on deep reinforcement learning to the forefront. Deep Q network, as a representative algorithm of deep reinforcement learning, is a combination of deep neural network and Q learning algorithm, which uses neural network to approximate the Q-value function in Q learning.

Q Learning Algorithm. In 1989, Watkins proposed a significant algorithm in the field of reinforcement learning, the Q-learning algorithm, which is a model-independent, off-policy reinforcement learning algorithm. Q learning can find an optimal action selection policy in the MDP problem, which can give the desired action based on the current state and the optimal policy [6].

In Q-learning, the intelligence(Agent has no prior knowledge and does not know which actions should be selected in the current state. Therefore, a reward R is usually set to represent the reward value from the current state S to the next state, and the reward value is used to calculate the Q table that guides the

Agent's behavior. q table acts as the brain of the intelligence, and each row of it represents the state of the Agent (state), and each column represents the action taken by the Agent (action). In the initialization stage, all Q-value elements in the Q table can be initialized to 0, which means that there is no information in the brain of the intelligence (Agent) at this time, and when the action a, is selected, the Q-value is updated as:

$$S_t Q\left(s_t, a_t\right) \leftarrow Q\left(s_t, a_t\right) + \alpha\left[r_{t+1} + \gamma \max_a Q\left(s_{t+1}, a\right) - Q\left(s_t, a_t\right)\right]$$

A deformation of the equation yields:

$$Q\left(s_t, a_t\right) \leftarrow (1 - \alpha)Q\left(s_t, a_t\right) + \alpha\left[r_{t+1} + \gamma \max_a Q\left(s_{t+1}, a\right)\right]$$

where a is the learning rate and γ is the discount factor. The role of learning rate a is that it determines the update of new and old information in the learning process, and generally the learning rate takes the value in [0.1]. When a takes the value of 0, the algorithm does not perform any learning, no information is updated, and the Q value is not updated; when a takes the value of 1, the algorithm only focuses on new training information and discards the old training. The role of the discount factor is that it determines the importance of future reporting on the current state value, and the general discount factor is also taken in [0.1], when the value of γ is 0, the intelligence only considers the current reward; when the value of γ is 1, the intelligence mainly considers the future reward.

Neural Network Design. In this paper, we change the Convolutional Neural Networks (CNN) used in the original DQN algorithm and adopt Multilayer Perceptron (MLP) as the part of the neural network [7]. Multilayer perceptron, also called multilayer perceptual neural network, is a multilayer deep feedforward neural network, which usually consists of three parts: an input layer composed of a set of perceptual units, a hidden layer composed of one or more layers of computational nodes, and an output layer composed of one layer of computational nodes, and its network structure is shown in Fig. In MLP networks, the different structural layers are fully connected to each other, i.e., any node in the upper layer of the network is connected to all nodes in the lower layer of the network, and each connection is equipped with a corresponding weight.

1. Input layer Input: The input layer consists of individual input nodes that input the information provided by the external environment. In the input layer, no computational processing of any kind is performed on the input information and it only serves to pass information to the hidden layer.
2. Hidden layer: The hidden layer consists of hidden nodes or hidden units, which do not have direct contact with the external environment. In each hidden layer, the information from the input layer or the previous hidden layer is computed and processed, and the processed information is passed to the next layer until it is finally passed to the output layer. For a general

feedforward neural network, there can be no hidden layers in the network, or it can have more than one hidden layer. However, in MLP networks, at least one hidden layer is required.

3. Output: The output layer consists of individual output nodes. In the output layer, the information passed from the hidden layer is computed and processed again, and then the information is passed to the external environment (Fig. 1).

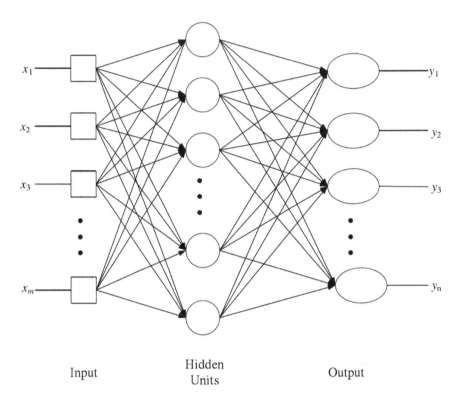

Fig. 1. MLP neural network topology

2.3   Conflict Brokering Strategy Model Training

The deep learning part uses MLP multilayer perceptual neural network, and the reinforcement learning part uses DQN algorithm composed of Q-learning method for solving the problem of control conflict deployment. Since refueling aircraft generally use civil aviation flight paths, the real flight plan data of Chinese civil aviation is selected for the generation of training samples, and the complete flight path flight process is extracted through the air traffic operation simulation system's simulation of aircraft operation for all flight plans. The flight trajectory is projected to be 5 min long, i.e., the trajectory of the aircraft in the next 5 min is calculated each time. At the same time, the spatial data query technology R-tree method is used for flight conflict detection, with a detection time step of 1 s. The total number of flight plan data used in this paper is 12,065, and the total number of conflict scenarios generated by simulation is 1783.

The design of hyperparameter values in the algorithm is shown in the Table 1:

Table 1. DQN algorithm hyper-parameter value design table.

Model parameters	Parameters number
Learning rate	0.001/0.0005
Total time step	30000
Experience pool size	50000
Batch size	16
Exploration decay rate	0.1
Last step exploration rate	0.02
Discount rate	0.99
Target network update frequency	500
Number of nodes in the hidden layer of the neural network	64
Number of hidden layers of the neural network	2

2.4   Analysis of Training Experiments

Stability Analysis. The dynamics of the algorithmic network during the learning process can be analyzed from the changes in the significant values recorded during the training of the model.

The algorithm in this paper analyzes the model with the average reward value reward and the average maximum Q. The stability analysis experiment is performed in Episodes, where one Episode represents a conflict scenario from input to final termination, and the reward value is calculated once for every 100 Episodes performed; 10,000 Episodes are performed for each group training in the stability analysis. The average reward value and the average maximum Q value are calculated; the average reward value is recorded as the average of the rewards per 100 Episodes, and the average maximum Q value is recorded as the average of the maximum Q values per 100 Episodes. Also consider different learning rate lr has different training results, the experiment for different learning rate lr was trained, from the training learning process reward value and maximum Q value, as shown in the figure, the average reward value and average maximum Q value in the learning rate lr = 0.001, the reward value curve and maximum Q curve overall show an upward trend, but there is still a certain magnitude of oscillation, the algorithm The stability of the model is poor; when the learning rate lr=0.0005, the reward value convergence rate is basically unchanged, and the convergence and stability of the algorithm model is better relative to the learning rate of 0.001; the maximum Q curve presents a higher blending strategy score at this time, and the blending strategy is more appropriate; therefore, if the learning rate lr of the conflict blending strategy solving algorithm is set near 0.0005, it is more Therefore, if the learning rate lr of the conflict policy solution algorithm is set around 0.0005, it is more suitable for the training of the policy model in this paper (Figs. 2 and 3).

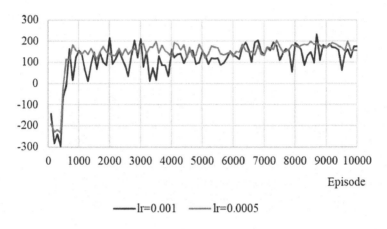

Fig. 2. Average reward function value

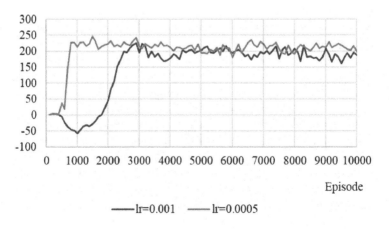

Fig. 3. Average maximum Q curve

3   Conclusion

Considering the high dimensional data generated by air traffic operation, a solution method of control conflict deployment strategy model based on deep Q network is proposed; the components of deep Q network one by one Q learning and neural network and its principle are analyzed, which is an effective means to solve the complex MDP model. The value of the reward function in the model is used as the basis to update the Q value of the action value function in the Q learning algorithm, which is used to evaluate the goodness of the action strategy; the multilayer perceptual neural network is used to approximate the Q value to realize the Q calculation under high-dimensional data, and the parameters of the neural network are updated by the stochastic gradient descent method; the paradox of combining neural network and Q learning is solved by using the empirical replay technique and the dual network structure technique; finally, the Using the flight plan data to generate a large number of flight conflicts through simulation runs for the training learning of the model, the trend of the reward value and the maximum Q value changes through the training shows that the model acquires a stable and optimal conflict deployment strategy.

References

1. Meng, G., Qi, F.: Flight conflict resolution for civil aviation based on ant colony optimization. In: 2012 Fifth International Symposium on Computational Intelligence and Design (ISCID) (2012)
2. Hong, Y., Lee, S., Kim, Y.: Bi-objective optimization for aircraft conflict resolution using epsilon-constraint method and TOPSIS. In: 2018 18th International Conference on Control, Automation and Systems (ICCAS), Daegwallyeong, pp. 104–108 (2018)
3. Baycik, N.O., Sharkey, T.C., Rainwater, C.E.: A Markov decision Process approach for balancing intelligence and interdiction operations in city-level drug trafficking enforcement. Socio-Econ. Plan. Sci. **69**, 100700 (2019)
4. Yang, Y., Zhang, J., Cai, K., Prandini, M.: Multi-aircraft conflict detection and resolution based on probabilistic reach sets. IEEE Trans. Control Syst. Technol. **25**(1), 309–316 (2017)
5. Olga, R., Sridhar, B.: Conflict resolution for wind-optimal aircraft trajectories in North Atlantic oceanic airspace with wind uncertainties. In: AIAA/IEEE Digital Avionics Systems Conference-Proceedings, 35 DASC Digital Avionics Systems Conference 2016 (2016)
6. Bicchi, A., et al.: Decentralized air traffic management systems: performance and fault tolerance. In: Proceedings of the IFAC Workshop on Motion Control
7. Hu, J., Lygeros, J., Prandini, M., Sastry, S.: Aircraft conflict prediction and resolution using Brownian motion. In: Proceedings of the 38th IEEE Conference on Decision and Control, Phoenix, AZ, USA, vol. 3, pp. 2438–2443

Efficient Recommendation Algorithm for Employment of College Students for Various Majors

Yu He[ID] and Meiling Cai[(⊠)][ID]

College of Information Science and Engineering, Hunan Normal University, Changsha, Hunan, China
`cai.meiling@hunnu.edu.cn`

Abstract. Against the increasing severity of employment difficulties, job recommendation systems for college students are becoming increasingly important. As it is impossible to refer to the students' own employment data, relevant research based on the school's historical employment data provides a reference for students' employment. We proposes a method based on the school's historical employment data for job recommendation for college students. The specific ideas and characteristics are as follows: First, preprocess the collected data to generate the user portrait. In the user portrait construction process, we proposes using the AHP-Entropy Weight method to construct a weight vector of ability requirements for different positions, highlighting the focus of students' abilities in different positions. To improve computational efficiency, first, we uses clustering algorithms to construct different user groups with different characteristics. Then, we calculates the similarity between the students to be recommended and the user groups, followed by the similarity with the users in that group to improve computational efficiency. In particular, we prove that if the number of samples in the database is greater than or equal to 6, our algorithm will have a lower average time complexity than the traditional algorithm. To address the scarcity of employment market data for college students, we collects the real employment data of graduating classes of a major in a certain university to build the HNNU-JOB data set based on students' employment ability characteristics. Extensive experiments on HNNU-JOB show that the proposed method achieves remarkable performance of recommendation.

Keywords: Job recommendation · AHP-Entropy Weight · User portrait · Similarity · Efficient recommendation

1 Introduction

In recent years, youth groups mainly composed of college graduates have faced increasing difficulties in employment. With the rapid development of recommendation systems, they have gradually been applied to the field of job recommendation for students. Using personalized recommendation technology to assist college students in finding employment is an important research topic. An item-based CF method has been proposed for online job-hunting based on users' job application records [1]. It proves that CF method has remarkable effect on job recommendation. CF technique predicts which items users will choose according to a large amount of data collected from their past behaviors and records [2,3]. Most graduates are looking for a job for the first time and have no historical employment information. Hence, they have no occupational records and do not have any experience in finding a job. Therefore, CF method cannot be directly applied to recommend jobs for graduates. Hence, how to recommend jobs for graduates with no historical job records is an important problem. Nie et al. [4,5] proposed a data-driven framework for forecasting student career choice upon graduation based on their behavior in and around the campus. Recommendation algorithms based on students' on-campus behavioral data have difficulties in data acquisition, large data volume and randomness in some data. There are also some algorithms for recommendation based on personal historical work experience. For example, Zhu et al. [6] and Qin et al. [7] proposed some job recommendation methods based on historical work experience. These work experience based job recommendation algorithms are also not suitable for recommending jobs to college graduates.

Due to lack of work experience and historical job-seeking behavior, it is unrealistic to recommend suitable job for college graduates based on their own historical employment data. Parks [8] pioneered the use of historical employment data for student career planning by surveying and collecting multidimensional data on the employment status and salary of undergraduate alumni, and then proposed suggestions for future career path planning. Therefore, we consider using alumni historical employment data to recommend employment for college students. In addition, there are other special aspects to the job recommendation issue for college graduates. On the one hand, job recommendation is different from recommendation scenarios in e-commerce, social media and other fields. The ability requirements of enterprises for students and the focus of different types of enterprises on students' abilities are important issues in the employment recommendation system. On the other hand, when the scale of historical employment data of alumni is large, how to design an efficient job recommendation algorithm is also a problem that we need to consider.

This paper studies the employment recommendation problem for college graduates and proposes solutions to the above two problems. First, this paper constructs a user portrait for students. The purpose of constructing a user portrait is to analyze user data, establish quantitative characteristic information for users, and provide a basis for subsequent data inference and recommendation algorithms. This paper proposes a method to establish a user portrait for college graduates. The process of constructing an alumni employment data set is: first, data collection, desensitization, and normalization of various indicators to measure students' employment skills. Then, in order to solve the problem of different positions requiring different students, this paper proposes using the combination of Analytic Hierarchy Process (AHP) and Entropy Weight method [9] to construct weight vectors of students' ability requirements for different positions, highlighting the different focuses of different types of companies on students' abilities. Finally, combined with the priority vectors, a user portrait containing employment characteristics is generated. To address the scarcity of employment market data for college students, this paper collects the real employment data of graduating classes of a major in a certain university to build the HNNU-JOB data set based on students' employment ability characteristics. In order to improve the recommendation efficiency of the recommendation algorithm, this paper first uses the clustering algorithm to construct user groups with different characteristics. Then, we calculates the similarity between the students to be recommended and each user group, followed by the similarity with the users in that group to achieve multi-granularity recommendation, which improves the computational efficiency. We prove that the complexity of the method proposed in this paper is lower than the traditional recommendation algorithm in the case of big data.

Our contributions can be summarized as follows:

1. Since college students have no work experience, historical employment data can provide data support for employment recommendation research. This paper collects multi-dimensional data based on students' employment skills and characteristics, and constructs an employment data set HNNU-JOB for college students, which provides a basis for follow-up research in this field;
2. Using the AHP-Entropy Weight method to construct priority vectors highlights the different focuses of different positions on students' abilities, depicting the different requirements of different positions for students' abilities, and improving the accuracy of recommendations;
3. This paper proposes an algorithm to improve recommendation efficiency in the case of big data. In particular, we prove that if the number of samples in the database is greater than or equal to 6, our algorithm will have a lower average time complexity than the traditional algorithm.

The remainder of this paper is arranged as follows. Section 2 introduces the construction method of employment user profile for college student based on AHP-Entropy Weight method. In Sect. 3, this paper introduces the accelerated recommendation algorithm based on clustering algorithm proposed in this article and analyzes its time complexity. We demonstrated the advantages of the proposed method through experiments on real employment data sets in Sect. 4. This paper ends with conclusions.

2   AHP-Entropy Weight Method and User Portrait

This section mainly introduces the construction of student user portrait combining Analytic Hierarchy Process (AHP) and entropy weight method, in this paper, we call it AHP-Entropy Weight Method. First, we introduce the AHP-Entropy Weight method which combines subjective calculation of weight vector and objective calculation weight vector to construct weight vectors of students characteristics. Then, the values of students' characteristics are calculated using the weight vectors to obtain the student's user profile.

2.1   User Portrait

A. Cooper et al. [10] first proposed the concept of user portrait. He defined user portrait as "virtual representatives based on real user data." Amato [11] et al., Quintana et al. [12] described user profiles as "A set of images obtained from massive data and composed of user information." Through this set, it is possible to describe a user's needs, personalized preferences and user interests. The main purpose of user portrait construction is to provide a basis for subsequent data reasoning and recommendation algorithms, and to provide Big data analysis services.

This paper constructs user portrait of college graduates and conducts a comprehensive analysis and quantification of college students' employment characteristics. Establishing student job-seeking user portrait is divided into three parts: Obtain original student data; Screening feature information; Feature quantification. This step quantitatively represents the various features of the original data for subsequent operations. In order to depict the different requirements of different positions for students' abilities, this paper proposes using the AHP-Entropy Weight method to construct the weight vectors of students' ability characteristic, thereby highlighting the different degrees of importance attached by different positions to different characteristics of students in the employment process. Therefore, the following parts will elaborate on two parts: the construction of student job-seeking feature system and data set, and the construction of weight vectors using AHP-Entropy weight method to generate user portrait. The overall logical framework of the student job-seeking portrait applied to personalized employment recommendation in this paper is shown in Fig. 1.

For students' personal information during school, this paper extracts multidimensional information reflecting students' employment characteristics, and uses these features to construct students' user portrait, forming a computable "virtual representation" reflecting students' characteristics. Since the characteristic information reflecting college students' abilities is finite, the job seeking feature system can be obtained through questionnaires to companies. After determining the student job seeking feature system, we can organize the students' personal information data according to the various features in the feature system. Since students' basic information contain a lot of personal privacy information, data desensitization is needed when constructing the data set to prevent disclosure of students' personal information. Then, we start the step—quantification of the students' characteristic information. Table 1 gives an example of some features that affect students' employment and the rules of data desensitization and quantification.

In Table 1, the rule 'Quantitative score of university' means that we can quantify the information of students based on the ranking of universities. The meaning of 'Major code' is that we represent students' major information as their major code, and this kind of representation can facilitate our subsequent

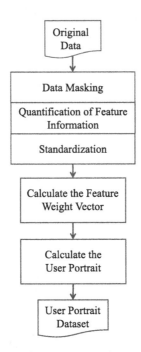

Fig. 1. Construction process of user portrait dataset

Table 1. Student Data Preprocessing Rules

Characteristic	Original Data	Rule
Name	Student's real name	Replace with a unique ID
Gender	Student's gender	Female 1 Male 0
Home Address	Student's Address	Student's home city
School	Name of the university	Quantitative score of university
Major	Name of student's major	Major code
Exam Scores	Grades for each subject	Grade Point Average
Competition Results	Award information	Number of times · Score
Internship Performance	Student's score	Student's score
Honors Obtained	Honors' information	Number of times · Score
CET4 Score	Official data	Highest score
CET6 Score	Official data	Highest score
employment information	Real employment data	Real employment data

calculations. In the item 'Competition Results', we quantify this information of a student as the score of the grade of the competition multiplied by the number of times they participated in all competitions. Among them, the award level for participating in the competition can refer to factors such as the influence of the competition. The quantitative rule for the item 'Honors Obtained' are similar to the rule of 'Competition Results'.

Since we make job recommendation based on the historical employment information of this major, the student's major information can be ignored in our method. In fact, the features reflecting a student's ability in the employment process are shown in Fig. 2.

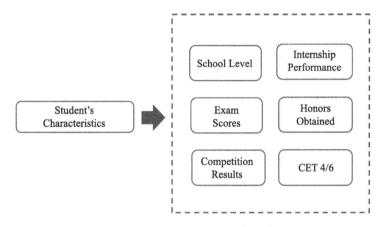

Fig. 2. Characteristic System for Evaluating Students' Comprehensive Employability

In the various indicators of the data set, there is a situation of dimensional inconsistency between different data. Hence, we need to perform data standardization to eliminate the influence of dimensions. We use the extremum transformation method to standardize the data. Since the indicators in this data set are all positive indicators, the formula for data standardization is as shown in Eq. (1).

$$y_{ij} = \frac{x_{ij} - \min_i(x_{ij})}{\max_i(x_{ij}) - \min_i(x_{ij})}, \tag{1}$$

where x_{ij} represents the initial value of the j-th feature of the i-th student in the database, and $\min_i(x_{ij})$ is the minimum value of the j-th feature. Similarly, $\max_i(x_{ij})$ is the maximum value of the j-th feature. y_{ij} is the value of the j-th feature of the i-th student after standardization.

2.2   Analytic Hierarchy Process Method

The previous section introduced the concept of user portrait and the definition of some indicators. The judgment matrix in AHP method is formulated by experts based on subjective personal experience, which has certain one-sidedness. Therefore, the objective evaluation method of Entropy Weight method is used again to objectively assign weights to each feature. Finally, this paper combines the weight vector obtained by the AHP method with the weight vector obtained by the entropy weight method to obtain the combined weight vector. After preprocessing the collected student data, this paper combines the subjective AHP method and the objective Entropy Weight method to construct weight vectors. In this way, for different positions, ability indicators with emphasis on students can be obtained. The Analytic Hierarchy Process (AHP) method is a simple, flexible and practical multi-criteria decision making method proposed by Saaty [13] in the early 1970s. It is a process of modeling and quantifying the decision-making thinking process of decision makers on complex systems. The main steps of the AHP method can be divided into three steps.

- **Build the hierarchy of the question.**
  In the AHP method, first, we need to hierarchize the problem and decomposes this problem into different levels according to the nature of the problem and the overall goal to form a multi-level structure model. The decomposition principle is applied by structuring a simple problem with the elements in a level being independent from those in succeeding levels, working downward from the focus in the top level, to criteria bearing on the focus in the second level, followed by subcriteria in the third level, and so on, from the more general (and sometimes uncertain) to the more particular and concrete [14]. The hierarchical structure of AHP method includes the focus layer, the criterion layer, and the scheme layer. The characteristic of the focus layer is that there is only one factor, which represents the highest evaluation standard or evaluation goal of the decision evaluation problem. The focus layer should be the highest level in the hierarchical model. The criterion layer contains many influencing factors that affect the decision target, also known as criteria. There are often two relationships between the criteria: one is that they do not affect each other at the same level, and the other is dominance, that is, the lower-level factors are subordinate to the upper-level related factors, constituting the so-called criteria and sub-criteria. The criterion layer is in the middle layer of the hierarchical model. In the college student job recommendation method proposed in this paper, the criterion layer includes factors such as academic performance, internship performance, etc. that affect students' employment. The scheme layer is relatively simple and easy to analyze. Its factors are all measures and decision plans proposed to achieve the factors in the target layer. The scheme layer has only one level and is the lowest level in the hierarchical model.

- **Establish a judgment matrix for pairwise comparison.**
  The hierarchical model reflects the interrelationships between the influencing factors in the decision evaluation problem, but we still need to know the

weights of the criterion layer factors relative to the focus layer. These weights need to be provided by the decision maker, and the weights given by different decision makers are generally different. When determining the weights of sub-factors that affect the factors at a higher level, evaluators often cannot quantify the proportions between them specifically due to the particularity of some factors. Moreover, the number of factors in the criterion layer is often too large to objectively and comprehensively determine the degree of influence of the sub-factors on that factor, resulting in a set of contradictory data, or even a set of data inconsistent with what the evaluator actually thinks.

How can we obtain credible relative weights between multiple factors? Saaty proposed a method of constructing a pairwise comparison matrix by comparing the relative importance of factors in pairs, assigning a numerical index to importance, and quantitatively depicting the relative importance of these factors. Assuming X is the next layer of Y, suppose there are n factors in the X layer, we use the set $\mathbf{x} = x_1, x_2, ..., x_n$ and we need their weights relative to the upper layer Y. At this step, we construct a $n \cdot n$ matrix A, which is called a pairwise comparison matrix or judgment matrix of $Y - X$. In this matrix, if the ratio of the weights of x_i and x_j relative to Y is a_{ij}, then the ratio of the weights of x_j and x_i relative to Y is $a_{ji} = 1/a_{ij}$. The value of a_{ij} is constructed by experts in the relevant fields according to Saaty's 1–9 scale method in Table 2 and the constructed weight matrix is tested for consistency to prevent excessive contradiction.

Definition 1. *Let $A = (a_{ij})$ be a $n \cdot n$ matrix that satisfies the following conditions:*

- $a_{ij} > 0$, $i, j \in 1, 2, ..., n$;
- $a_{ji} = 1/a_{ij}, i, j \in 1, 2, ..., n$.

Then, A is a positive reciprocal matrix.

- **Calculating the weight of a single element.**
  To derive the weight vector from the judgment matrix A, that is, the weight of the importance order of the factors related to this level relative to the upper level factors. Before introducing the method of calculating the weight vector, we need to introduce the consistency of the judgment matrix A. The judgment matrix obtained by the 1–9 scale may not satisfy the consistency, that is, $a_{ij} \cdot a_{jk} \neq a_{ik}$, $i, j, k = 1, 2, ...n$.
  Saaty [13] proposed that when the reciprocal matrix $A = (a_{ij})_{n \cdot n}$ is a consistent judgment matrix, the elements of matrix A have the following logical relationship with the weight vector $w = (w_1, w_2, ..., w_n)$:

$$a_{ij} = \frac{w_i}{w_j}, \forall i, j \in \{1, 2, ..., n\}. \tag{2}$$

If A is a consistent matrix, the normalized vector of its maximum eigenvalue is the weight vector. Let $w = (w_1, w_2, ..., w_n)^T$ be the weight vector of the judgment matrix. When the judgment matrix A satisfies complete consistency,

Table 2. The Fundamental Scale

Intensity of importance on an absolute scale	Definition	Explanation
1	Equal importance	Two activities contribute equally to the objective
3	Moderate importance of one over another	Experience and judgment strongly favor one activity over another
5	Essential or strong importance	Experience and judgment strongly favor one activity over another
7	Very strong importance	An activity is strongly favored and its dominance demonstrated in practice
9	Extreme importance	The evidence favoring one activity over another is of the highest possible order of affirmation
2,4,6,8	Intermediate values between the two adjacent judgement	When compromise is needed
Reciprocals	If activity i has one of the above numbers assigned to it when compared with activity j, then j has the reciprocal value when compared with i	
Rationals	Ratios arising from the scale	If consistency were to be forced by obtaining n numerical values to span the matrix

we have

$$A = \begin{pmatrix} 1 & w_1/w_2 & ... & w_1/w_n \\ w_2/w_1 & 1 & ... & w_2/w_n \\ ... & ... & ... & ... \\ w_n/w_1 & w_n/w_2 & ... & 1 \end{pmatrix} = \begin{pmatrix} w_1 \\ w_2 \\ ... \\ w_n \end{pmatrix} \cdot \begin{bmatrix} \frac{1}{w_1} & \frac{1}{w_2} & ... & \frac{1}{w_n} \end{bmatrix}.$$

Let λ_{max} be the maximum eigenvalue of A. When the judgment matrix A does not satisfy consistency, there must be $\lambda_{max} > n$. The higher the inconsistency of A, the larger the value of $\lambda_{max} - n$. The consistency test steps are as follows:

Step 1: Calculate the consistency index $CI = (\lambda_{max} - n)/(n - 1)$.

Step 2: Compare the value of CI to the Random Index (RI) for the same size matrix. For $n = 1...9$, the RI values are shown in Table 3. If $CI/RI \leq 0.1$, the inconsistency is acceptable. Otherwise, the judgments and matrix are invalid and must be revised. If the consistency of the judgment matrix A meets the consistency requirements, the next step is to calculate the weight vector. The eigenvalue method can be used to solve it. The characteristic equation is:

$$Aw = \lambda_{max} \cdot w, \tag{3}$$

where A is the judgment matrix, w is the characteristic vector corresponding to the maximum eigenvalue, and λ_{max} is the maximum eigenvalue. The characteristic vector w is normalized to calculate the weights of various factors. The value of λ_{max} exists and is unique. At present, there are many methods for calculating eigenvalues and eigenvectors, such as Power Iteration method and Inverse Iteration Method. The calculation methods for these quantities will not be described in detail here.

Table 3. Random Consistency Index

n	1	2	3	4	5	6	7	8	9	10
Random consistency index (R.I.)	0	0	0.58	0.90	1.12	1.24	1.32	1.41	1.45	1.49

2.3 Entropy Weight Method

In the 1960s, Clausius first proposed the concept of entropy and defined the degree of chaos of the system as entropy [15]. Later, Shannon [16] introduced the concept of entropy into information theory, which is used as a measure for random events. It can be used to measure the degree of uncertainty before the experiment, and it can also indicate the expected amount of information from an experiment.

Suppose an experiment has n results $x = x_i (i = 1, 2, 3, ..., n)$, where the probability of x_i occurring is $p(x_i)$. In information theory, the concept of entropy can be described as follows: the smaller $p(x_i)$ is, the greater the uncertainty. When $p(x_i)$ approaches 0, the uncertainty approaches infinity. The larger $p(x_i)$ is, the smaller the uncertainty. When $p(x_i)$ approaches 1, its uncertainty approaches 0. Therefore, $\ln(1/p(x_i))$ can measure this uncertainty very well. By weighting according to the probability of occurrence of events, the average uncertainty, that is, the information entropy $H(x) = -\sum_{i=1}^{n} p(x_i) \cdot \ln(p(x_i))$, can be obtained. Probability information will change due to obtaining information. Let H represent the original entropy and $H(I)$ represent the entropy after knowing information I. Since information I will reduce entropy, then $H(I) \leq H$. Therefore, the amount of information provided by information I can be measured by $H - H(I)$.

In information theory, entropy is a measure of uncertainty. The more information, the less uncertainty and the smaller the entropy; the less information, the greater the uncertainty and the greater the entropy. Based on the characteristics of entropy, we can use it as an objective weighting method by calculating the information entropy of indicators to determine their relative degree of change (discreteness). The greater the relative degree of change of the indicators, the greater the utility value of the information, and the greater the influence of the indicators on the overall system in the comprehensive evaluation. Higher weights are given to such indicators, otherwise lower weights are given.

The basic calculation idea of entropy weight method is as follows:

1. Select n evaluation objects and m indicators to construct an n-row m-column decision matrix X. In the decision matrix, x_{ij} is the value of the jth indicator of the ith evaluation object, where $i = 1, 2, ... n$, $j = 1, 2, ..., m$.
2. Standardization of indicator values. Since the meaning and calculation methods of each indicator are different, their units of measurement are not uniform. In order to eliminate the influence of dimensional and the magnitude of the indicator values themselves, standardization processing should be performed first. There are many methods for standardization, such as vector normalization, linear proportion, range transformation, etc. Each method has its

advantages and disadvantages. In order to eliminate the influence of variation dimension and variation range, and ensure that the data is compared under the same dimension, This article uses the range transformation method to standardize the data. The standardization method has already been described earlier and will not be explained in detail here.

3. Calculate the proportion of the ith evaluation object under the jth indicator:

$$p_{ij} = \frac{x_{ij}}{\sum\limits_{i=1}^{n} x_{ij}}, \quad i, j \in \{1, 2, ..., n\}. \tag{4}$$

4. Calculate the entropy value of the jth indicator:

$$e_j = -k \cdot \sum_{i=1}^{n} p_{ij} \cdot \ln(p_{ij}), \tag{5}$$

where $k = 1/\ln(n) > 0$, $e_j \geq 0$. According to information theory, the smaller the information entropy of an indicator, the more information it provides, the greater the discreteness, the greater the influence on the comprehensive evaluation, and the greater the weight should be given; on the contrary, smaller weights should be given.

5. Calculate the information utility of the jth indicator:

$$d_j = 1 - e_j. \tag{6}$$

6. Calculate the weights of various indicators using the following formula:

$$w_j = \frac{d_j}{\sum\limits_{j=1}^{m} d_j}, \quad 1 \leq j \leq m. \tag{7}$$

2.4   AHP-Entropy Weight Method

This paper uses the subjective analytic hierarchy process (AHP) method for calculating indicator weights and the objective entropy weight method to construct weight vectors of different ability requirements for different positions of students. The fusion method for weights obtained by AHP and Entropy Weight method is as follows:

The combined weight vector w obtained by fusing the subjective weight vector w' and the objective weight vector w'' is used as the final feature weight vector. This paper adopts the linear combination method to calculate the combined weight w. In order to eliminate the interference influence of larger numerical values and make the degree of difference between w' and w'' consistent with the degree of difference between the number α and β, the distance function is introduced to calculate the weight allocation coefficient α and β and obtain the combined weight. The distance formula between the ith item w'_i in the subjective weight vector and the ith item w''_i in the objective weight vector is shown in Eq. (8):

$$d(w'_i, w''_i) = [\frac{1}{2} \cdot \sum_{i=1}^{n}(w'_i - w''_i)^2]^{\frac{1}{2}}, \tag{8}$$

where n represents the number of indicators, that is, the dimension of the weight vector.

The difference between α and β is the difference between the allocation coefficients, as shown in the Eq. (9),

$$D = |\alpha - \beta|. \tag{9}$$

At the same time, we have $\alpha + \beta = 1$. In order to make the degree of difference between w' and w'' consistent with the degree of difference between α and β, combined with $d(w'_i, w''_i)$, we construct the following equation system:

$$\begin{cases} d(w'_i, w''_i)^2 = (\alpha - \beta)^2 \\ \alpha + \beta = 1 \end{cases}. \tag{10}$$

The combined weight w is

$$w = \alpha w' - \beta w''. \tag{11}$$

3 Accelerating Recommendation Algorithms Based on Clustering Algorithms

Process of Recommendation Algorithm Based on Clustering. As shown on the left side of Fig. 3, traditional employment recommendation algorithms suffer from slow inference due to the need to compare the features of the test sample with every sample in the item set in a traversal manner. To address this issue, this paper proposes a solution. Firstly, samples within the item set that have similar features are clustered using the MEAN-SHIFT [17] algorithm, forming different categories. Then, the features of samples within each cluster are averaged to form cluster features. Secondly, in the inference stage of employment recommendation, as shown on the right side of Fig. 3, this paper first compares the sample features with the cluster features and selects the class with the highest similarity. Then, it compares the sample with the samples within the selected cluster to find the user with the highest similarity, thus achieving the goal of employment recommendation.

Comparison of the Average Time Complexity Analysis Between Clustering Based Recommendation Algorithms and Traditional Algorithms. As shown in Fig. 3, although the algorithm proposed in this paper is slightly more complex in terms of the process compared to traditional algorithms, the average time complexity of the proposed algorithm is significantly lower than that of traditional algorithms. It is worth noting that the clustering operation performed by the MEAN-SHIFT [17] algorithm is carried out in

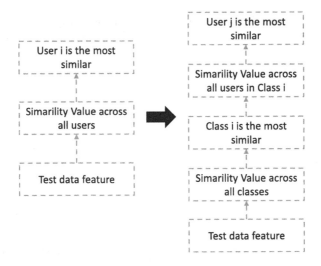

Fig. 3. On the left side is the inference process of traditional recommendation algorithms, and on the right side is the inference process of the recommendation algorithm proposed in this paper.

advance on the dataset and the clustering results are stored in a database, thus not participating in the algorithmic inference process between occupations.

In this paper, we assume that the number of users in the dataset is K, and the length of the feature vector for each user is N. After applying the MEAN-SHIFT algorithm to the dataset, it is classified into C_i clusters, where $1 \leqslant i \leqslant K$, $C_i = i$. Each cluster contains M_j samples, where $1 \leqslant j \leqslant C_i$, $1 \leqslant M_j \leqslant K$, and $K = M_0 + M_1 + \cdots + M_{C_i}$. Given that the time complexity of cosine similarity is $O(N^2)$, the average time complexity of the traditional algorithm is $K \cdot O(N^2)$. Our method has a time complexity of $C_i \cdot O(N^2) + M_j \cdot O(N^2) = (C_i + M_j) \cdot O(N^2)$. Next, let's calculate the average time complexity of the algorithm:

(1) When calculating the average time complexity, we first need to determine the possible scenarios for the number of samples in each class when there are C_i classes. This problem is equivalent to finding the number of solutions for the equation $K = M_0 + M_1 + \cdots + M_{C_i}$, which is also equivalent to finding the number of combinations of K in a multiset. Since $1 \leqslant M_j \leqslant K$, we perform a variable substitution.

$$L_i = M_i - 1. \tag{12}$$

Therefore, the equation becomes:

$$K - C_i = L_0 + L_1 + \cdots + L_{C_i}. \tag{13}$$

According to the properties of a multiset, the number of solutions for the equation when there are C_i classes is:

$$\binom{K - C_i + C_i - 1}{K - C_i} = \binom{K - 1}{K - C_i} = \binom{K - 1}{C_i - 1}. \tag{14}$$

Therefore, the total number of solutions is:

$$\sum_{i=1}^{K} \binom{K-1}{C_i - 1} = \binom{K-1}{0} + \binom{K-1}{1} + \cdots + \binom{K-1}{K-1} = 2^{K-1}. \tag{15}$$

(2) The sum of the time complexities of our method in all cases can be expressed by the formula:

$$\sum_{i=1}^{K} \sum_{j=1}^{C_i} (C_i + M_j) \cdot O\left(N^2\right)$$

$$= O\left(N^2\right) \cdot \sum_{i}^{K} C_i^2 + K = O\left(N^2\right) \cdot \left[\left(1^2 + K\right) + \left(2^2 + K\right) + \cdots + \left(K^2 + K\right)\right]$$

$$= O\left(N^2\right) \cdot K^2 + \frac{K \cdot (K+1) \cdot (2K+1)}{6}.$$

$$\tag{16}$$

(3) Based on formula 15 and formula 16, The average time complexity is:

$$O\left(N^2\right) \cdot \frac{K^2 + \frac{K \cdot (K+1) \cdot (2K+1)}{6}}{2^{K-1}} = O\left(N^2\right) \cdot \frac{2K^2 + 9K + 1}{3 \cdot 2^K}. \tag{17}$$

(4) In order to determine at which value of K our algorithm achieves a better average complexity compared to the traditional algorithm, we made the following judgment:

$$\frac{K^2 + \frac{K \cdot (K+1) \cdot (2K+1)}{6}}{2^{K-1} \cdot K} < 1$$

$$\Rightarrow \frac{2K^2 + 9K + 1}{3 \cdot 2^K} < 1. \tag{18}$$

It can be easily seen that the above equation holds when $K \geqslant 6$. In other words, when the number of samples in the dataset is greater than or equal to 6, the average time complexity of the algorithm proposed in this paper is lower than that of the traditional algorithm. In the era of big data, it is almost inevitable to have a dataset with a number of samples greater than or equal to 6.

4   Experiments

4.1   Dataset

The experiment in this paper utilized a newly created dataset called HNNU-JOB, which consists of 653 records of personal data and employment outcomes of students who signed contracts with the university over five years. As shown in Table 4, the dataset includes 7 individual basic information features and 6 academic achievement features for the students, as well as 3 enterprise information features for the employing companies.

Table 4. Feature information of the HNNU-JOB dataset.

Feature Object	Feature Type	Specific Features
Student Features	Personal Information	Name, Gender, Home Address, University Score, Faculty, Major, Employing Company
	Academic Achievements	Academic Performance, Internship Performance, Competition Results, Honors, CET4 Score, CET6 Score
Employing Company Features	Enterprise Information	Company Name, Company Category, Company Province

To incorporate the employment competency requirements of companies for students, the AHP-Entropy Weight Combination method is employed to further adjust the preprocessed dataset. This involves assigning combined weights to the evaluation indicators reflecting companies' considerations of students' employment capabilities. As different majors have varying emphases on the required competencies by companies, Table 5 presents the comprehensive competency evaluation indicator weights for students in the computer science field.

Table 5. Weighting of Comprehensive Evaluation Indicators for Enterprise-Computer Science Students.

Objective Level	Indicator Level	Weight		
		Analytic Hierarchy Process (AHP)	Entropy Weight Method	Combination Method (AHP-Entropy Weight Method.)
Employability Competency of Students	Gender	0.0128	0.0332	0.0224
	University Score	0.0869	0.1257	0.1052
	Academic Performance	0.2342	0.2479	0.2407
	Internship Performance	0.2156	0.2538	0.2336
	Competition Results	0.3147	0.2992	0.3074
	Honors	0.0459	0.0033	0.0258
	CET4 Score	0.0511	0.0242	0.0384
	CET6 Score	0.0439	0.0123	0.0290

Multiply the specific features of students in the dataset corresponding to the respective majors by their weights to adjust the dataset. In this experiment, 80% of the data in the dataset is randomly selected as the training set, and 20% of the data is used as the validation set.

4.2   Metrics

(1) This article refers to the reference and introduces the concept of Normalized Mutual Information (NMI), which is defined as follows:

$$\text{NMI} = \frac{\sum_{i=1}^{k} \sum_{j=1}^{m} n_{i,j}^{a,b} \cdot log \frac{n \cdot n_{i,j}^{a,b}}{n_i^a \cdot n_j^b}}{\sqrt{\left(\sum_{i=1}^{k} n_i^a \cdot log \frac{n_i^a}{n}\right) \cdot \left(\sum_{j=1}^{m} n_j^b \cdot log \frac{n_j^b}{n}\right)}}. \tag{19}$$

In Formula 20, m represents the number of clusters, n_i^a represents the total number of data points in cluster i of the clustering result, n_j^b represents the total number of data points in cluster j of the clustering result, and $n_{i,j}^{a,b}$ represents the number of data points that are assigned to cluster i but belong to the true label class j.

(2) Regarding the employment recommendation results, this article refers to the reference and introduces the concept of Relative Improvement (RelaImpr) to measure the gain of the employment recommendation method proposed in this article compared to other methods. For a random Gaussian classifier, $AUC = 0.5$. Therefore, the calculation formula for RelaImpr is as follows:

$$RelaImpr = \left(\frac{AUCOurModel - 0.5}{AUCOtherModel - 0.5} - 1\right) \times 100\%. \tag{20}$$

4.3   Experiment Results

Performance and Analysis of Clustering Algorithms. In order to obtain better recommendation results, this paper tested the clustering performance of three clustering algorithms on the HNNU-JOB dataset: MEAN-SHIFT [17], Affinity Propagation Algorithm (AP) [18], and Density-Based Algorithm for Discovering Clusters in Large Spatial Databases with Noise (DBSCAN)[?], which do not require input category information. Among them, samples employed in synonymous companies were considered as one category. Table 6 presents the evaluation results of these algorithms on the dataset using three evaluation metrics: ACC, NMI, and the average runtime of 10 runs. In order to visually display the clustering results of the three algorithms, this paper provides visualizations as shown in Fig. 4. Through analysis of the experimental results, the following conclusions can be drawn: (1) Based on the three evaluation metrics in Table 6, it can be observed that compared to the AP algorithm and DBSCAN algorithm, the Mean-shift algorithm has higher accuracy. It also slightly outperforms DBSCAN in terms of NMI and average runtime, and performs better than the AP algorithm. Figure 4 shows the clustering results of the three clustering algorithms on the self-made dataset. From the left, middle, and right parts of the figure, it can be seen that compared to the MEAN-SHIFT algorithm, the clustering results formed by AP and DBSCAN have fewer clusters and the clusters are not well-clustered. Therefore, in this paper, the MEAN-SHIFT algorithm, which has the best performance, is used for clustering analysis.

Table 6. Comparison of the performance of three clustering algorithms on HNNU-JOB dataset.

Method	ACC(%)	NMI	Mean Time(s)
AP	0.8749	0.7956	1.135
DBSCAN	0.8547	0.8738	1.117
MEAN-SHIFT (Our method)	**0.8935**	**0.8771**	**1.092**

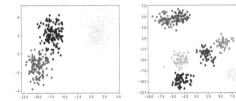 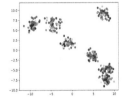

Fig. 4. It describes the visual comparison of clustering results using different algorithms on the HNNU-JOB dataset. Left: AP. Middle: DBSCAN. Right: Mean-shift.

Configuration Exploration. To further validate the effectiveness of the proposed employment recommendation algorithm, three ablation experiments were conducted in this study: 1) using the AHP method alone to calculate the weights of student employment indicators; 2) using the AHP-entropy method to calculate the weights of student employment indicators; 3) applying clustering before performing the employment recommendation algorithm. The Table 7 showed that: 1) Compared to the AHP method, the AHP-Entropy Weight method significantly improves the accuracy of the recommendation algorithm and reduces RelaImpr. This is because the AHP-Entropy Weight method can generate feature extraction matrices based on different companies' different requirements for students with different majors and abilities. The FPS remains unchanged because the generation of feature extraction matrices does not participate in the inference stage of the recommendation algorithm. 2) Compared to not using clustering algorithm, using clustering algorithm significantly improves the inference speed while slightly decreasing the accuracy and RelaImpr. This is due to the accuracy loss caused by the use of clustering algorithm.

Table 7. Results of the ablation experiments on student employment recommendation.

Method	RelaImpr(%)	ACC(%)	FPS
w/ AHP	8.89	69.31	149.56
w/ APH-Entropy Weight Method.	5.27	80.04	149.49
w/ Clustering	5.30	80.00	246.73

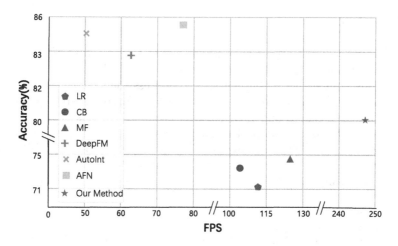

Fig. 5. Comparisons of different methods on HNNU-JOB dataset.

Comparison Against Other Methods. The employment recommendation method proposed in this paper is compared with LR, CB, MF, DeepFM [19], AutoInt [20], and AFN [21] recommendation methods. Table 8 presents the average results of 10 experiments for each recommendation method on the self-made dataset, with the best indicators highlighted in bold. From the experimental results, it can be observed that for the HNNU-JOB dataset, the proposed method significantly outperforms similar machine learning methods in terms of accuracy and FPS. Compared to deep learning-based algorithms, it may lag behind in terms of accuracy but exhibits a significant lead in terms of FPS. We also plot the scatter diagram on Fig. 5, which intuitively shows the superiority of our method.

Table 8. Classification FPS and accuracy comparison against state-of-the art on HNNU-JOB dataset.

Method	FPS	ACC(%)
LR	113.00	71.07
CB	105.99	73.41
MF	121.41	74.49
DeepFM	63.42	82.90
AutoInt	50.96	84.99
AFN	77.74	85.77
Our method	**246.73**	80.00

5   Conclusion

In this paper, we use the AHP-Entropy Weight method to generate corresponding feature weight vectors for students from different disciplines, considering their varying competency requirements. To address the slow feature matching problem in traditional algorithms, we significantly improve matching efficiency by first matching classes and then matching samples. In this paper, we prove that if the number of samples in the database is greater than or equal to 6, our algorithm will have a lower average time complexity than the traditional algorithm. Experimental results demonstrate that our proposed method outperforms previous algorithms in FPS.

Acknowledgements. This work was supported by National Students' Platform for Innovation and Entrepreneurship Training Program (202210542046) and Hunan Province General Higher Education Teaching Reform Research Project (HNJG-2021-0394).

References

1. Zhang, Y., Yang, C., Niu, Z.: A research of job recommendation system based on collaborative fltering. In: 2014 Seventh International Symposium on Computational Intelligence and Design, vol. 1, pp. 533–538. IEEE (2014)
2. Su, X., Khoshgoftaar, T.M.: A survey of collaborative filtering techniques. In: Advances in Artificial Intelligence (2009)
3. Wei, J., He, J., Chen, K., Zhou, Y., Tang, Z.: Collaborative filtering and deep learning based recommendation system for cold start items. Expert Syst. Appl. **69**, 29–39 (2017)
4. Nie, M., Yang, L., Sun, J., et al.: Advanced forecasting of career choices for college students based on campus big data. Front. Comput. Sci. **12**, 494–503 (2018)
5. Nie, M., Xiong, Z., Zhong, R., et al.: Career choice prediction based on campus big data-mining the potential behavior of college students. Appl. Sci. **10**(8), 2841 (2020)
6. Zhu, C., Zhu, H., Xiong, H., et al.: Person-job fit: adapting the right talent for the right job with joint representation learning. ACM Trans. Manag. Inf. Syst. (TMIS) **9**(3), 1–17 (2018)
7. Qin, H., Zhu, T., Xu, C., et al.: An enhanced neural network approach to person-job fit in talent recruitment. ACM Trans. Inf. Syst. **38**(2), 1–33 (2020)
8. Parks, J.B.: Employment status of alumni of an undergraduate sport management program. J. Sport Manag. **5**(2), 100–110 (1991)
9. Xie, C., Dong, D., Shengping, H., et al.: Safety evaluation of smart grid based on AHP-entropy method. Syst. Eng. Procedia **4**, 203–209 (2012)
10. Cooper A., Robert Reimann R., Cronin D.: About Face 3P: The Essentials of Interaction Design, pp. 19–22. Wiley Publishing Inc., New Jersey (2007)
11. Amato, G., Straccia, U.: User profile modeling and applications to digital libraries. In: Proceedings of the 3rd International Conference on Theory and Practice of Digital Libraries, Paris, France, pp. 184–197 (1999)

12. Quintana R.M., Haley S.R., Levick A., et al.: The persona party: using personas to design for learning at scale, In: Proceedings of the 2017 CHI Conference Extended Abstracts on Human Factors in Computing Systems (CHI EA 2017), pp 933–941 (2017)
13. Saaty, T.L.: A scaling method for priorities in hierarchical structures. J. Math. Psychol. **15**(3), 234–81 (1977)
14. Saaty, R.W.: The analytic hierarchy process-what it is and how it is used. Math. Model. **9**(3–5), 161–176 (1987)
15. Clausius, R.: On the moving force of heat, and the laws regarding the nature heat itself which are deducible therefrom. Philosoph. Mag. **2**(ser. 4), 1–21, 102–119 (1851)
16. Shannon, C.E.: A mathematical theory of communication. Bell Syst. Tech. J. **27**(3), 379–423 (1948)
17. Cheng, Y.: Mean shift, mode seeking, and clustering. IEEE Trans. Pattern Anal. Mach. Intell. **17**(8), 790–799 (1995)
18. Brendan, J.: Frey Delbert Dueck, clustering by passing messages between data points. Science **315**, 972–976 (2007)
19. Guo, H., Tang, R., Ye, Y., et al.: DeepFM: a factorization-machine based neural network for CTR prediction. In: Proceedings of the 26th International Joint Conference on Artificial Intelligence, 2782–2788 (2017)
20. Song, W., Shi, C., Xiao, Z., et al.: AutoInt: automatic feature interaction learning via self-attentive neural networks. In: Proceedings of the 28th ACM International Conference on Information and Knowledge Management. Association for Computing Machinery, New York, NY, USA, 1161–1170 (2019)
21. Xiao, J., Ye, H., He, X., et al.: Attentional factorization machines: Learning the weight of feature interactions via attention networks. arXiv: 1708.04617 (2017)

Coordinated Reconstruction Dual-Branch Network for Low-Dose PET Reconstruction

Yanyi Li, Pin Xu, Haoyuan Chen, Yufei Han, Guojian Xiao, Kuan Li,
and Jianping Yin$^{(\boxtimes)}$

Dongguan University of Technology, Dongguan 523808, Guangdong, China
jpyin@dgut.edu.cn

Abstract. Positron Emission Tomography (PET), known for its sensitivity and non-invasiveness in visualizing metabolic processes in the human body, has been widely utilized for clinical diagnosis. However, the procedure of PET imaging requires the administration of a radioactive tracer, which poses potential risks to human health. Reducing the usage of radioactive tracers leads to lower information content and increased independent noise. Therefore, the reconstruction of low-dose PET images becomes crucial. Existing reconstruction methods that learn a single mapping for low-dose PET reconstruction often suffer from over-denoising or incomplete information. To address this challenge, this work investigates the generation of realistic full-dose PET images. Firstly, we propose a simple yet reasonable low-dose PET model that treats each reconstructed voxel as a random variable. This model divides the reconstruction problem into two sub-problems: noise suppression and missing data recovery. Subsequently, we introduce a novel framework called the Coordinated Reconstruction Dual Branch Network (CRDB). The CRDB utilizes dual branches to separately perform denoising and information completion for PET reconstruction. Moreover, the CRDB leverages the Fast Channel Attention mechanism to capture diverse and unique information from different channels. Additionally, to emphasize pronounced distinctions, we adopt the Huber loss as the loss function. Quantitative experiments demonstrate that our strategy achieves favorable results in low-dose PET reconstruction.

Keywords: Low-Dose PET · PET reconstruction · image denoising

1 Introduction

Positron Emission Tomography (PET) is a valuable tool for cancer detection and evaluating treatment efficacy [1]. However, the usage of radioactive tracers

Data used in preparation of this article were obtained from the University of Bern, Dept. of Nuclear Medicine and School of Medicine, Ruijin Hospital. As such, the investigators contributed to the design and implementation of DATA and/or provided data but did not participate in analysis or writing of this report. A complete listing of investigators can be found at: "https://ultra-low-dose-pet.grandchallenge.org/Description/".

Z. Cai et al. (Eds.): NCTCS 2023, CCIS 1944, pp. 190–200, 2024.
https://doi.org/10.1007/978-981-99-7743-7_12

in PET imaging poses health risks [2], especially for vulnerable populations such as women and children. Insufficient tracer administration leads to noise, artifacts, and information gaps in the resulting images [3,4], which can mislead doctors in disease assessment. Additionally, reducing the dose of radiotracer in PET imaging can lead to several benefits. It can shorten the imaging time, reduce patient motion artifacts, increase the utilization of the imaging equipment, and lower the overall costs [5]. Thus, it is essential to develop methods to reconstruct low-dose PET images to resemble full-dose images closely.

Numerous studies have emerged aiming to generate full-dose PET images from low-dose PET scans. Deep learning, specifically Convolutional Neural Networks (CNNs), has gained popularity in medical images due to their ability to learn complex patterns [6,7]. In the context of PET image reconstruction, Xiang et al. [8] proposed a modified U-Net architecture, while Y. Wang et al. [9] utilized prior conditions to generate corresponding full-dose PET images. Additionally, by employing style modulation, [10] successfully generated images with more realistic textures. Nevertheless, existing neural networks commonly learn a single mapping to remove noise and complete missing information. This approach overlooks the fact that each voxel of a low-dose PET image follows a random variable distribution, resulting in either over-denoising or inadequate information in the final output.

To overcome these challenges, this work focuses on generating realistic full-dose PET images that provide clear and accurate information for medical professionals. We start by proposing a simple yet reasonable low-dose PET model that treats each reconstructed voxel as a random variable. This model divides the reconstruction task into two sub-problems: noise suppression and missing data recovery. To address these sub-problems, we introduce a novel Coordinated Reconstruction Dual Branch (CRDB) framework. After obtaining the feature maps using a CNN backbone, CRDB employs a dual branch to perform denoising and information completion separately, facilitating PET image reconstruction. Additionally, to enhance the extraction of relevant information from multiple feature maps, CRDB incorporates a lightweight yet efficient Fast Channel Attention (FCA) mechanism [11] in the dual branch. FCA selectively captures diverse information suitable for the reconstruction task from the aggregated features, providing more comprehensive representations for both denoising and reconstruction. Moreover, we adopt the Huber loss as our loss function to prioritize significant differences. Unlike the L1 loss, Huber loss [12] assigns higher weights to voxels with larger residuals, thus encouraging the network to focus more on challenging regions.

In conclusion, our contributions can be summarized into four points:

(1) We introduce a simple yet reasonable low-dose PET model that considers reconstructed voxels as random variables. This model effectively addresses the reconstruction problem by splitting it into two sub-problems: noise suppression and missing data recovery.

(2) We propose a novel framework, CRDB. By employing a dual branch approach, CRDB performs denoising and information completion separately to

achieve PET reconstruction. This approach ensures more accurate and reliable results.

(3) We customize an efficient dual-branch architecture and incorporate the FCA mechanism. FCA effectively captures diverse and relevant information from the final aggregated features, providing more comprehensive representations for both denoising and reconstruction processes.

(4) Through qualitative validation, we demonstrate that the PET images generated by our approach, CRDB, exhibit high similarity to real PET images in terms of intensity and distribution. This indicates the effectiveness of our proposed method.

2   Related Work

2.1   Machine Learning-Based Methods

The machine learning methods in PET reconstruction emerged earlier than deep learning methods. Kang et al. employed a regression forest method to extract features from low-dose PET and MRI images for predicting the full-dose image [13]. Wang et al. used the sparse coefficients estimated from the MRI and low-dose PET images to predict the standard PET image using a mapping strategy [14]. To further enhance the accuracy of sparse representation estimation, An et al. adopted a data-driven multilevel canonical correlation analysis scheme that involves multiple stages or levels of analysis [3]. To address the issue of incomplete training sample modalities, Wang et al. developed a semi-supervised triple dictionary learning method [15]. The experimental results in the paper demonstrate that incorporating the incomplete dataset is beneficial for the results. Therefore, if available, the incomplete dataset should be used.

2.2   Deep Learning-Based Methods

Traditional machine learning methods often suffer from long inference times when testing new cases, and the generated images may exhibit excessive smoothness [16]. As a result, deep learning-based methods have emerged as a promising alternative.

By employing a contextual strategy, multiple CNN modules are integrated to learn an end-to-end mapping between low-dose PET and T1 images as inputs and the corresponding full-dose PET images as outputs [17]. To better facilitate the contributions of different modalities at different positions in the image, an adaptive strategy for multimodal fusion is proposed [18]. The results indicate that this method outperforms traditional multimodal fusion approaches. Sanaei et al. demonstrated that using multiple different low-dose PET inputs for reconstruction yields better results compared to using a single low-dose PET [19]. Lei et al. using CycleGAN, the model learns both the transformation from low-dose PET to full-dose PET and the inverse transformation, which is the conversion from generated full-dose images to realistic low-dose PET images [20].

3   Methodology

As shown in Fig. 1, the pipeline of using CRDB to perform low-dose PET reconstruction consists of three parts: CNN backbone, reconstruction branch (RB), and denoised branch (DB). CNN backbone retrieves a sufficient representation that effectively captures the intrinsic content embedded in the image, it can be replaced by any network. Then two branches learn the distinctive content relevant to the feature map derived from a CNN output. By utilizing the distinctive content learned from the feature map, the RB addresses missing information, while the DB focuses on noise reduction. This coordinated reconstruction process ensures that the final output image is both accurate in terms of content and free from unwanted noise artifacts.

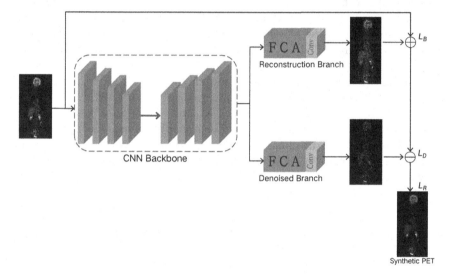

Fig. 1. The overall structure of CRDB. It is divided into (a) CNN backbone, (b) reconstruction branch, and (c) denoised branch.

3.1   Low-Dose PET Modelling

In the context of low-dose PET, it is widely acknowledged that the images obtained may not accurately and comprehensively depict the metabolic activity within the subject's body due to the limited radiation dose administered. While these images may lack the clarity and precision required for detailed analysis, they can still provide some valuable information about localized metabolic activity. Moreover, when the radiation dose is insufficient, the low-dose PET images may also contain disruptive noise, which can significantly interfere with the process of clinical diagnosis. Considering these factors, we can express the degradation model associated with low-dose conditions, including noise, in the following generic way:

$$x = y - I + N \tag{1}$$

where x and y represent low-dose PET and full-dose PET, respectively. I represent the information deduction and N is noise adding to low-dose PET.

3.2 Overall Framework

A common solution for (1) is to train the network to directly learn a mapping from x to y. However, this naive strategy often leads to sub-optimal results. For instance, excessive denoising can lead to insufficient information, or the presence of residual noise can result in information degradation.

To enable the network to simultaneously perform information completion and denoising, we propose training the network to learn two separate mappings corresponding to the aforementioned tasks. Therefore, we have designed a network architecture called the Coordinated Reconstruction Dual Branch Network(CRDB).

The CRDB architecture consists of several components. Firstly, we employ a simple CNN backbone to extract the latent content embedded in the low-dose PET, it can be replaced by any network as long as the final output convolution layer is removed. Next is the dual-branch module, which incorporates Fast Channel Attention(FCA) to improve the extraction of desired components from the various feature maps obtained by the CNN backbone. Finally, the network's output is given by:

$$\widehat{y} = x + \widehat{I} - \widehat{N} \tag{2}$$

where $\widehat{y}$ and x represent synthetic PET and low-dose PET, $\widehat{I}$ and $\widehat{N}$ are the outputs of the reconstruction branch and the denoised branch, respectively.

CNN Backbone. The CNN backbone is employed to extract features from low-dose images and comprises eight convolutional blocks with identical structures. Half of these blocks are dedicated to encoding, while the other half is used for decoding. The specific structure is as follows:

Encoder: The first convolutional block is responsible for increasing the dimensionality, while only the last three blocks utilize Max Pooling for downsampling. Each convolutional block consists of two $3 \times 3 \times 3$ convolutional layers followed by Batch Normalization and LeakyReLU.

Decoder: The decoder exhibits a similar structure to the encoder except the downsampling is replaced by upsampling using deconvolution. Moreover, there are skip connections between the corresponding layers of the encoder and decoder, which helps to alleviate the loss of valuable information during the encoding and decoding process.

Dual Branch. The dual-branch network is composed of a reconstruction branch and a denoising branch, serving the purpose of supplementing missing information and eliminating noise in low-dose PET images. Both branches share the same structure, consisting of an FCA module followed by a convolutional layer with kernel size 1.

We define the input feature as F_i, then FCA can be formulated as:

$$FCA\left(F_i\right) = F_i \cdot \left(1 + \sigma\left(F_i\left(GAP\left(F_i\right)\right)\right)\right) \tag{3}$$

where σ represents the Sigmoid activation function, GAP means global average pooling along the spatial wise, f_{1c} denotes Conv3d with kernel size 1.

3.3   Loss Function

A standard loss function for optimization in low-dose PET reconstruction is the L1 loss, minimizing the absolute deviations. The reason for not using L2 Loss is that L1 loss is more robust in the presence of outliers. PET data often contains a significant number of outliers, and L2 loss can amplify these outliers, leading to overall performance degradation. Although this produces good results in our test cases, we found that using the Huber as the loss function yields better results than L1.

$$HuberLoss(y, f(x)) = \begin{cases} \frac{1}{2}(y - f(x))^2, & \text{if } |y - f(x)| < \delta \\ \delta \cdot |y - f(x)| - \frac{1}{2}\delta, & \text{otherwise} \end{cases} \tag{4}$$

where y and $f(x)$ are the observed and predicted values, respectively. δ is the threshold.

The difference between the Huber loss function and the L1 loss is that the Huber loss imposes a relatively larger penalty for significant differences between the predicted and ground truth images. This characteristic enables the network to prioritize points with significant differences, directing its attention to the most important areas during the optimization process. In contrast, the L2 loss function's sensitivity to outliers can lead to excessive penalties for the same points with larger differences, potentially causing the network to overly emphasize these differences. By using the Huber loss function, excessive sensitivity to such differences is mitigated, preventing performance degradation, particularly in the case of whole-body PET images. This balanced approach ensures that the network maintains robustness while effectively capturing important features for accurate reconstruction.

3.4   Training Procedure

The training process of the model consists of three steps. Firstly, the backbone network is trained to extract potential content from the low-dose PET. At this stage, the denoised branch is fixed, and the model only produces the output from the reconstruction branch. The loss function for the backbone is as follows:

$$L_B = Huberloss(x + f_R(x), y) \tag{5}$$

where x and y represent low-dose PET and full-dose PET, respectively. f_R is the output of the reconstruction branch.

Secondly, the denoised network is trained for noise reduction using a method described in reference [21]. In this step, the low-dose PET is used as the label, while a noisy version of the low-dose PET is used as the input. At this stage, the trained backbone is fixed, and the model only produces the output from the denoised branch. Following the approach described in [22], the network does not directly output the denoised result, but instead estimates the noise present in the image.

$$L_D = Huberloss(f_D(x + n), n) \tag{6}$$

where x and n represent low-dose PET and injected noise, respectively. f_D is the output of the denoised branch.

Finally, the reconstructed network is trained with both the backbone and denoised branch fix. In that case, both the denoised branch and the reconstruction branch of the model have outputs, which together contribute to the final result.

$$L_R = Huberloss(x + f_R(x) - f_D(x), y) \tag{7}$$

where x and y represent low-dose PET and full-dose PET, respectively. f_R and f_D are the outputs of the denoised and reconstruction branches, respectively.

4   Materials and Experiments

4.1   Dataset Description

The datasets used in this study were obtained from the University of Bern, Dept. of Nuclear Medicine and School of Medicine, Ruijin Hospital [23]. The low-dose PET is synthesized at dose reduction factor DRF = 100 by randomly selecting 1/100 of the raw count list-mode datasets. Considering the limited number of training images, we extracted large 3D patches of size $192 \times 96 \times 96$ from each PET image.

The first dataset was acquired using a United Imaging Healthcare uExplorer whole-body PET/CT system. 294 patches were extracted from each image. We randomly selected 180 subjects for training, 10 for validation, and 69 for testing. The second dataset was acquired using a Siemens Biograph Vision Quadra whole-body PET/CT system. 485 patches were extracted from each image. We randomly selected 99 subjects for training, 10 for validation, and 50 for testing.

4.2   Experimental Settings

The CRDB was trained using a batch size of 22 with the Adam optimizer. We trained the backbone for 40 epochs, followed by an additional 10 epochs of training for the denoised branch and 10 epochs for the reconstruction branch. We employed a learning rate of 2e-4 that was linearly decreased with a factor of 0.1 and a patience of 5 epochs. To avoid overfitting, an early stopping strategy

Table 1. Quantitative comparison with four state-of-the-art SPET reconstruction methods in terms of PSNR, SSIM, and NRMSE.

Method	uExplorer dataset			Quadra dataset		
	PSNR	NRMSE	SSIM	PSNR	NRMSE	SSIM
1% dose PET	45.77	0.0079	0.9850	47.67	0.0053	0.9835
3D-Unet	51.13	0.0035	0.9907	53.54	0.0024	0.9956
3D-cGAN	48.92	0.0049	0.9743	49.36	0.0041	0.9854
DCITN	50.40	0.0038	0.9912	53.04	0.0026	0.9880
StyleGAN	51.33	0.0034	0.9904	54.15	0.0022	0.9963
Proposed	54.09	0.0026	0.9967	55.08	0.0021	0.9930

was applied and was used to terminate the training process when the learning rate exceeded 2e-6. All the experiments were conducted on a 49GB NVIDIA RTX A6000 GPU, with the PyTorch framework.

4.3 Comparison with Other Methods

We conducted comparisons between our proposed method and four existing methods: (1) 3D-Unet [8], (2) 3D-cGAN [9], (3) DCITN [24], (4)StyleGan [10]. 3D-Unet is an improved U-Net structure for unsupervised PET denoising.DCITN utilized dense connections for CT reconstruction. 3D-cGAN is proposed for PET image synthesis with GAN.StyleGan utilizing the latent space allows for the generation of image transformations with more realistic texture features. We use three indicators to study the performance of all methods, including normalized mean squared error (NRMSE), peak signal-to-noise (PSNR), and structural similarity index (SSIM). In Table 1, the experimental results indicate that our method outperforms other methods in the majority of the metrics. Compared to the second-ranked methods in the uExplorer dataset, CRDB shows an improvement of 2.73 db in PSNR, an increase of 0.0007 in NRMSE, and an enhancement of 0.0054 in SSIM.

To better demonstrate the effectiveness of each method, we have also provided visual comparisons in Fig. 2. The first row shows the comparison between the images generated by four different methods and our proposed method. The leftmost and rightmost images correspond to the low-dose image and the full-dose image, respectively. The second row displays the magnified results within the red box. It is evident that our method generates images that are closest to the full-dose image, exhibiting clear edges and fewer artifacts.

4.4 Ablation Study

To validate the proposed Coordinated Reconstruction method, as well as the effectiveness of the FCA module and Huber loss, we conducted experiments on the same dataset. For the Coordinated Reconstruction method, we trained the

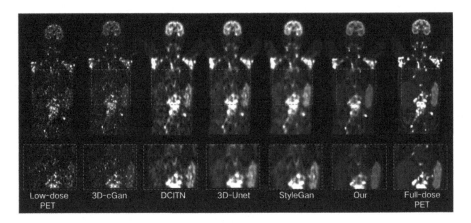

Fig. 2. Results of synthetic PET from five methods on uExplorer low-dose PET dataset.

two branches jointly. The low-dose images were used as inputs, while the corresponding full-dose images were used as labels. The final result was obtained by combining the low-dose input with the outputs from both branches. Regarding the FCA module, we created a separate network without this module and retrained it using the proposed method. As for the Huber loss, we replaced it with L1 loss to train the network. The results of the ablation experiments are presented in Table 2, demonstrating the effectiveness of our proposed method. It can be observed that our method outperforms the other control groups in all three metrics, indicating improvements in performance.

Table 2. Quantitative comparison of ablation concerning our methods.

Method	PSNR	NRMSE	SSIM
w/o Coordinated Reconstruction	53.48	0.0027	0.9951
w/o FCA	53.93	0.0027	0.9967
w/o Huberloss	53.59	0.0027	0.9953
CRDB(our)	54.09	0.0026	0.9968

5   Conclusion

Most of the research focuses on designing a network to reconstruct images using one mapping. In contrast, this work explores how generated images can contain more information with reduced noise. Firstly, we developed a model that treats low-dose images as the outcome of removing specific information from full-dose images and subsequently adding noise. Furthermore, we propose a novel framework CRDB that aims to accomplish information completion and noise reduction. To enhance performance and ensure network efficiency, we designed a dual-branch network following the CNN backbone. The experimental results demonstrate that our model outperforms others on the low-dose total-body PET dataset. In future work, our objective is to determine the optimal threshold for the Huber loss function.

Acknowledgements. This work was supported in part by the National Key Research and Development Program of China under Grant 2022YFF0606303, the National Natural Science Foundation of China under Grant 62206054, Research Capacity Enhancement Project of Key Construction Discipline in Guangdong Province under Grant 2022ZDJS028. Thanks to Xue Song, Kuangyu Shi & Axel Rominger, Dept. of Nuclear Medicine of the University of Bern, Hanzhong Wang, Rui Guo & Biao Li, Ruijin Hospital, Shanghai Jiaotong University for support of the source of the DATA.

References

1. Schrevens, L., Lorent, N., Dooms, C., Vansteenkiste, J.: The role of pet scan in diagnosis, staging, and management of non-small cell lung cancer. Oncologist **9**(6), 633–643 (2004)
2. Zhou, B., Tsai, Y.-J., Chen, X., Duncan, J.S., Liu, C.: MDPET: a unified motion correction and denoising adversarial network for low-dose gated pet. IEEE Trans. Med. Imaging **40**(11), 3154–3164 (2021)
3. An, L., et al.: Multi-level canonical correlation analysis for standard-dose pet image estimation. IEEE Trans. Image Process. **25**(7), 3303–3315 (2016)
4. Kaplan, S., Zhu, Y.-M.: Full-dose pet image estimation from low-dose pet image using deep learning: a pilot study. J. Digit. Imaging **32**(5), 773–778 (2019)
5. Xu, J., Gong, E., Pauly, J., Zaharchuk, G.: 200x low-dose pet reconstruction using deep learning. arXiv preprint arXiv:1712.04119 (2017)
6. Ronneberger, O., Fischer, P., Brox, T.: U-Net: convolutional networks for biomedical image segmentation. In: Navab, N., Hornegger, J., Wells, W.M., Frangi, A.F. (eds.) MICCAI 2015. LNCS, vol. 9351, pp. 234–241. Springer, Cham (2015). https://doi.org/10.1007/978-3-319-24574-4_28
7. Wang, T., et al.: Machine learning in quantitative pet: a review of attenuation correction and low-count image reconstruction methods. Physica Med. **76**, 294–306 (2020)
8. Cui, J., et al.: Pet image denoising using unsupervised deep learning. Eur. J. Nuclear Med. Mol. Imaging **46**, 2780–2789 (2019)
9. Wang, Y., et al.: 3D conditional generative adversarial networks for high-quality pet image estimation at low dose. Neuroimage **174**, 550–562 (2018)
10. Zhou, Y., et al.: 3D segmentation guided style-based generative adversarial networks for pet synthesis. IEEE Trans. Med. Imaging **41**(8), 2092–2104 (2022)
11. Cai, Y., Xiaowan, H., Wang, H., Zhang, Y., Pfister, H., Wei, D.: Learning to generate realistic noisy images via pixel-level noise-aware adversarial training. Adv. Neural. Inf. Process. Syst. **34**, 3259–3270 (2021)
12. Huber, P.J.: Robust estimation of a location parameter. In: Kotz, S., Johnson, N.L. (eds.) Breakthroughs in Statistics: Methodology and Distribution, pp. 492–518. Springer, New York (1992). https://doi.org/10.1007/978-1-4612-4380-9_35

13. Kang, J., Gao, Y., Shi, F., Lalush, D.S., Lin, W., Shen, D.: Prediction of standard-dose brain pet image by using MRI and low-dose brain [18f] FDG pet images. Med. Phys. **42**(9), 5301–5309 (2015)
14. Wang, Y., et al.: Predicting standard-dose pet image from low-dose pet and multimodal MR images using mapping-based sparse representation. Phys. Med. Biol. **61**(2), 791 (2016)
15. Wang, Y., et al.: Semisupervised tripled dictionary learning for standard-dose pet image prediction using low-dose pet and multimodal MRI. IEEE Trans. Biomed. Eng. **64**(3), 569–579 (2016)
16. Wangerin, K.A., Ahn, S., Wollenweber, S., Ross, S.G., Kinahan, P.E., Manjeshwar, R.M.: Evaluation of lesion detectability in positron emission tomography when using a convergent penalized likelihood image reconstruction method. J. Med. Imaging **4**(1), 011002 (2017)
17. Lei Xiang, Yu., Qiao, D.N., An, L., Lin, W., Wang, Q., Shen, D.: Deep auto-context convolutional neural networks for standard-dose pet image estimation from low-dose pet/MRI. Neurocomputing **267**, 406–416 (2017)
18. Wang, Y., et al.: 3D auto-context-based locality adaptive multi-modality GANs for pet synthesis. IEEE Trans. Med. Imaging **38**(6), 1328–1339 (2018)
19. Sanaei, B., Faghihi, R., Arabi, H., Zaidi, H.: Does prior knowledge in the form of multiple low-dose pet images (at different dose levels) improve standard-dose pet prediction? In: 2021 IEEE Nuclear Science Symposium and Medical Imaging Conference (NSS/MIC), pp. 1–3. IEEE (2021)
20. Lei, Y., et al.: Whole-body pet estimation from low count statistics using cycle-consistent generative adversarial networks. Phys. Med. Biol. **64**(21), 215017 (2019)
21. Zhang, M., Liu, L., Jiang, D.: Joint semantic-aware and noise suppression for low-light image enhancement without reference. Signal Image Video Process. **17**, 3847–3855 (2023)
22. Zhang, K., Zuo, W., Chen, Y., Meng, D., Zhang, L.: Beyond a gaussian denoiser: residual learning of deep CNN for image denoising. IEEE Trans. Image Process. **26**(7), 3142–3155 (2017)
23. Xue, S., et al.: A cross-scanner and cross-tracer deep learning method for the recovery of standard-dose imaging quality from low-dose PET. Eur. J. Nucl. Med. Mol. Imaging **49**, 1843–1856 (2021). https://doi.org/10.1007/s00259-021-05644-1
24. Huang, G., Liu, Z., Van Der Maaten, L., Weinberger, K.Q.: Densely connected convolutional networks. In: 2017 IEEE Conference on Computer Vision and Pattern Recognition (CVPR), pp. 2261–2269 (2017)

Networks and Security

Link Prediction in Dynamic Networks Based on Topological and Historical Information

Erfei Jia[1], Dongwen Tian[1], Tian Nan[2], and Longjie Li[1,3(✉)] (iD)

[1] School of Information Science and Engineering, Lanzhou University, Lanzhou 730000, China
ljli@lzu.edu.cn

[2] State Grid Gansu Electric Power Company Material Company, Lanzhou 73050, China

[3] Key Laboratory of Media Convergence Technology and Communication, Lanzhou 730000, Gansu, China

Abstract. Many real-world networks are dynamic ones whose structure keeps changing over time. Link prediction in dynamic networks is more challenging and complex than that in static ones due to their dynamic nature. However, effectively using the information carried by dynamic networks can make notable enhancements to prediction accuracy. To solve the problem of dynamic network link prediction, this paper proposes a new supervised method, named THILP. This method treats link prediction as a regression problem. In this regard, both elaborate topological and historical features are extracted from multiple snapshots to represent node pairs, and the RandomForestRegressor algorithm is adopted to train a prediction model. Extensive experiments are executed on nine benchmark networks to investigate the effectiveness of the THILP method. The results show that THILP behaves remarkably better than baseline methods.

Keywords: Link prediction · Dynamic networks · Topological features · Historical features

1 Introduction

Nowadays, complex networks are ubiquitous, which range from social networks to collaboration networks, from biological networks to technological networks, and from communication networks to transportation networks. As a consequence, the research of complex networks has been capturing increasing attention of researchers from diverse disciplines. Among these researches, link prediction, which aims to uncover missing links in static networks and foretell future connections in dynamic networks, has become an important branch due to its wide range of applications, such as friendships recommendation in online social networks, route planning for material delivery, and protein interactions analysis in biological networks.

Z. Cai et al. (Eds.): NCTCS 2023, CCIS 1944, pp. 203–220, 2024.
https://doi.org/10.1007/978-981-99-7743-7_13

To address the problem of link prediction, considerable efforts have been made by researchers [14,29]. Approaches in the literature can be mainly categorized as similarity-based methods and supervised learning-based methods [22,26,30]. Similarity-based methods hypothesize that *nodes with higher similarity scores are more likely to form connections*. Therefore, these methods usually design effective similarity indexes based on the observed structural information including common neighbors [1,32], paths [2,28], triangles [4,7,41], and community structures [3,38]. For example, the Common Neighbors index [32] defines the similarity between two nodes as the number of the shared neighbors. Moreover, the Local Path index [28] considers not only the number of common neighbors but also the number of paths with length 3 between two nodes. On the other hand, supervised learning-based methods assess the connections of node pairs by using some machine learning algorithms [16,23,37,42]. For instance, Fire et al. [16] proposed a supervised link prediction framework, which trains prediction models by adopting a set of structural features including nodes features and link features, and three classification algorithms like RandomForest to predict missing links in social networks. Xiao et al. [42] presented a prediction method based on convolutional neural network. Their method integrates multiple features obtained by network embedding and word embedding techniques. Li et al. [23] proposed an ensemble link prediction algorithm, in which four similarity indexes are assembled and two models trained by Logistic Regression and XGBoost are fused.

Actually, most of networks in the real-world keep evolving with time. For example, in a social network, the connections between individuals are usually varying dynamically according to the behaviors of their social partners [20]. These kind of networks are called *dynamic networks*, which are more precise in characterizing the complex systems [44]. Compared to link prediction in static networks, link prediction in dynamic networks is a challenge and complex process because of the complex dynamic structure and non-linear varying nature of dynamic networks [14,36]. On the other hand, the evolution history of a dynamic network can provide more information to detect potential or future links. In this regards, Soares and Prudêncio [39] proposed an event-based method that predicts future links based on the historical information of node pairs. Xu et al. [43] proposed a label propagation-based distributed temporal link prediction algorithm, which considers the dynamical properties of the interactions between nodes. Wu et al. [40] presented a similarity-based dynamic network link prediction method. This method measures the similarity between nodes based on node ranking and predicts the future similarity between each node pair using the historical similarity series. Chiu and Zhan [12] proposed a deep learning-based approach, in which traditional similarity metrics and weak estimators are employed to represent features of node pairs. Chen et al. [11] designed a supervised link prediction method for dynamic networks based on the change of the topological characteristics of two nodes between adjacent snapshots.

In this paper, we propose a L̲ink P̲rediction method for dynamic networks based on both T̲opological and H̲istorical I̲nformation (THILP). THILP is a supervised method that gauges the probability of a future connection between two nodes using a prediction model. The motivation behind the proposed method is to integrate not only topological features of node pairs extracted from multiple snapshots but also the historical connecting states of node pairs. In this regards, the proposed THILP method represents a node pair by the elaborate topological and historical features, and then trains a forecasting model using the RandomForestRegressor [6]. The effectiveness of the proposed method is evaluated on a group of dynamic networks with various topological characteristics. The experimental results show that our method outperforms the baselines including methods designed for both static and dynamic networks.

2   Problem Definition

To better depict the link prediction problem in dynamic networks, this section describes the formal definition of dynamic networks and formalizes the problem of dynamic network link prediction.

For simplicity, this study only considers unweighted and undirected networks. Let $G = (V, E)$ be a network, where V is the node set and $E \subseteq V \times V$ denotes the link (or edge) set. A dynamic network is represented as a series of snapshot networks, and the length of time period between any two adjacent snapshots is supposed to be fixed.

Definition 1. *(Dynamic networks). A dynamic network $\mathcal{G}$ is constituted of a sequence of networks, i.e., $\mathcal{G} = \{G_1, G_2, \cdots, G_T\}$, where $G_k = (V_k, E_k)$ $(1 \leq k \leq T)$ is a snapshot at time stamp k, and T represents the number of time stamps to record the snapshots of $\mathcal{G}$. Here, node sets across different snapshots are assumed to be the same, i.e., $V_1 = V_2 = \cdots = V_T = V$. But, links may appear or disappear over time. The adjacency matrix of snapshot G_k is presented as A_k, in which the element $A_k(i, j) = 1$ if there is a link between nodes v_i and v_j at time stamp t, and $A_k(i, j) = 0$ otherwise.*

Because the network structure of a static network is fixed, link prediction method can only reveal the unobserved links by using the known structural information of the network. While the structure of a dynamic network changes over time. Link prediction in a dynamic network can predict new links on the basis of the structural and temporal information extracted from the network. In this paper, we use a sequence of snapshots with length L, i.e., $\{G_{t-L}, G_{t-L+1}, \cdots, G_{t-1}\}$, to predict G_t [9,10].

Definition 2. *(Dynamic network link prediction). For a dynamic network with L snapshots, denoted as $\mathcal{G} = \{G_{t-L}, G_{t-L+1}, \cdots, G_{t-1}\}$, the task of dynamic network link prediction is to predict the network structure at time stamp t according to the information of previous L snapshots.*

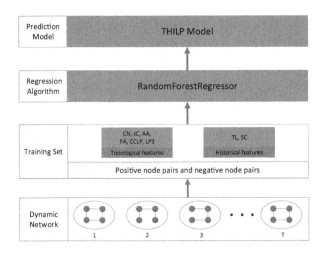

Fig. 1. Flowchart of the THILP method.

3   The Proposed Method

In this work, we propose the THILP method for link prediction in a dynamic network, which extracts the features of node pairs from both topological and historical information of the network, and employs the algorithm of Random-ForestRegressor [6] to train a prediction model. Figure 1 shows the basic idea of the proposed THILP method. The detail description of the method will be presented in what follows.

3.1   Features of Node Pairs

In general, features of node pairs play a crucial role in a supervised link prediction method. Therefore, we elaborate a set of features of node pairs for the THILP method by considering both topological and historical information from the network. In the following, both types of features are separately depicted.

Topological Features. Topological features that characterize the relationship between nodes according to the structures of snapshot networks are commonly used in many supervised link prediction methods [11,12,45]. As aforementioned, a host of similarity indexes have been devised for link prediction in static networks. In our proposed method, we carefully select six efficient similarity indexes to represent the affinities between nodes from various aspects of the topological structure of a snapshot.

Let G_k be a snapshot of the dynamic network $\mathcal{G}$, the six topological features of a node pair (v_i, v_j) extracted from G_k are explained as follows.

(1) *Common neighbors* (CN) [32]. This feature calculates the number of common neighbors between v_i and v_j, which is defined as

$$CN_k(i,j) = |\Gamma_k(i) \cap \Gamma_k(j)|, \tag{1}$$

where $\Gamma_k(i)$ denotes the neighbor set of node v_i in G_k.

(2) *Jaccard coefficient* (JC) [27]. This feature estimates the affinity between v_i and v_j as the ratio of shared neighbors to their total neighbors. The formal expression reads as

$$JC_k(i,j) = \frac{|\Gamma_k(i) \cap \Gamma_k(j)|}{|\Gamma_k(i) \cup \Gamma_k(j)|}. \tag{2}$$

(3) *Adamic-Adar* (AA) [1]. The AA index computes the relationship between v_i and v_j by penalizes the large-degree common neighbors, which is measured as

$$AA_k(i,j) = \sum_{v_l \in \Gamma_k(i) \cap \Gamma_k(j)} \frac{1}{\log d_k(l)}, \tag{3}$$

where $d_k(l)$ is the degree of node v_l in G_k.

(4) *Preferential attachment* (PA) [5]. The value of PA index is the product of the degrees of v_i and v_j, which reads as

$$PA_k(i,j) = d_k(i) \cdot d_k(j). \tag{4}$$

(5) *Clustering coefficient for link prediction* (CCLP) [41]. This feature sums the clustering coefficients of common neighbors between v_i and v_j. The formal definition is

$$CCLP_k(i,j) = \sum_{v_l \in \Gamma_k(i) \cap \Gamma_k(j)} CC_k(l), \tag{5}$$

where $CC_k(l)$ is the clustering coefficient of node v_l in G_k, which is computed as

$$CC_k(l) = \frac{2\Delta_k(l)}{d_k(l)(d_k(l) - 1)},$$

where $\Delta_k(l)$ is the number of triangles passing through v_l in G_k.

(6) *Local path with length 3* (LP3). This measure counts the number of paths with length 3 connecting v_i and v_j, which is calculated as

$$LP3_k(i,j) = \sum_{v_l \in \Gamma_k(i)} |\Phi_k(l) \cap \Gamma_k(j)|, \tag{6}$$

where $\Phi_k(l) = \Gamma_k(l) - \{v_i\}$.

Historical Features. Intuitively, links are more likely to generated between nodes that have connected before [20, 25]. For example, researchers tend to collaborate with others who have co-authored papers. Accordingly, historical states of node pairs act an important part in link prediction for dynamic networks [39]. In this paper, we define two historical features that capture the previous connection states of node pairs for the THILP method.

(1) *Temporal label* (TL). This feature records the connection state of a node pair in each snapshot of the dynamic network. For node pair (v_i, v_j), its value of TL in snapshot G_k is defined as

$$TL_k(i,j) = \begin{cases} 1, \text{ if } A_k(i,j) = 1 \\ 0, \text{ otherwise} \end{cases} \tag{7}$$

(2) *State change* (SC). The connection state of a node pair may change constantly during the evolution of a dynamic network. With the passage of time, new links may appear and existing links may disappear. To characterize the changes of connection state of node pairs, we define the feature of SC, which is estimated using two adjacent snapshots. For node pair (v_i, v_j), there are four cases of the change of its connection state from time $k-1$ to k: (1) creation of a new link; (2) removal of the existing link; (3) always connection; and (4) always unconnection. The formal value of SC is assigned as

$$SC_k(i,j) = \begin{cases} 1, \text{ if } A_{k-1}(i,j) = 0 \text{ and } A_k(i,j) = 1 \\ -1, \text{ if } A_{k-1}(i,j) = 1 \text{ and } A_k(i,j) = 0 \\ 2, \text{ if } A_{k-1}(i,j) = 1 \text{ and } A_k(i,j) = 1 \\ -2, \text{ if } A_{k-1}(i,j) = 0 \text{ and } A_k(i,j) = 0 \end{cases} \tag{8}$$

3.2 Algorithm of the Proposed Method

The THILP method is a supervised learning method. Thus, to train the prediction model, a training set is a necessary. Algorithm 1 describes the construction of training set. The input of this algorithm is a sequence of network snapshots $\{G_{t-L}, G_{t-L+1}, \cdots, G_{t-1}, G_t\}$, where G_t is used to generate and label node pairs in training set, and $\{G_{t-L}, G_{t-L+1}, \cdots, G_{t-1}\}$ are employed to extract features for each node pair. In this algorithm, we put all connected node pairs in G_t, i.e., E_t, into the training set X. To ensure that X contains balanced classes, we randomly sample the same number of unconnected node pairs as E_t from G_t. Those node pairs are denoted as H_t. Both of E_t and H_t compose the samples in X. Afterward, the feature vector of each node pair in X is calculated and its class is labeled. If there is a link between two nodes in G_t, the label is positive (denoted by 1); otherwise, the label is negative (denoted by 0). In total, the length of the feature vector of a node pair is $8L-1$. Here, L is a hyper-parameter that denotes the number of concerned snapshots. The testing set Y is constructed in a similar way to the training set, except that the snapshot sequences are composed of $\{G_{t-L+1}, G_{t-L+2}, \cdots, G_t, G_{t+1}\}$.

Then, we analyze the time complexity of the algorithm for constructing training set. Let N denote the number of nodes in the dynamic network and $\langle k \rangle$ be

---

Algorithm 1. Construction of training set

Input: A sequence of network snapshots $\{G_{t-L}, G_{t-L+1}, \cdots, G_{t-1}, G_t\}$
Output: Training set X
 1: $U \leftarrow$ all node pairs
 2: $E_t \leftarrow$ all connecting node pairs in G_t
 3: $\bar{E}_t \leftarrow U - E_t$
 4: $M \leftarrow$ size of E_t
 5: $H_t \leftarrow$ sample(M node pairs from $\bar{E}_t$)
 6: $X \leftarrow E_t \cup H_t$
 7: **for** $(v_i, v_j) \in X$ **do**
 8:     **for** $k = t - L$ to $t - 1$ **do**
 9:         Compute 6 topological features for (v_i, v_j) in G_k
10:         Compute $TL_k(i,j)$
11:         **if** $k > t - L$ **then**
12:             Compute $SC_k(i,j)$
13:         **end if**
14:     **end for**
15:     **if** $(v_i, v_j) \in E_t$ **then**
16:         (v_i, v_j) is labeled as 1
17:     **else**
18:         (v_i, v_j) is labeled as 0
19:     **end if**
20: **end for**
21: **return** X

---

the average degree of all nodes in each snapshot. The time complexity of line 1 for generating U is $O(N^2)$, and those of lines 2 ∼ 6 are not larger than $O(N^2)$. Given a node pair, we can conclude that the computational complexity for computing its feature vector is $O(L \langle k \rangle^3)$ based on the analysis in Ref. [37]. With the help of adjacency matrix, the time complexity for labeling the node pair is $O(1)$ (lines 15 ∼ 19). Since $L \ll M$, where M is the size of E_t, the time complexity of lines 7 ∼ 20 is $O(M \langle k \rangle^3)$. As a result, the time complexity of Algorithm 1 is $O(N^2 + M \langle k \rangle^3)$.

After getting the training set and testing set, we feed the training set to RandomForestRegressor [6] to train a prediction model. Then the probability that a testing node pair belongs to positive class is predicted by the trained model.

4   Performance Evaluation

In this section, we evaluate the performance of the THILP method experimentally on nine dynamic networks in comparison with seven baseline methods. All link prediction algorithms in our experiments are implemented in Python 3.6^1 with the graph package of NetworkX^2 and the machine learning package of

---

[1] https://www.python.org/.
[2] http://networkx.github.io/.

Table 1. The basic topological characteristics of nine networks. $|V|$ and $|E|$ denote the number of nodes and unique links, respectively. ρ represents the network density and C is the average clustering coefficient. $\langle k \rangle$ and H indicate the average degree and degree heterogeneity [29], respectively. τ and T_N are the length of time period and the number of snapshots, respectively.

Networks	$\|V\|$	$\|E\|$	ρ	C	$\langle k \rangle$	H	τ	T_N
Rado	167	3,251	0.2345	0.59	38.93	1.66	1 month	9
DNC	1,891	4,465	0.0025	0.21	4.72	15.52	2 months	6
Vast	400	895	0.0112	0.04	4.47	2.41	1 day	10
Forum	899	7,046	0.0175	0.06	15.68	2.16	1 month	5
Reality	96	2,539	0.5568	0.75	52.9	1.14	1 month	7
Hyper	113	2,196	0.3470	0.53	38.87	1.22	6 h	7
Mess	1,899	15,737	0.0087	0.11	16.57	3.18	1 month	6
Enron	151	1,612	0.1423	0.52	21.35	1.36	6 months	9
Digg	30,398	86,312	0.0002	0.01	5.68	4.95	3 days	5

scikit-learn[3]. In THILP, most of the parameters of RandomForestRegressor are set as the default values except random_state and max_features. The value of random_state is set to be 10, and the value of max_features is determined by the GridSearch algorithm. The candidate range of max_features is [0.4, 1].

4.1 Datasets, Baselines and Evaluation Metrics

Datasets. To verify the superiority of the THILP method, nine dynamic networks are used in our experiments. (1) Radoslaw-email (Rado): This is an internal email communication network between employees of a mid-sized manufacturing company [31]. A link presents an email communication from one employee to another. This network contains email interactions from January 2010 to September 2010. (2) DNC-email (DNC): This is email network leaked from the Democratic National Committee (DNC) in 2016 [35]. Nodes in the network correspond to persons. A directed edge denotes that a person has sent an email to another person. It covers the period from January to December 2016. (3) Vast: This is a cellphone communication network deriving from the VAST 2008 Challenge, which recorded cellphone calls of 400 people during 10 d [18]. (4) UCI-forum (Forum): This network was collected from an online social forum of students at University of California, Irvine in 2004 [33]. The network recorded student's activity in the forum between May and October 2004. (5) Reality-Mining (Reality): This network is composed of cellphone calls between a small set of students at the Massachusetts Institute of Technology, collected by the Reality Mining experiment performed in 2004 [15]. The network contains data from September 2004 to January 2005. (6) HyperText (Hyper): This network describes the

---

[3] https://scikit-learn.org/stable/.

face-to-face contacts of the attendees of the ACM Hypertext 2009 conference in Turin, Italy over three days from June 29 to July 1, 2009 [21]. (7) UCI-messages (Mess): Similar to Forum, this network records the sent messages between the students from the University of California, Irvine in an online community [34]. It covers the period from April to October 2004. (8) Enron-email (Enron): This is an email communication network between the employees of Enron company in the period from January 1999 to July 2002 [35]. (9) Digg: This is a reply network of the social website Digg [13]. In the network, nodes represent users and directed edges denote replays between users. The dataset covers a period from October 29 to November 13 2008.

In this study, all benchmark networks are treated as unweighted and undirected ones. The basic topological characteristics of these networks are summarized in Table 1. It is worth pointing out that this table only lists the number of unique links in each network. In addition, to represent a network as a series of snapshots according to the time window τ, some snapshots are merged into adjacent ones due to data incomplete. In Table 1, T denotes the number of snapshots in each network after necessary merging operations. From this table, we can observe that the characteristics of these networks are diverse. For instance, Reality is a very small network, but Digg is a large one; Reality has an extremely high clustering coefficient, whereas the coefficients of Vast, Forum and Digg are exceedingly low; Vast contains 10 snapshots, while Forum and Digg have only five snapshots.

Next, a training set and a testing set are generated for each benchmark network. To construct the training set, we use the sequence of $[G_1, G_2, \cdots, G_{T-1}]$. As demonstrated in Algorithm 1, node pairs in the training set are extracted from and labeled according to G_{T-1}. The features of these node pairs are computed from $[G_1, G_2, \cdots, G_{T-2}]$. Similarly, the testing set is obtained based on $[G_2, G_3, \cdots, G_T]$.

Baseline Methods. In our experiments, the proposed THILP method is compared with four static methods, i.e., CN [32], JC [27], PA [5] and AA [1], and three dynamic methods, i.e., event-based score method (EVENT) [39], DTLPLP [43] and DyLiP [11]. For the method of EVENT, there are three constant factors (c, i and r), and a decay factor (α). In our experiments, we adopt the best values experimentally verified in Ref. [39]. That is, $c = 0.25$, $i = 1$, $r = -0.5$, and $\alpha = 0.05$. The DTLPLP method has two parameters, namely decay factor δ and the weight influence factor α. According to the experimental results in Ref. [43], DTLPLP performs best when $\delta = 0.6$ and $\alpha = 0.2$. The same parameter settings are used in this work.

Evaluation Metrics. To quantify the accuracy of link prediction methods, three commonly used metrics, namely, *AUC* [29], *Precision* [19], and *Ranking score* [8], are adopted in this study.

In this paper, AUC measures the probability that a randomly selected positive node pair has a higher similarity score than a randomly selected negative node pair. In implementation, if among n times of independent comparisons, there are n_1 times that the positive node pair has a higher score and n_2 times that they have the same score, then AUC value is computed as

$$AUC = \frac{n_1 + 0.5 \times n_2}{n}. \tag{9}$$

Precision is defined as the proportion of correctly predicted links among the predicted ones. In implementation, we sort all node pairs in testing set in descending order according to their connection probabilities or similarity scores. If among the top-R node pairs, r node pairs are correctly predicted, then Precision is computed as

$$Precision = \frac{r}{R}. \tag{10}$$

In this paper, R is the number of all positive links in testing set.

In the case in this paper, Ranking score focuses on the ranks of positive links in the ranked list of all testing node pairs in descending order based on their connection probabilities. The formal calculation of Ranking score is

$$RS = \frac{1}{|E_p|} \sum_{e \in E_p} \frac{r_e}{|Y|}, \tag{11}$$

where E_p is the set of positive links in testing set Y, and r_e denotes the rank of a positive link e.

4.2   Results and Analysis

Analysis of Different Features. The proposed THILP method uses six structural features (i.e., CN, JC, AA, PA, CCLP, and LP3) and two temporal features (i.e., TL and SC) to represent a node pair as a vector. In this subsection, we experimentally analyze the importance of these features. Figure 2 shows the importance of each feature, under the measure of Gini coefficient, for different networks. The value of each feature is the average over different snapshots. From this figure, one can see that the importance of each feature fluctuates strongly over networks. There is no feature that is always important. For the network of Vast, temporal features, especially SC, are very important, whereas structural features except PA are extremely unimportant. On the contrary, structural features are more significant than temporal features on the networks of Hyper and Enron. What's more, PA has higher importance than other structural features in most cases; the importance of SC is always higher than that of TL. In general, SC and PA are two most important features. SC has the highest importance on Rado, Vast, and Forum, while PA has the highest importance on DNC, Reality, Hyper, Mess, and Digg. Meanwhile, most structural features except PA have higher importance on Hyper and Enron than other networks. From Table 1, we

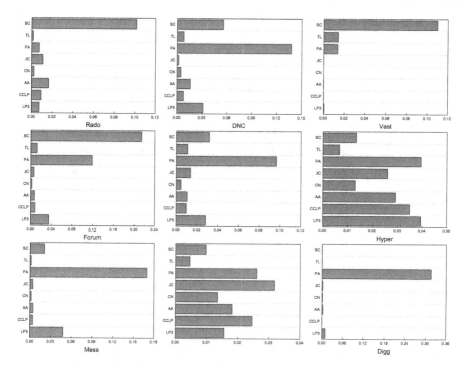

Fig. 2. Importance of each feature in terms of Gini coefficient.

observe that the topological characteristics of Rado, Vast, and Forum are diverse. In our opinion, this phenomenon is the normal case because SC is a temporal feature, which has no close relationship with topological characteristics. However, the topological characteristics of DNC, Reality, Hyper, Mess, and Digg, on which PA is most important, are also very different. From Fig. 2, we find that the importance values of PA on these networks are also inconsistent. For example, the value on Reality is less than 0.1, whereas that on Digg is more than 0.3. It is rational that the topological characteristics of Reality and Digg have large differences. Although the values of PA on DNC and Reality are very close, these two networks differ widely in their topological characteristics. In addition, the other structural features, e.g., CCLP, get high importance on Hyper and Enron maybe caused by the high clustering coefficients and large average degrees of these networks. However, Rado and Reality also have high clustering coefficients and large average degrees, CCLP is not important on them. In conclusion, the factors that give rise to the importance of features are very complex.

Subsequently, we perform another experiment to verify the advantage of adopting both topological information and historical information in the proposed THILP method. In this experiment, three versions of the proposed method, i.e., using only topological information (denoted as THILP1), using only historical information (denoted as THILP2), and using both kinds of information (denoted

Table 2. Accuracy of three versions of the proposed method. THILP1 uses only topological information, THILP2 uses only historical information, and THILP3 uses both kinds of information.

Networks	THILP1		THILP2		THILP3	
	Precision	AUC	Precision	AUC	Precision	AUC
Rado	0.833	0.910	0.869	0.904	**0.874**	**0.946**
DNC	0.654	0.811	0.608	0.728	**0.680**	**0.841**
Vast	0.669	0.739	0.972	0.983	**0.981**	**0.997**
Forum	0.781	0.839	0.788	0.870	**0.871**	**0.932**
Reality	0.841	0.909	**0.868**	0.921	0.858	**0.925**
Hyper	0.527	0.547	**0.580**	**0.634**	0.556	0.585
Mess	0.709	0.785	0.614	0.643	**0.722**	**0.791**
Enron	0.804	0.864	0.793	0.814	**0.821**	**0.874**
Digg	0.608	**0.687**	0.387	0.503	**0.610**	0.686

as THILP3), are considered. The experimental results measured by Precision and AUC are outlined in Table 2. It is evident from the table that using both topological and historical information simultaneously in the proposed method (i.e., THILP3) obtains the best results except on Reality, Hyper, and Digg. On Digg, the accuracy of both THILP1 and THILP3 is exceedingly close and is much larger than that of THILP2. The reasons caused these outcomes can be found from Fig. 2, which manifests that the feature of PA is overwhelmingly important, while the features of SC and TL have almost no importance on Digg. On Reality, THILP3 has the best AUC, and the second best Precision. On the network of Hyper, all three versions of the proposed method achieve very low accuracy. Figure reffig:importance shows that the importance scores of all features are very smaller on Hyper. On the other side, Hyper is a face-to-face contacts network of the attendees of a conference. So, there is a certain degree of randomness in the appearance of links. As a consequence, it is hard to predict new contacts for this network.

Comparison with Baselines. In summary, the above experimental results suggest that considering both topological and historical information simultaneously in the proposed method is a proper choice.

In this subsection, we perform an experiment to evaluate the accuracy of the proposed method in comparison with baselines. The prediction results, in terms of Precision, AUC, and Ranking score, of the proposed method and baselines on these networks are shown in Fig. 3. From the Precision results in Fig. 3(a), one can see that the proposed THILP method achieves the best performance on all networks except Hyper and Enron. Specially, on DNC, Vast, Forum, and Mess, THILP remarkably outperforms baselines. On the network of Vast, the Precision score of THILP is up to 0.981. In other words, THILP can correctly predict more

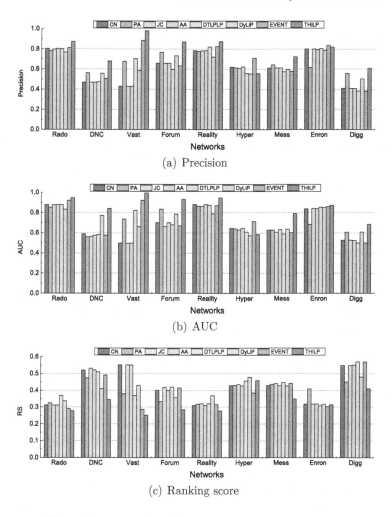

(a) Precision

(b) AUC

(c) Ranking score

Fig. 3. Accuracy of THILP and baselines on 9 networks.

than 98% links that will appear in Vast. The Vast network is composed of call data of 400 people within 10 d. In such a network, historical information plays an important role to predict new links. If two people frequently contacted each other in the last 9 d, they are likely to contact again in the 10th day. According to Table 1, this network is prediction unfriendly [17] since its clustering coefficient is very small. Therefore, common neighbors-based methods, such as CN and AA, fail to uncover future links [24]. Because considering both topological and historical information, and the topological information containing more than common neighbors-based features, the THILP method attains excellent performance under the metric of Precision on the network of Vast. Similarly, the EVENT method also obtains very high Precision on Vast since it also takes historical features into account. But the Precision results of DTLPLP and DyLip

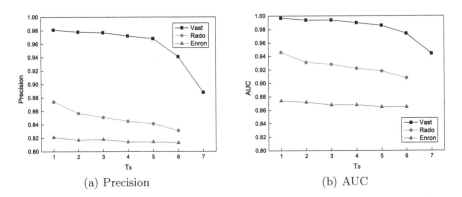

Fig. 4. Accuracy of THILP with different number of snapshots.

are not so decent over Vast. For the network of Forum, due to the high importance of both SC and PA, the proposed THILP method attains the Precision score of nearly 0.9, which is much larger than those of baselines. In addition, most methods perform well on Rado, Reality, and Enron owing to their high clustering coefficients.

Figure 3(b) demonstrates the AUC results of all methods on these nine networks. From this figure, it can be found that the THILP method is superior to baselines in terms of AUC except on Hyper. As aforementioned, the formation of links in Hyper has randomness to some extent. Thus, all methods get low AUC scores over the network. On Vast, THILP still achieves the extremely high accuracy; the AUC score approximates 1. And the AUC of EVENT is second only to that of THILP. What's more, the improvements of THILP on Forum and Mess are apparent. Although both networks have similar characteristics (see Table 1), historical features play a vital role in Forum while topological features act a pivotal part in Mess. In addition, PA performs the best among all baselines on Forum and Digg caused by the intense importance of PA in these two networks.

Finally, Fig. 3(c) displays the Ranking scores of all methods. It worthwhile to note that Ranking score is the smaller the better. Similar with the results in Figs. 3(a) and 3(b), the results in terms of Ranking score in Fig. 3(c) show that the THILP method performs better than baselines in most cases. Specifically, on DNC and Vast, the Ranking scores of THILP are conspicuously lower than those of baselines.

In summary, the THILP method is greatly superior to the baselines under the three metrics in most of cases.

Influence of Network Snapshots. In Definition 2, link prediction in dynamic networks is defined as predicting future links according to the information of previous L snapshots. In this experiment, we test the prediction accuracy of the THILP method with different number of previous snapshots. To this end, we select the networks of Rado, Vast and Enron since they have more snapshots than others. The experimental results are presented in Fig. 4, in which T_s denotes the time stamp of the start snapshot. It can be seen from the figure that both Precision and AUC show a downward trend with the increase of T_s. This indicates that the loss of snapshot information will lead to a decrease in prediction accuracy.

Furthermore, the changing trends of three networks are not similar. The accuracy of Enron is relatively stable with different number of snapshots, whereas Vast shows a obviously downward trend especially when $T_s > 5$. This circumstance is caused by the different length of time period of a snapshot. The time period of Vast is very short, which is only 1 day. Reducing the number of snapshots will drastically decrease the available information. In result, the prediction accuracy over Vast drops significantly when less snapshots are used. Oppositely, the network of Enron has a particularly long time period, which is 6 months. Accordingly, a small number of snapshots can also provide sufficient information. As a result, the prediction performance over Enron decreases slowly when reducing the number of snapshots. Meanwhile, the changing trend of Rado network is between the trends of Vast and Enron because the size of the time period of Rado is also between them of Vast and Enron.

In summary, it can be concluded that the prediction accuracy will be reduced when decreasing the number of snapshots. However, for networks with long time period, we can appropriately reduce the number of snapshots to improve computational efficiency.

5   Conclusion

In this paper, we investigated the problem of link prediction for dynamic networks. We proposed to address the problem by regarding it as a supervised learning problem, in which the connection probability of a future link is gauged. To this end, we elaborated a set of features that integrates both topological and historical information to represent node pairs. Then, a prediction model was trained using the RandomForestRegressor algorithm.

To analyze the performance of the proposed method, extensive experiments were implemented on nine benchmark networks in comparison with seven baseline methods. Experimental results manifested that (1) the importance of different features in the proposed method is diverse; (2) using both topological and historical features is a proper choice; (3) the proposed method outperforms baselines in most cases; and (4) reducing the number of snapshots will decrease the prediction accuracy.

Acknowledgments. This study was supported in part by the Science and Technology Program of Gansu Province (Nos. 21JR7RA458 and 21ZD8RA008), and the Supercomputing Center of Lanzhou University.

References

1. Adamic, L.A., Adar, E.: Friends and neighbors on the Web. Soc. Netw. **25**(3), 211–230 (2003)
2. Ayoub, J., Lotfi, D., El Marraki, M., Hammouch, A.: Accurate link prediction method based on path length between a pair of unlinked nodes and their degree. Soc. Netw. Anal. Min. **10**(1), 9 (2020)
3. Bai, S., Fang, S., Li, L., Liu, R., Chen, X.: Enhancing link prediction by exploring community membership of nodes. Int. J. Mod. Phys. B **33**(31), 1950382 (2020)
4. Bai, S., Li, L., Cheng, J., Xu, S., Chen, X.: Predicting missing links based on a new triangle structure. Complexity **2018**, 1–11 (2018)
5. Barabási, A.L., Albert, R.: Emergence of scaling in random networks. Science **286**(5439), 509–512 (1999)
6. Breiman, L.: Random forests. Mach. Learn. **45**, 5–32 (2001)
7. Cannistraci, C.V., Alanis-Lobato, G.G., Ravasi, T.: From link-prediction in brain connectomes and protein interactomes to the local-community-paradigm in complex networks. Sci. Rep. **3**(1), 1613 (2013)
8. Chen, B., Chen, L.: A link prediction algorithm based on ant colony optimization. Appl. Intell. **41**(3), 694–708 (2014)
9. Chen, J., Lin, X., Jia, C., Li, Y., Wu, Y., Zheng, H., Liu, Y.: Generative dynamic link prediction. Chaos An Interdis. J. Nonlinear Sci. **29**(12), 123111 (2019)
10. Chen, J., et al.: E-LSTM-D: a deep learning framework for dynamic network link prediction. IEEE Trans. Syst. Man Cybern. Syst. **51**, 3699–3712 (2019)
11. Chen, K.J., Chen, Y., Li, Y., Han, J.: A supervised link prediction method for dynamic networks. J. Intell. Fuzzy Syst. **31**(1), 291–299 (2016)
12. Chiu, C., Zhan, J.: Deep learning for link prediction in dynamic networks using weak estimators. IEEE Access **6**, 35937–35945 (2018)
13. De Choudhury, M., Sundaram, H., John, A., Seligmann, D.D.: Social synchrony: predicting mimicry of user actions in online social media. In: Proceedings of the 2009 International Conference on Computational Science and Engineering, vol. 4, pp. 151–158. IEEE Computer Society, USA (2009)
14. Divakaran, A., Mohan, A.: Temporal link prediction: a survey. N. Gener. Comput. **38**, 213–258 (2020)
15. Eagle, N., (Sandy) Pentland, A.: Reality mining: sensing complex social systems. Personal Ubiquit. Comput. **10**(4), 255–268 (2006)
16. Fire, M., Tenenboim-Chekina, L., Puzis, R., Lesser, O., Rokach, L., Elovici, Y.: Computationally efficient link prediction in a variety of social networks. ACM Trans. Intell. Syst. Technol. **5**(1), 1–25 (2013)
17. Gao, F., Musial, K., Cooper, C., Tsoka, S.: Link prediction methods and their accuracy for different social networks and network metrics. Sci. Program. **2015**, 1–13 (2015)
18. Grinstein, G., Plaisant, C., Laskowski, S., O'Connell, T., Scholtz, J., Whiting, M.: VAST 2008 Challenge: introducing mini-challenges. In: Proceedings of 2008 IEEE Symposium on Visual Analytics Science and Technology, pp. 195–196. IEEE (2008)
19. Herlocker, J.L., Konstan, J.A., Terveen, L.G., Riedl, J.T.: Evaluating collaborative filtering recommender systems. ACM Trans. Inf. Syst. (TOIS) **22**(1), 5–53 (2004)
20. Ibrahim, N.M.A., Chen, L.: Link prediction in dynamic social networks by integrating different types of information. Appl. Intell. **42**(4), 738–750 (2015)
21. Isella, L., Stehlé, J., Barrat, A., Cattuto, C., Pinton, J., Van den Broeck, W.: What's in a crowd? analysis of face-to-face behavioral networks. J. Theor. Biol. **271**(1), 166–180 (2011)

22. Kumar, A., Singh, S.S., Singh, K., Biswas, B.: Link prediction techniques, applications, and performance: a survey. Phys. A **553**, 124289 (2020)
23. Li, K., Tu, L., Chai, L.: Ensemble-model-based link prediction of complex networks. Comput. Netw. **166**, 106978 (2020)
24. Li, L., Xu, S., Leng, M., Fang, S., Chen, X.: Predicting top-L missing links: an improved local naïve Bayes Model. IEEE Access **7**, 57868–57880 (2019)
25. Li, T., Zhang, J., Yu, P.S., Zhang, Y., Yan, Y.: Deep dynamic network embedding for link prediction. IEEE Access **6**, 29219–29230 (2018)
26. Li, Z., Fang, X., Sheng, O.R.L.: A survey of link recommendation for social networks. ACM Trans. Manag. Inf. Syst. **9**(1), 1–26 (2017)
27. Liben-Nowell, D., Kleinberg, J.: The link-prediction problem for social networks. J. Am. Soc. Inform. Sci. Technol. **58**(7), 1019–1031 (2007)
28. Lü, L., Jin, C.H., Zhou, T.: Similarity index based on local paths for link prediction of complex networks. Phys. Rev. E **80**(4), 046122 (2009)
29. Lü, L., Zhou, T.: Link prediction in complex networks: a survey. Phys. A **390**(6), 1150–1170 (2011)
30. Martínez, V., Berzal, F., Cubero, J.c.: A Survey of Link Prediction in complex networks. ACM Comput. Surv. **49**(4), 1–33 (2017)
31. Michalski, R., Palus, S., Kazienko, P.: Matching organizational structure and social network extracted from email communication. In: Abramowicz, W. (ed.) BIS 2011. LNBIP, vol. 87, pp. 197–206. Springer, Heidelberg (2011). https://doi.org/10.1007/978-3-642-21863-7_17
32. Newman, M.E.: Clustering and preferential attachment in growing networks. Phys. Rev. E **64**(2), 4 (2001)
33. Opsahl, T.: Triadic closure in two-mode networks: redefining the global and local clustering coefficients. Soc. Netw. **35**(2), 159–167 (2013)
34. Opsahl, T., Panzarasa, P.: Clustering in weighted networks. Soc. Netw. **31**(2), 155–163 (2009)
35. Rossi, R.A., Ahmed, N.K.: The network data repository with interactive graph analytics and visualization. In: Proceedings of the Twenty-Ninth AAAI Conference on Artificial Intelligence, pp. 4292–4293. AAAI Press (2015)
36. Selvarajah, K., Ragunathan, K., Kobti, Z., Kargar, M.: Dynamic network link prediction by learning effective subgraphs using CNN-LSTM. In: Proceedings of 2020 International Joint Conference on Neural Networks (IJCNN), pp. 1–8. IEEE (2020)
37. Shan, N., Li, L., Zhang, Y., Bai, S., Chen, X.: Supervised link prediction in multiplex networks. Knowl.-Based Syst. **203**, 106168 (2020)
38. Singh, S.S., Mishra, S., Kumar, A., Biswas, B.: CLP-ID: community-based link prediction using information diffusion. Inf. Sci. **514**, 402–433 (2020)
39. Soares, P.R., Prudêncio, R.B.: Proximity measures for link prediction based on temporal events. Expert Syst. Appl. **40**(16), 6652–6660 (2013)
40. Wu, X., Wu, J., Li, Y., Zhang, Q.: Link prediction of time-evolving network based on node ranking. Knowl.-Based Syst. **195**, 105740 (2020)
41. Wu, Z., Lin, Y., Wang, J., Gregory, S.: Link prediction with node clustering coefficient. Phys. A **452**, 1–8 (2016)
42. Xiao, Y., Li, R., Lu, X., Liu, Y.: Link prediction based on feature representation and fusion. Inf. Sci. **548**, 1–17 (2021)
43. Xu, X., et al.: Distributed temporal link prediction algorithm based on label propagation. Futur. Gener. Comput. Syst. **93**, 627–636 (2019)

44. Yang, M., Liu, J., Chen, L., Zhao, Z., Chen, X., Shen, Y.: An advanced deep generative framework for temporal link prediction in dynamic networks. IEEE Trans. Cybern. **50**(12), 4946–4957 (2020)
45. Yang, Y., Lichtenwalter, R.N., Chawla, N.V.: Evaluating link prediction methods. Knowl. Inf. Syst. **45**(3), 751–782 (2015)

Link Prediction in Multiplex Network Based on Regression and Conditional Probability

Na Shan[1], Wenxin Yang[1], Zhaozhi Zhang[2], and Longjie Li[1,3](✉) (iD)

[1] School of Information Science and Engineering, Lanzhou University, Lanzhou 730000, China
ljli@lzu.edu.cn
[2] State Grid Gansu Electric Power Company Material Company, Lanzhou 73050, China
[3] Key Laboratory of Media Convergence Technology and Communication, Lanzhou 730000, Gansu, China

Abstract. Multiplex networks are often used to describe the relationship of different properties between the same group of entities in real complex system, in which nodes represent entities and links in different layers represent connections of different properties between entities. The key to link prediction in multiplex networks lies in (1) making full use of the information provided by each layer of a network; (2) effectively fusing the information provided by each layer of the network together. In this paper, we propose a method based on regression and conditional probability, called MRCP, in which the feature vectors of node pairs are the vectors proposed in our previous work. This method combines intralayer probability and interlayer information to predict missing links in multiplex networks. Firstly, the intralayer probability is calculated by using regression algorithm based on intralayer information. Then the conditional probability of link existence is calculated by using the auxiliary layer information. Finally, both probabilities are combined for link prediction. In order to verify the effectiveness of the method, we conducted experiments on 8 real datasets. The experimental results show that the prediction performance of this method is better than compared methods.

Keywords: Link prediction · Multiplex networks · Supervised regression · Feature extraction

1 Introduction

Many complex systems in the real world can be modeled as complex networks, such as social networks [12,31], biological networks [6,11], and collaboration networks [36]. The study of complex networks can help us understand the nature of real systems. Link prediction, which aims to predict missing or upcoming links in a network, has become a hotspot in complex network analysis and drawn increasing attention of researchers from various disciplines [16,25]. Link prediction has

Z. Cai et al. (Eds.): NCTCS 2023, CCIS 1944, pp. 221–236, 2024.
https://doi.org/10.1007/978-981-99-7743-7_14

a wide range of applications in both reality and theory, such as recommending new friends for users, suggesting products to customers, planning routes for material delivery, and investigating network evolution mechanisms.

In the past, a majority of link prediction approaches focused on single-layer networks, in which all node belong to the same type and all links are also of the same kind. However, the connection types between entities in a host of real world systems are not limited to one type, but may include multiple types. For instance, the same group of people might have different relationships because they are friends, family members or colleagues. This kind of systems can be modeled as *multilayer networks* [2,14]. Particularly, if the nodes across different layers in a multilayer network are the same, this network is a *multiplex network* [4]. Therefore, a multiplex network is a special multilayer network. In this paper, we concentrate on the link prediction problem in multiplex networks.

Some researches [5,17,24] have reported that the topological characteristics of different layers in a multiplex network are indeed interrelated to some extent. As a consequence, link prediction in multiplex networks should make full use of the structure information of all layers. A number of recent studies [20,22,35] have proved that the prediction accuracy in a multiplex network can be enhanced by leveraging the structure information of all layers. Thereby, traditional link prediction methods that only adopt the structure information derived from single-layer networks are unable to efficaciously solve the link prediction problem in multiplex networks. On the other hand, how to effectively integrate the information drew from different layers is still a big challenge.

To date, many scholars begin to study the problem of link prediction in multiplex networks. Abdolhosseini-Qomi et al. [1] proposed a method called ML-BNMTF to solve the problem of link prediction in multiplex networks, which considers the inter-layer community overlap. Rezaeipanah et al. [26] used supervised classification to solve the problem of link prediction in multiplex networks including Twitter and Foursquare, and proposed three groups of features based on node structure, self-path and meta path. Tang et al. [31] developed an iterative degree penalty algorithm, named IDP, for inter-layer link prediction in multiplex networks. Sharma et al. [29] predicted the possibility of target links in the target layer according to whether there are links in other layers. Yao et al. [35] proposed a method called NSILR, which combines the topology information between layers and within layers to predict links by calculating the correlation between layers. Najari et al. [22] put forward a probability-based model, which uses Logistic Regression to obtain the probability of link existence based on intra-layer features. Samei et al. [27] defined a similarity index that combines intra-layer similarity and inter-layer similarity to predict spurious links in a multiplex network. Luo et al. [20] designed a new multi-attribute decision-making method to solve the link prediction problem in multi-layer networks.

The key to link prediction in multiplex networks lies in (1) making full use of the information provided by each layer of network; (2) effectively fusing the information provided by each layer of network together. In this paper, we propose a method based on regression and conditional probability using the feature vector proposed in our previous work, referred to as MRCP (**M**ultiplex network link prediction based on **R**egression and **C**onditional **P**robability). The MRCP method combines the intra-layer probability and the inter-layer information. The intra-layer probability is calculated by using regression calculation on the intra-layer information, and the inter-layer information considers the connection state of the node pairs in auxiliary layers. In order to prove the effectiveness of the MRCP method, we conducted experiments on 8 real networks. The experimental results show that the prediction performance of MRCP is better than baseline methods.

2   Preliminaries

2.1   Problem Description

To better understand the link prediction problem in multiplex networks, this section introduces the concept of multiplex networks and formalizes the problem of link prediction.

A multiplex network with k layers and N vertices can be denoted by $G = (G_1, G_2, \ldots, G_k)$, where $G_i = (V_i, E_i)$ represents the network of layer i, and each layer of the network G has the same set of nodes, i.e., $|V_1| = |V_2| = \cdots = |V_k| = N$. Let the layer α be the target layer network, denoted as G_α, and the remaining layers as the auxiliary layers, denoted as $G_{\beta_1}, G_{\beta_2}, \ldots, G_{\beta_k - 1}$. The link prediction problem in multiplex networks is to forecast the missing or future links in any layer by using information extracted from intra-layer and inter-layer.

2.2   Link Prediction Method in Single Layer Networks

Common Neighbors (CN). [23] measures the similarity of two nodes by calculating the number of paths of length 2 between them, which is

$$CN\,(x, y) = |\Gamma\,(x) \cap \Gamma\,(y)|,\tag{1}$$

where $\Gamma\,(x)$ denotes the neighbor set of node x.

Resource Allocation (RA). [38] is inspired by the process of resource propagation and believes that the similarity between node x and y is related to the number of resources that x can propagate to y through their common neighbors. The specific definition is

$$RA\,(x, y) = \sum_{z \in \Gamma(x) \cap \Gamma(y)} \frac{1}{k_z},\tag{2}$$

where k_z is degree of node z.

Jaccard Coefficient (JC). [18] considers the influence of the sum of the degrees of the two endpoints on the basis of CN. For two pairs of nodes with the same value of CN, the greater the sum of the endpoint degrees, the less likely a link will be generated between them. Namely,

$$JC(x,y) = \frac{CN(x,y)}{|\Gamma(x) \cup \Gamma(y)|}. \tag{3}$$

Preferential Attachment(PA). [3] calculates the similarity of two nodes as the product of the degrees of these two nodes, which is

$$PA(x,y) = k_x \cdot k_y. \tag{4}$$

2.3 Link Prediction Method in Multiplex Networks

NSILR (Node Similarity Index Based on Layer Relevance). [35] indicates that the similarity scores of node pairs in target layer α are not only contributed by the intra-layer structure information from layer α, but also depend on the inter-layer structure information extracted from other layers. The higher the correlation between layer β_i and layer α, the greater the contribution of layer β_i [35]. For a node pair (x,y) in target layer α, NSILR first calculates its similarity score within each layer based on the traditional existing methods, such as CN and RA. Then, all scores are aggregated to estimate the similarity of node pair (x,y) in the multiplex network, which is defined as

$$S^\alpha(x,y) = (1-\varphi)\,sim^\alpha(x,y) + \varphi \sum_{i=1,\beta_i \neq \alpha}^{k} \mu^{\alpha\beta_i} sim^{\beta_i}(x,y), \tag{5}$$

where $sim^*(x,y)$ is the similarity score depending on the intra-layer information from layer $*$. $\mu^{\alpha\beta_i}$ denotes the relevance between layers α and β_i, which can be acquired by calculating the Global Overlap Rate (GOR) or Pearson Correlation Coeffcient (PCC) between layers. The tunable parameter φ, which lies in the interval $[0,1]$, is used to adjust the influence of information from intra-layer and inter-layer.

LAA (Likelihood Assignment Algorithm). [29] also takes the information from all auxiliary layers of the network into account. The final score is assigned as a weighted combination of scores of different layers. The weights are estimated by checking the link correspondence between two layers using likelihood of a link being present in the target layer given the link is present in the auxiliary layer [29]. The formal definition is

$$S^\alpha(x,y) = \sum^{k} w_{\beta_i} I(x,y,\beta_i), \tag{6}$$

where w_{β_i} is the weight of layer β_i. If the link (x,y) is found to be present in layer β_i, the value of $I(x,y,\beta i)$ is 1; otherwise, the value is 0.

LPIS (Link Prediction Accounting Interlayer Similarity). [22] proposes a probabilistic-based model to calculate the probability of link existence by using intra-layer features. Then these probabilities along with inter-layer similarity are used to obtain the final probabilities of link existence [22]. The mathematical expressio of LPIS is

$$S^{\alpha}(x, y) = (1 - \varphi) S^{\alpha}_{intra}(x, y) + \varphi S^{\alpha}_{inter}(x, y), \qquad (7)$$

$$S^{\alpha}_{inter}(x, y) = \begin{cases} \sum_k S^{\alpha}_{intra}(x, y) \times R^{\alpha\beta_i}(x, y), & \text{if } I(x, y, \beta_i) = 1 \\ \sum_k (1 - S^{\alpha}_{intra}(x, y)) \times (1 - R^{\alpha\beta_i}(x, y)), & \text{if } I(x, y, \beta_i) = 0 \end{cases} \qquad (8)$$

where $S^{\alpha}_{intra}(x, y)$ is the existence probability of link (x, y) in target layer α. $R^{\alpha\beta_i}$ is the similarity of link (x, y) between layers α and β_i, which can be obtained by calculating Average Similarity of the Neighbors (ASN) [37] or Asymmetric Average Similarity of the Neighbors (AASN) [22].

3   The Proposed Method

We propose a link prediction method based on regression and conditional probability, named MRCP, for multiplex networks. The motivation of MRCP is making full use of the information of all layers of a multiplex network can obtain better prediction performance.

3.1   Intra-layer Predictor Based on Regression

When we calculate the probability that the target node pair has links in the target layer, we still use the features proposed in our previous work [28]. Among them, the feature FAL (Friendship in auxiliary layers) reflects the relationship between the node pairs in the auxiliary layers, so we do not consider it when calculating the probability in the layer. Therefore, this paper extracts eight features CN, RA, JC, PA, LA, ACC, CCLP and FoN (Friendship of neighbors) from the target layer to construct the feature vector of the node pair, and uses the regression algorithm to calculate the probability of the existence of links between nodes.

3.2   Interlayer Information Based on Conditional Probability

In this study, MRCP considers two cases when combining the auxiliary layer information. (1) the probability of the existence of links in the target layer when there are links in the auxiliary layer. (2) The probability of link existence in the target layer when there is no link in the auxiliary layer. Let $P^1_{\beta_i}$ and $P^2_{\beta_i}$ denote the possibility of the existence of links in the target layer with and without links in the auxiliary layer, respectively. The formula is as follows,

$$P^1_{\beta_i} = P(edges\ in\ layer\ \alpha | edges\ in\ layer\ \beta_i) = \frac{|E_\alpha \cap E_{\beta_i}|}{|E_{\beta_i}|}, \qquad (9)$$

$$P_{\beta_i}^2 = P\left(edges\ in\ layer\ \alpha | edges\ not\ in\ layer\ \beta_i\right) = \frac{\left|E_\alpha \cap \bar{E}_{\beta_i}\right|}{\left|\bar{E}_{\beta_i}\right|}, \quad (10)$$

where E_α and E_{β_i} represent the set of existing edges in layer α and layer β_i, respectively. $\bar{E}_{\beta_i}$ denotes the set of nonedges in layer β_i.

3.3   Definition of MRCP

In MRCP, the similarity score of a node pair is mainly composed of two parts. (1) Intralayer infomation: Use the information extracted from the target layer to construct the feature vector of the node pair, and then use the regression algorithm to calculate the probability of the link in the target layer; (2) Interlayer information: In the case of whether there is a link between the target node pair in the auxiliary layer, the probability that there is a link between the node pair in the target layer. After obtaining the conditional probability of the node's contribution to the existence of the target layer and the auxiliary layer information, MRCP is finally defined as:

$$MRCP^\alpha(x,y) = \varphi S_{intra}^\alpha(x,y) + (1-\varphi)\sum_{i=1}^{k-1} P_{\beta_i}, \quad (11)$$

$$P_{\beta_i} = \begin{cases} P_{\beta_i}^1, & \text{if } I(x,y;\beta_i) = 1 \\ P_{\beta_i}^2, & \text{if } I(x,y;\beta_i) = 0 \end{cases}$$

where φ is an adjustable parameter with a value range of $[0,1]$, which is used to adjust the influence of target layer information and auxiliary layer information. k represents the number of layers of the multiplex network, $S_{intra}^\alpha(x,y)$ is the probability of existence of link (x,y) in layer α, P_{β_i} is the contribution of the auxiliary layer β_i.

4   Datasets and Evaluation Metrics

4.1   Datasets

In order to fairly measure the performance of the link prediction method, in this article, we select 8 real multiplex networks from different fields, and their brief descriptions are as follows:

(1) Vicker [32]: Multiplex social network among 29 seventh graders in a school in Victoria, Australia. It is composed of 3 layers of sub-networks, corresponding to contact, best friend and co-working.

(2) CS [21]: A multiplexsocial network among 61 employees of the Department of Computer Science of Aarhus University. The network consists of 5 types of online and offline relationships, namely Facebook, leisure, work, cooperation, and lunch.

(3) CKM [8]: A multiplex interactive network between doctors. It is composed of 246 nodes and 3 layers, and each layer of sub-network corresponds to asking for advice, discussing cases, and friends.

(4) Lazega [10,30]: A multiplex network of partners. It is composed of 71 nodes and 3 layers of sub-networks, which correspond to co-working, friendship and advice.

(5) CElegans [7,9]: A multilplex neuron network of Caenorhabditis elegans. It is composed of 279 nodes and 3 layers of sub-networks, each layer of network corresponds to different synaptic connection methods: electrical, chemical, and multiple.

(6) Krackhardt [15] :The multiplex network consists of 3 layers, each of which represents the relationship of seeking advice, friends, and reporting work among 21 high-tech company managers.

(7) Kapferer [13]: This multiplex network describes the interaction between workers in a tailor shop in Zambia. It contains a total of 39 nodes and 4 layers, of which two layers record the interactions related to work and assistance; the other two layers represent friendship and social emotional relationships.

(8) TF [22]: A multiplex network composed of 1565 users and 2 layers of sub-networks, each layer of sub-networks is collected from Twitter and Foursquare.

This article treats all networks as undirected and unweighted networks, and their basic structure information is listed in Table 1. In addition, Fig. 1 shows the overlap rates between layers of each network.

4.2 Evaluation Metrics

We use Precision and AUC (Area Under Curve) to measure the effectiveness of our method.

(1) *Precision* First, we rank each edge according to its probability score of existence. The precision value refers to the proportion of the actual number of edges l among the top L edges. Namely,

$$Precision = \frac{l}{L}. \tag{12}$$

(2) *AUC* Randomly take one link from E_α^P and one link from $P_\alpha - E_\alpha^P$, then compare the scores of this two links. In n-times comparison, the number of times that the link in E_α^P has a higher score is $n1$, and the number of times that the two have the same score is $n2$. Then the calculation formula of AUC is:

$$AUC = \frac{n1 + 0.5 * n2}{n}. \tag{13}$$

Table 1. Basic structure information of 8 multiplex networks. N represents the number of nodes, $|E|$ represents the number of links in each layer of the network, and r and C represent the assortativity coefficient [38] and the clustering coefficient [33], respectively. $\langle k \rangle$ is the average degree, $\langle H \rangle$ represents degree heterogeneity $(\langle H \rangle = \langle k^2 \rangle / \langle k \rangle^2)$ [19], e represents network efficiency.

Network	layer	N	$|E|$	r	C	$\langle k \rangle$	$\langle H \rangle$	e
Vicker	1	29	240	−0.161	0.754	16.552	1.099	0.796
	2	29	126	−0.152	0.681	8.690	1.275	0.635
	3	29	152	−0.110	0.713	10.483	1.250	0.666
CS	1	60	193	0.005	0.673	6.433	1.213	0.398
	2	32	124	0.003	0.540	7.750	1.227	0.591
	3	25	21	0.017	0.268	1.680	1.389	0.097
	4	47	88	−0.010	0.392	3.745	1.514	0.347
	5	60	194	−0.213	0.640	6.467	1.665	0.475
CKM	1	215	449	−0.137	0.260	4.177	1.494	0.122
	2	231	498	−0.098	0.260	4.312	1.348	0.115
	3	228	423	0.102	0.211	3.711	1.237	0.100
Lazega	1	71	717	0.020	0.522	20.197	1.166	0.633
	2	69	399	0.079	0.498	11.565	1.314	0.528
	3	71	726	−0.079	0.509	20.451	1.167	0.640
CElegans	1	253	517	−0.116	0.202	4.087	2.163	0.253
	2	260	888	−0.081	0.186	6.831	1.788	0.331
	3	278	1703	−0.078	0.288	12.252	1.668	0.409
Krackhardt	1	21	145	−0.265	0.765	13.810	1.064	0.845
	2	21	79	−0.224	0.566	7.524	1.225	0.684
	3	21	20	−0.672	0.000	1.905	1.916	0.404
Kapferer	1	39	158	−0.183	0.458	8.103	1.347	0.567
	2	39	223	−0.051	0.498	11.436	1.226	0.638
	3	35	76	−0.082	0.310	4.343	1.506	0.470
	4	37	95	−0.165	0.335	5.135	1.556	0.446
TF	1	1564	14090	−0.098	0.131	18.018	3.386	0.327
	2	1508	18471	−0.041	0.344	24.497	3.775	0.353

5 Experimental Results and Analysis

5.1 Experimental Setting

The division of training set and test set in this paper is the same as our previous work. In the next experiment, we randomly select 80% of the edges from E_α as E_α^T, and the remaining edges are marked as E_α^P. All experimental results are the average of 10 independent experiments. We use the Networkx package to

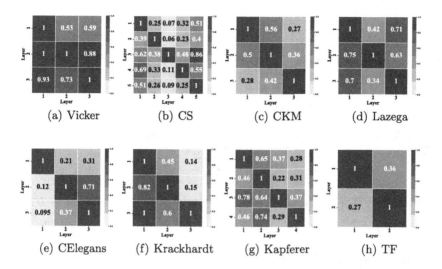

Fig. 1. Interlayer overlap rates of 8 multiplex networks.

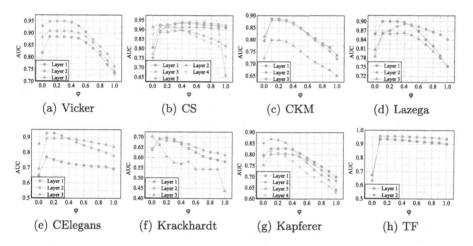

Fig. 2. The change of AUC value of MRCP under different value of φ.

extract features, select the RandomForest Regressor algorithm to calculate the probability of link existence in the target layer, and use the scikit-learn machine learning package to implement the regression algorithm. The value of L when calculating Precision is set to $|E_\alpha^P|$.

5.2   Influence of Parameter φ

The free parameter φ included in the MRCP method ranges from 0 to 1, and is used to adjust the contribution of the information in the target layer and the information of auxiliary layers. In this section, we set the value of φ to

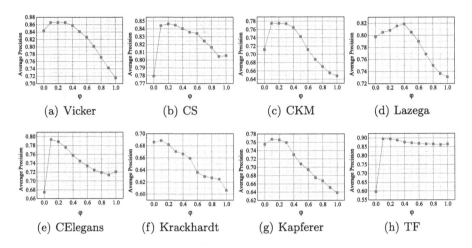

Fig. 3. The change of Precision value of MRCP under different value of φ.

$[0.0, 0.1, ..., 1.0]$. By observing the changes of AUC and Precision at different values of φ, we analyze the influence of the parameter φ on the performance of MRCP and determine the best value of φ.

Figure 2 shows the prediction results of MRCP in eight networks with different values of φ when AUC is used as the evaluation index. When the value of φ is 0.0, it is equivalent to using only the information of auxiliary layers; when the value of φ is 1.0, it is equivalent to using only the information of target layer.

Figure 3(a) shows the AUC value obtained by the MRCP method under different values of φ in Vicker. It can be seen from the figure that when each layer of Vicker are used as the target layer, the AUC value shows the same changing trend with the change of the value of φ. As the value of φ increases, the value of AUC gradually increases, and then gradually decreases after reaching the peak. This shows that when each layer of Vicker is used as the target layer, combining the information of target layer and auxiliary layers at the same time can get a better prediction effect. In addition, the AUC value when $\varphi = 0.0$ is higher than the AUC value when $\varphi = 1.0$, which shows that using only the auxiliary layers information in the Vicker network will obtain a better prediction effect than using only the target layer information. This discovery is very useful for solving the cold start problem [35]. In each layer of the remaining 7 networks, most of the predicted results have the same trend as Vicker, so the same conclusion can be obtained.

It can be seen from Fig. 3(b) that the change trend of the third layer and fourth layer of CS is consistent with that of Vicker network, but in the first layer, the second layer and the fifth layer, the AUC value when φ is 0.0 is lower than that when φ is 1.0. Combined with Table 1 and Fig. 1(b), we can find that the AUC value of layer 1, layer 2 and layer 5 of CS is lower than that when φ is 1.0. The overlap rate of this layers is lower than other layers, but the links in this layers are dense. Using only the target layer can obtain more information than only using the auxiliary layers, so that better prediction results can be obtained. In addition, in all sub-networks of CS, the change trend of AUC first increases to the peak value and then decreases with the increase of the value of φ, which indicates that the better effect can be obtained by combining the information within and between layers in CS network. The same phenomenon can be observed in all layers of TF, the first layers and the third layer of celegans and the second layer of lazega.

In addition, it is worth noting that Fig. 3(f) shows that in Krackhardt's third layer, the AUC value decreases almost all the time with the increase of the value of φ, and the prediction effect obtained by using only the auxiliary layer information (when $\varphi = 0.0$) is much better than that obtained by using only the target layer information (when $\varphi = 1.0$). From Table 1, we can find that Krackhardt's third layer contains very few links, so the information obtained from the target layer is very limited. In addition, Fig. 1(f) shows that all the links in Krackhardt' third layer exist in first layer, and 60% of the links appear in layer 2. The super high overlap rate with the auxiliary layer leads to more auxiliary layer information, which can better improve the prediction effect.

Specifically, when $\varphi = 1.0$, the AUC values of CS's third layer and Krackhardt's third layer have a larger decrease, which is very different from the other layers. From Table 1, we found that the third layers of both networks are extremely sparse. Without the help of other layers (i.e., $\varphi = 1.0$), there are no enough information to predict links in these layers.

Figure 3 shows the prediction results of MRCP in eight networks with different values of φ when precision is used as the evaluation index. It can be seen from the figure that the average precision value of MRCP in the eight networks increases first with the change of φ value, and then decreases gradually after reaching the peak value. CS, celegans and TF networks are slightly different from the other five networks. The average precision of MRCP method at $\varphi = 0.0$ is less than that at $\varphi = 1.0$. It can be seen from Fig. 1(f) that the overall network overlap rates of the three networks are low, so the prediction effect is not good only by using the auxiliary layer information.

In summary, we can get two conclusions. (1) Compared with using only the target layer information ($\varphi = 1.0$), the addition of auxiliary layer information can improve the performance of link prediction; (2) When $\varphi = 0.1$, MRCP can get the best prediction effect in most networks. Therefore, in the next experiment, we set the value of φ to 0.1.

5.3   Comparison with Other Multiplex Network Methods

In this section, we compare MRCP with LAA, LPIS and NSILR to prove the effectiveness of MRCP. In the experiment, we use AUC and Precision to measure the experimental results. In addition, the parameters selection in NSILR method and LPIS are consistent with the previous articles [28].

The results shown in Table 2 are the prediction performance of MRCP and these 3 existing multiplex network link prediction methods in 8 networks when

Table 2. AUC value of each method on 8 multiplex networks.

Network	Layer	MRCP	LAA	LPIS	NSILR
Vicker	1	**0.8856**	0.8196	0.7125	0.8455
	2	**0.9486**	0.9299	0.7960	0.8372
	3	**0.9094**	0.8833	0.7766	0.8808
	Average	**0.9145**	0.8776	0.7617	0.8545
CS	1	**0.9232**	0.8051	0.9201	0.9294
	2	0.8924	0.7517	**0.9194**	0.9090
	3	**0.9260**	0.9140	0.7340	0.6500
	4	**0.9133**	0.8776	0.8281	0.8075
	5	**0.8872**	0.7720	0.8616	0.8797
	Average	**0.9084**	0.8241	0.8526	0.8351
CKM	1	**0.8858**	0.7949	0.6676	0.6787
	2	**0.8803**	0.8134	0.6705	0.7118
	3	**0.7990**	0.7235	0.6273	0.6755
	Average	**0.8550**	0.7773	0.6551	0.6887
Lazega	1	**0.9010**	0.8521	0.7897	0.8390
	2	0.8623	0.7850	0.8703	**0.8743**
	3	**0.8601**	0.8069	0.7884	0.8189
	Average	**0.8745**	0.8147	0.8161	0.8441
CElegans	1	**0.7699**	0.6500	0.6278	0.6720
	2	**0.9263**	0.8576	0.7304	0.7350
	3	**0.8922**	0.6935	0.7991	0.8317
	Average	**0.8628**	0.7337	0.7191	0.7462
Krackhardt	1	0.6908	0.6415	0.6713	**0.7093**
	2	0.6923	0.6367	0.7041	**0.7092**
	3	0.6625	**0.7031**	0.4938	0.4125
	Average	**0.6819**	0.6604	0.6231	0.6103
Kapferer	1	**0.8266**	0.7871	0.6843	0.7897
	2	**0.8013**	0.7524	0.6837	0.7914
	3	**0.8703**	0.8511	0.5815	0.6864
	4	**0.8134**	0.7848	0.6465	0.7236
	Average	**0.8279**	0.7939	0.6490	0.7478
TF	1	**0.9346**	0.6738	0.8021	0.8149
	2	**0.9571**	0.6324	0.9176	0.9400
	Average	**0.9459**	0.6531	0.8599	0.8775

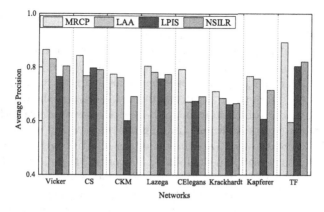

Fig. 4. Average Precision value of each method on 8 multiplex networks.

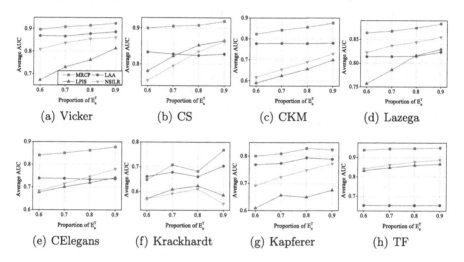

(a) Vicker   (b) CS   (c) CKM   (d) Lazega

(e) CElegans   (f) Krackhardt   (g) Kapferer   (h) TF

Fig. 5. The change of the average AUC value of MRCP under different training set ratios.

AUC is used as the evaluation index. The results are the average of 10 independent experiments. We boldly indicate the optimal value of each layer of the network and the optimal value of the average value of each layer of the network. It can be seen intuitively from Table 2 that when AUC is used as an evaluation index, the overall performance of the MRCP method is the best. In all networks, the highest average AUC is obtained by the MRCP method. Figure 4 shows the average Precision value of these 4 methods on 8 multiplex networks. From the figure, we can see that the average Precision value obtained by the MRCP method in the 8 networks is the best among the 4 methods. In summary, the MRCP method can solve the link prediction problem in multi-layer networks more effectively than the other three methods.

To further compare the performance of these four multiplex network link prediction methods, we set the proportions of the training set to 90%, 80%, 70% and 60% respectively, and observe the performance of the four methods in different training set proportions. The results are shown in Figures 1–5. The results in the figures are the average of 10 independent experiments. Observing Fig. 5, we can see (1) As the proportion of the training set increases, the overall trend of the average AUC value of the four methods in each network is gradually increasing. This is because more sufficient training information will make the increase of n_1 and the decrease of n_2 (see the definition of AUC in Formula 13). This phenomenon is also reflected in single-layer networks [34], indicating that single-layer networks and multiplex networks are the same in some properties, so it is valuable to consider extending the methods in single-layer networks to multiplex networks. (2) Regardless of how the proportion of the training set changes, the MRCP method performs optimally in all networks except Karackhardt, which reflects the effectiveness of the MRCP method. (3) When the proportion of the training set is reduced from 90% to 60%, in the 7 networks except Karackhardt, the change of the AUC value of the MRCP method is very small compared with the NSILR and LPIS methods, which shows that the MRCP method has Better robustness. In addition, as the proportion of the training set changes, the AUC value of the LAA hardly changes. This is because the LAA method mainly calculates the possibility of the existence of the link in target layer based on the existence of the link in auxiliary layers. Therefore, the change in the percentage of deleted links in the target layer has little effect on its results.

In summary, compared with LAA, LPIS and NSILR, MRCP has better prediction performance. In addition, compared with the NSILR and LPIS methods, the MRCP method has better robustness. Since the MRCP method uses the same feature vector as our work [28] when calculating the intralayer probability, the outstanding performance of the MRCP method once again illustrates the effectiveness of our extracted features.

6   Conclusion

In this paper, we proposed a link prediction method MRCP based on regression and conditional probability for multiplex networks, which combines intra-layer probability and inter-layer information to predict missing links in the network. In order to prove the effectiveness of the MRCP method, we conducted experiments on 8 real networks and compared them with the three methods, namely LAA, LPIS and NSILR. The experimental results show that our MRCP achieves superior performance compared to baseline methods. In the future, leveraging the technique of graph neural networks to perform link prediction in multiplex networks will be a research trend.

Acknowledgments. This study was supported in part by the Science and Technology Program of Gansu Province (Nos. 21JR7RA458 and 21ZD8RA008), and the Supercomputing Center of Lanzhou University.

References

1. Abdolhosseini-Qomi, A.M., Yazdani, N., Asadpour, M.: Overlapping communities and the prediction of missing links in multiplex networks. Phys. A **554**, 124650 (2020)
2. Aleta, A., Moreno, Y.: Multilayer networks in a nutshell. Ann. Rev. Condens. Matter Phys. **10**(1), 45–62 (2019)
3. Barabási, A.L., Albert, R.: Emergence of scaling in random networks. Science **286**(5439), 509–512 (1999)
4. Battiston, F., Nicosia, V., Latora, V.: Structural measures for multiplex networks. Phys. Rev. E **89**(3), 1–14 (2014)
5. Bródka, P., Chmiel, A., Magnani, M., Ragozini, G.: Quantifying layer similarity in multiplex networks: a systematic study. R. Soc. Open Sci. **5**(8), 171747 (2018)
6. Cannistraci, C.V., Alanis-Lobato, G.G., Ravasi, T.: From link-prediction in brain connectomes and protein interactomes to the local-community-paradigm in complex networks. Sci. Rep. **3**(1), 1613 (2013)
7. Chen, B.L., Hall, D.H., Chklovskii, D.B.: Wiring optimization can relate neuronal structure and function. Proc. Natl. Acad. Sci. **103**(12), 4723–4728 (2006)
8. Coleman, J., Katz, E., Menzel, H.: The diffusion of an innovation among physicians. Sociometry **20**(4), 253 (1957)
9. De Domenico, M., Porter, M.A., Arenas, A.: MuxViz: a tool for multilayer analysis and visualization of networks. J. Complex Netw. **3**(2), 159–176 (2015)
10. Emmanuel, L.: The Collegial Phenomenon: the Social Mechanisms of Cooperation Among Peers in a Corporate Law Partnership. Oxford University Press, Oxford (2001)
11. Guimerà, R., Sales-Pardo, M.: Missing and spurious interactions and the reconstruction of complex networks. Proc. Natl. Acad. Sci. **106**(52), 22073–22078 (2009)
12. Jalili, M., Orouskhani, Y., Asgari, M., Alipourfard, N., Perc, M.: Link prediction in multiplex online social networks. R. Soc. Open Sci. **4**(2), 160863 (2017)
13. Kapferer, B.: Strategy and Transaction in an African Factory: African Workers and Indian Management in a Zambian town. Manchester University Press, Manchester (1972)
14. Kivelä, M., Arenas, A., Barthelemy, M., Gleeson, J.P., Moreno, Y., Porter, M.A.: Multilayer networks. J. Complex Netw. **2**(3), 203–271 (2014)
15. Krackhardt, D.: Cognitive social structures. Soc. Netw. **9**(2), 109–134 (1987)
16. Kumar, A., Singh, S.S., Singh, K., Biswas, B.: Link prediction techniques, applications, and performance: a survey. Phys. A **553**, 124289 (2020)
17. Lee, K.M., Min, B., Goh, K.I.: Towards real-world complexity: an introduction to multiplex networks. Eur. Phys. J. B **88**(2), 48 (2015)
18. Liben-Nowell, D., Kleinberg, J.: The link-prediction problem for social networks. J. Am. Soc. Inform. Sci. Technol. **58**(7), 1019–1031 (2007)
19. Lü, L., Zhou, T.: Link prediction in complex networks: a survey. Phys. A **390**(6), 1150–1170 (2011)
20. Luo, H., Li, L., Zhang, Y., Fang, S., Chen, X.: Link prediction in multiplex networks using a novel multiple-attribute decision-making approach. Knowl.-Based Syst. **219**, 106904 (2021)
21. Magnani, M., Micenkova, B., Rossi, L.: Combinatorial analysis of multiple networks (2013)
22. Najari, S., Salehi, M., Ranjbar, V., Jalili, M.: Link prediction in multiplex networks based on interlayer similarity. Phys. A **536**, 120978 (2019)

23. Newman, M.E.: Clustering and preferential attachment in growing networks. Phys. Rev. E Stat. Phys. Plasmas Fluids Relat. Interdiscip. Topics **64**(2), 4 (2001)

24. Nicosia, V., Bianconi, G., Latora, V., Barthelemy, M.: Growing multiplex networks. Phys. Rev. Lett. **111**(5), 058701 (2013)

25. Pandey, B., Bhanodia, P.K., Khamparia, A., Pandey, D.K.: A comprehensive survey of edge prediction in social networks: techniques, parameters and challenges. Expert Syst. Appl. **124**, 164–181 (2019)

26. Rezaeipanah, A., Ahmadi, G., Sechin Matoori, S.: A classification approach to link prediction in multiplex online ego-social networks. Soc. Netw. Anal. Min. **10**(1), 27 (2020)

27. Samei, Z., Jalili, M.: Discovering spurious links in multiplex networks based on interlayer relevance. J. Complex Netw. **7**(5), 641–658 (2019)

28. Shan, N., Li, L., Zhang, Y., Bai, S., Chen, X.: Supervised link prediction in multiplex networks. Knowl.-Based Syst. **203**, 106168 (2020)

29. Sharma, S., Singh, A.: An efficient method for link prediction in complex multiplex networks. In: 2015 11th International Conference on Signal-Image Technology & Internet-Based Systems (SITIS), pp. 453–459. IEEE (2015)

30. Snijders, T.A.B., Pattison, P.E., Robins, G.L., Handcock, M.S.: New specifications for exponential random graph models. Sociol. Methodol. **36**(1), 99–153 (2006)

31. Tang, R., Jiang, S., Chen, X., Wang, H., Wang, W., Wang, W.: Interlayer link prediction in multiplex social networks: an iterative degree penalty algorithm. Knowl.-Based Syst. **194**, 105598 (2020)

32. Vickers, M., Chan, S.: Representing Classroom Social Structure. Victoria Institute of Secondary Education, Melbourne (1981)

33. Watts, D.J., Strogatz, S.H.: Collective dynamics of small-world networks. Nature **393**(6684), 440–442 (1998)

34. Yang, J., Zhang, X.D.: Predicting missing links in complex networks based on common neighbors and distance. Sci. Rep. **6**(1), 1–10 (2016)

35. Yao, Y., et al.: Link prediction via layer relevance of multiplex networks. Int. J. Mod. Phys. C **28**(08), 1750101 (2017)

36. Yu, Q., Long, C., Lv, Y., Shao, H., He, P., Duan, Z.: Predicting co-author relationship in medical co-authorship networks. PLoS ONE **9**(7), e101214 (2014)

37. Zhao, D., Li, L., Peng, H., Luo, Q., Yang, Y.: Multiple routes transmitted epidemics on multiplex networks. Phys. Lett. A **378**(10), 770–776 (2014)

38. Zhou, T., Lü, L., Zhang, Y.C.: Predicting missing links via local information. Eur. Phys. J. B **71**(4), 623–630 (2009)

A Zero Trust Model for Networked Self-Service Terminals

Boya Liu[1]([✉]) [iD], Haitao Ye[1] [iD], Jizhou Chen[2,3], Yong Xia[2], and Jieren Cheng[3] [iD]

[1] School of Information Technology and Electrical Engineering, Southern Cross University of Australia, Military Rd, East Lismore, NSW 2480, Australia
18975804657@163.com
[2] Guangdong Provincial Administration of Government Services and Data, Guangzhou 510030, Guangdong Province, China
[3] School of CyberSecurity and Crypt-Ology, Hainan University, Haikou 570228, Hainan Province, China

Abstract. Networked self-service terminals (NSST) are intelligent devices that are widely used in various fields. They can provide convenient services and interactions, but they also face various security threats. Traditional security protection models are often based on the division of trust boundaries, treating the internal of the terminal as a trusted area, and the external of the terminal as an untrusted area. However, in the application scenarios of self-service terminals, the concepts of internal and external have become blurred, and the security problems have gradually emerged. The traditional boundary security model can no longer meet their security needs. To solve this problem, a zero-trust model for NSST is proposed. This model is based on the security framework of the NIST zero-trust model, which no longer assumes that any area or component is trustworthy, but instead uses multi-level, multi-dimensional, and dynamic security policies to achieve comprehensive and real-time monitoring and protection of the terminal. On this basis, the characteristics and security requirements of NSST are analyzed, and the overall architecture and core components of the zero-trust model are designed, including identity authentication, access control, data encryption, behavior audit, permission management and other aspects. The protection of NSST is achieved by the collaboration of components.

Keywords: Zero trust model · Self-Service Terminal · Network Security · Security Protection

1 Introduction

1.1 Research Background and Motivation

With the continuous progress of internet technology and the popularization of intelligent hardware devices, more and more devices are connected to the internet, making the transmission of information more convenient and efficient. Connected devices are widely used in various fields due to their advantages of self-service, efficiency, and convenience. However, the openness, interconnectivity, and programmability of Networked

Z. Cai et al. (Eds.): NCTCS 2023, CCIS 1944, pp. 237–247, 2024.
https://doi.org/10.1007/978-981-99-7743-7_15

Self-Service Terminals (NSST) have also made them targets for hackers and malicious software intrusion, resulting in security risks for these interconnected devices.

In addition, with the rise of mobile internet and the IoT, the application scenarios of connected self-service devices are becoming increasingly widespread, such as in fields such as banking, hospitals, catering, retail, etc. Although their popularization and use have improved work efficiency and service quality, they have brought more security risks. For example, on a bank ATM, malicious software can steal user account information and passwords; On hospital self-service registration machines, hackers can cause serious consequences by tampering with the system. These security issues also pose increasingly serious security threats and challenges to these networked self-service terminals.

1.2 Research Purpose and Significance

This article aims to design a Zero Trust Model (ZTM) for NSST to improve their security and reliability. On the basis of the existing ZTM, combined with the characteristics and security requirements of NSST, a feasible and referential Zero trust security model is proposed to provide more comprehensive and rigorous technical support and guarantee for the security of self-service terminals. Through the relevant research in this article, new ideas can be provided to address the security threats and challenges faced by NSST, improve the security and reliability of self-service terminals, and ensure the privacy of users and the security of enterprise data.

Theoretically, the Zero trust security model is a technical means based on authentication, authorization, encryption, audit, etc., which transfers the basic point of network security from traditional border defense to fine-grained control of data flow, and realizes the comprehensive coverage of network security. Compared to traditional boundary defense models, ZTMs pay more attention to data security protection and can better adapt to the changes in security threats and attack methods in modern network environments [1]. In network terminals such as NSST, the ZTM can improve data security, reduce the occurrence of security vulnerabilities, and reduce security risks.

In a practical sense, the security issues of online self-service devices have attracted widespread attention and attention. With the popularization of the Internet and the development of technology, online self-service devices have become an indispensable part of people's lives, involving important fields such as finance, healthcare, and transportation, and their security is particularly important. The Zero trust security model can effectively solve the security problem of NSST, improve the security and reliability of devices, and protect users' privacy and asset security. Therefore, adopting the Zero trust security model can provide more comprehensive and rigorous security guarantee for NSST, protect user information and enterprise data from threats, and maintain social stability and security.

1.3 Research Status and Issues

With the continuous development of network security technology, Zero Trust Models (ZTMs) have gradually become one of the current research hotspots. Domestic and foreign scholars have achieved a series of achievements in the research of ZTMs.

Among them, the Beyond Corp model proposed by Google and the ZTM proposed by Forrester are representative ZTMs. Google's Beyond Corp model is a ZTM based on cloud computing and network security technology, aimed at protecting Google's internal network and cloud services through a borderless security architecture. This model achieves fine-grained control of the network by using a unified authentication and authorization mechanism to control user access rights and authenticate and authorize devices and applications [2]. Forrester's ZTM emphasizes fine-grained control over devices, users, applications, and data to improve network security. This model achieves security protection of data by using multiple authentication and access control techniques [3].

Domestic researchers of China have also been involved in the research of ZTMs, but compared to foreign countries, they are still in the early stages. At present, the domestic research mainly focuses on the theory, and has not formed a relatively mature Zero trust security model.

Although the ZTM has achieved certain results in network security, it still has significant results in only some areas. Firstly, most of the existing ZTMs are designed for centralized network environments such as data centers and cloud computing, without in-depth research in the field of NSST. Secondly, the existing ZTM lacks an effective defense mechanism against security issues in NSST, such as identifying and defending security vulnerabilities in old operating systems used by NSST. Therefore, these unsafe factors that may expose a large area of the internal network at any time are the starting point of this study. This study will provide new ideas for eliminating security threats in NSST through the basic theory of existing zero trust models.

2 Overview of the Zero Trust Model

2.1 The Origin and Evolution of the Zero Trust Model

At present, more and more organizations and enterprises have established their own information systems on the network, and these information systems often need to interact with external networks, which makes the network security problem more complex and serious. The traditional boundary security concept believes that there is a clear boundary between the internal network and the external network. By setting firewall, intrusion detection, access control and other security measures on this boundary, the security of the internal network can be effectively protected. However, with the rise of cloud computing, mobile office and other emerging technologies, the boundary between the internal network and the external network is gradually blurred, which makes the traditional boundary security concept more and more difficult to meet the challenges of network security. In order to address this challenge, ZTMs have emerged.

2.2 The Core Concept of the Zero Trust Model

ZTM is a network security architecture based on minimizing trust. Its core idea is not to trust any user, device, application or network traffic, but to require authentication and access control in every link [4]. The emergence of the ZTM indicates that traditional border security concepts are no longer able to meet the requirements of today's network security, and a more advanced and flexible security architecture is needed.

3 Analysis of Security Issues in NSST

3.1 Application Scenarios and Characteristics of NSST

Networked self-service terminal is a terminal device that can provide various self-service services. It is connected to the backend server through the internet, and users can purchase goods, query information, and handle various services through these terminal devices. These terminal devices can be deployed in various public places or within enterprises, such as shopping malls, stations, airports, hospitals, banks, etc. At stations and airports, NSST can provide services such as flight and train schedules, ticket purchases, boarding, and pick-up. In hospitals, NSST can provide services such as registration, payment, drug collection, and medical reimbursement. In banks, NSST can provide services such as withdrawal, transfer, and account inquiry. It can be said that NSST have a wide range of application scenarios in various industries, providing users with a more convenient service experience. Under the widespread application of NSST, it also has some characteristics:

1. Self-service: NSST provide self-service, allowing users to freely choose the required service content without manual intervention, thereby reducing labor costs and waiting time.
2. Intelligent: The online self-service terminal is equipped with various sensing devices, scanners, speech recognizers, etc., which can identify user needs and provide corresponding services, achieving intelligent interaction.
3. Efficiency: NSST can operate 24 h a day without interruption, with a wide range of services and the ability to provide services to multiple users simultaneously, thereby improving service efficiency.
4. Scalability: NSST can access and control remote servers through network connections, and service content can be expanded and updated at any time.

However, the widespread application of NSST has also brought some security issues. Due to the connection between NSST and the internet, they may face the threat of being invaded by network attackers.

3.2 Analysis of the Current Situation of Security Issues in NSST

In modern society, more and more self-service terminals use the Internet for data transmission and interaction to meet people's various needs. The widespread application of NSST has brought many security threats and attack methods, but the existing security defense measures are insufficient to resist these potential risks. Therefore, NSST are prone to posing threats to data and software in the following aspects [5]:

1. **Network Security**: The operating system and software versions are too old: Many NSST use operating systems and software versions that are too old and vulnerable to known vulnerabilities. Hackers can use these vulnerabilities to invade the system or obtain sensitive information. Unable to upgrade patches in a timely manner: Even with new vulnerability patches, many NSST cannot upgrade in a timely manner. This allows hackers to exploit vulnerabilities to attack systems, while terminal operators or enterprises fail to fix vulnerabilities in a timely manner and cannot respond quickly

to attack events. Improper device management: Many NSST have improper device management, such as using weak passwords, not changing default passwords, and not configuring firewalls correctly, which can easily allow hackers to invade the system.

2. **Software Security**: Security issues with third-party software: Many NSST require the installation of third-party software or applications, which may have inherent vulnerabilities or security risks. Hackers can exploit these vulnerabilities for attacks.

   Security issues with their own software: The software used by NSST may also have vulnerabilities or security risks, such as lack of good code specifications, lack of security testing, and other issues. Lack of timely software updates: Software suppliers may not update their software in a timely manner, resulting in known vulnerabilities not being repaired in a timely manner, leading to opportunities for hackers to exploit.

3. **Manage Security**: Data management: NSST usually require users to provide personal sensitive information, such as account number, password, ID number, etc. If the user information management of NSST is not in place or there are insufficient security measures to protect users' sensitive information, there is a risk of information leakage. In terms of device management: The management of NSST is also prone to problems, such as untimely maintenance, inadequate security measures, and administrators' excessive trust in the system. These management problems may lead to a decline in system security, which may lead to Data breach or other security problems.

3.3   Security Threats and Attack Methods of NSST

With the increase in the number of NSST, the security threats and attack methods they face are becoming increasingly diverse and complex. By analyzing the security threats and attack methods faced by NSST, it can provide a basis for the subsequent design of ZTMs.

1. **Network Security:**

   DDoS attack: Hackers may exhaust the network bandwidth of self-service devices by sending a large amount of malicious traffic to the network where the devices are located, resulting in the devices being unable to function properly.

   Malicious software attack: Hackers may inject malicious software (such as viruses, trojans, etc.) into self-service devices, causing them to be controlled or stealing internal data.Port scanning attack: Hackers may scan the open ports of self-service devices to identify vulnerabilities and exploit them for attacks.

   Man-in-the-middle attack: hackers may obtain or tamper with the communication content by cheating the communication between self-service devices and servers to steal data or control the devices.Identity authentication attack: Hackers may obtain the login password of self-service devices through violent cracking or social engineering attacks, thereby gaining control of the device.

2. **Software Security:**

   Buffer overflow attack: hackers may send data exceeding the buffer capacity to the device, crash the device program and run malicious code to control the device.

   SQL injection attack: hackers may attack the database of the device and steal or tamper with data by injecting malicious SQL statements.

XSS attack: Hackers may inject malicious script code into the device to attack the device's web application, achieving the goal of controlling the device or stealing user data.

Reverse engineering attack: hackers may find vulnerabilities or weaknesses in equipment through Reverse engineering of equipment programs, and use these vulnerabilities or weaknesses to attack.

Encryption algorithm attack: Hackers may attack the data security of devices by analyzing the encryption algorithm or key used, such as stealing encrypted data or tampering with encrypted data.

3. **Manage Security:**

Unauthorized access attack: Hackers may obtain unauthorized access to self-service devices by deceiving or attacking administrator credentials, in order to obtain sensitive data or control the device.

Remote attack: Hackers may control devices or steal sensitive information by remotely accessing administrator accounts or management interfaces.

4 Design of a ZTM for NSST

4.1 Analysis of Security Requirements for NSST

Network and information security refer to a three-dimensional system structure that involves multiple aspects of content, based on the structural characteristics of the network, taking different measures from different network levels and system applications to improve and defend [6]. Therefore, it is necessary to analyze the security requirements of NSST and provide ideas for future security solutions based on the ZTM. For the security needs of NSST, the following aspects can be considered:

1. **Authentication and Authorization:** NSST require authentication and authorization of users, and only users who have passed the authentication and authorization can perform corresponding operations. Therefore, it is necessary to deploy effective identity authentication and authorization mechanisms on devices, such as the use of multi factor identity authentication (MFA) and other technologies to ensure the legitimacy and credibility of user identities.
2. **Data Protection:** NSST typically involve the collection and processing of user sensitive information, so a series of technical measures need to be taken to protect the security and privacy of these data. For example, technologies such as encrypted transmission, data classification and labeling, data backup and recovery are used to ensure the security of data during transmission and storage.
3. **Malicious Behavior Detection and Prevention:** NSST need to have the ability to detect and prevent malicious behavior, such as intrusion detection, threat intelligence analysis, antivirus software, and other technologies. These technologies can effectively prevent hacker attacks, malicious software, and other threats.

4. **Operational Audit and Risk Assessment:** NSST need to have the ability to conduct operational audit and risk assessment, track users' operational behavior, and conduct risk assessment and threat analysis on devices. These technologies can detect abnormal operations and risk events in a timely manner and take timely measures to handle them.

5. **Management and Operation:** NSST need to have effective management and operation measures, such as device configuration management, vulnerability management, software updates, backup and recovery measures. These measures can ensure the stability and safety of equipment operation, and promptly handle equipment failures and safety incidents.

4.2 Design of a Security Solution for NSST Based on ZTM

The core idea of the ZTM based on the NIST framework is "never trust, always verify", which means that no device, user, or request should be trusted by default, but each access request should be fully authenticated, authorized, and encrypted to protect resources and data [7]. At the same time, based on the characteristics of self-service, intelligence, efficiency, and scalability of NSST, as well as the analysis of the security requirements of networked autonomous terminals, a specific security solution based on the ZTM will be designed from the following aspects.

1. **Develop access strategies:** sort and classify NSST and related resources, identify all sensitive and non sensitive data and applications in the system, and establish corresponding asset lists. Develop access policies based on asset inventory, including authentication, access authorization, and access restrictions for different users and devices.

2. **Implement network segmentation:** By isolating NSST from other devices, network segmentation is implemented to prevent horizontal movement attacks.

3. **Strengthen identity authentication:** Use multi factor identity authentication to verify the user's identity, and protect the user's identity information through hardware, software, and other technical means.

4. **Implement permission management:** implement the Principle of least privilege based on the roles and responsibilities of users to ensure that users can only access the resources they need.

5. **Monitoring and response:** Detect and respond to security events by implementing real-time monitoring and response mechanisms to prevent hacker intrusion and Data breach.

6. **Implement data encryption:** Encrypt sensitive data to ensure its security during transmission and storage.

4.3 Security Framework and Process for NSST

Based on the above security scheme design, in order to address the security issues of NSST, this study designed a security framework based on the ZTM to adapt to the scenarios of NSST. Firstly, in this model framework, users, terminals, and data are considered untrustworthy. The security framework is shown in Fig. 1 and consists of the following components:

244 B. Liu et al.

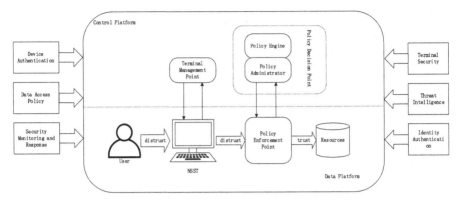

Fig. 1. Safety framework based on NIST ZTM

1. Core components:
   A. Data: All data involved in the scenario of NSST.
   B. User: A person who uses an online NSST.
   C. Device: The NSST device used by the user.
   D. Resources: Network resources that need to be accessed by NSST.
   E. Self-service terminal: A NSST device provided to users.
   F. Policy Engine: A system that evaluates and authorizes access requests from users, devices, and NSST based on predefined rules and conditions.
   G. Policy administrator: The person or system responsible for defining and updating access policies.
2. Logic components:
   A. Policy Execution Point (PEP): A system or software module that executes access control between users, devices, or NSST and resources.
   B. Policy Decision Point (PDP): A system or software module that allows or denies access requests based on the output of the policy engine.
   C. Policy Management Point (PMP): A system or software module responsible for distributing access policies defined by policy administrators to various PEPs and PDPs.
   D. Policy Information Point (PIP): Refers to a system or software module that provides relevant information required by the policy engine.
   E. Terminal Management Point (TMP): Refers to the system or software module responsible for managing the configuration, updates, monitoring, and maintenance of NSST.
3. Functional components:
   A. Identity authentication: The process of verifying the identity of users, devices, and NSST, such as using multi factor authentication technology.
   B. Device authentication: The process of verifying whether devices and NSST meet security requirements.
   C. Data access strategy: The process of protecting data from leakage or tampering during transmission and storage, such as using encryption, signature, hash, and other technologies.

    D. Security monitoring and response: refers to the process of monitoring Réseau Sentinelles activities, detecting and responding to potential security threats, such as using log analysis, intrusion detection, alarm notification and other technologies.

    E. Terminal security: The process of protecting the hardware and software of NSST from attacks and damage, such as using physical locks, cameras, firewalls, and other technologies.

    F. Threat intelligence: Collect, process, and analyze data to understand the motives, targets, and attack behaviors of threat actors, helping us make faster, wiser, and more data-supported security decisions.

Compared to the NIST, the main difference of this security architecture is the addition of self-service terminal components and the addition of terminal management points for centralized management of NSST, as well as terminal security functions to protect the security of NSST in real-time.

The process of this security framework in the scenario of NSST is as follows:

1. Users use devices to connect to NSST and initiate requests to access resources.
2. PEP intercepts requests and sends access requests and related information to PDP, such as the identity, attributes, status, etc. of users, devices, and NSST.
3. PDP evaluates and authorizes access requests based on the output of the policy engine, and returns the decision to allow or deny to PEP.
4. The policy engine evaluates and authorizes access requests based on the access policies defined by the policy administrator and relevant information obtained from PIP, such as threat intelligence, SIEM system analysis results, etc.
5. PEP executes PDP's decisions, and if access is allowed, forwards the request to the resource; If access is denied, an error message is returned to the user.
6. Data access policies protect data from leakage or tampering during transmission and storage, such as using encryption, signature, hashing, and other technologies.
7. Terminal security protects the hardware and software of NSST from attacks and damage, such as using physical locks, cameras, firewalls, and other technologies.
8. TMP manages the configuration, update, monitoring, and maintenance of NSST to ensure their normal operation.

5   Discussion and Outlook

5.1   Discussion on the Advantages and Disadvantages of a ZTM for NSST

The traditional network boundary-based security protection model determines the security level of the object to be protected based on the sensitivity of business and information, and divides it into security zones. Then, relevant technologies are used for security isolation to achieve protection for each security zone [8]. However, due to the inability of traditional security models to adapt to higher intensity attack scenarios targeting NSST, this paper proposes a ZTM for NSST, which emphasizes the verification and authorization of all devices and users, and even within the internal network, all traffic needs to be audited and restricted, thereby improving the security and reliability of the system. Here are the advantages and disadvantages of the ZTM:

1. **Advantages:**

More secure: The ZTM can better protect the security of the system and reduce the risk of malicious attacks by verifying and authorizing devices and users.

More reliable: The ZTM can better ensure the reliability of the system and reduce the risk of system failure by auditing and limiting all traffic.

More flexible: The ZTM does not rely on specific network structures or devices, can adapt to different network environments and device requirements, and has more flexible deployment methods.

More controllable: The ZTM audits and restricts all access requests, enabling better management of user and device access permissions and enhancing system controllability.

2. **Disadvantages:**

Single point risk: Zero trust is a strong control architecture, and the control of resources is concentrated on the gateway. Therefore, once a Single point of failure occurs, the whole business will be interrupted.

Risk of centralized permissions: The zero trust architecture converges and concentrates many risks, reducing management costs. However, if centralized management is out of control, it will also bring greater risks;

Complexity risk: The ZTM requires auditing and limiting all traffic, requiring the deployment of a large number of security devices and technologies, which increases the complexity of the system.

High cost risk: The ZTM requires verification and authorization on all devices and users, requiring a significant investment of cost and effort.

5.2 Future Development Prospects of ZTM for NSST

The ZTM for NSST is the future development direction in the field of security for NSST. On the one hand, in terms of technology, the future ZTM will rely more on the support of advanced technologies such as security chips, artificial intelligence, and blockchain to improve security and credibility. The development of these technologies will provide more possibilities and support for the application of ZTMs. On the other hand, in terms of application, future ZTMs will pay more attention to the expansion and adaptability of application scenarios. ZTMs for NSST can be applied to more fields, such as smart homes, industrial control, and so on.

Overall, the ZTM for NSST is the development direction in the future security field of NSST, and will become an important means of ensuring the security of NSST.

6   Conclusions

This article proposes a ZTM for NSST based on the NIST zero trust architecture. Through the collaboration of core components, multiple logical components, and rich functional components, it achieves continuous identity verification and authorization of terminals, encryption of data, minimization and differentiation of access, and restriction and audit of operation and maintenance operations. The ZTM proposed by the relevant research institute in this article can provide more efficient and secure security solutions for NSST, providing useful reference and guidance for practical applications in related fields.

References

1. Assunção, P.: A zero trust approach to network security; proceedings of the. 2010 In: Proceedings of the Digital Privacy and Security Conference, F, (2019)
2. Ward, R., Beyer, B.: Beyondcorp: A new approach to enterprise security (2014)
3. Kindervag, J.: Build security into your network's dna: The zero trust network architecture. Forrester Res. Inc. 27 (2010)
4. Feng, J.Y., Yu, T.T, Wang, Z.Y., et al.: Edge ZTM for Resisting the Threat of Lost Terminals in Power IoT Scenarios. Comput. Res. Dev. (2022)
5. Shao, L., Niu, W.N., Zhang, X.S.: Self-service terminal network security threat assessment and response in IoT application scenarios. J. Sichuan Univ. Nat. Sci. Ed. **60**(1), 11 (2023)
6. Hu, Z.: Network and Information Security. Tsinghua University (2006)
7. NIST has released the second draft of SP 1800–35: Implementing a Zero Trust Architecture. Inf. Technol. Standard. (1): 1 (2023)
8. Wang, S.L., Feng, X., Cai, Y.B, et al.: Analysis and application of Zero trust security model. Inf. Secur. Res. **6**(11) (2020)

Modeling and Verification of WPA3 Security Protocol Based on SPIN

Meihua Xiao⬛, Shanshan Qiao(✉)⬛, Tao Liu⬛, Ke Yang⬛, Zehuan Li⬛,
and Dongming Zhan⬛

School of Software, East China Jiaotong University, Nanchang 330013, China
`falseshanshanqiao2023@163.com`

Abstract. Wi-Fi Protected Access 3 (WPA3) is the latest generation of Wi-Fi encryption protocol, and a comprehensive and systematic analysis of its security properties is of great significance for ensuring the security of network information transmission. In this paper, model checking technology is used to formalize analysis and verification of WPA3 protocol's authentication and secrecy. Abstract modeling principles are proposed, initiator, responder and intruder models are constructed, authentication and secrecy are formally defined through operational semantics, and a state reduction strategy is proposed, that is, according to the protocol message set, static analysis strategy is used to reduce the invalid message attacks of attackers, and the problem of state explosion is effectively alleviated. Experimental results show that there is a key reinstallation attack in the protocol, and the corresponding solution is given. The method proposed in this paper can provide guideline for analyzing similar network security protocols.

Keywords: Model Checking · SPIN · WPA3 · Formal Verification

1 Introduction

The Wi-Fi Alliance introduced the WPA3 encryption protocol in 2018, which mainly implements data encryption through asymmetric key working principle. Due to objective factors, the Wi-Fi Alliance announced in 2020 that all Wi-Fi certified products need to be updated to the latest WPA3 encryption protocol [1]. Because WPA3 protocol has a great degree of update compared with the previous generation WPA2 protocol, so far scholars have only carried out scattered research on WPA3 protocol, it is necessary to systematically analyze the security of WPA3 protocol. As an important part of WPA3 protocol, security analysis of the 4-way handshake has naturally become an important research issue.

Formal methods are widely used in the design, development and verification of computer systems, and mathematical methods are used to improve the correctness, reliability, robustness and security of computer systems. Domestic researchers have carried out in-depth and fruitful research on formal methods and achieved a series of research results. The National Natural Science Foundation of China (NSFC) has also provided long-term support in this field. Many researchers have grown into experts in this field through the support of NSFC funds [2].

Z. Cai et al. (Eds.): NCTCS 2023, CCIS 1944, pp. 248–265, 2024.
https://doi.org/10.1007/978-981-99-7743-7_16

Related work

Model checking technology began in the early 1980s.Its basic idea is to abstract a process or system into a finite state model and analyze and verify it [3]. Lowe and other scholars used this method to find the vulnerabilities of NSPK protocol, which proved the feasibility of model checking technology in the direction of security protocol analysis [4]. The Belgium security team found a KRACK reinstallation security vulnerability in the WPA2 protocol [5], as a direct response to this vulnerability, the Wi-Fi Alliance urgently organized a global upgrade patch for Wi-Fi products and devices. Symmetric key-based encryption [6] will eventually become a thing of the past. In 2018, the Wi-Fi Alliance introduced a new generation of Wi-Fi encryption protocol, WPA3 [7]. As a Wi-Fi encryption scheme based on the asymmetric key design principle [8], the standard encryption algorithm of WPA3 protocol adopts SAE encryption scheme [9], at the same time, it combines the Diffie-Hellman encryption scheme based on elliptic curve [10]. In the case of supporting digital signature function, WPA3 protocol adopts asymmetric encryption mode, which greatly improves its security and reliability, and can effectively avoid data information being tampered and forged by illegal users. Meanwhile, SAE encryption algorithm improves the calculation amount of brute force cracking, which cannot be cracked within effective time, eliminates dictionary attack [11] and other problems, and solves the problems of insecure key distribution and difficult key management. Starting in 2020, all Wi-Fi Alliance certified devices have been updated to the latest WPA3 encryption scheme. Wireless network communication has entered a new fourth-generation encryption stage. Karim Lounis implement an attack that exploits the vulnerability using the Linux software utilities hostapd-2.7 and wpa_supplicant-2.7 on Raspberry Pis and show the impact of the attack on a legitimate WPA3 network and provide a countermeasure to mitigate the attack [12]. The main contribution of this paper [13] is to analyze the technology offered in the new Wi-Fi Protected Access III (WPA3) security scheme and provide the first comprehensive security analysis and discussion to determine whether it has addressed the vulnerabilities of its predecessor. An interesting finding of this paper is that WPA3 still lacks in addressing all the issues existing in WPA2 and exploring other mitigations for future research [13].

In this paper, the authentication and secrecy of WPA3 protocol are studied by using model checking technology. The security protocol specification is defined by operational semantics, which provides a theoretical basis for verifying WPA3 protocol. The intruder model is formally defined, and the four-way handshake process of WPA3 protocol is modeled and verified by SPIN tool.

2   Formal Description of WPA3 Four-Way Handshake

Sequence of role behavior of both sides of WPA3 four-way handshake communication.

$$
\begin{aligned}
Initiator = [&send(AP, STA, \{Non\}) \\
&recv(STA, AP, \{Non, M\}) \\
&send(AP, STA, \{Non + 1, M\}PTK) \\
&recv(STA, AP, \{Non + 1, M\}PTK) \\
&claim(AP, STA, \{auth, sec\})]
\end{aligned}
\tag{1}
$$

$$Responder = [recv(AP, STA, \{Non\})$$
$$send\,(STA, AP, \{Non, M\,\})$$
$$recv(AP, STA, \{Non + 1, M\,\}PTK) \tag{2}$$
$$send\,(STA, AP, \{Non + 1, M\,\}PTK)$$
$$claim(STA, AP, \{auth, sec\})]$$

Although the role behavior sequence roughly gives the interaction flow of the protocol, the details are still not clearly displayed. Therefore, through the specific analysis of the WPA3 protocol operation specification, combined with the abstract modeling principle, the protocol four-way handshake flow is given in Fig. 1.

It is assumed that at the beginning of the protocol session, the STA can always complete the SAE handshake phase and the association phase with the AP, and the connection is successfully entered into the four-way handshake phase. It can be seen from the WPA3 protocol four-way handshake model in Fig. 1 that the protocol is abstracted and formally expressed, and the protocol interaction process is as shown in (3).

$$AP \rightarrow STA : Anonce, r;$$
$$STA(\{Anonce, Snonce, r\}GETKEY) \rightarrow AP : Snonce, r, \{MIC\}EDCRYPTKey;$$
$$AP(\{Anonce, Snonce, r\}GETKEY) \rightarrow STA : r + 1, \{MIC, GTK\}EDCRYPTKey;$$
$$STA \rightarrow AP : r + 1, \{MIC\}EDCRYPTKey$$

$$\tag{3}$$

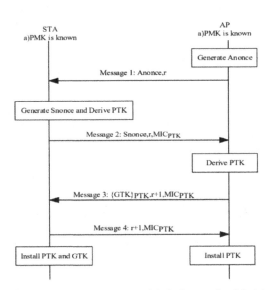

Fig. 1. WPA3 Four-way Handshake Interaction Model

3   Model Construction

3.1   Modeling Honest Agents

The syntax structure of Promela is similar to C language, which constructs a protocol model by describing the behavior of protocol entities. This language mainly represents entities and their behaviors through processes, and information transmission between different entities is represented as information exchange between processes, implemented through predefined channels. In order to improve the accuracy of protocol models and alleviate the state explosion problem, it is necessary to properly abstract the protocol interaction flow and exclude irrelevant content before using model checking method to analyze and verify the security properties of protocols. For the WPA3 protocol communication parties to exchange keys and other functions by sending messages, it is necessary to reasonably abstract and simplify the operation of the communication messages. Therefore, the following abstract modeling principles are proposed:

1. Two entities on both sides of WPA3 communication: Client (Station) and Server (Access Point).For the convenience of description, they are respectively simplified as STA and AP.
2. When describing the protocol abstractly, it is necessary to describe the key used in the protocol uniformly, and use Key to represent it. When it comes to specific modeling, the encryption keys need to be distinguished to distinguish different ciphertexts.
3. Define a key generation function GETKEY(),which can realize the function of generating a key between the client and the server. The key is used to encrypt the communication messages of both parties after the connection is established.
4. Because the data frame loss problem, that is, the operation of both parties after the loss of data packets, is usually not considered in the abstract model, it is necessary to supplement the protocol model by analyzing the state machines of both parties.
5. Assuming that the key system for encrypting the protocol is perfect, that is, the intruder cannot obtain the key by brute force attack, and defines it as the EDCRYPT() function, the encryption and decryption operations of the protocol have no loopholes. When studying whether there is a logical loophole in the protocol design, it is necessary to add a dangerous operation setting, that is, some operations do not directly disclose the key, but increase the risk of key disclosure.

According to the IEEE 802.11 standard, the state machines of AP and STA are given, and the specific contents are shown in Fig. 2 and Fig. 3.

1. The construction of message channel

By analyzing the communication messages of the protocol, a complete set of data items is constructed to facilitate the representation of various messages. The complete set of data includes the protocol entity name, message items, key information, random data, generic data and placeholders. The complete definition is as follows;

mtype = {AP,STA,Intruder,Anonce,Snonce,gD,NULL}; // Data Representation in WPA3

where {AP,STA,Intruder,Anonce,Snonce,gD,NULL} refers to the message item in the protocol interaction process, Anonce is the random number generated by the AP at the server side, Snonce is the random number generated by the STA at the user side, gD represents generic data, and NULL represents a placeholder used to fill the empty space in the message.

According to different information structures, the message channels constructed are different. In order to simplify the program, it is necessary to specify the message format and reduce the number of channels. The message specification format is shown in Table 1.

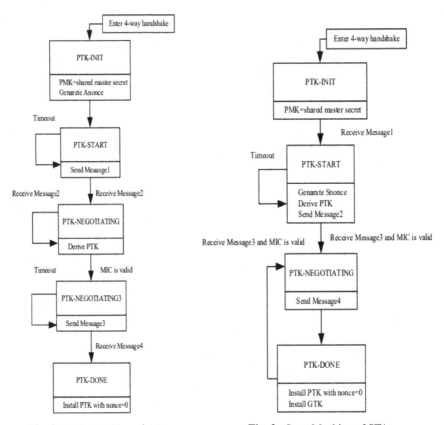

Fig. 2. State Machine of AP   **Fig. 3.** State Machine of STA

So far, the specific definition for the adversary control channel is introduced.

chan syn = [0] of {mtype,mtype,mtype,byte,byte,byte};

The syn channel is used to transport message items. When sending the statement syn ! $x1,x2,x3,x4,x5,x6$, $x1$ represents the sender of the message, $x2$ represents the receiver of the message, $x3$ represents a random number, $x4$ represents the encrypted ciphertext of the message, $x5$ represents a replay counter, and $x6$ is used for message integrity checking. The message receiving statement syn ? eval(x1),eval(x2),x3,x4,x5,x6,the eval() function evaluates the received value. If the value is the same as the target value, the information is received; otherwise, the information is discarded. The specific format is shown below:

Table 1. Four-way handshake message specification format

message	conventionalization
Anonce,r	AP,STA,Anonce,NULL,r,NULL
Snonce,r,{MIC}EDCRYPTKey	STA,AP,Snonce,NULL,r,{MIC}EDCRYPTKey
{GTK}EDCRYPTKey,r + 1, {MIC}EDCRYPTKey	AP,STA,NULL,{GTK}EDCRYPTKey,r + 1, {MIC}EDCRYPTKey
r + 1,{MIC}EDCRYPTKey	STA,AP,NULL,NULL,r + 1,{MIC}EDCRYPTKey

syn!AP, STA, Anonce, NULL, r, NULL; //Message sending statement

syn?eval(x1), eval(x2), x3, x4, x5, x6; //Message receiving statement

By introducing the eval() function, the problem of state explosion can be alleviated effectively [14]. Using Promela language to model WPA3 protocol into a concurrent system, the state transition of the system increases rapidly due to the existence of cross-execution operations between different processes in the system, which is easy to produce state explosion problem. The eval() function can effectively reduce the number of invalid states in a system, because the recipient can use the eval() function to determine which messages are valid for it and which are not valid for it, invalid messages can be discarded.

In order to verify the dangerous behavior during the four-way handshake and implement the verification function by using security assertions, a channel needs to be defined for the information transmission between the two parties after the four-way handshake is completed. The format is as follows:

$$chan\, comm\ =\ [0]\, of\, \{byte\};$$

2. The description of honest agents' behavior

Before describing the agent behavior, define the honest agent of the WPA3 protocol's four-way handshake process. The two honest agents in WPA3 protocol are server AP and client STA. The honest agent processes are defined and named proctype PIni() and proctype PRes() respectively.

At the beginning of the WPA3 protocol interaction, server AP and client STA will generate random numbers respectively. Function DerPTK() is used to generate the key for encrypting communication information. The honest subject sends and receives corresponding messages through syn and comm channels. Considering that packet loss may occur during protocol interaction in a real environment due to network faults and other problems, Therefore, messages like {NULL,NULL,NULL,0,0,0} are used to notify the AP or STA to resend the information, and finally completing identity authentication and key transmission. Process PIni and PRes specific implementation code can be found in Appendix A.

The code in an atomic block is executed sequentially and does not block for external reasons. The proctype PIni() and proctype PRes() processes define corresponding operation statements by using atomic block statements, thus reducing the number of state space [15] transitions and alleviating the state explosion problem to a certain extent.

3.2 Modeling Intruder

This section is mainly based on the traditional Dolev-Yao model, combined with the characteristics of the WPA3 four-way handshake. According to the communication model assumptions, through the introduction of adversary control communication and expanding network communication channels, the communication protocol is analyzed. Under this model assumption, the PI of the intruder process is defined. Under the assumption of adversary control communication, agents can exchange messages with each other through syn and comm channels. Correspondingly, the intruder process PI can also receive information transmitted by other agents and send related information to other corresponding agents through syn and comm channels.

In that process of constructing the intrude, it is assumed that the two parties participating in the four-way handshake process are honest agents, and the messages encrypted by the honest agents in the interaction process can be decrypted only by using the corresponding keys; Intruders control the entire communication environment and can always intercept the information transmitted between the server AP and the user STA. Next, we will mainly introduce the construction of the corresponding knowledge base of the intruder and describe the ability of the intruder.

1. Construction of intruder knowledge set

The construction of the intruder's knowledge base mainly depends on two basic elements, the set of basic knowledge items and the set of knowledge items that the intruder can learn. The basic knowledge item set is mainly the initial knowledge of the intruder, including the role identity of the two communication parties, the format of the communication message, etc. The set of knowledge items that an intruder can learn is defined as the set of knowledge items that an intruder can learn by analyzing the intercepted communication messages, distinguishing the data items according to the known message format, and using the obtained data items to deduce and decrypt the new knowledge. For the data items that cannot be decrypted, the intruder can store them completely in the knowledge base.

In order to alleviate the state explosion problem, it is necessary to simplify the intruder's knowledge set, eliminate the repeated invalid data items, and further reduce the number of system state transitions. When building a knowledge base, intruders often only need to record valuable data items. Usually, these data items are used by intruders to forge communication messages to achieve man-in-the-middle attacks, so it is necessary to analyze the set of data items that should be available to achieve this attack, which is called the set of knowledge items that need to be learned. The set of knowledge items that the intruder can learn (SetE) and the set of knowledge items that need to be learned (SetN) are intersected to obtain valuable data items.

Set of SetE: The set of knowledge items that the intruder can learn. This refers to the message items that the intruder intercepts in the communication channel through monitoring. The intruder deduces and decrypts new knowledge from these message items based on the known knowledge. The data items that cannot be decrypted are stored completely in this set. When analyzing the four-way handshake process, it is important to note that the encryption key used between the client STA and the server AP has already been pre-shared through the SAE handshake. As a result, the intruder cannot directly decrypt the ciphertext without knowing the key and can only store the intercepted ciphertext completely in the set.

Set of SetN: The knowledge items that the intruder needs to learn, that is, the set of knowledge items that the intruder needs to construct the message for man-in-the-middle attack by analyzing the format of the communication message. Since it is impossible to confirm the message content for man-in-the-middle attack in advance, it is necessary to list all the message items that can be forged, and then exclude invalid and unreasonable message items.

In that formal analysis of the WPA3 four-way handshake, the knowledge that an intruder can learn by listening to the message in the communication channel is shown in Table 2. Since the intruder cannot decrypt the ciphertext without the corresponding key, it can only learn the entire message.

Table 2. Knowledge that intruder can learn

interceptable message	learnable knowledge
AP,STA,Anonce,NULL,r,NULL	Anonce,r
STA,AP,Snonce,NULL,r,{MIC}EDCRYPTKey	Snonce,r,{MIC}EDCRYPTKey
AP,STA,NULL,{GTK}EDCRYPTKey,r + 1, {MIC}EDCRYPTKey	{GTK}EDCRYPTKey,r + 1, {MIC}EDCRYPTKey
STA,AP,NULL,NULL,r + 1,{MIC}EDCRYPTKey	r + 1,{MIC}EDCRYPTKey

By analyzing the sentences received by AP and STA, the knowledge that the intruder needs to learn is analyzed.

$$syn?eval(self),\ g2,\ eval(Key),\ g3,\ eval(Key);$$

The value range of the receiving statements g1, g2 and g3 is $\{(AP,STA),(Anonce,Snonce),(r,r + 1)\}$. Assuming that the intruder controls the whole communication channel, the number of messages that the intruder can forge is 24. The messages that an intruder can forge and the knowledge items required to learn are shown in Table 3.

The intersection operation is performed on the corresponding second column of information in Table 2 and Table 3, and information items having value to the intruder can be obtained, and the specific knowledge item set thereof is shown as follows:

$\{AP,STA,Anonce,r\}$; $\{MIC\}EDCRYPTKey$; $\{r + 1,\{GTK\}EDCRYPTKey\}$.

Table 3. Knowledge that invaders can learn

falsifiable message	knowledge to be learned
AP,STA,Anonce,NULL,r,NULL	AP,STA,Anonce,Snonce,r,r + 1
STA,STA,Anonce,NULL,r,NULL	{GTK}EDCRYPTKey,{MIC}EDCRYPTKey
AP,STA,Snonce,NULL,r,NULL	STA,STA,Anonce,NULL,r,NULL
AP,STA,Anonce,NULL,r + 1,NULL	AP,STA,Snonce,NULL,r,NULL
STA,STA,Snonce,NULL,r,NULL	AP,STA,Anonce,NULL,r + 1,NULL
STA,STA,Anonce,NULL,r + 1,NULL	STA,STA,Snonce,NULL,r,NULL
AP,STA,Snonce,NULL,r + 1,NULL	STA,STA,Anonce,NULL,r + 1,NULL
STA,STA,Snonce,NULL,r + 1,NULL	AP,STA,Snonce,NULL,r + 1,NULL
STA,AP,Snonce,NULL,r,{MIC}EDCRYPTKey	STA,STA,Snonce,NULL,r + 1,NULL
AP,AP,Snonce,NULL,r,{MIC}EDCRYPTKey	AP,AP,Snonce,NULL,r,{MIC}EDCRYPTKey
STA,AP,Anonce,NULL,r,{MIC}EDCRYPTKey	STA,AP,Anonce,NULL,r,{MIC}EDCRYPTKey
STA,AP,Snonce,NULL,r + 1,{MIC}EDCRYPTKey	STA,AP,Snonce,NULL,r + 1, {MIC}EDCRYPTKey
AP,AP,Anonce,NULL,r,{MIC}EDCRYPTKey	AP,AP,Anonce,NULL,r,{MIC}EDCRYPTKey
AP,AP,Snonce,NULL,r + 1,{MIC}EDCRYPTKey	AP,AP,Snonce,NULL,r + 1, {MIC}EDCRYPTKey
STA,AP,Anonce,NULL,r + 1,{MIC}EDCRYPTKey	STA,AP,Anonce,NULL,r + 1, {MIC}EDCRYPTKey
AP,AP,Anonce,NULL,r + 1,{MIC}EDCRYPTKey	AP,AP,Anonce,NULL,r + 1,{MIC}EDCRYPTKey
AP,STA,NULL,{GTK}EDCRYPTKey,r + 1, {MIC}EDCRYPTKey	STA,STA,NULL,{GTK}EDCRYPTKey,r + 1, {MIC}EDCRYPTKey
STA,STA,NULL,{GTK}EDCRYPTKey,r + 1, {MIC}EDCRYPTKey	AP,STA,NULL,{GTK}EDCRYPTKey,r, {MIC}EDCRYPTKey
AP,STA,NULL,{GTK}EDCRYPTKey,r, {MIC}EDCRYPTKey	STA,STA,NULL,{GTK}EDCRYPTKey,r, {MIC}EDCRYPTKey
STA,STA,NULL,{GTK}EDCRYPTKey,r, {MIC}EDCRYPTKey	AP,AP,NULL,NULL,r + 1,{MIC}EDCRYPTKey
STA,AP,NULL,NULL,r + 1,{MIC}EDCRYPTKey	STA,AP,NULL,NULL,r,{MIC}EDCRYPTKey
AP,AP,NULL,NULL,r + 1,{MIC}EDCRYPTKey	AP,AP,NULL,NULL,r,{MIC}EDCRYPTKey
STA,AP,NULL,NULL,r,{MIC}EDCRYPTKey	
AP,AP,NULL,NULL,r,{MIC}EDCRYPTKey	

2. Description of intruder behavior

Based on Dolev-Yao's idea of intruder modeling and the principle of abstract modeling, adversary-controlled communication channel is introduced to simulate the communication environment of intruder-controlled network, and the communication protocol is analyzed. Combined with the methods mentioned above, the ability of the intruder is analyzed, and the specific behavior of the intruder is formally modeled by Promela language. Intruder model construction is divided into three parts, respectively, the interception of the message, knowledge representation and learning, message forgery and sending.

a. Message interception: Syn for receiving statement? eval(x1),x2,x3,x5,x5,x6 is used to define that intruders can steal all messages sent by honest agents. In this case, eval(x1) in a statement means that eval() is called. Only statements that meet the criteria will be accepted by the honest principal.
b. The representation and learning of knowledge items: After listening to and obtaining communication messages, the intruder uses the old messages to deduce and decrypt, and learns new knowledge. Use {g6,STA,g7,0,g8,0} to represent the message after the protocol. The first two items represent the sender and receiver, the middle two items represent the random number and encrypted ciphertext, and the last two items represent the replay counter and message integrity check. Record new knowledge with AddToKnowledge().
c. Message forging and sending: The intruders combine basic knowledge with new knowledge to forge communication messages and send them to both parties to achieve a man-in-the-middle attack. It is important to note that only critical information can be used to forge valid messages.

The intruder process is defined as PI to describe the intruder's behavior. In the code of the intruder process PI, the 'do' keyword is used to implement the loop function, and the operations in the loop body are repeatedly executed until the 'break' keyword is triggered to break out of the loop. The purpose of using loop structure is twofold: firstly, to allow the intruder to constantly learn new knowledge and forge new messages, and secondly, to enable the intruder to join the interaction process at any time and send messages to both parties.

3.3 Formal Specification of Security Properties

1. Authentication

Two rules for authentication are used in this article: One is to execute the protocol steps in the correct order, and the other is that after the protocol is executed, the participants should agree on something. Based on these two rules, this paper gives an informal description of the authentication of the four-way handshake, where the correct execution of the four-way steps is crucial, and it ensures that the AP and STA have the same information after the handshake is completed. The formal description is shown in (4).

$$\forall \pi \in traces(P) :$$
$$\forall i, 1 \le i \le |\pi|; \pi[i] = x \Rightarrow \exists j, 1 \le j \le i; \tag{4}$$
$$\pi[j] = \overleftarrow{x} \wedge t = |\pi| : cont(r, \pi[t]) = cont(t/\pi[t])$$

where P represents the protocol, traces(P) is the finite set of traces of the protocol P, $\overrightarrow{x}$ representing events that precede x in execution order, and the cont() function returns information owned by the protocol participants.

2. Secrecy

Secrecy means that the specific message sent by the honest agent cannot be known by the intruder when it is transmitted over the channel. Based on the preceding contents, this paper provides an informal description of the secrecy of the four-way handshake: during the four-way handshake process, the intruder cannot directly obtain the exact information, assuming that all participants in this process are honest. The formal description is shown in (5).

$$\forall \pi \in traces(P):$$
$$\forall r \in \pi: \tag{5}$$
$$honest(r) \Rightarrow I \nrightarrow m$$

where r represents the participants of the protocol, $honest()$ represents the honest predicate, I represents the intruder, and m represents the specific information.

3. Authentication and Secrecy of Protocols Defined by LTL Formulas

After providing the formal description of the security properties, we need to utilize LTL formulas to describe the security properties of the protocol.

As a Wi-Fi security protocol, the goal of the WPA3 four-way handshake process is to complete identity authentication between the AP and the STA, and implement corresponding key generation and delivery operations. Therefore, it is necessary to describe the authentication and secrecy of the protocol. The authentication refers to the completion of identity authentication between the AP and the STA. Secrecy means that after the session between the AP and the STA is completed, the key transferred by the AP will not be leaked, that is, the key used by the AP and the STA to encrypt the communication information will not be obtained by a third party.

To describe the authentication of the protocol, atomic predicates are needed [16]. Promela language is used to describe the authentication of the protocol, and some corresponding global variables are constructed by definition.

$$bit\,IniRunAS\,=\,0;\ bit\,IniCommitAS\,=\,0;$$
$$bit\,ResRunAS\,=\,0;\ bit\,ResCommitAS\,=\,0;$$

In this context, IniRunAS indicates that the STA participates in a session to the AP, IniCommitAS indicates that the STA submits a session to the AP, ResRunAS indicates that the AP participates in a session to the STA, and ResCommitAS indicates that the AP submits a session with the STA; An initial value of 0 indicates that the session is not engaged or committed, whereas a value of 1 indicates that the session is engaged or committed.

Once the global variable is defined, it is essential to update the value of each atomic predicate correspondingly. This can be achieved through the utilization of macro definitions. The pertinent macro definition is provided below.

#define IniRun(a,b)if:: ((a == AP)&&(b == STA))- > IniRunAS = 1:: else skip fi
#define ResRun(a,b) if:: ((a == AP)&&(b == STA))- > ResRunAS = 1:: else skip
fi

#define IniCommit(a,b)if:: ((a = = AP)&&(b = = STA))- > IniCommitAS = 1::
else skip fi

#define ResCommit(a,b)if:: ((a = = AP)&&(b = = STA))- > ResCommitAS = 1::
else skip fi

The confidentiality of the protocol is described by atomic predicate method. The corresponding global variable definitions are as follows:

bit GTKI = 0; bit GTKS = 1;

The corresponding macro definition is shown below:

$$\#defineSecInt(GTKI! = GTKS).$$

#define SecInt(GTKI! = GTKS).

In the given context, GTKI represents a key obtained by an intruder, while GTKS represents a key sent by the AP to the STA. When GTKI is different from GTKS, it indicates that the key transferred from the AP to the STA is not obtained by the intruder, thus satisfying confidentiality. Conversely, when GTKI is the same as GTKS, it means that the key transferred from the AP to the STA is obtained by the intruder, thereby failing to meet the requirements of confidentiality.

Moving on, let's delve into a more detailed description of the authentication and secrecy aspects of WPA3. By utilizing the defined atomic predicates, the protocol authentication is defined as follows: the AP authenticates the STA, meaning that the ResRunAS value must be true before IniCommitAS. Similarly, the STA needs to authenticate to the AP, thus requiring the IniRunAS value to be true before ResCommitAS. Protocol secrecy, on the other hand, implies that SecInt is always true.

To represent the aforementioned security attributes, they are converted into LTL formulas as depicted in (6).

$$-[](([]!IniCommitAS)||(!IniCommitAS \cup IniCommitAS \cup ResRunAS))$$
$$-[](([]!ResCommitAS)||(!ResCommitAS \cup IniRunAS)) \qquad (6)$$
$$-[]SecInt$$

At this point, the security attributes of WPA3 have been fully characterized.

3.4 Analysis of Experimental Results

After defining each process, formal verification of the WPA3 protocol's four-way handshake process is conducted using SPIN version 6.4.9 in the SPIN environment built on the Ubuntu 20.04 TLS system. The experimental results are depicted in Fig. 4.

It can be seen from Fig. 4 that the formal verification is performed on the WPA3 protocol four-way handshake, the search depth reaches 43 layers, the total number of state transitions is 1845, the verification result is that an error is found, and the attack sequence diagram is given, as shown in Fig. 5.

```
(Spin Version 6.4.9 -- 17 December 2018)
Warning: Search not completed
            + Breadth-First Search
            + Partial Order Reduction

Full statespace search for:
            never claim        - (not selected)
            assertion violations +
            cycle checks       - (disabled by -DSAFETY)
            invalid end states +

State-vector 108 byte, depth reached 43, errors: 1
      1107 states, stored
                231 nominal states (stored-atomic)
       738 states, matched
      1845 transitions (= stored+matched)
       876 atomic steps
hash conflicts:      0 (resolved)
```

Fig. 4. WPA3 Four-way Handshake Model Verification Result

After analysis, the four-way handshake process meets the authentication and confidentiality required by the protocol, but there is a dangerous operation, i.e., key reinstallation. The reason for this operation is that STA confirms the completion of handshake after sending Message 4, then installs PTK, resets the nonce to 0, encrypts the message and sends it, while the intruder prevents AP from receiving Message 4, AP will resend Message 3 due to timeout, STA will repeat the above operation after receiving Message 3, because the nonce is reset and the duplicate encryption key is used.

4   The Improved WPA3 Protocol

The key reinstallation operation can be avoided by setting a flag amount, which is initially 0 and is set to 1 when the STA installs the PTK for the first time. The STA will check the flag amount each time the PTK is installed. It will reset the nonce when the flag amount is 0, and will not reset it when the flag amount is 1. Additionally, the flag amount will be reset to 0 when the AP disconnects from the STA. Since the AP also needs to use nonce encryption, the nonce value needs to be passed in Message 4. The improved handshake flow is shown in (7).

$(1)AP \rightarrow STA : Anonce, r;$

$(2)STA(\{Anonce, Snonce, r\}GETKEY) \rightarrow AP : Snonce, r, \{MIC\}ECRYPTKey$

$(3)AP(\{Anonce, Snonce, r\}GETKEY) \rightarrow STA : r + 1, \{MIC, GTK\}EDCRYPTKey$

$(4)STA \rightarrow AP : r + 1, \{MIC, nonce\}EDCRYPTKey$

$$(7)$$

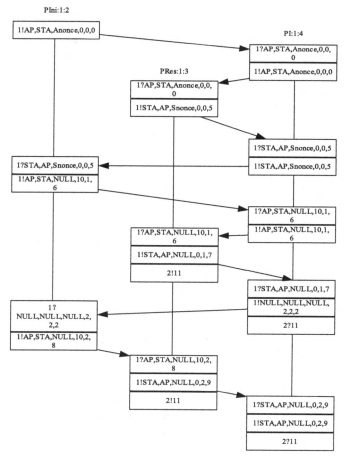

Fig. 5. Attack Path

Correspondingly, the state machines of the AP and the STA need to be improved. The specific content is shown in Fig. 6 and Fig. 7.

The improved four-way handshake model has been formally verified, with a search depth of 9999 layers and a total number of state transitions equal to 738057. The verification result confirms that there are no vulnerabilities in the improved protocol.

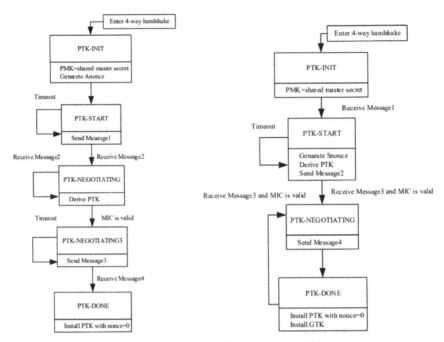

Fig. 6. Improved State Machine of AP   **Fig. 7.** Improved State Machine of STA

5   Conclusion

The main research work of this paper is as follows: it provides a detailed introduction to all stages of the WPA3 protocol, with a specific focus on the interaction process of the four-way handshake. It introduces operational semantics to define the security protocol specification and proposes the principle of protocol abstract modeling. The multi-party communication in wireless networks is simplified into two entities, the key representation is simplified, and the key generation function is defined. Under the assumption of a perfect key system, the WPA3 four-way handshake interaction process is reasonably abstracted and simplified, enabling formal representation. The characteristics of the WPA3 four-way handshake interaction process are thoroughly studied, and the four-way handshake process is modeled by analyzing the behavior of both parties with a fine granularity using a state machine. The Dolev-Yao model is used, introducing an adversary-controlled communication channel to fully explore the ability of intruders to control the communication network. Additionally, a static analysis strategy is combined to reduce invalid messages and alleviate state explosion. The ability of intruders is analyzed and an intruders model is constructed based on the principle of abstract modeling. The security of the four-way handshake model is verified using the SPIN tool. The experimental structure confirms the preservation of authentication and confidentiality in the protocol. However, it identifies a dangerous operation of key reinstallation and proposes a solution. The improved model's verification results demonstrate the absence of key reinstallation.

Future research directions can be explored from the following aspects: by establishing a standard protocol description language, the protocol can be automatically modeled to enhance the level of automation. The intruders model constructed in this paper requires manual analysis of messages and manual forging of messages during man-in-the-middle attacks. An algorithm can be developed to enable automatic message forging and improve the attack efficiency of intruders. Theorem proving methods can be employed to verify the security properties of the WPA3 protocol, as these methods can handle infinite state spaces.

Appendix a

```
//Process Initiator
proctype PIni(mtype self;mtype party;mtype nonce){
end:
do
::atomic{
startflag==0->syn!self,party,nonce,0,counterIni,0;
startflag=-1;
}
::atomic{
syn?eval(NULL),eval(NULL),eval(NULL),eval(0),ev
al(0),eval(0)->
counterIni=counterIni+1;
syn!self,party,nonce,0,counterIni,0;
}
::atomic{
syn?g1,eval(self),eval(Snonce),eval(0),eval(counterIni
),g2->ResRun(self,g1);
PTK=derPTK(0,Anonce,Snonce);
MICIni=PTK;
PTKA=PTK;
PTKS=g2;
counterIni=counterIni+1;
equal(g2,MICIni)->MICIni=MICIni+1;
syn!self,g1,NULL,Encrytion(PTK,5),counterIni,MICI
::atomic{
syn?eval(NULL),eval(NULL),eval(NULL),eval(1),ev
al(1),eval(1)->
MICIni=MICIni-1;
counterIni=counterIni+1;
syn!self,g1,NULL,Encrytion(PTK,5),counterIni,MICI
ni;
MICIni=MICIni+1;
}
ni;
ResCommit(self,g1);
MICIni=MICIni+1;
}
::atomic{
```

```
syn?eval(NULL),eval(NULL),eval(NULL),eval(2),ev
al(2),eval(2)->
counterIni=counterIni+1;
MICIni=MICIni+1;
syn!self,g1,NULL,Encrytion(PTK,5),counterIni,MICI
ni;
MICIni=MICIni+1;
}
::atomic{
syn?g1,eval(self),eval(NULL),eval(0),eval(counterIni)
,eval(MICIni)->
printf("success");
AuthEnd=1;
SecEnd=1;
}
od;
}
//Process Responder
proctype PRes(mtype self;mtype nonce){
end:
do
::atomic{
syn?g3,eval(self),g4,eval(0),g5,eval(0)->counterRes=
g5;
PTK=derPTK(0,Anonce,Snonce);
MICRes=PTK;
syn!self,g3,nonce,0,counterRes,MICRes;
IniRun(g3,self);
counterRes=counterRes+1;
MICRes=MICRes+1;
}
::atomic{
syn?g3,eval(self),eval(NULL),g5,eval(counterRes),ev
al(MICRes)->
IniCommit(g3,self);
MICRes=MICRes+1;
GTK=g5-PTK;
GTKS=GTK;
syn!self,g3,NULL,0,counterRes,MICRes;
counterRes=counterRes+1;
MICRes=MICRes+1;
comm ! Encrytion(PTK,6);
}
```

References

1. Kwon, S., Choim, H.K.: Evolution of Wi-Fi protected access: security challenges. IEEE Consum. Electron. Mag. **99**, 1–1 (2020)

2. Ting, C., Guozheng, W., Liu, Z., Geguang, P., Zhao, R., Liu, K.: Analysis of NSFC formal methods field fund applications. Prospective Technol. **2**(01), 132–140 (2023)
3. Tian, C., Deng, Y., Jiang, Y.: Introduction to the special topic on formal methods and applications. J. Soft. **32**(06) (2021)
4. Lowe, G.: Breaking and fixing the Needham-Schroeder public-key protocol using FDR. Soft. Concepts Tools. **17**, 93–102 (1996)
5. Vanhoef, M., Piessens, F.: Key reinstallation attacks: Forcing nonce reuse in WPA2. In: Proceedings of the 2017 ACM SIGSAC Conference on Computer and Communications Security, ACM (2017)
6. Wang, W., Liu, Z.: The development and improvement of cryptography and encryption technology. Digital Technol. Appl. **40**(01), 237–239 (2022)
7. Hyun, N.J., Yeop, L.J., Hui, K.S., Kee, C.H.: Comparative analysis on security protocols of WPA3 standard for secure wireless LAN environments. J. Korean Inst. **44**(10), 1878–1887 (2019)
8. Yao, S.: Analysis of asymmetric encryption technology. Electron. Technol. **49**(07), 50–51 (2020)
9. Harkins. D.: Simultaneous authentication of equals: a secure, password-based key exchange for mesh networks. In: Proceedings of the 2008 Second International Conference on Sensor Technologies and Applications, IEEE (2008)
10. Heng, W.G., Lin, Q.Y, Wei, F.: An Improved Security authentication protocol for lightweight RFID based on ECC. J. Sens. **2022** (2022)
11. Liu, C., Liang, L., Chen, R.: Analysis and research of wireless attack vulnerability based on WPA/WPA2 protocol. Netw. Secur. Technol. Appl. **231**(03), 71–72 (2020)
12. Lounis, K, Zulkernine, M.: Bad-token: denial of service attacks on WPA3. SIN '19. In: Proceedings of the 12th International Conference on Security of Information and Network, vol. 15, pp. 1–8 (2019)
13. Kohlios, C.P., Hayajneh, T.: Comprehensive attack flow model and security analysis for Wi-Fi and WPA3. Electron. **7**(11), 284 (2018)
14. Clarke, E.M., Grumberg, O., Peled, D.: Model checking. MIT press, Cambridge (1999)
15. Bell Labs. What is spin [EB/OL]. http://spinroot.com/spin/what.html. 1:17 (2019)
16. Zhong, X., Xiao, M., Li, W.: Formal analysis and improvement of RFID ultra-lightweight authentication protocol RCIA. Comput. Eng. Sci. **40**(12), 2183–2192 (2018)

Author Index

Z. Cai et al. (Eds.): NCTCS 2023, CCIS 1944, p. 267, 2024.
https://doi.org/10.1007/978-981-99-7743-7

Printed in the United States
by Baker & Taylor Publisher Services